ANALYTICAL TECHNIQUES IN CONFLICT MANAGEMENT

To the Children of the World and
their future children and grandchildren
May they live in peace

Also by Manas Chatterji

Economics of International Security (co-editor), forthcoming.
Economic Issues of Disarmament (co-editor), forthcoming.
Disarmament, Economic Conversion and Management of Peace (co-
    editor).
New Frontiers in Regional Science (co-editor).
Dynamics and Conflict in Regional Structural Change (co-
    editor).
Technology Transfer in the Developing Countries (editor).
Hazardous Materials Disposal: Siting and Management (editor).
Health Care Cost Containment Study: An Econometric Study.
Spatial, Environmental and Resource Policy in the Development
    Countries (co-editor).
Energy and Environment for the Developing Countries (editor).
Management and Regional Science for economic Development.
Space Location and Regional Development (editor).
Energy, Regional Science and Public Policy (co-editor).
Environment, Regional Science and Interregional Modeling (co-
    editor).

Analytical Techniques in Conflict Management

MANAS CHATTERJI
Professor of Management
State University of New York, Binghamton

Dartmouth
Aldershot · Brookfield USA · Hong Kong · Singapore · Sydney

Published by
Dartmouth Publishing Company Limited
Gower House
Croft Road
Aldershot
Hants GU11 3HR
England

Dartmouth Publishing Company
Old Post Road
Brookfield
Vermont 05036
USA

A CIP catalogue record for this book is available from the British Library and the US Library of Congress

ISBN 1 85521 221 8

Printed and bound in Great Britain by
Billing and Sons Ltd, Worcester

Contents

Preface

At the same time that there is widespread poverty throughout much of the world, a small portion of humanity lives affluently. To bridge this gap and to bring the unfortunate millions to par with the fortunate few, a sustained effort in economic development is necessary. International cooperation, and internal and external peace between and within countries are basic ingredients for this to occur. Peace, however, should not be viewed as a passive condition, that is, merely as the absence of violence. It should be used as an active, aggressive weapon so that peace and non-violence can lead to a better social, psychological and moral climate. Increased cooperation can also lead to a higher level of material well-being. Innovative ideas in the social sciences and new tools of analysis need to be developed for this purpose. This study is a small step in that direction. I discuss herein a number of techniques and show how they can be used for analysing conflict problems, freely using my and others' research. I have placed a heavy emphasis on statistics since I believe that to be crucial. Wherever possible, I have given an example and computer program. While it is difficult to present much of this material in layman's language, I have tried to limit myself to a low level of mathematical sophistication. Obviously, it is not possible to be exhaustive in the treatment. As a result, many sections are quite brief and are in need of more detailed explanation.

I am indebted to the National Institute of Dispute Resolution, Washington, DC, USA for providing modest but necessary financial support and to Dr Thomas Kelly, formerly Dean of the School of Management, and presently Vice-President of External Affairs, State University of New York at Binghamton, for providing facilities. I am grateful to Anna Sefcovic and Bernadette Bobal for typing and to Michael Horan, Frank Egereonu, Indrajit De and my daughter, Pinka Chatterji, a student at Cornell University, for editorial assistance.

Manas Chatterji   SUNY-Binghamton, June 1992

Introduction

Conflict management and peace have always been of great
interest to mankind since the earliest days of civilization.
Seeds of these thoughts are rooted in the great religions,
while development of these concepts has taken place in a
number of directions.

The application of conflict management and peace studies
to human interaction was initially investigated from religious
and ethical perspectives. Considerable development of them
has taken place in theological literature, some of which has
been adapted to practical life through methods such as
transcendental meditation. From time immemorial religious
leaders and social transformers have relentlessly spread the
gospel of peace and tranquility.

In the academic disciplines, the greatest impetus has
come in the peace studies area where learned societies are
formed, books have been written, and international issues of
peace and conflict resolution are discussed at conferences.
Interest in these issues culminated in peace movements which
have been quite prominent in the second half of the twentieth
century. The quest for peace and the hope that it is imminent
has never been stronger than in recent years as a result of
superpower convergence. But the hopes for peace dimmed again
as a result of conflict in the Middle East.

In modern times concern over peace and war is more than
an ethical or religious question; it is interwoven in the
social, economic and political fabric of the global community.
Therefore, it is vital that we develop a theoretical basis for
conflict management and peace analysis and indicate how
techniques of social sciences can be applied to solve
practical, real-life problems in such areas as: personal-
family conflicts; societal problems such as race relations;
ethical problems; planning problems such as housing,

1

transportation, etc.; and, of course, international relations.
Peace Science tries to provide the basis for an inter-
disciplinary social science discipline. Isard (1982) attempts
to give a definition of the new discipline of Peace Science in
stating that:

> In the past, we and others have variously defined the
> field as conflict theory and analysis, conflict
> management, and conflict resolution; or as embodying
> those efforts designed to cope with conflict and to
> establish world order and order within societies of
> different sizes and structures. We have frequently
> emphasized the field's cross-disciplinary character. We
> have claimed that it draws upon the existing concepts,
> tools, theories, models, and techniques of diverse
> fields-economics, mathematics, psychology, sociology,
> anthropology, political science, industrial relations,
> regional science, geography, biology, and law-and
> attempts to fuse the better elements of these. Nowhere,
> as far as we are aware, do we proceed further and detail
> concretely this fusion process and suggest a conceptual
> framework that embodies and explicates all the links
> among variables, approaches, and theories. We shall,
> however, attempt to do so.... We take the position that
> once fields become established and institutionalized
> they lose their flexibility. With time, they
> cumulatively, though never completely, lose ability to
> absorb new ideas and theories and move along drastically
> new directions. In contrast, a new field such as Peace
> Science which has yet to find a definition, core, and
> boundaries acceptable to many scholars, is completely
> free to identify and embrace an optimal combination of
> concepts, tools, theories, models, and techniques. For
> at least a few years, until its scholars become widely
> recognized and acquire vested interests, it may redefine
> itself without constraint. It can draw upon the strong
> elements of existing fields while discarding sterile,
> excessively refined models, theories, and abstractions,
> and obsolete techniques and knowledge, thereby promising
> to achieve much in unifying and integrating social
> science and related knowledge (p. 489).

During the last two decades considerable advances have
taken place in the development of a peace science theory,
particularly under Isard's leadership. In his introductory
book on Peace Science (Isard, 1988) he covers the following
subjects:

1.   Procedures for situations with a small number of options
      where participants can only rank outcome.
2.   Procedures for situations with many options where the
      participants can only rank outcome.
3.   Procedures for situations where the participants can
      value outcome in relative terms.
4.   Procedures for situations with a small number of options
      where the participants can assign precise values to
      outcome.
5.   Procedures for situations with many options where the
      participants can assign precise values to outcome.

6.   Multi-objective programming and multi-criteria analysis.
7.   Matching conflict situations and conflict management
      procedures-static framework.
      He has then taken a super-power conflict area, namely the
armament race, and extended his theoretical framework to show
how the problem can be handled using the abovementioned
framework (Isard, 1988).
      Isard starts with the topics of individual and group
behaviour under crisis and non-crisis situations, gives a
formal cognitive framework for individual and group behaviour,
decision-making behaviour under major psychological stress,
learning, problem solving, negotiation, mediation leadership,
etc., and indicates how these can be put into a world system
model of disarmament.   Just as Isard has integrated the
different theories of economics, sociology, psychology and
political science into a new area of social science called
"Peace Science", my objective in this study will be to put
together the different tools of statistics, econometrics and
operations research to indicate how these methods can be used
to analyse real-life problems. Although these tools are quite
general, my main focus will be on their application to pubic
sector conflict management, and, in particular, international
relations.
      A great potential for the application of these tools also
exists in private sector (business) conflict management.   In
acknowledging this, I wish to present some material in this
area following Aggarwal (1981) closely.   My study will serve
to describe further the conceptual framework for the
discipline of peace science by investigating the application
of quantitative methods to behavioural science.   It is no
secret that different types of conflict abound in business
enterprise and that managers and business executives devote a
considerable amount of time (some estimate about 30%) to
dealing with them.   This conflict may be personal or
interpersonal; it may be between different departments of a
company (e.g. about transfer pricing); or it may be an
international conflict involving a business.   It can, of
course, be various other types as well, such as:
1.   Conflict of interest, i.e. insider trading in a
      brokerage house, public defender, judge and jury, etc.
      In this case an ethical code is an effective instrument
      with which to deal with the conflict.
2.   Multinational: National interests often clash with
      those of the multinational corporations, not only over
      resource use, pricing, import substitution, and rate of
      return, but also such matters as environment and
      "bribes", etc. Individuals working in the multinational
      scene also face conflict with personal goals, national
      goals and company goals.
3.   Government regulations and business practices: In all
      governments, large numbers of regulations (controlling
      health, welfare, safety, hiring practices, affirmative
      action, etc.), constitutional changes, and judicial
      decrees determine how the business should be organized.
      Some of these dictates are often conflicting.
4.   Role conflict: Individuals assume different roles in
      different environments, for instance, in the family or
      at work. The higher the intensity of responsibility,

3

say for physicians, accountants, salesmen, etc., the more painful is the conflict.

5.   Goal conflict: This type of conflict may arise from role conflict or conflicts of interest. The goals of individuals, groups, organizations, etc. may be at conflict with respect to such issues as environment or weapons, etc.

6.   Channels conflict: Channels or distribution links that flow through information or trade may lead to conflict if they do not correspond to the decision tree.

7.   Encroachment: Since responsibilities in a complex organization are overlapping, there are always conflicts over crossing jurisdictional lines. Lawyers, accountants, and finance people frequently disagree over issues of control.

8.   Miscellaneous conflict:
     (i)   Industrial scientists vs. bureaucrats
     (ii)   Media control and public benefits
     (iii) Mergers and employee participation
     (iv)   Consultant's own ethical standards vs. client's need
     (v)   Power of lines manager vs. staff manager

It would be an exhaustive chore to list all the potential conflict situations of a business setting. Although many resolution strategies may have been used in individual circumstances, the more frequently used strategies are topically listed as follows:

1.   Legal
2.   Third party intervention - arbitration
3.   Bargaining
4.   Counselling
5.   Code of ethics

It is difficult to match a particular conflict management strategy with a given conflict situation. Aggarwal (1981) gives a list of some strategies used in the literature.

1.   Splitting-off to solve corporate ownership problems
2.   Training in communication skills
3.   Placing the responsibility of labour problem solutions on both labour and management
4.   Increasing the share of minority personnel
5.   Using graph algorithm for field operations
6.   Codifying customs of bargaining
7.   Identifying the relationship between conflict resolution methods and managerial effectiveness
8.   Using outside intervention when the conflict is not so intense
9.   Somatic conflict
10. Confrontation
11. Interpersonal contact, mentoring and dialogue

It should not be presumed that all conflicts are undesirable, since social change evolves through conflict. Some conflicts, of course, can never be solved. Non-violent conflict resolution is the focus of this investigation.

4

With this background information in business conflict I shall now list different techniques that can be used effectively in conflict analysis. I shall explain each technique, give an example and suggest a computer program whenever possible. Due to the lack of time and limitation of space, I shall present some techniques in detail and others only briefly.

1 Statistical Methods in Conflict Management

A. Descriptive Statistics

The development of conflict between contesting parties depends greatly on chance and probability. As such, the science of probability, namely statistics, has a leading role to play in any technique. The enumerations and elaboration of technique that follow in Chapters 2-8 are non-stochastic. The introduction of descriptive statistics and statistical inference in this chapter will greatly complement the latter material.

Conflict management strategies are designed to make appropriate policy decisions within the framework of multivariate analysis in the face of uncertainty. Decisions are based on the value of the variables. Some of them, such as population, income, arms expenditure, etc. are quantitative, while others, such as power, motivation, love and rectitude, are qualitative. The variables can be classified as discrete when it takes a specified number of values, usually integers, such as the number of riots, number of wars, number of persons injured, etc. Other variables, such as population, income, unemployment rate, educational level, etc. are continuous variables, which can take into account any value within a certain range. As mentioned before, the variables in any conflict situation are stochastic, i.e. they take certain values with some probabilities such that the total probability is equal to one. The objective in any scientific inquiry is to estimate the mean value of the variable $\mu = E(X)$; e.g. expected number of riots, expected number of terrorist activity and its variance $V(X) = E(X-\mu)^2$. We shall elaborate this point later.

One characteristic of the variables involved in the conflict management area is that they are a mixture of discrete and continuous variables, qualitative and quantitative, and they therefore pose measurement problems. The variables scale of measurements can be (1) nominal (2) ordinal (3) interval and (4) ratio. In the nominal case, we have a yes-no (binary type) or 1,2,3... type variables. In the case of ordinal variables, the variables can be ranked. In the interval scale the magnitude of the distance between any pair of consequentive integers is equal to the distance between any other pair. For example, we can say that John is five inches taller than Robert. In the ratio scale there is an absolute zero point - say temperature. However, interval scale measurements are sufficient for statistical methods.

As I mentioned before, conflict management decisions are based on multivariate considerations. However, for the sake of simplicity, we first deal with a univariate situation where only one variable is concerned. Whether the variable is discrete or continuous, quantitative and qualitative, and whether the measurements are made on nominal, ordinal, interval or ratio scales, there are two basic tasks in statistics. First, we need to organize the data into a manageable form and construct descriptive structures, and then estimate its parameters, its probability distribution, etc. in the population based on sample characteristics. Population is a collection of all possible values which a variable can take. For example, the variable the number of riots theoretically can take any value whatsoever. In most situations, the population is infinite or it does not exist. Usually, we have a sample, i.e. an occurrence of a number of riots. On the basis of sample observations, we are required to estimate the population value, say from the sample mean $X = \Sigma\ X_i/N$ estimate the population mean μ, and sample standard deviations where

$$S = \sqrt{\frac{\Sigma(X - \bar{X})^2}{n - 1}}$$ to estimate the population standard deviation,

$$\sigma = \sqrt{\frac{\Sigma(X - \mu)^2}{N}} = E(X - \mu)^2$$ where N, and n denote the number of

observations in the population and sample respectively.

The first step is the organization of data into a manageable form. This may be achieved by organizing the ungrouped data into a frequency table and graphically representing it by the histogram (frequency curve) or frequency polygon (in the case of discrete variable) as in Fig. 1.1. The frequency curve is a limiting form of the histogram when the histogram is drawn on the basis of relative frequencies. The curve can be represented by an equation.

Although these have been drawn for the sample data, similar constructions may be made for the population values. However, the population values are not available. If they were, there would be no need to take a sample.

Although frequency tables and their graphic representations assist us in visualizing the situation, they are not very helpful since they are very descriptive. What we really need is some objective quantifiable characteristics of the sample. One such characteristic is a measure of central tendency, namely the are relative frequencies.

$$\bar{X} = \text{sample mean} = \Sigma X_i/n \qquad \text{(ungrouped)}$$

$$\bar{X} = \Sigma X_i f_i/n = \Sigma X_i p_i \qquad \text{(grouped) where } p_i = f_i/n$$

When we are dealing with the qualitative variables, the median rather than the mean can denote the central tendency. The median is the value of the variable such that 50% of the values fall below it and 50% fall above it. Whether we use mean or median, they represent the sample. Obviously, all other values cannot be equal to it. So we need an index of

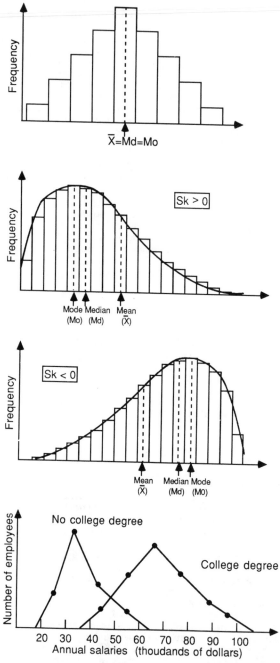

Figure 1.1 Histogram and Frequency Polygon

8

measurement of variability which is given by the sample standard deviation

$$S = \sqrt{\frac{\Sigma(X - \bar{X})^2 f}{n-1.}}$$

The sample arithmetic mean ($\bar{X}$) is a better estimate of the population mean μ rather than the sample median since it has the least variability over repeated samples. Besides, according to Chebysheff's inequality, $\bar{X}$ + 2S will cover 80% of the values in the sample. In summary, the ultimate objective is to estimate

$$E(\bar{X}) = \text{population mean } \mu = \Sigma X_i f_i/N = \Sigma X_i\, P_i$$

$$\text{population S.d. } \sigma = \sqrt{\sum_{i=1}^{N}(X - \mu)^2\, fi/N}$$

$$= \sqrt{\Sigma(X-\mu)^2\, P_i}$$

$$= E\,(X - \mu)^2$$

with the help of sample mean

$$\bar{X} = \sum_{i=1}^{n} X_i\, f_i/n = \Sigma X_i\, P_i \qquad \text{and}$$

$$S = \sqrt{\sum_{i=1}^{n}(X_i - \bar{X})^2 f_i/n} = \sqrt{\sum_{i=1}^{n}(X_i - \bar{X})^2 P_i}$$

The crux of the problem is to estimate the population probabilities P_i; i.e. the probability that there will be 1,2,3... riots. [1] Of course they can be estimated by p_i; i.e. sample estimates based on past observations. However, for a better understanding of estimating the probability, I intend to present a short description of probability in the following section.

Example 1
The following data represent the number of customers Rex Department store lost, per month, over a 12 month period and the associated number of lost case sales.

Number of customers lost: 25, 22, 17, 31, 15, 19, 22, 26, 22, 32, 12, 16.

Lost sales (in cases): 20, 18, 16, 26, 14, 15, 17, 20, 18, 27, 8, 10.
a.   Find the mean for each variable.
b.   Find the standard deviation for each variable.
c.   Find the variance for each variable.
d.   Display the customer and the lost sales data on a chart.
        a.   Find the mean
        b.   Find the mode
        c.   Find the median
        d.   Find the variance
        e.   Find the standard deviation

9

Answer to Example 1 by SAS Computer Program

```
DATA PAGE15;
INPUT   LOSTSALE   CUSTOMER;
* LOSTSALE = LOST SALES (IN CASES);
* CUSTOMER = NUMBER OF CUSTOMERS LOST;
CARDS;
25        20
22        18
17        16
31        26
15        14
19        15
22        17
26        20
22        18
32        27
12        8
16        10
;
PROC   MEANS DATA=PAGE15;
       VAR LOSTSALE CUSTOMER;
TITLE "PROC MEANS ON LOSTSALE AND CUSTOMER";
PROC   CHART DATA=PAGE15;
       VBAR LOSTSALE;
TITLE "PROC CHART OF LOSTSALE";
PROC   CHART DATA=PAGE15;
       VBAR CUSTOMER;
TITLE "PROC CHART OF CUSTOMER";
PROC   PRINT DATA=PAGE15;
TITLE1 "NUMBER OF LOST SALES PER MONTH AT REX BROS";
TITLE2           "AND NUMBER OF CUSTOMERS LOST";
```

PROC MEANS ON LOSTSALE AND CUSTOMER

VARIABLE	N	MEAN	STANDARD DEVIATION	MINIMUM VALUE	MAXIMUM VALUE
LOSTSALE	12	21.58333333	6.20056205	12.00000000	32.00000000
CUSTOMER	12	17.41666667	5.58338987	8.00000000	27.00000000

11

FREQUENCY BAR CHART

```
FREQUENCY

   4 +     *****     *****
     |     *****     *****
     |     *****     *****
     |     *****     *****
     |     *****     *****
     |     *****     *****
     |     *****     *****
     |     *****     *****
     |     *****     *****
     |     *****     *****
   3 +     *****     *****
     |     *****     *****
     |     *****     *****
     |     *****     *****
     |     *****     *****
     |     *****     *****
     |     *****     *****
     |     *****     *****
     |     *****     *****
     |     *****     *****
   2 +     *****     *****     *****     *****
     |     *****     *****     *****     *****
     |     *****     *****     *****     *****
     |     *****     *****     *****     *****
     |     *****     *****     *****     *****
     |     *****     *****     *****     *****
     |     *****     *****     *****     *****
     |     *****     *****     *****     *****
     |     *****     *****     *****     *****
     |     *****     *****     *****     *****
   1 +     *****     *****     *****     *****
     |     *****     *****     *****     *****
     |     *****     *****     *****     *****
     |     *****     *****     *****     *****
     |     *****     *****     *****     *****
     |     *****     *****     *****     *****
     |     *****     *****     *****     *****
     |     *****     *****     *****     *****
     |     *****     *****     *****     *****
     |     *****     *****     *****     *****
     ----------------------------------------------
           15        20        25        30
```

LOSTSALE MIDPOINT

FREQUENCY BAR CHART

FREQUENCY

```
4 +                  *****     *****
  |                  *****     *****
  |                  *****     *****
  |                  *****     *****
  |                  *****     *****
  |                  *****     *****
  |                  *****     *****
  |                  *****     *****
  |                  *****     *****
  |                  *****     *****
3 +                  *****     *****
  |                  *****     *****
  |                  *****     *****
  |                  *****     *****
  |                  *****     *****
  |                  *****     *****
  |                  *****     *****
  |                  *****     *****
  |                  *****     *****
  |                  *****     *****
2 +       *****      *****     *****     *****
  |       *****      *****     *****     *****
  |       *****      *****     *****     *****
  |       *****      *****     *****     *****
  |       *****      *****     *****     *****
  |       *****      *****     *****     *****
  |       *****      *****     *****     *****
  |       *****      *****     *****     *****
  |       *****      *****     *****     *****
  |       *****      *****     *****     *****
1 +       *****      *****     *****     *****
  |       *****      *****     *****     *****
  |       *****      *****     *****     *****
  |       *****      *****     *****     *****
  |       *****      *****     *****     *****
  |       *****      *****     *****     *****
  |       *****      *****     *****     *****
  |       *****      *****     *****     *****
  |       *****      *****     *****     *****
  |       *****      *****     *****     *****
  --------------------------------------------------
          10         15        20        25
```

CUSTOMER MIDPOINT

NUMBER OF LOST SALES PER MONTH AT REX BROS
AND NUMBER OF CUSTOMERS LOST

OBS	LOSTSALE	CUSTOMER
1	25	20
2	22	18
3	17	16
4	31	26
5	15	14
6	19	15
7	22	17
8	26	20
9	22	18
10	32	27
11	12	8
12	16	10

B. Probability Theory and Probability Distribution

Probability Theory

In management science we make decisions for a number of variables such as price, advertisement, etc. in the face of uncertainty. After organizing the sample data into a manageable form, the next most important step is to make inferences about the population characteristics (say, the population mean and variance) on the basis of sample information. Here are some examples: (1) On the basis of the data concerning average monthly sales of a sample of ten branch stores, we may want to make statements about the average monthly sales of all the stores in the chain, or, (2) on the basis of a store's sales during the last ten months we may need to predict the sales of that store for the next month. In the stock market, the objective may be to predict the stock price of a company at a future date on the basis of the stock prices for the last ten time periods. In economic analysis, we may be interested in the future values of some key economic variables, such as gross national product, inventory level and rate of inflation, based on the information gained from past sample observations of these and related variables. All these variables in question are stochastic, i.e. they assume different values with some specific probabilities.

Formally speaking, we are given the sample mean and variance of the variable X, which are defined as follows:

$$\bar{X} = \sum_{i=1}^{n} X_i \, (f_i/n) \tag{1}$$

$$s^2 = \sum_{i=1}^{n} (X - \bar{X})^2 \, (f_i/n)$$

where (f_i/n) is the sample relative frequency in the ith class. The objective is to estimate the population mean and variance as defined by

$$\mu = \sum_{i=1}^{N} X_i \, (f_i/N) \tag{2}$$

$$\sigma^2 = \sum_{i=1}^{N} (X_i - \mu)^2 \, (f_i/N)$$

where f_i/N are the corresponding population relative frequencies in the ith class, i.e. the probability that a value falls in the ith class.

The reason we do not know μ and σ^2 is that we did not examine all the observations in the population, i.e. f_i/N, in the population, although in the sample, (f_i/n), are known.

When the population is large or infinite, the population relative frequency denotes the chance or probability that a particular variate value will fall into a certain class. Thus, to make any statement about μ on the basis of $\overline{X}$, it will be necessary to make an estimate of this probability. These are the reasons why we need to study the theory of probability. In this section we will do it only briefly.

DEFINITION OF PROBABILITY OF AN EVENT

An experiment results in an event. For example, the experiment "throwing a coin" produces an event – say, "heads". In situations in business and economics, we can usually see an event, say, the sales volume of a store. The probability of an event E, P(E), is defined as

$$P(E) = \frac{\text{Number of outcomes in the experiment favourable to the event E}}{\text{Total number of possible outcomes of the experiment}} \qquad (3)$$

For example, if the experiment involves tossing a coin, and E designates "getting a 'heads', the numerator of EQ (3) is 1, the denominator is 2, and P(E) = 1/2.

However, since in most real world situations, the real world experiments are not controlled, the computation of P(E) from EQ (3) becomes difficult.

Alternatively, the probability of an event can be defined as the limiting form of the relative frequency when the sample size is large, i.e.

$$P(E) = \lim_{n \to \infty} \frac{n_1}{n} \qquad (4)$$

where n_1 denotes the number of outcomes favourable to a given event, and n is the number of replication of the event. Applying this frequency theory to the tossing experiment, we see that in a sample of 20 tosses, we may not get exactly ten heads; nevertheless, as number of tosses increases, the ratio of number of heads to the total number of tosses approaches 1/2. Although in many situations, the computation of probability through EQ (3) is difficult and will need some algebraic manipulations, that definition is crucial for the understanding of the theory of probability. This can be seen in reference to some examples. To work out these examples we need some background regarding (a) factorial notation, (b) permutation and combination, (c) the principle of independent joint actions, and (d) sample space and outcome trees.

(a)   FACTORIAL NOTATION

A factorial of a number, say, 5, denoted by 5!, is defined as

$$5! = 5 \times 4 \times 3 \times 2 \times 1 = 120$$

Similarly, 4! = 4 x 3 x 2 = 24.

It is seen from above that

$$5! = 5 \times 4!$$

Similarly, then

$$r! = 1 \times 2 \times 3 \ldots \times (r-1) \times r \text{ and}$$

$$r! = r (r-1)!$$

When r is large, say, r = 52, r! can be computed by the use of a computer.

(b)   COMBINATIONS AND PERMUTATIONS

If there are three balls, marked A, B, C, in a box, in how many ways can two balls be taken out of the box? The obvious answer is three: AB, AC and BC.   When, as in this case, we are not making any distinction between AB and BA, the process is known as "combination" and is denoted by $3c_2$.   In general cases, when r objects are taken out of n objects, the number of combinations, or ways, we can do the job is denoted by n_{cr}

$$n_{cr} = \frac{n!}{r!(n-r)!} \tag{6}$$

In the above example n = 3, and r = 2, so $3C_2 = \frac{3!}{2!(3-1)!} = 3$, which is the same answer that we found from simple arrangements
       When we are interested in the <u>order</u> of the arrangement, i.e., noting that AB is <u>not</u> the same as BA, then the process is known as permutation, and denoted by $n_{pr} = n_{cr} \times r!$

(c)   PRINCIPLE OF INDEPENDENT JOINT ACTIONS

If the first job can be done in m ways, and after we perform the first job, a second job can be done in n ways, then the two jobs can be done in m x n ways when the two jobs are independent.   For example, if there are three ways to travel from Binghamton to Syracuse, and there are four ways to go from Syracuse to Buffalo, then there are 3 x 4 = 12 ways to travel from Binghamton to Buffalo.

(d)   SAMPLE SPACE AND OUTCOME TREES

Consider the "experiment" in which we are taking a sample of three machine parts from a production line where each part can be either defective (D) or non-defective (N).   A possible outcome of this process is (NNN) where all the items are non-defective.   Obviously, there are eight possible outcomes, as shown below:

```
                                        Prob. (outcome)
        (DDD) = ℓ₁  = 1/2  1/2  1/2 = 1/8
        (DDN) = ℓ₂
        (DND) = ℓ₃
        (DNN) = ℓ₄
        (NDD) = ℓ₅
        (NDN) = ℓ₆
        (NND) = ℓ₇
        (NNN) = ℓ₈  = 1/2  1/2  1/2 = 1/8
```

The list of all possible outcomes, namely ℓ_1, ℓ_2, ℓ_3, ℓ_4, ℓ_5, ℓ_6, ℓ_7, ℓ_8 is known as the sample space or outcome set. In non-technical terms, we can say that the sample space consists of all possible outcomes of the experiment. If we assume that the probability of getting a defective or non-defective item is the same, and that the selections are independent (getting a defective item the first time does not affect the probability of subsequently selecting a defective one), then all of the outcomes have equal chance of occurrence. Since the total probability must add up to 1, we must have

$$P(\ell_1) = P(\ell_2) = P(\ell_8) = 1/8$$

Sometimes it is not easy to compute the probability of an outcome as in the above case. In those cases, we use the outcome, or probability tree as shown in Fig. 1.2. In that figure, we assume that the probability of getting a defective machine part is .1, and getting a non-defective part is .9. For example, if we want to compute the probability of the outcome (DND), we notice from the first branching of the tree in Fig. 1.2 that 10% of the parts will be defective. Of all those cases where the first item is defective, 90% will report non-defective for the second item, and of these 10% will be defective in the third drawing. So the probability of the outcome (DND) will be 1/10 of the 9/10 of 1/10 = 9/1000 as shown in Fig. 1.2.

Geometrically, an outcome can be denoted by a point on a Venn Diagram, as shown in Fig. 1.3. In many situations we need to compute the probability of an "event" rather than an outcome. An event is a subset of the outcome set. For example, the event, E, may denote

    E: not less than two defectives
i.e. $E = \{\ell_1, \ell_2, \ell_5\}$. If we want to compute the probability, $P(E)$, then we notice that ℓ_1 will take place 1/8 of the time, ℓ_2 will take place 1/8 of the time, and ℓ_5 will take place one third of the time, so that E will take place 1/8 + 1/8 + 1/8 = 3/8 of time, one way or another. Thus, the probability of an event is the sum of the probabilities of the outcomes included in the event. The event, E, which can be broken down to other outcomes, (such as ℓ_1, ℓ_2, ℓ_5) is called a composite event, whereas the outcomes, ℓ_1, ℓ_2, ℓ_5, are called simple events.

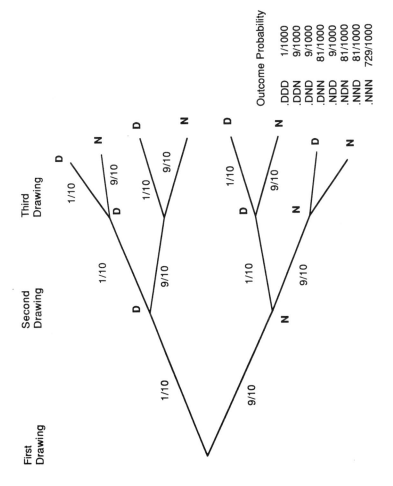

First Drawing

Second Drawing

Third Drawing

Outcome Probability

.DDD	1/1000
.DDN	9/1000
.DND	9/1000
.DNN	81/1000
.NDD	9/1000
.NDN	81/1000
.NND	81/1000
.NNN	729/1000

Figure1.2 Outcome Tree

Color

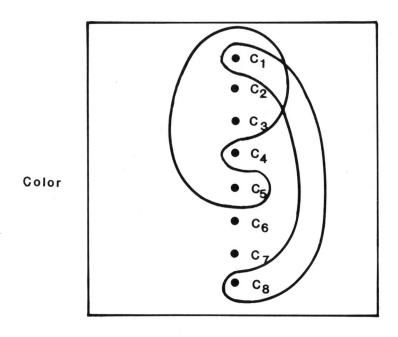

Figure 1.3 Venn Diagram for Union (U)

20

Example 1.
From the historical data, it has been found that of 2000 stores of a certain size class, 789 stores had average yearly sales of over one million dollars. What is the probability that if a store is selected at random from this group, its sales will be more than one million dollars? Assume all stores have the same probability of being selected.

Answer: By definition (3) the probability is given by

$$P(\text{Sales} > \$1m) = \frac{\text{No. of favourable cases}}{\text{Total number of cases}} = \frac{789}{2000}$$

Example 2.
A box has a white and b black balls. A certain number of balls, say, n, were removed and their colour unnoticed. Then one ball was taken at random. What is the probability that the ball is white?

Answer: Since the colour of balls has not been noticed, the information that the n balls were taken is of no value. Thus, the probability remains the same as it was before, namely,

$$P(W) = \frac{\text{Total number of favourable cases}}{\text{Total number of possible cases}} = \frac{a}{a+b}$$

Example 3.
Suppose six cards are taken at random without replacement from a full deck. What is the probability that out of these six cards, three will be red and three will be black?

Answer: If there were only three cards A, B, and C, in the deck, there can be $3! = 6$ total arrangements. The arrangements will be:

ABC	BAC
ACB	CAB
BCA	CBA

From the 52 cards, the total number of ways to take six cards will be 52_{c6} which is, of course, a large number.
We also know that there are 26 black cards and 26 red cards. Out of the 26 black cards, there are 26_{c3} ways we can take three black cards. Similarly, there are 26^3 ways to take three red cards. Similarly, there are 26_{c3} ways to take three red cards. Since taking out the red cards is independent of taking out black cards, applying the independence principle, we can say that the total number of ways the two tasks can be accomplished (taking three white cards and taking three black cards) is $26_{c3} \times 26_{c3}$. This is the total number of favourable cases. As mentioned before, the total number of all possible cases is 52_{c6}. So by definition EQ (3), the probability is given by

$$P(3W, 3B) = \frac{26_{c3} \times 26_{c3}}{52_{c6}}$$

Example 4.
There are 500 companies listed in the Fortune 500 listing. Of these companies, 360 made a profit last year, and the remaining companies did not make a profit. Suppose 20 companies are taken at random. What is the probability that out of 20 only 13 have made a profit and seven have not? Notice that since the companies have been chosen at random, they are "independent".

Answer: The total number of possible cases is 500_{c20}
    To decide the total number of favourable cases we notice that 13 profit making companies can be selected 360_{c13} ways out of all profit-making companies, and the remaining seven companies can be selected in 140_{c7} ways. Since these two cases are independent, following the independence action formula, the total number of favourable cases is

$360_{c13} \times 140_{c7}$. So, from the definition (3) of probability the required probability is given

$$P(13 \text{ profit making}, \\ 7 \text{ non-profit making}) = \frac{360_{c13} \times 140_{c7}}{500_{c20}}$$

Example 5.
There are N balls in a box out of which a are white and b are black, and n balls are chosen at random without replacement. What is the probability that out of n balls x balls will be white and (n-x) balls will be black?

Answer: Using the same principle as in (3), the required probability is given by

$$P(x \text{ White, } n-x \text{ black}) = \frac{a_{cx} \times b_{cn-x}}{N_{cn}}$$

    The above probability is known as hypergeometric probability.

ADDITION AND MULTIPLICATION RULES OF PROBABILITY

It is clear that probability, defined as a relative frequency, is always non-negative and less than or equal to one, i.e.
$$0 \leq P(E) \leq 1 \qquad (7)$$

since the number of favourable cases cannot be more than the total number of outcomes.
    Again, since the relative frequencies also add up to 1, we have
$$P(E_1) + P(E_2) + \ldots\ldots + P(E_n) = 1 \qquad (8)$$

where E_1, E_2 ... E_n are the exhaustive ways an event, E can take place. Any two events are called mutually exclusive, or pairwise disjoint, when they cannot take place at the same time.

So far, we are considering the probability of a simple event. However, in the die-throwing example, if the question is to find out the probability of getting either 1 or 2 points, the situation is different. This probability is denoted by

$$P(E_1 \cup E_2)$$

where $\cup$ stands for "union", E_1 is the event that a "1" point will come up on the die, and E_2 is the event that a "2" point will appear on the die.

When two events, E_1 and E_2, are mutually exclusive, they cannot take place at the same time and the same place. Symbolically, we write $E_1 \cap E_2 = \emptyset$, where the symbol $\cap$ is read as "intersection".

For mutually exclusive events it can be proved that:

$$P(E_1 \cup E_2) = P(E_1) + P(E_2) \qquad (9)$$

The above formula states that the probability of occurrence of either of the events E_1 and E_2 is the sum of their individual probabilities. In the die-throwing example, events E_1 and E_2 are obviously mutually exclusive, i.e. in this case "one" and "two" points cannot appear at the same time. This probability is given by

$$P(E_1 \cup E_2) = 1/6 + 1/6 = 2/6 = 1/3$$

Nevertheless, there can be situations involving events which are not mutually exclusive. Consider, for example, two light bulbs in a room. It is possible that either one of the two bulbs or both will burn out at a given time. In that case the events E_1 (the first bulb will burn out) and E_2 (the second bulb will burn out) are not mutually exclusive. Mutual exclusiveness should not be confused with independence of two events. In this case, the two events are independent since the probability concerning whether the first bulb will be burned out or not does not depend upon what happened to the second bulb. If two events are mutually exclusive, it implies that they are dependent. When the events E_1 and E_2 are not mutually exclusive, it can be proved that (9) becomes

$$P(E_1 \cup E_2) = P(E_1) + P(E_2) - P(E_1 \cap E_2) \qquad (10)$$

The expression, $P(E_1 \cap E_2)$, read as "E_1 and E_2" or "E_1 intersection E_2" denotes the joint probability of the occurrence of E_1 and E_2. In this case, it refers to the probability that both the bulbs will be fused at the same time and in the same place.

It can be shown that when the events E_1 and E_2 are independent, the joint probability is given as follows:

$$P(E_1 \cap E_2) = P(E_1) \cdot P(E_2) \qquad (11)$$

For example, the joint probability that both the bulbs will be fused in the probability that the first bulb will be fused (.6), multiplied by the probability that the second bulb will be fused (.3) i.e. .6 x .3 = .18. Thus the probability that either the first or second bulb will be fused will be given by (10) as

$$P(E_1 \cup E_2) = .3 + .6 - .18 = .72$$

In this connection, we should mention that $P(E_1)$ and $P(E_2)$ are called marginal probabilities. More examples of marginal possibilities will be given later.

Example 6.
A die is thrown. What is the probability that it will turn up with one or three points?

Answer: Let E_1 denote the event that the die has one point, and E_2 denote the event that the die has three points. Obviously, these two events are mutually exclusive, i.e. they cannot take place at the same time. Following (9),

$$P(E_1 \cup E_2) = P(E_1) + P(E_2) = 1/6 + 1/6 = 1/3$$

Example 7.
Suppose we have a group of men and women of different ages. The probability that a woman will be selected is .60, and the probability that the age of the selected person will be less than 35 is .40. What is the probability that a person selected at random will be either (1) a female, (2) of age less than 35, or (3) both?

Answer: Let E_1 denote the event that the person selected is female, and E_2 be the event that the person is less than 35 years old. Assume that E_1 and E_2 are independent. So the required probability according to (10) is given by

$$P(E_1 \cup E_2) = P(E_1) + P(E_2) - P(E_1 \cap E_2)$$
$$= .60 + .40 - (.60)(.40)$$
$$= .76$$

Example 8.
Firms may be classified according to size and profitability. Suppose that the probability that a company will have a certain size class (500-1000 workers) is .53, and the probability that the profit will be more than $1 million is .64. What is the probability that a company selected at random will be either (a) of this size class, (b) with sales over $1 million, or (c) both?

Answer: Let E_1 denote the event that the company selected will be in the size class (500-1000 workers), and E_2 be the event that the profit will be more than $1 million. Assume that E_1 and E_2 are independent. Then the required probability is

given
$$P(E_1 \cup E_2) = P(E_1) + P(E_2) - P(E_1 \cap E_2)$$
$$P(E_1) = .53 \text{ and } P(E_2) = .64$$

24

$$P(E_1 \cap E_2) = P(E_1)P(E_2) = (.53)(.64) = .34$$
finally
$$P(E_1 \cup E_2) = .53 + .64 - .34 = .83$$

Example 9.
What is the probability of getting two sixes consecutively when throwing a die?

Answer: Let E_1 denote the event of getting a six on the first throw, and E_2 denote the event of getting a six on the second throw. Obviously, these two events are independent. So the probability is

$$P(E_1 \cap E_2) = P(E_1) \cdot P(E_2),$$

$$= \frac{1}{6} \cdot \frac{1}{6} = 1/36$$

Example 10.
What is the probability that the stock price of both IBM and GAF will go up tomorrow when the probability that IBM will go up is .5 and that GAF will go up is .3?

Answer: Let E_1 be the event that the stock price of IBM will go up tomorrow, and E_2 be the same for GAF. Assume that E_1 and E_2 are independent. The joint probability of these events taking place is

$$P(E_1 \cap E_2) = P(E_1)P(E_2) = .5 \times .3 = .15$$

CONDITIONAL PROBABILITY

It has been mentioned before that when two events are independent, the probability of the occurrence of one event is not influenced by the occurrence or non-occurrence of the other event. In symbolic language, if $P(E_1|E_2)$ (read as the "conditional probability of E_1, given that E_2 has taken place") is the same as $P(E_1)$ (whether E_2 has taken place or not), then the events E_1 and E_2 will be considered independent. Thus the technical definition of independence of two events E_1 and E_2 is

$$P(E_1|E_2) = P(E_1) \text{ or alternatively}$$
$$P(E_1 \cap E_2) = P(E_1) P(E_2) \tag{12}$$

When the equation (12) is not satisfied, the events will be called dependent.
Under the assumption of independence, the joint probability that the two events E_1 and E_2 will take place simultaneously is given by (as mentioned in [11]) the product of the individual probabilities, i.e. $P(E_1 \cap E_2) = P(E_1) P(E_2)$.

Example 11.
Three boxes contain 2 white and 3 black balls, 4 white and 3 black, and 2 white and 5 black balls, respectively. One ball is taken from each box. What is the probability that among these balls 2 are white and 1 is black?

Answer: This event of getting 2 white balls and 1 black ball can be accomplished in the following way. The required probability is the sum of the probabilities of the individual cases.

	Box 1	Box 2	Box 3
Case 1	W	W	B
Case 2	B	W	W
Case 3	W	B	W

In case 1, the probability of getting a white ball from Box 2 is dependent on the colour of the ball obtained from Box 1. The same is true in the case of Box 3. Thus we are dealing with a conditional probability situation. The required probability as computed from (11) is

$$\frac{2}{5} \times \frac{4}{7} \times \frac{5}{7} = \frac{40}{245}$$

Notice that individual probabilities have been multiplied, since taking a ball from one box is independent of taking a ball from another box. Similarly, the probability in Case 2 is

$$\frac{3}{5} \times \frac{4}{7} \times \frac{5}{7} = \frac{60}{245}$$

The probability in Case 3 is

$$\frac{2}{5} \times \frac{3}{7} \times \frac{2}{7} = \frac{12}{245}$$

So the total probability according to (9) is

$$\frac{40}{245} + \frac{60}{245} + \frac{12}{245} = \frac{112}{245}$$

Example 12.
Let A = event of getting double six on a roll of two die.

then $P(A) = (1/6)^2 = 1/36$

$$P(\bar{A}) = (1 - \frac{1}{36}) = 35/36$$

Similarly, P (at least one double six in n tosses)

= 1 − P(no double sixes in n tosses)
= 1 − $(35/36)^n$

We may be interested in knowing how many times, n, we have to throw two dice so that with a 50% probability, we can expect double six at least once. To find out the value of n we can put P = .50 in the above equation and solve the value of n using logarithms.

DEFINITION OF CONDITIONAL PROBABILITY

Consider the example of a box containing 3 white balls and 7 black balls. The probability of getting a white ball (event E_1) is 3/10. If the ball taken is white and is not returned, then the probability of drawing another white ball (event E_2) will be 2/9. Obviously E_2 is dependent on E_1 since the probability of E_2 depends on whether E_1 has taken place or not. When such is the case, then the conditional probability as stated before is denoted by $P(E_2|E_1)$. It can be shown that when two events are not independent, the joint probability is

$$P(E_1 \cap E_2) = P(E_1) \cdot P(E_2|E_1) \qquad (13a)$$

i.e. the joint probability is the product of the unconditional probability of E_1 (also known as marginal probability) multiplied by the conditional probability of E_2, given E_1 has taken place. The concept of conditional probability can also be explained in terms of probability trees as mentioned before. Eq. (13a) can be written in the alternative form

$$P(E_1 \cap E_2) = P(E_2) \cdot P(E_1|E_2) \qquad (13b)$$

The conditional probability formula can thus be written as

$$P(E_2|E_1) = \frac{P(E_1 \cap E_2)}{P(E_1)}$$

or $\qquad (13c)$

$$P(E_1|E_2) = \frac{P(E_1 \cap E_2)}{P(E_2)}$$

Example 13.
          The events are defined as follows:

A_1 The person buys the product A
A_2 The person does not buy the product A
B_1 The person is a college graduate
B_2 The person is not a college graduate

On the basis of past information, it is given that

$$P(A_1) = .40$$
$$P(B_2) = .55$$
$$P(B_1|A_2) = .60$$

          (i) Explain in words the meaning of $P(A_1|B_2)$ and compute it.
          (ii) Do you think that the level of education is independent of the decision to buy product A?

Answer: (i) $P(A_1 \cap B_1) + P(A_2 \cap B_1) = P(B_1)$
          $P(A_1 \cap B_1) + P(A_2) \cdot P(B_1|A_2) = P(B_1)$
          $P(A_1 \cap B_1) + (.6) (.6) = .45$
          $P(A_1 \cap B_1) = .09$

27

$$\text{(ii)} \ P(A_1 \cap B_2) + P(A_2 \cap B_2) = P(B_2)$$
$$P(A_1 \cap B_2) + P(A_2) \ P(B_2|A_2) = P(B_2)$$
$$P(A_1 \cap B_2) + (.6)(.4) = .45$$
$$P(A_1 \cap B_2) = .21$$

$$P(A_1|B_2) = \frac{P(A_1 \cap B_2)}{P(B_2)} = \frac{.21}{.55}$$

Example 14.

The probability that a consumer will buy coffee is .10. If the person buys coffee, the probability that he/she will also buy cream is .4. The probability that he/she will buy cookies (whether he buys coffee or cream) is .6.

a.   What is the probability that the person will buy both coffee and cream?

b.   What is the probability that the person will buy coffee and cookies?

Answer: a. $P(C \cap CR) = P(C)P(CR/C) = .10 \times .4 = .040$

            b. $P(C \cap CK) = P(C) \ P(CK) = .10 \times .6 = .060$

BAYES' THEOREM

In scientific inquiry in general and management science in particular, policy decisions are made on the basis of changing the strategy in the light of new information. For example, the market share of a company selling coffee may have been stable at .20 for the last three months. Obviously, its market share is influenced by the sales strategy of its competitors. The company may wish to revise the market share estimate on the basis of information acquired through the use of a market survey. This revision can be accomplished through the use of Bayes' Theorem.

Bayes Theorem is an application of the conditional probability. Consider the following examples:

Example 15.

In a company with three factories, suppose 40% of the product is produced by Factory 1, 50% by Factory 2, and 10% by Factory 3. In Factory 1, 10% of the goods produced are defective; in Factory 2, 5%; and in Factory 3, 2%. A customer of this company purchased the product, which was found to be defective. What is the probability that it was produced by Factory 3?

Answer: The solution to this problem can be expressed in tabular form, as follows:

Events	$P(C)$ Probability of events	x	$P(E\|C)$ Cond. Prob.	=	$P(E \cap C)$ Joint Prob.
C_1 (Factory 1)	.40	x	.10	=	.040
C_2 (Factory 2)	.50	x	.05	=	.025
C_3 (Factory 3)	.10	x	.02	=	.002
				Total $P(E)$ =	.067

28

The required conditional probability $= P(C_3/E) = \dfrac{P(C_3 \cap E)}{P(E)}$

$$P(C_3|E) = \frac{.002}{.067} = .03$$

Example 16.

There are boxes marked B_1, B_2, and B_3.

B_1 has 3 white balls and 5 black balls.
B_2 has 4 white balls and 3 black balls.
B_3 has 3 white balls and 6 black balls.

A box is chosen at random, and a ball is taken and found to be white. What is the probability that the first box was chosen?

Answer: It should be noticed that the question asked here is the reverse of what is usually asked. The question that is normally asked is this: if a ball is taken from one of the boxes, what is the probability that it will be white? The answer to that question is simple. The probability of choosing a white ball, given that the first box was selected is

$$P(W|B_1) = 3/8$$

Similarly,

$P(W|B_2) = 4/7$
$P(W|B_3) = 3/9$. But we need to compute $P(B_1|W)$. For that, we proceed as follows. Each box has an equal chance of being selected, i.e.

$$P(B_1) = P(B_2) = P(B_3) = 1/3$$

So $P(W)$, the probability of getting a white ball, will be obtained by simply adding the joint probability, i.e.

$P(W) = P(B_1) \cdot P(W|B_1) + P(B_2) \ P(W|B_2) + P(B_3) \cdot P(W|B_3)$
$= [(1/3)] \cdot [3/8)] + [(1/3)] \cdot [(4/7)] + [(1/3)] \cdot (3/9)]$
$= .43$

It is noted that

$$P(W|B_1) = 3/8$$

However, the question that is asked in this example is

$$P(B_1|W) = ?$$

To answer the question, we use Bayes' Theorem, which is given by

$$P\ (B_1|W) = \frac{P(B_1)\ P(W|B_1)}{P(W)} = \frac{1/3 \cdot 3/8}{.43} = .29$$

It should be carefully noted that the answer in Example (15) is different from $P(B_1) = 1/3$. When we do not know the colour of the ball, there is an equal probability of selecting a box, i.e. 1/3. Once we know the colour of the ball, this probability changes. Obviously, if a box has relatively more white balls, the probability of selecting that box will be higher than 1/3.

Bayes' Theorem helps us to modify the estimate of an initial or a priori probability with the aid of new information. The a priori probability can be either a subjective probability, or one that has been established on the basis of past experience. Suppose that it has been established that over the last five years the market share of any product has been steady at 20%. A competitor has introduced a new product, and we wish to know how it will affect our market share.

For that purpose we can conduct a sample survey and use its results to modify the initial probabilities with the help of Bayes' theorem, as we have applied it in Examples (14) and (15).

We usually have a difficulty in identifying a Bayes' Theorem problem. In such a problem, the initial probability, such as $P(E/C_3)$, is given, and we want just the opposite, namely, $P(C_3/E)$. Once we identify a Bayes' Theorem problem, the computation is straightforward, particularly when the tabular formulation of Example 15 is followed.

Summary Review of Section B

Key Words

Sample Mean
Variance
Sample Relative Frequency
Probability
Factorial Notation
Permutation and Combination
Independent Joint Actions
Mutually Exclusive (pairwise disjoint)
Union
Intersection
Joint Probability
Marginal Probabilities
Conditional Probability
Independent Events
Bayes' Theorem
Outcome
Sample Space

<u>Formulas</u>

1. $\mu = \sum\limits_{t=1}^{N} X_i \ (f_i/N)$

2. $\sigma^2 = \sum\limits_{t=1}^{N} (X_i - \mu)^2 \ (f_i/N)$

3. $P(E) = \dfrac{\text{\# of outcomes in the experiment favourable to event}}{\text{total number of possible outcomes of the experiment}}$

4. $P(E) = \lim\limits_{n\to\infty} \left(\dfrac{n_1}{n}\right)$

5. $r! = r(r-1)!$

6. $n_{cr} = \dfrac{n!}{n!(n-r)!}$

7. $n_{pr} = n_{cr} \cdot r!$

8. $P(E_1) + P(E_2) + \ldots + P(E_n) = 1$

9. $P(E_1 \ U \ E_2) = P(E_1) + P(E_2)$ when E_1 and E_2 are mutually exclusive

10. $P(E_1 \ U \ E_2) = P(E_1) + P(E_2) - P(E_1 \cap E_2)$ when E_1 and E_2 are not mutually exclusive.

11. $P(E_1 \cap E_2) = P(E_1) \cdot P(E_2)$

12. $P(E_1 \cap E_2) = P(E_1) \cdot P(E_2/E_1)$

Bayes' Theorem: $P(E|F) = \dfrac{P(E) \cdot P(F|E)}{P(F)}$

where $P(F) = P(E) \cdot P(F/E) + P(\overline{E}) \cdot P(F/\overline{E})$,

$\overline{E}$ being the complementary event of E

Probability Distributions

The basic problem in statistics is that the possible values of the variable(s) in the population are numerous. As such, it is only possible for us to make a probability statement, such as, the number of riots will take a value within a certain range. The computation of the population mean $\mu = \Sigma x\ (\pi)$ and $\sigma = \Sigma(x - \mu)^2\ (\pi)$ depends upon the value of (π). If we are dealing with a discrete variable, such as number of riots, and certain assumptions of independence and the constancy of the probability of occurrence of the events are assumed, then this probability can be obtained from the binomial distribution by using the probability function

$$P_{b(x)} = \frac{n!}{x!\ (n-x)!} \qquad \pi^x(1 - \pi)^{n-x}$$

where n denotes the number of confrontations and "p" is the probability of a riot. This function will give the probability that out of, n = 10 confrontations, x = 3 will result in riots where the probability of riots p = .3 (for example). In the case of binomial distribution it is assumed that the successive events are independent and the probability of riots does not change from trial to trial. If the probability "p" of such an event, e.g. war, is very small, but the number of confrontations that may lead to war "n" is large, so that m = np is finite, then the probability of that x = 0,1,2... war will take place, can be obtained from the Poisson distribution by the formula

$$P_p(x) = e^{-m} \cdot \frac{m^x}{x!}$$

If the variable under consideration is continuous (all variables can be assumed to be continuous) then the probability that the variable "x" will take values within a small range X ± dx can be computed by the probability function of the normal distribution

$$P_N(x) = \frac{1}{\sqrt{2\pi}\ \sigma} - \text{Exp}\ (x - \mu)^2/2\sigma^2)$$

where μ, σ denote the population mean and the standard deviation respectively. It can be shown that when n is large the binomial and Poisson converges to normal. Most of the events in the international conflict arena can be characterized by binomial, Poisson and normal distributions or their extensions.

Supplementary Examples

1. An urn contains a white balls and b black balls. If a + b balls are drawn from this urn, find the probability that among them there will be exactly a white and b black balls.

2. From an urn containing a white balls and b black one, a certain number of balls, k, is drawn, and they are laid aside, their colour unnoted. Then one more ball is drawn; and it is required to find the probability that it is a white or a black ball.

3. Two dice are thrown n times in succession. What is the probability of obtaining double six at least once?

4. Two urns contain respectively 3 white, 7 red, 15 black balls, and 10 white, 5 red, 9 black balls. One ball is taken from each urn. What is the probability that they both will be of the same colour?

5. What is the probability that of 6 cards taken from a full pack, 3 will be black and 3 red?

6. Ten cards are taken from a full pack. What is the probability of finding among them (a) at least one ace; (b) at least two aces?

7. The face cards are removed from a full pack. Out of the 40 remaining cards, 4 are drawn. What is the probability that they belong to different suits?

8. Under the same conditions, what is the probability that the 4 cards belong to different suits and different denominations?

9. Three urns contain respectively 1 white and 2 black balls; 3 white and 1 black balls, 2 white and 3 black balls. One ball is taken from each urn. What is the probability that among the balls drawn there are 2 white and 1 black?

10. Cards are drawn one by one from a full deck. What is the probability that 10 cards will precede the first ace?

11. Urn 1 contains 10 white and 3 black balls; urn 2 contains 3 white and 5 black balls. Two balls are transferred from No. 1 and placed in No. 2 and then one ball is taken from the latter. What is the probability that it is a white ball?

12. Two urns identical in appearance contain respectively 3 white and 2 black balls; 2 white and 5 black balls. One urn is selected and a ball taken from it. What is the probability that this ball is white?

13. What is the probability that 5 tickets drawn in the French lottery all have one-digit numbers?

14. What is the probability that each of the four players in a bridge game will get a complete suite of cards?

15. In how many ways can all the letters of the word Mississippi be arranged?

16. 6 cards are chosen at random from a pack of 52; what is the probability that 3 will be black and 3 red?

17. 2 dice are thrown; what is the probability that the sum shown will be 7 or 11?

18. A die is thrown 12 times; what is the probability that the face 4 will appear just twice?

19. A throws 3 coins, B throws 2; what is the chance that A will throw a greater number of heads than B?

20. A card is drawn at random from a pack and replaced, then a second drawing is made, and so on. How many drawings must be made in order to have a chance of $\frac{1}{2}$ that the ace of spades shall appear at least once?

21. In how many throws with a single die is there an even chance that the number 6 will appear at least once?

22. 2 dice are thrown; in how many turns is there an even chance that double sixes will appear at least once?

23.

Colossal Supermarket stores are located throughout the United States as follows:

Population of City	Geographic Area					
	NE	SE	Central	NW	SW	US
	B_1	B_2	B_3	B_4	B_5	
A_1 Under 20,000	3	5	6	5	6	25
A_2 20,000–under 50,000	5	11	16	9	9	50
A_3 50,000–under 100,000	29	12	3	7	24	75
A_4 100,000 and over	63	12	10	4	11	100
All Cities	100	40	35	25	50	250

a. What is the symbolic notation for the probability that a store selects at random to participate in an experimental program is located:

1. In a Southeastern city under 20,000 population?
2. In a city in the Central US with population 50,000-under 100,000?
3. In the Northeast?
4. In a city with population 100,000 or more?
5. In the Northeast given that the experimental store is to be in a city with population 20,000-under 50,000?

b. Explain in words the probability designated by each of the following symbolic forms:

1. $P(A_3|/b_4)$ 4. $P(B_2)$

2. $P(A_3 \text{ and } B_2)$ 5. $P(A_1 \text{ and } B_5)$

3. $P(A_1)$

c. What is each of the probabilities in a?

d. What is each of the probabilities in b?

e. How do you interpret any of your probability statements in c and d?

f. Which of the probabilities in a is a joint probability? A marginal probability? A conditional probability?

g. Derive the marginal probability distribution by size of city. Explain the meaning of this distribution.

h. Derive the conditional probability distribution by geographic area, given that the size of the city is 50,000-under 100,000. Explain the meaning of this distribution.

i. Find the following probabilities by the multiplication theorem or the probability directly from the distribution of stores.

1. $P(A_1 \text{ or } B_4)$ 4. $P(A_4 \text{ and } B_3)$

2. $P(A_2 \text{ and } B_1)$ 5. $P(A_1 \text{ and } A_3)$

3. $P(B_2 \text{ or } B_5)$ 6. $P(A_3 \text{ and } B_1)$

j. Are the two variables (size of city and geographic area) statistically independent in the population of 250 stores? Explain fully how you arrived at your answer.

k. If the two variables are independent, of what significance is this? If they are not independent, what is the nature of the relationship between them?

24. Given: A_1 Person reads Magazine A

                             A_2 Person does not read Magazine A

                             B_1 Person is male

                             B_2 Person is female

and that in the population under study:

$$P(A_1) = .40 \qquad\qquad P(B_1|A_2) = .60$$
$$P(B_2) = .55$$

a.   Find $P(A_1 \text{ and } B_1)$. What probability is designated by this symbolic form?

b.   Find $P(A_2|B_1)$. What probability is designated by this symbolic form?

c.   Find $P(A_2 \text{ and } B_2)$. What probability is designated by this symbolic form?

d.   Are the two variables (readership and sex) independent in this population? Explain fully the basis for your answer.

3.   The probability that a customer entering a supermarket buys spaghetti is .10. If the customer buys spaghetti, the probability that he will also buy spaghetti sauce is .4. Whether or not the customer buys spaghetti, the probability is .5 that he will buy milk.

     a.   What is the probability that a customer will buy both spaghetti and spaghetti sauce? Explain the basis for your answer.

     b.   What is the probability that the customer will buy both spaghetti and milk? Explain the basis for your answer.

25. A has three pennies, B has two. The coins are all thrown, and it is agreed that the player showing the greatest number of heads shall win all; in case of a tie, B shall win. How is this game from A's point of view?

C.   Statistical Inference

The theory of statistical inference helps in making judgements about a parameter on the basis of a sample statistic. The parameters characterize the population distribution, and the statistic is a function of sample observations. Point and interval estimation theory gives us an idea about the numerical value of the population parameter. Once this estimation is performed with a given amount of confidence, it can be used for different types of management decision making, e.g. the product design, increasing/decreasing advertisement outlay, changing the price, etc. Nevertheless, the process of estimation is not conducted in the complete absence of any <u>a priori</u> information. For example, an engineer may not know exactly the average life of all light bulbs produced, but on the basis of his experience he has some idea about the number of hours a light bulb will last, for example, 1200 hours. Naturally, he wants to test - on the basis of a sample of light bulbs - whether he is right or wrong.

More importantly, the engineer may be interested in testing a new method of manufacturing to find out whether it will increase the life of the light bulb. Similarly, an economist may try to evaluate the effect of a particular monetary policy on the inflation rate, an accountant may need to tell whether a particular auditing procedure has decreased the number of errors, or a personnel officer may have to find out whether a particular organization design has increased the workers' productivity. In short, on the basis of sample observations, we want to know whether a population parameter has a particular value or whether it has changed from a previous known value as a result of some new policy decisions made by the decision maker. Such questions can be answered by the Theory of Testing of Hypotheses.

In this case, making a hypothesis about either one or a set of parameters is called parametric testing. If there is more than one parameter, and we are testing for all of them, then it will be a simple hypothesis. For example, for the distribution $f(X, \theta_1, \theta_2)$, the null hypothesis, $\theta_1 = 2$, $\theta_2 = 3$, will be a simple hypothesis.

Thus, in the above case, $H_0: \theta_1 = 2$, $\theta_2 < 3$, will be a composite hypothesis. In the example concerning the light bulb we are testing for the average life-hours in the population (μ). If we assume that the population variance, σ^2, is known, or that an estimate is used, then it will be a simple hypothesis; if however, we are making a hypothesis about μ and σ^2 simultaneously, it will be a composite hypothesis. We are, of course, assuming here that the population distribution can be characterized by two parameters only, namely, mean (μ) and variance (σ^2). If the population distribution is normal, this will be the case. In some situations, the population distribution may not be known. In that case, it will be called a non-parametric distribution. For example, any hypothesis regarding the population median will be a non-parametric hypothesis since the probability distribution of the median does not involve any parameter. In this chapter, we shall be interested only in the simple parametric testing of the hypothesis and shall assume (unless otherwise stated) that in the case of a continuous variate the

37

population distribution is normal with mean μ and variance σ^2, and that when samples are taken from the population, the drawings are independent with replacements.

TESTING FOR THE POPULATION MEAN (μ) WHEN THE POPULATION STANDARD DEVIATION (σ) IS KNOWN

Following the same example just provided, let us suppose that the engineer believes that the population mean value (μ) of the life of the light bulb is 1200 hours. He wants to test whether he is right. From past experience he may know definitely that the population value of the standard deviation (σ) is 3. Symbolically, the situation can be specified by what is known as the null hypothesis,

$$H_o \ (\mu_o = 1200)$$

(1)

If on the basis of sample observations and a proper test procedure (defined in Equation (4) the null hypothesis cannot be supported, then H_o in (1) will be rejected. The alternative hypothesis, H_1, that the population mean value is not equal to 1200, will be accepted. Symbolically, the alternative hypothesis can be written as

$$H_1 \ (\mu_o \neq 1200)$$

(2)

Obviously, in this case, the alternative hypothesis is two-sided (or two-tailed, as it is often called) since the average life hours in the population can be more than or less than 1200.

If the engineer has adopted a new manufacturing technique and expects that, as a consequence, the life-hours have increased, then the alternative hypothesis will be one-sided (in this case, right-tailed), namely,

$$H_1 \ (\mu > 1200)$$

(3)

The null hypothesis is always written in terms of equality, i.e. $H_o(\mu=\mu_o)$. Whether the alternative hypothesis is two-tailed or one-tailed (left or right) will depend upon the statement of the problem. For example, a store has recently hired an MBA graduate in the marketing department and expects that this will lead to an increase in sales. Before the hiring the monthly sales were $1000. The manager now has sales data for 14 months subsequent to the hiring. He wants to test whether the hiring has increased the sales. Obviously, the null hypothesis in this case is H_o ($\mu = 1000$) and the alternative hypothesis is H_1 ($\mu > 1000$). The alternative hypothesis is one-sided upper-tailed since the manager is expecting the rise in sales. Similarly, in testing the effectiveness of posting a guard to reduce vandalism, the alternative hypothesis is one-sided left-tailed. On the other hand, with regard to testing the effectiveness of a drug, the hypothesis is two-sided both-tailed, since we do not know whether it is an improvement or detriment over an existing drug.

For the sake of simplicity, let us start with the case of a two-tailed alternative. Our objective is to choose a decision procedure (or a test statistic as it is often called) to test the null hypothesis H_o ($\mu = \mu_o$) against H_1 ($\mu \neq \mu_o$) on the basis of a sample of size n of the variable X, i.e. X_1, $X_2, \ldots X_n$ (say, n = 49). The simplest approach will be to compute the sample mean -- a consistent, efficient and unbiased estimate of the population mean.

$$\overline{X} = \frac{X_1 + X_2 + X_n}{n} = 1209 \text{ (say)}$$

We then see whether the difference between this best estimate of the parameter and its hypothesized value, i.e. ($X = \mu_o$), is large or not compared with the standard error of X, i.e. $\sigma/\sqrt{n}$. The reason we compare the difference with the standard error is because standard error is by definition the amount of variation in estimates we can expect due to random (not intrinsic) causes. Thus, particularly for large n (n > 30 by convention), the test procedure is to compute the test statistic

$$Z = \frac{\overline{X} - \mu_o}{\sigma/\sqrt{n}} \qquad (4)$$

and see whether the value of Z is too large or too small in reference to a normally distributed variate. The frequency function of that variate is shown in Figure 1.4.

If X's are normally distributed, Z in (4) will also be normally distributed for any n. Even if X's are not normally distributed, by the central limit theories, for large n, Z will be so distributed. Basically, then, to test the null hypothesis against an alternative hypothesis (one-tailed or two-tailed), we need to compute the test statistic in (4) and read the probability of getting such a value from a normal table. For example, if, for a hypothetical case, the value of Z is 2.04, then we find from such a table that the probability (known as the Prob-Value) of getting 2.04 or more (if the null hypothesis is true) equals .0207, which is quite small. Usually a cutoff value of α = .05 and the corresponding Z = ± 1.96 are chosen. This α is known as the level of significance, or probability of a Type I error.

Thus, to test the null hypothesis (1) with the two-tailed alternative hypothesis (2), given α = .05 and known σ, we simply need to compute (4) and reject H_o when Z > 1.96 or Z < -1.96. Otherwise, we accept H_o. When Z is either > 1.96 or < -1.96, the set of values for Z > 1.96 and Z < -1.96 is known as the rejection area, or critical region.

Of course, when the value of α changes, the cutoff value of Z also changes. For example, when α = .01, the value of Z is ± 2.58, As can be seen from a normal probability table in any statistics book, for values of α = .10, .15, .20, and .30, the corresponding values for Z are ± 1.64, ± 1.44, ± 1.28, and ± 1.04. We should note carefully that to obtain a value of Z

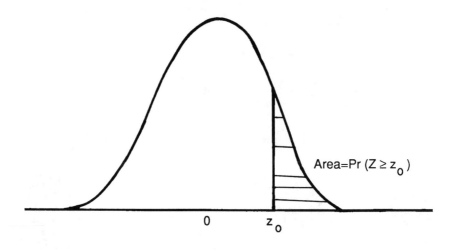

Figure 1.4: Frequency Function of a Normally Distributed Variate

for a given α we should look for the $\alpha/2$ value in the body of the table and then read off the corresponding value of Z from the first column, since we are dealing with a two-tailed alternative hypothesis in this example. In some texts, the two-tailed combined values of the probabilities are given so that one does not have to divide by 2. It is more important to understand how to get the probability from the chart rather than merely to follow a mechanical process. Thus it is highly beneficial that we practise the computation of Z values for different values of α.

In a situation where many null hypotheses are tested routinely (as in the department of statistical quality control in a company), the repeated use of (4) may be time-consuming. Instead, after a little manipulation the rule (4) may be written as follows:

$$\text{if } \bar{X} \geq \mu_o + 1.96 \ \sigma/\sqrt{n}$$
$$\text{Reject } H_o \qquad\qquad (4a)$$
$$\text{or } \bar{X} \leq \mu_o - 1.96 \ \sigma/\sqrt{n}$$

Otherwise, accept H_o.

An alternative method of testing a two-tailed hypothesis is to construct an interval estimation, $\bar{X} \pm 1.96 \ \sigma/\sqrt{n}$, for μ, and examine whether the hypothetical population parameter, μ_o, falls within the interval. If that is the case, H_o is accepted. In the light bulb example ($\mu_o = 1200$, $\sigma = 3$), let us suppose, for a sample of size, $n = 49$, $\bar{X} = 1209$. The interval estimate of μ will be $\bar{X} \pm 1.96 \ \sigma/\sqrt{n}$ (assuming $\alpha = .05$), i.e. 1209.16 to 1209.84. Since the hypothetical value, $\mu_o = 1200$, falls in this region, the null hypothesis is accepted, and we conclude that the average life in bulb hours has not changed from 1200 hours.

When the alternative hypothesis is one-sided, say, H_1: ($\mu > 1200$), the procedure of (4) still applies except that the critical value, Z (say Z_o) is chosen in such a way that $P(Z > Z_o)$ is .05. From normal table, it is seen that this value is $+1.64$. Note that since the alternative hypothesis is one-tailed, we look for $\alpha = .05$ (and not $\alpha/2$) in the body of the table. If the computed value from (4) is more than 1.64, we reject H_o. When the alternative hypothesis is left-tailed, i.e. H_1 ($\mu < 1200$), the critical value is -1.64. Thus when the computed value (4) is less than -1.64, we reject the null hypothesis, H_o. If the value of α changes, the critical values will change, just as they did in the case of the two-sided test.

Geometrically, the rejection area (outside Z = ± 1.96), or the shaded area in Fig. 1.4, is known as the critical region. If the value of the test statistic Z falls in that region, the null hypothesis is rejected. The probability of the test statistic falling in this region when the null hypothesis is true is $\alpha = .025 + .025 = .05$, as we have seen from a normal table.

In essence, if we repeat the test procedure (4) a very large number of times, we shall make an error 5% of the time, i.e. we shall reject the hypothesis when it is to be accepted five times out of 100. In terms of the light bulb example, good lots (average life of more than 1200 hours) will be defective 5% of the time. The situation is similar to rejecting a good machine part. This type of error is called a Type I error. The size of this error, representing the area of the critical region, is known as the level of significance, denoted by α. The quantity $1-\alpha$, denoting the proportion of correct decisions, is known as the confidence level, and the value of α is usually predetermined.

If we want to decrease the size of α, we have to increase the value of Z, say, from ± 1.96 to ± 2.58. As seen from the normal table, the Type I error will then be .01. One danger with this decision is that another type of error creeps in. With a high cutoff value of Z, H_o is rejected less often, i.e. (average life $\neq$ 1200 hrs.) i.e. bulbs pass as non-defective. This error is more troublesome to the engineer since defective items will more often cause adverse customer reactions. This type of error, denoted by β, namely, the probability of accepting the null hypothesis when it is to be rejected, is known as the Type II error. Fig. 1.6 shows Type I and Type II errors.

For a fixed sample size, Type I and Type II errors cannot be controlled simultaneously. The smaller the Type I error, the greater the Type II error. The best we can do is to devise a test procedure (decision rule) by means of which the Type II error will be minimized for a given amount of Type I error. It can be proved, using the Neyman–Pearson Lemma, that the best test procedure is given by (4). In a subsequent section, we shall discuss how to compute the Type II error for a given amount of Type I error we define Type I and Type II errors in the following way which is easy to memorize. Fig. 1.6 explains the errors graphically.

Decision/Event	Null Hypothesis is True	Null Hypothesis is not True
Accept H_o	No Error	Type II error = β
Reject H_o	Type I Error (α)	No Error

Example 1.
A Company producing a packaged food item wants to make sure that the average weight of the item is <u>exactly</u> 16 ounces. From past experience, it is found that the standard deviation of the weights is 3 ounces. To keep production under control, the foreman took a sample of n = 49 items and found the average weight to be 14.2 ounces. On the basis of this information, can he conclude that the production is under control? (use α = .05).

Answer: The null hypothesis of this problem is H_o (μ = 16) and the alternative hypothesis is

$$H_1 \ (\mu \neq 16)$$
$$\alpha = .05; \ n = 49, \ \overline{X} = 14.2$$

To test the null hypothesis, H_o, we compute

$$Z = \frac{\overline{X} - \mu_o}{\sigma/\sqrt{n}} = \frac{14.2 - 16.0}{3/\sqrt{49}} = -4.2$$

For $\alpha = .05$, $Z_{.025} = \pm 1.96$.

Since computed $Z = -4.2$ falls within the critical region, the null hypothesis, H_o, is rejected. The production is not under control.

TESTING FOR THE POPULATION MEAN WHEN THE POPULATION STANDARD DEVIATION IS UNKNOWN

In the previous example it was assumed that the population standard deviation was known. However, if σ is not known (as is usually the case), procedure (4) needs modification. If σ is not known, but the sample size (n) is large (n > 30), we can still use (4) on the strength of the large sample theory. This is known as the large sample test. We just replace σ by its sample estimate, $s = \sqrt{\Sigma(X-\overline{X})^2/n-1}$.

However, when σ is not known, but X is still normally distributed, then Z in (4) is <u>not</u> distributed normally, i.e. the probability that Z will take a specified range of values cannot be computed from the normal probability function. Instead we use the Student's "t" distribution, and the test statistic becomes

$$t = \frac{\overline{X} - \mu_o}{s/\sqrt{n}} \quad \text{with degrees of freedom} = n-1 \quad (5)$$

(5) is the same as (4) except that σ is now replaced by s, and the t distribution is used instead of normal distribution. In Fig. 1.5, the frequency curve of the t distribution is superimposed on the frequency curve of the normal distribution. It is seen from this figure that the critical value of t has to be higher (since we lack information for the value of σ) than the Z value corresponding to the same size (α) of the critical region. For example, when the probability is .025 while Z = 1.96, the corresponding value of t (from 't' table) is 1.98 with degrees of freedom (d.f.) equal to 120. The degree of freedom is defined as the number of observations in the sample minus one, since s^2 is an unbiased estimate of σ^2 only when the sum of squares is divided by (n-1). The reason for the greater stringency of the test is the availability of less information as a result of replacing the unknown σ with s. It is to be noted that when the X's are <u>not</u> normally distributed, and the value of n is large, t is normally distributed with zero mean and unit standard deviation i.e. t approaches Z.

43

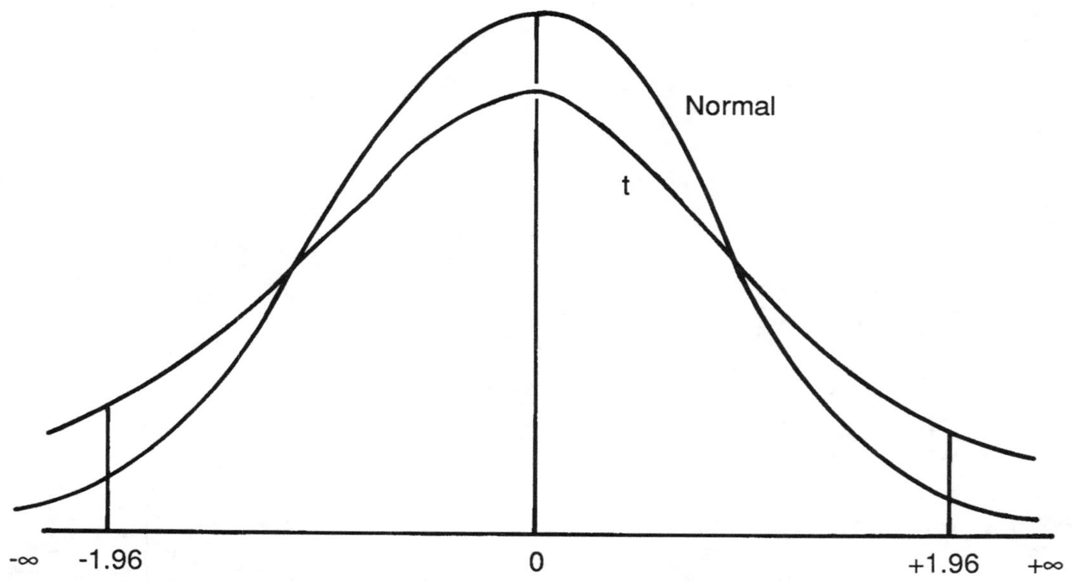

Figure 1.5: Comparison of t and Normal Distributions

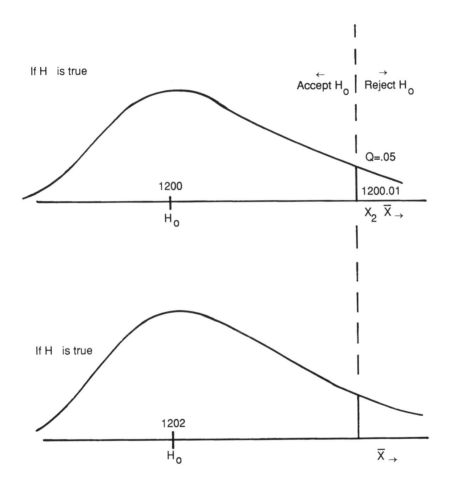

If H is true

$\leftarrow$ Accept H_0 | $\rightarrow$ Reject H_0

Q=.05

1200

1200.01

H_0

X_2 $\overline{X}_{\rightarrow}$

If H is true

1202

H_0

$\overline{X}_{\rightarrow}$

Figure 1.6: Graphical Explanation of Type I and Type II Errors

Example 2.
A machine in a certain plant has historically produced 500
items daily with a variance of 64. An energetic salesperson
suggests that management sell a new type of machine, which,
according to him, can produce more than 500 items daily. The
management agrees to try out the machine. Over a 9-day
period, the average daily production was found to be 509. Do
you think the salesperson has a better machine? ($\alpha = .05$).
Assume the variance for the new machine is 64.

Answer: The null and alternative hypotheses for this
problem are:

$$H_o \ (\mu = 500)$$
$$H_1 \ (\mu > 500)$$

Since we expect that the salesperson will
deliver a better quality, or at least a
same quality product.

$$\overline{X} = 509,$$

and $\sigma = \sqrt{64} = 8$

Following (4) and test activities,

$$Z = \frac{\overline{X} - \mu_o}{\sigma/\sqrt{n}} = \frac{509 - 500}{\sigma/\sqrt{9}} = 3.37$$

The right-tailed value for Z for $\alpha = .05$ is $+ 1.64$. Since the
computed value of $Z = 3.37$, which is greater than the critical
value, we reject the null hypothesis, H_o, and conclude that
the new machine is better.

Example 3.
The price-earning ratio (P/E) for a company is defined as the
shares price divided by the earnings per share. In the last
year the average of price-earning ratios for all industries in
manufacturing was 7.0. In the current year, there is a
suspicion that this ratio has declined. To test this, a
sample of 40 companies was taken, and the following ratios
were computed. Test whether the suspicion is true or false.

Price-earning Ratio (P/E) for n = 40 companies

7	6	11	12	13	6	10	12
8	9	6	9	12	11	12	13
1	17	8	13	14	16	20	13
12	12	13	6	12	11	10	12
8	9	13	12	18	16	18	13

Answer: The null and alternative hypotheses,
respectively, are given as

$$H_o \ (\mu = 7.0) \text{ and}$$
$$H_1 \ (\mu < 7.0)$$

The population standard deviation σ is not known. However, since n = 40 is large (n > 30), we can still use (4) as a normal variate, replacing σ by s. From the data we obtain $\bar{X}$ = 11.35, and s = 3.8

$$Z = \frac{11.5 - 7.0 = 7.5}{3.8/\sqrt{40}}$$

Since the value of Z is more than 1.64, we reject the null hypothesis, H_a, and conclude that the ratio has declined.

Example 4.
A variable denoting the number of errors per page follows Poisson distribution. For the sake of simplicity, let us assume that it is normally distributed. An auditor adopts a new sampling technique and wants to know whether it has changed the detection of the average number of errors per page in an accounting report. For a number of years, this average was found to be 8. For a sample of 20 pages, he finds that the average is 6.5, with a standard deviation of 1.3. Do you think that his new technique has changed the average detection number, given α = .05? Assume that only the new sampling procedure may be responsible for this change.

Answer: The data given in the problem are n = 20, $\bar{X}$ = 6.5, and s = 1.3.   The null hypothesis to be tested is
H_o (μ = 8) against the alternative H_1 (μ < 8). This is a one-tailed alternative hypothesis. Since the sample size is less than 30, and the population standard deviation is not given, the appropriate test to be used is the one-tailed t test

$$t = \frac{\bar{X} - \mu_o}{s/\sqrt{n}} \quad d.f. = n-1 = 20-1 = 19$$

$$= \frac{6.5 - 8}{1.3/\sqrt{20}} = -5.16$$

With degrees of freedom = 20 - 1 = 19, the left-tailed 5% value of t is -1.729. Since our computed result, t = -5.16 is less than this value, we reject the null hypothesis and conclude that the new technique has changed the average number detected.

Example 5.
     The liquidity of a company is measured by what is known as the "current ratio". This ratio is attained by dividing the current assets (cash and other assets) by the current liability, namely as the short-term debt. For the last 15

years the average of the ratios was found to be quite stable at 1.2. A sample of ten companies was selected, and the value of the 1980 ratio was found to be as recorded below. Test whether the hypothesis that the ratio was declined can be accepted. (α = .05).

Company	Current Ratio
1	1.3
2	.8
3	1.2
4	1.8
5	1.6
6	2.6
7	1.5
8	.7
9	.6
10	.7

Answer: From the given data, we have n = 10, $\bar{X}$ = 1.28, and s = 1.88. Since the sample size is less than 30, and the population standard deviation is not known, the proper test to use is the t test. The null hypothesis to be tested is

H_o (μ = 1.2) against the alternative H_1 (μ < 1.2). The test is

$$t = \frac{\bar{X} - \mu_o}{s/\sqrt{n}} = \frac{1.28 - 1.2}{1.88/3.16}$$

With degrees of freedom = 9, and α = .05, the critical value of t = −1.83. Since our computed value of t is more than this critical value, we reject H_o and conclude that the ratio has changed.

Example 6.
The average monthly sales of a company was found to be 40 units. To increase the sales the company launched an advertisement program. For the next 7 months the average sales figure increased to 42.9 units with a standard deviation of 1.2. Do you think the advertisement has been effective? (α = .10). From the given data

n = 7, $\bar{X}$ = 42.9, and s = 1.2.

The null hypothesis to be tested is

H_o (μ = 40) against

H_1 (μ > 40)

The test to use is the t test

$$t = \frac{\bar{X} - \mu_o}{s/\sqrt{n}} = \frac{4.29 - 40}{1.2/\sqrt{7}} = 6.39$$

48

With degrees of freedom = 6 - 1 = 5, the right-tailed table value of t at 5% levels of significance is 1.943. Since our computed value, t = 6.39, is more than this value, we reject the null hypothesis and conclude that the advertisement has been effective.

TESTING FOR THE DIFFERENCE BETWEEN THE TWO INDEPENDENT POPULATION MEANS WHEN THE POPULATION STANDARD DEVIATIONS ARE KNOWN

So far, we have been concerned with one population, namely, all possible values of the life-hours of light bulbs. In the case of the production of machine parts, the population may be the average length of the part. In the case of the stock market, it may be the average value of the stock in a particular portfolio. In the case of marketing, for example, it may be the average monthly sales of the stores in the Northeast. However, in many instances we may want to compare two independent populations. For example, we may want to compare the average life-hours of bulbs produced by two processes, the stock prices of two portfolios, or the average monthly sales of two sets of stores, one on the East Coast and one on the West.

Taking the last example, we postulate the null hypothesis as

$$H_o(\mu_1 = \mu_2) \text{ or } H_o(\mu_1 - \mu_2 = 0) \tag{6}$$

where μ_1 is the population average sales of <u>all</u> the stores in the East, and μ_2 stands for the population average of all the stores in the West. The alternative hypotheses (assuming two-tailed formulation) can be written as

$$H_1 (\mu_1 \neq \mu_2) \text{ or}$$
$$H_1 (\mu_1 - \mu_2 \neq 0) \tag{7}$$

Realistically, the alternative hypothesis is one-tailed, i.e. the sales in one region are more or less than the sales in the other region. But in (7) the two-tailed formulation has been taken for the sake of simplicity since we may not know which region has the higher sales.

To test the above hypothesis (7), we recall the general principle and compute

$$Z = \frac{\text{Best Estimate of the parameter} - \text{Hypothesized Value}}{\text{Standard error of the estimate}} \tag{8}$$

Then we see from the normal table whether Z falls in the critical region. The parameter in this case is $\mu_1 - \mu_2$, and the hypothetical value is 0. The best estimate of $\mu_1 - \mu_2$ will be $(\bar{X}_1 - \bar{X}_2)$ where $\bar{X}_1$ is the mean of n_1 sample observations from the first population, and $\bar{X}_2$ is the mean of n_2 sample observations from the second population. Let us assume that both n_1 and n_2 are large (say, greater than 30).

It can be shown that the square of the (standard error)^2 of $\bar{X}_1 - \bar{X}_2$, i.e. $\sigma^2(\bar{X}_1 - \bar{X}_2) = \text{VAR}(\bar{X}_1 - \bar{X}_2) = \sigma_1^2/n_1 + \sigma_2^2/n_2$ where σ_1, σ_2 are population variances, respectively, assumed to be known. With this information, (8) becomes

$$Z = \frac{\bar{X}_1 - \bar{X}_2}{\sqrt{\dfrac{\sigma_1^2}{\sqrt{n_1}} + \dfrac{\sigma_2^2}{\sqrt{n_2}}}} \tag{9}$$

With $\alpha = .05$ and a two-tailed alternative hypothesis (7), the critical value of $Z = \pm 1.96$. Even if μ_1, μ_2 are not known and are estimated by sample variances, s_1 and s_2, we can still use normal distribution, provided both n_1 and n_2 are large (> 30). It may be mentioned in passing that the stipulated "hypothetical" value of the parameter in equation (7) need not be zero. If it is hypothesized that the average sales in the first region are $4 million more than those in the other region, then the appropriate null and alternative hypotheses will be

$$H_o \ (\mu_1 - \mu_2 = \$4m)$$
$$H_1 \ (\mu_1 - \mu_2 > \$4m)$$

The test statistics becomes $Z = \dfrac{\bar{X}_1 - \bar{X}_2 - 4}{\sqrt{\dfrac{\sigma_1^2}{\sqrt{n_1}} + \dfrac{\sigma_2^2}{\sqrt{n_2}}}}$

Obviously, the alternative hypothesis need not be always two-tailed. However, the same test procedure applies except that we use different critical Z values. The above hypothesis can also be tested with the help of interval estimation of $\mu_1 - \mu_2$. The interval estimate ($\alpha = .05$) in this case is

$$(\bar{X}_1 - \bar{X}_2) \pm 1.96 \ (\sqrt{\sigma_1^2}/n_1 + \sqrt{\sigma_2^2}/\sqrt{n_2})$$

If the hypothetical stipulated value, 0, in (6) lies within the interval, the hypothesis is accepted.

Example 7.
A company uses two machines manufactured by two different sources. One is domestic and the other foreign. The manager is thinking of making a major purchase of new machines and wants to know whether there is any difference in the average length of the parts produced by the two machines. He takes two random samples of 35 and 45 units manufactured by domestic and foreign machines, respectively. The sample average lengths of the machine parts are 2.40 and 2.36, and the population standard deviations are .13 and .24, respectively. Do you think the performance of the machines is equal? ($\alpha = .05$).

Answer: From the problem the following data is known:

$$n_1 = 35 \text{ and } n_2 = 45, \ \overline{X}_1 = 2.40 \text{ and}$$

$$\overline{X}_2 = 2.36, \ \sigma_1 = .13 \text{ and } \sigma_2 = .24.$$

The null hypothesis to be tested is H_o
$(\mu_1 \neq \mu_2)$ or $H_1 \ (\mu_1 - \mu_2 \neq 0)$

Since sample sizes are more than 30 and the population standard deviations are given, the test to be applied is the normal test.

$$\frac{\overline{X}_1 - \overline{X}_2}{\sqrt{\sigma_1^2} + \sqrt{\sigma_2^2}} = \frac{2.40 - 2.36}{\sqrt{(.13)^2} \ \sqrt{(.26)^2}} = .95$$

The two-tailed 5% value of Z is 1.96. Since our computed value, Z = .95, is less than this value, we accept the null hypothesis and conclude that the performance of the machines is equal.

Example 8.
An auditor hypothesizes that the average number of errors per report of a small firm is always two more than that of a large firm. From past experience he knows that the standard deviation of the number of errors in the two types of firms is 1.24 and 1.36, respectively. He chooses 15 large firms and 25 small firms and finds the averages are 12 and 10, respectively. Do you think the auditor's hypothesis is correct? (Assume $\alpha = .05$).

Answer: From the problem it is given that $n_1 = 15$, $\overline{X}_1 = 12$, $n_2 = 25$, $\overline{X}_2 = 10$, $\sigma_1 = 1.24$, and $\sigma_2 = 1.36$. The null hypothesis to be tested is

$$H_o \ (\mu_1 - \mu_2 = 2)$$

where μ_1 and μ_2 denote the population average number of errors for small and large firms, respectively. The alternative hypothesis is given by

$$H_1 \ (\mu_1 - \mu_2 \neq 2)$$

Since the population standard deviations are given, we use the normal test.

$$Z = \frac{\overline{X}_1 - \overline{X}_2}{\sqrt{(\sigma_1^2/n_1 + \sigma_2^2/n_2)}} = \frac{12 - 10 - 4}{.1764} = 11$$

51

Since the computed value of Z is less than -1.96, we reject the null hypothesis and conclude that there are differences in the number of errors per report for a small firm as compared to a large firm.

TESTING FOR THE DIFFERENCE BETWEEN TWO INDEPENDENT POPULATION MEANS WHEN THE POPULATION STANDARD DEVIATIONS ($\sigma_1 \sigma_2$) ARE NOT KNOWN (VARIABLES ARE ASSUMED TO BE NORMALLY DISTRIBUTED).

As is usually the case, when we make a hypothesis about the quality of their mean values, μ_1 and μ_2, the two population standard deviations are unknown, and the numbers of the observations in the samples n_1 and n_2 are frequently small. In that situation the test statistic in (9) cannot be used since it is no longer distributed normally. To construct a valid test we have to assume that the population standard deviations are equal, i.e. $\sigma_1 = \sigma_2 = \sigma$ and then obtain a pooled estimate, s_p, on the basis of sample standard deviations s_1 and s_2. The pooled estimate is given as

$$s_p = \sqrt{\left\{ \frac{(n_1-1)\ s_1^2 + (n_2-1)\ s_2^2}{n_1 + n_2 - 2} \right\}} \tag{10}$$

With the assumption of equality of variance and the estimate of this common standard deviation variance, the equation (9) can be written as:

$$t = \frac{\bar{X}_1 - \bar{X}_2 - 0}{s_p \sqrt{\left(\frac{1}{n_1} + \frac{1}{n_2}\right)}} \qquad d.f. = n_1 + n_2 - 2 \tag{11}$$

Notice that since σ_1, σ_2 are unknown, and n_1, n_2 are small, we are using t in place of Z. With d.f. = $n_1 + n_2 - 2$, we can find the critical value of t from 't' table given in any book on statistics. If the computed value of t in (11) is more than the table value, then we reject the null hypothesis that the population means are equal. Alternatively, if we are interested in using the method interval estimate of $\mu_1 - \mu_2$ for testing the same hypothesis, the appropriate interval is

$$(\bar{X}_1 - \bar{X}_2) \pm t_{.025}s_p \tag{12}$$

If 0 falls in this interval, we accept the null hypothesis, $H_0(\mu_1 - \mu_2 = 0)$, and reject the alternative hypothesis, $H_1 (\mu_1 - \mu_2 \neq 0)$. In (12), $t_{.025}$ denotes the two-tailed $\alpha = .05$ value of the t distribution obtained from 't' table with degrees of freedom $n_1 + n_2 - 2$.

In the above analysis, we assumed that the two samples are independent. In some cases, this need not be the case. For example, we may want to compare the sales figures for the

same stores and test whether these figures for two time periods are the same. This situation, termed as matched sample, needs a slightly different approach (see Example 10).
    The two sample cases can be generalized to a K sample situation, where K > 2. For example, we may want to test whether the population average monthly sales figures of stores located in 20 geographical regions are the same. The null hypothesis to be tested is

$$H_o \; (\mu_1 = \mu_2 = \mu_3 \; ... \; = \mu_{20}) \qquad (13)$$

The hypothesis (13) involving more than two means can be tested by the analysis of variance (ANOVA) technique.

Example 9.
A businessman invests some money in some stocks and bonds, and he thinks that the rate of return on the stocks is more than the rate of return on the bonds. He chooses at random 11 portfolios of stocks and 13 of bonds and observes the following returns. Test whether the businessman is correct in his thinking.

Rate of returns on stocks		Rate of return on Bonds (in %)	
Stock	(in %)	Bonds	
1	6	1	8
2	8	2	9
3	9	3	10
4	10	4	6
5	8	5	9
6	7	6	10
7	6	7	5
8	9	8	8
9	8	9	10
10	3	10	8
11	2	11	7
		12	7
		13	13

Answer: Stocks   Bonds

$\overline{X}_1 = 6.9$ $\overline{X}_2 = 8.38$

$s_1 = 7.93$ $s_2 = 7.42$

$n_1 = 11$ $n_1 = 13$

                                   $H_o \; (\mu_1 = \mu_2)$

                                   $H_1 \; (\mu_1 > \mu_2)$

$$t = \frac{\overline{X}_1 - \overline{X}_2}{s \sqrt{\dfrac{1}{n_1} + \dfrac{1}{n_2}}} = \frac{6.9 - 8.38}{s \sqrt{\dfrac{1}{11} + \dfrac{1}{13}}} > -t_{.05}$$

$$\text{where} \quad s^2 = \frac{(n_1-1)\ s_1^2 + (n_2-1)\ s_2^2}{n_1 + n_2-2}$$

$$t_{.05} = 1.717$$

Accept H_o

Example 10.
A pharmaceutical company is interested in testing the effectiveness of a new medicine over an old one administered to reduce blood pressure. Ten patients in a hospital were given the medicines in two consecutive months. The reduction of their blood pressures was reported as follows. Test whether the new medicine is more effective than the old one. (α = .05).

Patient	X_1 Blood pressure index with old medicine	X_2 Blood pressure index with new medicine
1	90	110
2	120	130
3	130	125
4	110	135
5	115	110
6	125	106
7	112	113
8	130	114
9	120	115
10	114	113

Answer: Since the experiment is conducted on the same patients, the two samples are not independent. It is a case of a matched sample with a small sample size and an unknown standard deviation. To work out the matched sample case, we proceed as follows. The null hypothesis to be tested is

$$H_o\ (\mu_1 - \mu_2 = 0)$$

$$H_1\ (\mu_1 - \mu_2 \neq 0)$$

Patient No.	X_1	X_2	$d_i = X_1 - X_2$
1	90	110	−20
2	120	130	−10
3	130	125	5
4	110	135	−25
5	115	110	5
6	125	106	19
7	112	113	− 1
8	130	114	16
9	120	115	5
10	114	113	1

$$\bar{d} = \sum_{i=1}^{n} d_i/n = -.5$$

$$s_d = \sqrt{\Sigma\ (d_i - \bar{d})^2/(n-1)} = 3.51$$

The appropriate test (using the values of d and s_d) is

$$t = \frac{\bar{d} - 0}{s_d/\sqrt{n}} = -.117 \text{ with d.f.} = n-1=9.$$

The one-sided 5% value of t is -1.83. Since the computed t is more than this value, H_o is accepted and we conclude that the new medicine is not more effective.

TESTING FOR THE POPULATION PROPORTION WHEN THE NUMBER OF OBSERVATIONS IN THE SAMPLE IS LARGE

So far we have discussed several tests about the population mean value of a variate X, such as total monthly sales. However, in management science and economics, questions often arise about the proportion of cases where the variate X has certain attributes. For example, in the production of a machine part we may want to know the value of the proportion of defective parts (π) in the population. Obviously, it is not possible for us to inspect all units produced. We take a sample of, say, n = 50 units. On the basis of the sample population defectives (p) we want to know whether in the population, the percentage defective, π, has a particular hypothetical value, say, π_o = .03. Thus the null hypothesis in this case is

$$H_o\ (\pi = .03) \tag{14}$$

and the two-tailed alternative hypothesis is

$$H_1\ (\pi \neq .03)$$

Alternatively, the company may have chosen a special production process by which it hopes to reduce the percentage defective from the previous figure of 3%.
In this case the null hypothesis to be tested is

$$H_o\ (\pi = .03) \tag{14a}$$

and the alternative hypothesis is

$$H_1\ (\pi < .03)$$

which is one-tailed. To test the above hypothesis we use the same principle we discussed before. We compute the sample best estimate minus the corresponding population hypothetical value, divide by the standard error of the estimate, and use it as a normal deviate for a large sample.
In this case the population hypothetical value of .03, and its best estimate is the sample proportion defective,

$p = \dfrac{m}{n}$, where m is the number of defectives in a sample of size

n. The standard error of p is

$$\sigma_p = \frac{\sqrt{\pi\ (1-\pi)}}{\sqrt{n}} \tag{15}$$

So when the null hypothesis is true, the test statistic is

$$Z = \frac{P-\pi_o}{\sqrt{\pi_o(1-\pi_o)/n}}$$

For a two-tailed alternative hypothesis with α = .05, the critical value of Z is ± 1.96. If our computed value of Z is more than 1.96 or less than −1.96, we shall reject the null hypothesis (14). For a given value of α, if the alternative hypothesis is one-sided, then the critical value of Z will be different, as determined from the normal table. When the sample size n is small, say, n < 30, the testing procedure (15) is not valid. For large n the hypothesis can be tested with the interval estimate method, namely,

$$P \pm 1.96 \ x \ \frac{\sqrt{\pi_o\ (1-\pi_o)}}{\sqrt{n}} \tag{16}$$

If π_o falls in the interval, the null hypothesis is accepted; otherwise, we reject it.

Example 11.
A machine producing a certain part is said to be under control if the proportion defective is about .030. To test whether the machine is under control or not, a sample of size 100 was taken, and four defectives were found. Do you think that the machine is under control? (α = .05).

Answer: From the problem it is given that n = 100 and that
             p = 4/100, or .04. The null hypothesis to be tested is H_o (π = .03) against the two-tailed alternative hypothesis H_1 ($\pi \neq .03$). The test to use is

$$Z = \frac{P - \pi_o}{\sqrt{\dfrac{\pi_o\ (1-\pi_o)}{n}}} = \frac{.04\ -\ .03}{\dfrac{\sqrt{.03\ (.97)}}{\sqrt{10}}}$$

$$Z = .185$$

             Since the computed value of Z is less than the 5% critical value of 1.96, we accept H_o and conclude that the production is under control.

TESTING THE DIFFERENT BETWEEN TWO POPULATION PROPORTIONS WHEN THE SAMPLE SIZES ARE LARGE

When we have two machines the question may arise whether the proportion of defectives (π_1) by machine 1 is equal to the proportion (π_2) produced by machine 2.
The null hypothesis in this case is

$$H_o \ (\pi_1 = \pi_2) \text{ or } H_o \ (\pi_1 - \pi_2 = 0)$$

and the alternative hypothesis is

$$H_1 \ (\pi_1 \neq \pi_2) \text{ or } H_1 \ (\pi_1 - \pi_2 \neq 0)$$

On the other hand, the first machine may be new, and we may want to know whether it is more efficient, i.e. whether the percentage defective, π_1, is less than π_2. The null and alternative hypothesis in this case can be written as

$$H_1 \ (\pi_1 < \pi_2) \text{ or} \tag{17}$$

$$H_1 \ (\pi_1 - \pi_2 < 0)$$

The best estimate of $\pi_1 - \pi_2$ will be $P_1 - P_2$, the difference between the sample proportions in the independent samples of size n_1 and n_2 $(n_1, n_2 > 30)$. The standard error of $P_1 - P_2$ will be

$$\sigma_{p1 - p2} = \frac{\sqrt{\pi_1 \ (1 - \pi_1)}}{\sqrt{n_1}} + \frac{\sqrt{\pi_2 \ (1 - \pi_2)}}{\sqrt{n_2}} \tag{18}$$

so that the test statistic becomes

$$Z = \frac{P_1 - P_2}{\sqrt{\dfrac{\pi_1 \ (1-\pi_1)}{n_1} + \dfrac{\pi_2 \ (1-\pi_2)}{n_2}}} \tag{19}$$

Since π_1 and π_2 are both unknown, we construct a null hypothesis that they are equal, i.e. $H_o \ (\pi_1 = \pi_2 = \pi)$. The best estimate of the common value, π, is

$$\overline{P} = \frac{n_1 P_1 + n_2 P_2}{n_1 + n_2}$$

and the test formula (19) becomes

$$Z = \frac{P_1 - P_2}{\overline{P}(1-\overline{P}) \ (\dfrac{1}{\sqrt{n_1}} + \dfrac{1}{\sqrt{n_2}})} \tag{20}$$

For n > 30 and α = .05, the critical values of Z are again $\pm$ 1.96. For other values of α (one-tailed or two-tailed), the appropriate critical value of Z will have to be determined from a normal table. When the sample sizes are small, then the procedure (20) cannot be used.

Example 12.
A company has two offices, one in the centre city and the other in a suburb. A sample of 40 employees in the city revealed a preference about the working conditions. Nine per cent of the people are dissatisfied with the working conditions. The figure for the suburbs was .08, obtained on the basis of a sample of 50 employees. Do you think that the workers in the city are less dissatisfied with the working conditions? (α = .05)

Answer: H_o $(\pi_1 - \pi_2 = 0)$
H_1 $(\pi_1 - \pi_2 < 0)$

$$Z = \frac{.09 - .08}{.08(.92) \left(\frac{1}{40} + \frac{1}{50}\right)} = .17$$

Since Z is more than -1.96, the null hypothesis is rejected, and we conclude that the people who live in the city are equally dissatisfied with working conditions as those who live in the suburbs.

TESTING FOR THE POPULATION VARIANCE

We recall that the variate under consideration was assumed to have a normal distribution with two parameters, namely, the population mean, μ, and the population variance, σ^2. So far we have tested the hypothesis regarding μ for one and two samples. However, we may be interested in testing a hypothesis regarding the population variance, σ^2. For example, a financial officer in a small firm may be interested in the cash flow problem of the organization. On the basis of his past experience he has found that the variability, as measured by the variance of the average daily cash flows, is $9000. In recent months he has taken some steps to change the cash flow situation. After the steps were taken, on the basis of the cash flow experience of n = 10 days, how can we test whether the cash flow situation has changed or not? (α = .05).

In this case, the null hypothesis to be tested is

H_o $(\sigma^2 = \sigma^2_o = 9000)$

(21)

and the alternative hypothesis is

H_1 $(\sigma^2 \neq \sigma^2_o \neq 9000)$

The test procedure is as follows. On the basis of ten sample months, we compute the sample variance

$$s^2 = \frac{1}{n-1} \Sigma(X - \bar{X})^2 \text{ and then compute the statistic } \chi^2$$

$$\chi^2 = \frac{(n-1)s^2}{\sigma_o^2} \qquad \text{(read as chi-square)} \qquad (22)$$

The χ^2 distribution, unlike the normal and t distributions, is not symmetrical. For degrees of freedom = n-1, we shall find (from χ^2 table given in a statistics book) two critical values, χ^2 for $\alpha=.05$. If the χ^2 value in (22) falls within these two table values, then the hypothesis H_o is accepted. Otherwise, it will be rejected.

Example 13.
The variability of the daily cash flow in a company determines the cash flow management policy. A company experiencing cash flow problems adopts a new policy. The variability as measured by the variance of the flow was found to be 300,000 for a sample of 10 days. Before the policy was taken, it was found to be 350,000. Do you think that the policy has reduced the variability? ($\alpha = .05$).

Answer: The null hypothesis is H_o: ($\sigma^2 = 350,000$) and the alternate hypothesis is: H_1: ($\sigma^2 < 350,000$)
            $n = 10$, $s^2 = 300,000$
            Following (22) $\chi^2 = \dfrac{(n-1)s^2}{\sigma_o^2} = 6.61$ with d.f.

            $(n_1-1) = 9$, from a χ^2 table in a statistics book we find:

            $\chi^2_{05} = 16.92$ d.f. = 9

            Thus the computed value of $\chi^2 = 6.61$ is statistically insignificant. We accept H_o, and conclude that the variability has not been reduced.

TESTING HYPOTHESIS CONCERNING EQUALITY OF TWO VARIANCES

In the stock market, investors are not only interested in the average return but also in the variability of a number of portfolios. In a hypothetical situation, suppose the sample standard deviation variance measuring risk of one portfolio is $s_1 = 3$, and in another portfolio it is $s_2 = 4$, while the sample sizes are $n_1 = 10$ and $n_2 = 15$, respectively. With this information, we want to test whether in the populations the variances are equal. The null hypothesis is
       H_o $(\sigma_1^2 = \sigma_2^2)$ (23)
The alternative hypothesis is
       H_1 $(\sigma_1^2 \neq \sigma_2^2)$ (24)
Usually, we assume the independence of the two samples and the normality of the population. To test (23) we use the F

distribution, which is again a non-symmetrical probability distribution, where

$$F = \frac{s_1^2}{s_2^2}$$ (25)

with degrees of freedom = $n_1 - 1$, $n_2 - 1$ where s_1^2 and s_2^2 are variances, respectively. Depending on the value of n_1 and n_2, the critical values of the F distribution can be obtained from the F table given in any book on statistics. If the computed value of F from (25) falls within this range, the hypothesis is accepted; otherwise, it is rejected.

Example 14.
It is often argued that although the average value of the stocks of two computer companies, A and B, are approximately equal, the variability of Stock A is higher than the variability of Stock B. To test this hypothesis random samples of $n_1 = 25$ and $n_2 = 25$ of the two stocks were taken and the corresponding sample variances, $s_1^2 = 1.24$, and, $s_2^2 = .51$ were obtained. Do the data show that Stock A has more variability?

Solution: $H_o \ (\sigma_1^2 = \sigma_2^2)$

and
$H_1 \ (\sigma_1^2 > \sigma_2^2)$

For $\alpha = .045$, we shall reject H_o when $F > F_{.045} = 1.98$ obtained from F table. So to test the hypothesis, we compute:

$$F = \frac{s_1^2}{s_2^2} = \frac{1.04}{51} = 2.04.$$

Since computed F > the table value of F = 1.98, we reject H_o and conclude that Stock 1 has more variability.

TYPE I AND TYPE II ERRORS RECONSIDERED

The tests discussed before are based on the Neyman-Pearson Lemma, which offers a procedure that minimizes the Type II error for a stipulated amount of Type I error. As mentioned before, for a given sample size, the two types of error cannot be reduced simultaneously. Let us take an example to clarify some points related to the computation of the Type II error. Suppose in the light bulb example ($\sigma = 3$, $n = 49$) the null hypothesis is

$H_o \ (\mu = 1200)$ (26)

and the alternative hypothesis is
$H_1 \ (\mu \neq 1200)$

(27)

With α = Type I error = .05, we want to test the null hypothesis. With the standard test procedure the statistic to use is

$$Z = \frac{\bar{X} - \mu_o}{\sigma/\sqrt{n}}$$ (28)

In this case μ_o = 1200, σ = 3, and n = 49. If Z is more than 1.96 or less than -1.96, we reject H_o; otherwise, we accept H_o.

It may be well to remember that the Type II error (ß) is the probability of accepting H_o when it should be rejected, i.e. when H_o is accepted but μ_o is different from 1200. The nearer the alternative value of μ to the null hypothetical value, the larger will be the Type II error since it is difficult to differentiate two values when they are close.

To illustrate the computation of the Type II error, let us set the upper-tail alternative hypothesis as

$$H_1 \ (\mu = 1202), \qquad\qquad\qquad (29)$$

We first find the critical value of X, which is given by

$$
\begin{aligned}
\overline{X} &= \mu_o + Z\ \sigma\sqrt{n} \\
&= 1200 + 1.645.\ (3/\sqrt{7}) \\
&= 1200 + .705 \\
\overline{X} &= 1200.705
\end{aligned}
$$

Then the Type II error is given by

$$P\ (Z < \frac{1200.7 - 1202}{3/\sqrt{n}}) = .01$$

as seen from the normal probability table. In a similar fashion, for different values assumed in the alternative hypothesis in (29) the Type II error can be plotted, as in Fig. 1.7. This curve is known as a Type II error curve. It is seen from this figure that as we move further from the null hypothesis value of μ, namely μ_a, the Type II error decreases.

The power (γ) of the test is defined as equal to 1-ß. 1-Type II error; i.e. it gives us the probability of rejecting H_o when it should be rejected. When the power is plotted against alternative values of the parameter, we get what is known as the power curve. A hypothetical power curve is shown in Fig. 1.8. A decision as to which test procedure is best to choose can be made from the corresponding power curves.

Example 15.

Suppose the monthly sales (X) of a store are distributed normally with mean, μ, and standard deviation σ = 7. A sample of 49 months is chosen, and the sales for each month is noted. We wish to test the hypothesis (α = .05).

$$
\begin{aligned}
H_o &= (\mu = \$1000) \\
H_1 &= (\mu = \$\ 900)
\end{aligned}
$$

a.   Calculate the type II error, ß, and the power of the test.

b.   What is the probability of accepting H_1 when μ = \$990?

Answer: The critical value (see 4a) X_1 is given by

$$\overline{X}_1 = \mu_o - Z_2\ \sigma/\sqrt{n}\ =\ 1000 - 1.645 = 998.35$$

$$ß = p\ (Z > \frac{998.35 - 990}{25/\sqrt{49}}) = .01$$

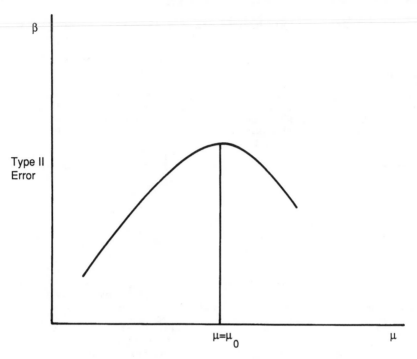

Figure 1.7: (Type II Error)

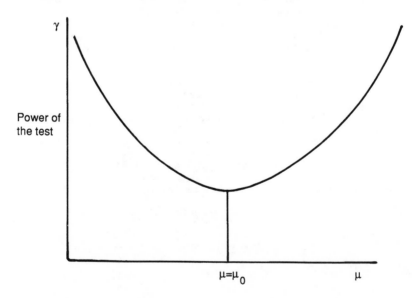

Figure 1.8: Power Curve

SAMPLE INSPECTION PLANS -- OPERATING CHARACTERISTIC CURVE

The Type II curve is also known as the Operating
Characteristics Curve (OC) for a sampling plan. It gives the
probability of accepting a specific lot for different values
of the population parameter. For example, suppose lots
supplied to the manufacturer contain 100 machine parts each.
The manufacturer is willing to accept a 3% (p = .03)
proportion as defective. If the proportion defective is more
than .03, then the manufacturer wants to reject the lot.

Obviously, the manufacturer cannot check every item in
every lot. He adopts a sampling inspection plan. A sample of
n items is drawn from the lot. If the number of defectives in
the sample is more than a certain number, say, m, the lot is
rejected; otherwise, it is accepted. The value of the number
m is based on the acceptable proportion defective, p, and is
known as the single sampling inspection plan. The parameters
which determine a sampling plan are n, the sample size, and m,
the acceptance number. Given the values of, say, n = 10 and
m = 0, we can compute the probability of accepting a lot when
the fraction defective can take different values, i.e. π = .1,
.3, etc. For example, when π = .1,
$$P \text{ (accepting the lot) } = 10 \ (.1)^0 \ (.9)^{10}$$
$$= 10 \ (.9)^{10}$$
Thus for each value of π, we can compute the probability of
acceptance. When the probabilities are plotted against the
alternative values of π, we get the Operating Characteristic
Curve (OC). In this sample, it is clear that the probability
of acceptance will be zero when π = 0. The steeper the
falling of the OC curve, the better the sampling inspection
plan. Other types of sampling plans, such as double sampling,
are also used in statistical quality control work.

Example 16.
For a company producing light bulbs over a period
of the last 10 years, the mean life has been
found to be equal to μ = 1500 hours, and the
standard deviation, σ = 300 hours. A new process
has recently been developed. For a sample of 100
bulbs, the average number of hours, X, produced
by this process is found to be 1550. Test
whether the new process is really better than the
old. Compute the Type II error for the
alternative hypothesis, μ = 1540. Also draw the
operating characteristic curve.

Answer: The null hypothesis is $H_o(\mu = 1500)$. The
alternative hypothesis is $H_o(\mu > 1500)$.

$$\text{(a) PR } (\bar{X} \geq 1,265) = \text{PR } \left(\frac{\bar{X} - \mu_o}{\sigma/\sqrt{n}} \geq \frac{1550 - 1500}{300/\sqrt{100}}\right)$$
$$= \text{PR } (Z \geq 1.66) - .049$$
Since the Z is more than 1.64, the H_o (μ =
1500) is rejected.
(b) The critical value of X, corresponding
to the critical Z value can be obtained as
follows:

63

$$\frac{\overline{X} - \mu_o}{\sigma/\sqrt{n}} = 1.64 = \text{critical Z}$$

The critical value of $\overline{X}$ = 1549.

The Type II error can be computed as

$$\text{Pr } (\overline{X} < 1249) = \text{Pr } (\frac{\overline{X} - \mu_1}{\sigma/\sqrt{n}} < \frac{1549 - 1540}{300/\sqrt{100}})$$

$$= \text{Pr } (Z < .30) = .62 = \beta$$

Following in a procedure similar to that above, we can compute the Type II error corresponding to alternative values of μ = 1540, 1580, 1620, etc. When we plot this Type II error corresponding to different values of μ we get the operating characteristic curve. As the alternative values of μ moves further away from the hypothetical values of μ_o, the Type II error decreases, i.e. it is easier to discriminate.

Example 17   In many production processes, the items come in lots. It is not possible to accept or reject the lot on the basis of complete inspection. Naturally, a sample of n items is examined, and the number of defectives, X, is counted. If X exceeds a particular acceptance number, say, a, the lot is rejected; otherwise, it passes as a good lot. Each sampling plan is characterized by the sample size n and the acceptance number, a. The quality of the sampling plan (defined by n and a) is measured by the probability of accepting the lot for various hypothetical fraction defectives in the lot. Suppose, for example, we take a sample of n = 20 and the acceptance number, a = 2. The hypothetical fraction of defectives may be equal to p = .1, .2, .3, .4, .5.

Then, using the binomial table, we can compute the probability of acceptance as follows:

P (accept when P = .1) = .677
P (accept when P = .2) = .206
P (accept when P = .3) = .035
P (accept when P = .4) = .004
P (accept when P = .5) = .000

Plotting these probabilities for the corresponding value of P, we may draw the Operating Characteristic Curve for the sampling plan (similar to Fig. 1.9).

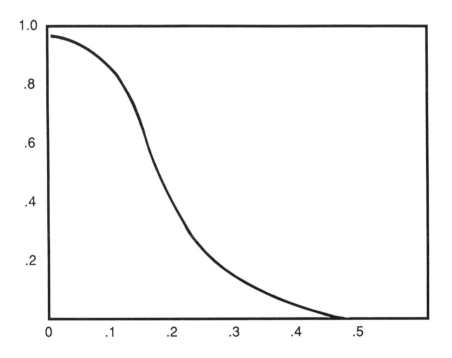

Figure 1.9

Operating Characteristic Curve

n=15,　a=1

In the classical testing of hypotheses, the sample size n is fixed and all the units in the sample are taken at one time. However, we can take samples one by one, and the number of samples necessary to make a decision can be determined by the accumulation of information. In this method, acceptance or rejection of a hypothesis may be accomplished with lower sample size and, consequently, less cost compared with the classical "one time only" sampling. In this case, instead of having only one acceptance number, m, we have two numbers, A and B. If the number of rejections is more than B, the lot is rejected. If it is less than A, it is accepted. If it is inbetween A and B and we are undecided, we take another sample lot and try to make a decision on the basis of the combined sample.

Example 18.   An example of Sequential Sampling (SPRT)

In the classical theory of the testing of a hypothesis, the number of observations, i.e. the size of the sample, is usually constant. In contrast, in sequential testing, the number of observations is a random variable. A sequential test gives us a rule at any stage of the experiment (say, m^{th}, m = 1,2,3...) to determine whether to accept, reject, or continue the experiment. This can be illustrated by the following simple example. Let X be a random variable. The probability that X = 1 is denoted by P, the value of which is unknown. The distribution of X is given by the function, f(X,P). It is defined for only two values of X, namely, X = 0 and X = 1; i.e. $f(1,P) = P$ and $f(0,P) = 1-P$. The null hypothesis is H_o ($P = P_o$) and the alternative hypothesis is H_1 ($P = P_1$). A rule of sequential analysis known as the sequential probability ratio test (SPRT) is given as follows.
Compute:

$$Z_i = \frac{f(X_i,P_1)}{f(X_i,P_o)} = \log \frac{P_1}{P_o} \text{ if } X_i = 1$$

$$= \log \frac{1-P_1}{1-P_o} \text{ if } X_i = 0$$

and

$$Z_1 + \ldots + Z_m = m^* \log \frac{P_1}{P_o} + (m-m^*) \log \frac{1-P_1}{1-P_o}$$

where m^* denotes the number of 1's in the sequence of the first m observations. We accept H_o, if

$$m^* \log \frac{P}{P_o} + (m - m^*) + \log \frac{1-P_1}{1-P_o} \geq \log A$$

We continue the experiment by taking an additional observation if

$$\log B < m^* \log \frac{P_1}{P_o} \quad (m-m^*) \log \frac{1-P_1}{1-P_o} > \log A.$$

The constants, A and B, are related to the Type I error (α) and Type II error (β). Although the above procedure looks mathematically complicated, it is in fact simple and very powerful. Following the same procedure of the Neyman-Pearsonian Testing of hypothesis, we can construct the operating characteristic of the SPRT rule. We can also compute ASN (Average Sample Number) for making a decision. Since it costs money to take a sample, if ASN is less than n (fixed sample size), then SPRT will be preferred to the classical test. The crucial point to note is that using the sequential testing method, we may get the same conclusion with much fewer sample observations.

D.   Analysis of Variance, Co-variance and Design of Experiments

So far we have discussed how to test the equality of the mean of two populations, i.e. $Ho(\mu_1 = \mu_2)$. An example will be to test whether the average number of communal religious riots in countries like India and Pakistan are the same. The process can be extended to $Ho(\mu_1 = \mu_2 ..... = \mu_k)$, where the means in "k" populations are equal. For example, in East European countries, we can test whether the values of political variables for each country are equal. This can be tested by what is known as the analysis of variance. In the case of one-way analysis of variance (ANOVA) we may be interested to test whether incidents of riots in different states of India differ significantly. For that purpose we have to organize the data $i = 1, ... n$ in $j = 1 ... k$ states and see whether the between states variation sums of square differ significantly from error variation.

In symbols, $SS_y = \Sigma_j \Sigma_i (Y_{ji} - \overline{Y})^2$ in which $\overline{Y}$ is the mean of Y over the whole sample (known as grand mean), and the summations are over all individual cases in each category j

$$SS_{between} = \Sigma N_j (Y_{j*} - \overline{Y})^2$$

in which $\overline{Y}_{1*}$ is the mean of Y in the category j, and N_j is the number of cases in category j.

$$SS_{within} = \Sigma\Sigma (Y_{ji} - \overline{Y}_{j*})^2$$

$SS_A = SS(between)$ is the position of the SS in Y due to jth classification (states). $SS(error) = SS(within)$ is the amount of variation within each category j (states) which is not explained by variation due to states. As such it is called error sums of squares. Comparing the SS_A with $SS(error)$ rather than with mean SS_A and mean SS_e we can decide whether the classification of the states has any impact on the variable Y.   Instead of taking a single variable of classification, namely states, we can take classifications with respect to such variables such as language, income, etc., and decide whether such variables affect riot variables significantly.

A natural extension as the ANOVA technique is the subject matter of Design of Experiments.   Here we have a number of factors, say, military, economics, political and social, in connection with a conflict problem.   Each factor has a number of levels, e.g. high, how, medium.   The objective of this is to combine appropriate levels of different factors so that the outcome is most desired, (peaceful).

E.   Non Parametric Testing of Hypothesis and χ^2 Test
Since most of the variables in conflict analysis are qualitative where the population distribution does not have any parameters the test procedure discussed before may not be applicable.   For that purpose, tests, such as Run test, Spearman Rank Correlation, Kruskal–Wallis test, Wilkinson test and χ^2 test.   The objective is to test whether the observed frequencies vary significantly from the expected frequencies by computing

$$\chi^2 = \Sigma \frac{(O - E)^2}{E} \qquad \qquad d.f. = (r - 1)(C - 1)$$

where r and c denote the number of rows and column of the 2x2 contingency table as follows

$$\begin{array}{c|cc}
 & C_1 & C_2 \\
\hline
R_1 & & \\
\hline
R_2 & &
\end{array}$$

O denotes the observed frequencies in each cell and the expected frequencies are computed by multiplying the marginal frequencies and then divided by the total number of operations.

F.   Multivariate Distribution
So far we have discussed statistical procedures with one variable.   But, in practice, a problem may involve more than one variable.   For that purpose, we can use multivariate procedures where the multivariate normal distributions is of crucial importance.

Key Words in Section C

Parameters
Hypothesis Testing
Composite Hypothesis
Population Variance
Non–Parametric Distribution
Null Hypothesis
One–Tailed Hypothesis/Two–Tailed Hypothesis
Type I Error
Critical Region

Interval Estimation
Confidence Coefficient
Neyman-Pearson Lemma
t distribution
Frequency Curve
Pooled Estimate
Degrees of Freedom
ANOVA
Standard Error of the Estimate
Proportion Test
χ Square
F distribution
Non-Symmetrical Probability Distribution
Power Curve
Operating Characteristic Curve
Sequential Sampling

The TTEST Procedure

Operating systems: All

G.   Computer Programs

ABSTRACT

The TTEST procedure computes a t statistic for testing the hypothesis that the means of two groups of observations in a SAS data set are equal.

INTRODUCTION

Means for a variable are computed for each of the two groups of observations identified by values of a classification or CLASS variable. The t test tests the hypothesis that the true means are the same. This can be considered as a special case of a one-way analysis of variance with two levels of classification.

TTEST computes the t statistic based on the assumption that the variances of the two groups are equal and also computes an approximate t based on the assumption that the variances are unequal. For each t, the degrees of freedom and probability level are given; Satterthwaite's (1946) approximation is used to compute the degrees of freedom associated with the approximate t. An F' (folded) statistic is computed to test for equality of the two variances (Steel and Torrie 1980).

The TTEST procedure was not designed for paired comparisons. See **Examples** below for a method of using the MEANS procedure to get a paired-comparisons t test.

Note that the underlying assumption of the t test computed by the TTEST procedure is that the variables are normally and independently distributed within each group.

SPECIFICATIONS

The statements used to control the procedure are

PROC TTEST *option*;
  CLASS *variables*;
  VAR *variables*;
  BY *variables*;

No statement may be used more than once. There is no restriction on the order of the statements after the PROC statement. The CLASS statement is required.

PROC TTEST Statement

PROC TTEST *option*;

The following option can appear in the PROC TTEST statement:

DATA=*SASdataset*
     names the SAS data set for the procedure to use. If DATA= is not given, PROC TTEST uses the most recently created SAS data set.

CLASS Statement

CLASS *variable*;

A CLASS statement giving the name of the grouping variable must accompany the PROC TTEST statement. The grouping variable must have two, and only two, values. PROC TTEST divides the observations into the two groups for the *t* test using the values of this variable.

You can use either a numeric or a character variable in the CLASS statement. If you use a character variable longer than 16 characters, the value is truncated and a warning message is issued.

VAR Statement

VAR *variables*;

The VAR statement gives the names of the dependent variables whose means are to be compared. If the VAR statement is omitted, all numeric variables in the input data set (except a numeric variable appearing in the CLASS statement) are included in the analysis.

BY Statement

BY *variables*;

A BY statement can be used with PROC TTEST to obtain separate analyses on observations in groups defined by the BY variables. When a BY statement appears, the procedure expects the input data set to be sorted in order of the BY variables. If your input data set is not sorted in ascending order, use the SORT procedure with a similar BY statement to sort the data, or, if appropriate, use the BY statement options NOTSORTED or DESCENDING. For more information see the discussion of the BY statement in "Statements Used in the PROC Step" in the *SAS User's Guide: Basics*.

DETAILS

Missing Values

An observation is always omitted from the calculations if it has a missing value for either the CLASS variable or for the variable to be tested.

Computational Method

The usual t statistic for testing the equality of means $\bar{x}_1$ and $\bar{x}_2$ from two independent samples with n_1 and n_2 observations is

$$t = (\bar{x}_1 - \bar{x}_2) / \sqrt{s^2(1/n_1 + 1/n_2)}$$

where s^2 is the pooled variance

$$s^2 = \{(n_1 - 1)s_1^2 + (n_2 - 1)s_2^2\} / (n_1 + n_2 - 2)$$

and where s_1^2 and s_2^2 are the sample variances of the two groups. The use of this t statistic depends on the assumption that $\sigma_1^2 = \sigma_2^2$, where σ_1^2 and σ_2^2 are the population variances of the two groups.

You can use the folded form of the F statistic, F', to test the assumption that the variances are equal, where

$$F' = (\text{larger of } s_1^2, s_2^2) / (\text{smaller of } s_1^2, s_2^2) .$$

A test of F' is a two-tailed F test since we do not specify which variance we expect to be larger. The printout value of PROB $>$ F gives the probability of a greater F value under the null hypothesis that $\sigma_1^2 = \sigma_2^2$.

Under the assumption of equal variances, the t statistic is computed with the formula given above, using the pooled variance estimate s^2.

Under the assumption of unequal variances, the approximate t is computed as

$$t = (\bar{x}_1 - \bar{x}_2) / \sqrt{(s_1^2/n_1 + s_2^2/n_2)}$$

The formula for Satterthwaite's (1946) approximation for the degrees of freedom is as follows:

$$df = \frac{(s_1^2/n_1 + s_2^2/n_2)^2}{(s_1^2/n_1)^2 / (n_1 - 1) + (s_2^2/n_2)^2 / (n_2 - 1)}$$

Refer to Steel and Torrie (1980) and *SAS for Linear Models* (Freund and Littell 1981) for more information.

Printed Output

For each dependent variable included in the analysis, the TTEST procedure prints the following statistics for each group

1. the name of the dependent variable
2. the levels of the classification variable
3. N, the number of nonmissing values
4. the MEAN or average
5. STD DEV, the standard deviation
6. STD ERROR, the standard error

72

7. the MINIMUM value
8. the MAXIMUM value.

Under the assumption of unequal variances, the TTEST procedure prints

9. T, an approximate t statistic for testing the null hypothesis that the means of the two groups are equal
10. DF, Satterthwaite's approximation for the degrees of freedom
11. PROB > |T|, the probability of a greater absolute value of t under the null hypothesis. This is the two-tailed significance probability.

Under the assumption of equal variances, the TTEST procedure prints

12. T, the t statistic for testing the null hypothesis that the means of the two groups are equal
13. DF, the degrees of freedom
14. PROB > |T|, the probability of a greater absolute value of t under the null hypothesis. This is the two-tailed significance probability.

PROC TTEST then gives the results of the test of equality of variances:

15. the F' (folded) statistic (see the **Details** section above)
16. the degrees of freedom, DF, in each group
17. PROB > F', the probability of a greater F value.

EXAMPLES

Comparing Group Means: Example 1

The data for this example consist of golf scores for a physical education class. We want to use a t test to determine if the mean golf score for the males in the class differs significantly from the mean score for the females.

The grouping variable is SEX, and it appears in the CLASS statement.

The numbers on the sample output correspond to the statistics described above.

```
DATA SCORES;
   INPUT SEX $ SCORE @@;
   CARDS;
F 75  F 76  F 80  F 77  F 80  F 77  F 73
M 82  M 80  M 85  M 85  M 78  M 87  M 82
;
PROC TTEST;
   CLASS SEX;
   VAR SCORE;
   TITLE 'GOLF SCORES';
```

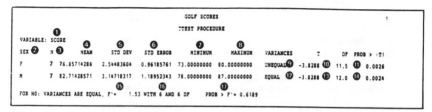

```
                                    GOLF SCORES                                          1
                                  TTEST PROCEDURE
VARIABLE: SCORE
   ❶
SEX ❷   N ❸    MEAN        STD DEV      STD ERROR      MINIMUM       MAXIMUM    VARIANCES      T      DF   PROB > |T|
          ❹        ❺          ❻           ❼           ❽
F       7  76.85714286   2.54483604   0.96185761   73.00000000   80.00000000   UNEQUAL❾ -3.8288 ❿  11.5 ⓫  0.0026
M       7  82.71428571   3.14718317   1.18952343   78.00000000   87.00000000   EQUAL   ⓬ -3.8288 ⓭  12.0 ⓮  0.0024
                          ⓯                   ⓰                           ⓱
FOR HO: VARIANCES ARE EQUAL, F'=   1.53 WITH 6 AND 6 DF      PROB > F' = 0.6189
```

Paired Comparisons Using PROC MEANS: Example 2

For paired comparisons, use PROC MEANS rather than PROC TTEST. You can create a new variable containing the differences between the paired variables and use the T and PRT options of PROC MEANS to test whether the mean difference is significantly different from zero.

This is useful if you have a PRETEST and POSTTEST value for each observation in a data set and you want to test whether there is a significant difference between the two sets of scores.

Following the INPUT statement in the DATA step is an assignment statement to create a new variable DIFF by subtracting PRETEST from POSTTEST. Then, you use PROC MEANS with the T and PRT options to get a *t* statistic and a probability value for the null hypothesis that DIFF's mean is equal to zero.

```
DATA A;
   INPUT ID PRETEST POSTTEST;
   DIFF=POSTTEST-PRETEST;
   CARDS;
1   80   82
2   73   71
3   70   95
4   60   69
5   88  100
6   84   71
7   65   75
8   37   60
9   91   95
10  98   99
11  52   65
12  78   83
13  40   60
14  79   86
15  59   62
;
PROC MEANS MEAN STDERR T PRT;
   VAR DIFF;
   TITLE 'PAIRED-COMPARISONS T TEST';
```

74

		PAIRED-COMPARISONS T TEST			1
VARIABLE	MEAN	STD ERROR OF MEAN	T	PR>|T|	
DIFF	7.93333333	2.56434651	3.09	0.0079	

REFERENCES

Freund, R.J. and Littell, R.C. (1981), *SAS for Linear Models: A Guide to the ANOVA and GLM Procedures*, Cary, NC: SAS Institute Inc.

Satterthwaite. F.W. (1946), "An Approximate Distribution of Estimates of Variance Components," *Biometrics Bulletin*, 2, 110-114.

Steel, R.G.D. and Torrie, J.H. (1980), *Principles and Procedures of Statistics*, Second Edition, New York: McGraw-Hill Book Company.

Analysis of Variance

by Kathryn A. Council

What is analysis of variance?

Analysis of variance is a statistical technique that is used to study the variability of experimental data. For example, you might observe that using different fertilizers on tomato plants results in the production of different amounts of tomatoes. This difference in tomato yield is the *variability*. You can use analysis of variance to see if such factors as the fertilizer contribute to that variability.

The basic process that takes place when you use analysis of variance is testing hypotheses about your data—for example, you might hypothesize that the fertilizer does not significantly affect the tomato yield.

The hypotheses are often stated in terms of the equality of group means. For example, you might classify the yields from the tomato plants into three groups, one for each fertilizer you used, and then state your hypothesis as, "The mean tomato yield does not differ significantly among the three fertilizer groups."

A typical experiment

Let's follow the tomato plant experiment through the experimental stage and into the analysis phase.

You buy a dozen tomato plants of the same variety. To reduce the variability from factors other than fertilizer, you choose plants that are as alike as possible and pot them in the same type of soil.

You select four of the plants at random and use fish-oil emulsion as the fertilizer, applying it weekly. Four other plants receive Magic-Grow fertilizer weekly. The last four plants are allowed to grow with just the nutrients in the soil—no fertilizer. During the growing season, you record the weight of the tomatoes produced by each plant, and after the first frost you calculate the total weight for each plant. This total weight is the plant's *yield*.

Now you formulate the hypothesis that the mean yield does not differ significantly among the three fertilizer groups, and you use the SAS procedure ANOVA to test your hypothesis.

Terminology

In the terminology of analysis of variance, the tomato plants in this experiment are *experimental units*. The yield is the *response variable* or the *dependent variable*. The fertilizer is the *treatment variable*, or *independent variable* or factor or classification variable.

The variance in plant behavior from treatment to treatment is the *between-group variance*; our hypothesis states that this variance is not significant.

Another kind of variation is also occurring due to the natural variations in the tomato plants, say in their insect infestations. Although you try to reduce this variation by choosing similar plants and potting them in the same soil, it can't be eliminated entirely. This variation is important because it influences the outcome of the experiment, but can't be attributed to the fertilizer treatment. This variance is the *within-group variance*, because it occurs from plant to plant within each treatment group rather than from treatment to treatment. It is also known as the *experimental error*, or the *error*.

How to use the SAS System for analysis of variance

To use SAS for analysis of variance you need a PROC ANOVA statement, a CLASSES statement giving the classification or grouping variables, and a MODEL statement describing the experiment you are investigating. Here are the statements needed for the tomato plant experiment:

PROC ANOVA;
  CLASSES FERTILZR;
  MODEL YIELD = FERTILZR;

The CLASSES statement gives the variable FERTILZR, since we are classifying the experimental units into groups according to which fertilizer treatment they received.

In the MODEL statement, the word MODEL is followed by the variable whose behavior you are studying—the dependent variable or response variable. In this case, you are studying the YIELD. Then comes an equal sign, then the treatment variable, FERTILZR.

The statements

DATA TOMATO;
  INPUT PLANT FERTILZR $ YIELD;
  CARDS;
data lines go here
PROC ANOVA;
  CLASSES FERTILZR;
  MODEL YIELD = FERTILZR;
  TITLE 'TOMATO PLANT EXPERIMENT';

produce the output shown in figure 11-1.

77

Tomato Plant Experiment

Analysis of Variance Procedure

Class Level Information

Class	Levels	Values
Fertilizer	3	F M M

Number of Observations in Data Bet = 12

Dependent Variable: Yield

Source	DF	Sum of Sources	Mean Square	F Value
Model	2	405.5	202.75	84.03
Error	9	38.5	3.16	PR > F
Corrected Total	11	438.0		0.0001

R-Square	CV	Root M	Yield Mean
0.934332	19.7724	1.779	9.000

Source	DF	ANOVA F Value	PR > F	
Fertilzr	2	405.500	64.02	0.0001

Figure 11-1

Balanced vs. unbalanced data	When all the subgroups of your data contain the same number of observations, you can use PROC ANOVA.

If the subgroups contain different numbers of observations, or if some subgroups contain no observations, use PROC GLM. (ANOVA may be used for unbalanced data when you have only one treatment variable). All MODEL statements discussed in the following sections çan be used with both PROC ANOVA and PROC GLM.

Experimental   It's possible to specify anv experimental units completely at random. Our tomato plant experiment is an example of a completely randomized design. In this case, the treatment variable, fertilizer, defines the groups. The treatment means, the mean yields of tomatoes per plant for each fertilizer treatment, can be tested for equality:

```
PROC ANOVA;
  CLASSES FERTILZR;
  MODEL YIELD = FERTILZR;
```

INTRODUCTION

Frequency tables show the distribution of variable values. For example, if a variable A has six possible values, a frequency table for A shows how many observations in the data set have the first value of A, how many have the second value, and so on.

Crosstabulation tables show combined frequency distributions for two or more variables. For example, a crosstabulation table for the variables SEX and EMPLOY shows the number of working females, the number of non-working females, the number of working males, and the number of non-working males.

One-Way Frequency Tables

If you want a one-way frequency table for a variable, simply name the variable in a TABLES statement. For example, the statements

```
PROC FREQ;
   TABLES A;
```

produce a one-way frequency table giving the values of A and the frequency of each value.

Two-Way Crosstabulation Tables

If you want a crosstabulation table for two variables, give their names separated by an asterisk (*). Values of the first variable form the rows of the table, and values of the second variable form the columns. For example, the statements

```
PROC FREQ;
   TABLES A*B;
```

produce a crosstabulation table with values of A down the side and values of B across the top.

For some pairs of variables, you may want information about the existence and/or the strength of any association between the variables. With respect to the existence of an association, PROC FREQ computes statistics that test the null hypothesis of no association. With respect to the strength of an association, PROC FREQ computes measures of association that tend to be close to zero when there is no association, and close to the maximum (or minimum) value when there is perfect association. You can request the computation and printing of these statistics by specifying one or more options in the TABLES statement. For information on specific statistics computed by PROC FREQ, see the section entitled **Tests and Measures of Association**.

In choosing measures of association to use in analyzing a two-way table, you should consider the study design (which indicates whether the row and column variables are dependent or independent), the measurement scale of the variables (nominal, ordinal, or interval), the type of association that each measure is designed to detect, and any assumptions required for valid interpretation of a measure. It is important to exercise care in selecting measures that are appropriate for your data. For more information to guide you in choosing measures of association for a specific set of data, see Hayes (1963) and Garson (1971). For an advanced treatment, refer to Goodman and Kruskal (1979), or Bishop, Fienberg, and Holland (1975, Chapter 11).

Similar comments apply to the choice and interpretation of the test statistics. For example, the Mantel-Haenszel chi-square statistic requires an ordinal scale for both variables, and is designed to detect a linear association. The Pearson chi-square, on the other hand, is appropriate for all variables and can detect any kind of association but it is less powerful for detecting a linear association because its power is dispersed over a greater number of degrees of freedom (except for 2 by 2 tables).

N-Way Crosstabulation Tables

If you want a three-way (or *n*-way) crosstabulation table, give the three (or *n*) variable names separated by asterisks in the TABLES statement. Values of the last variable form the columns of a contingency table; values of the next-to-last variable form the rows. Each level (or combination of levels) of the other variables form one stratum, and a separate contingency table is produced for each stratum. For example, the statements

```
PROC FREQ;
    TABLES A*B*C*D / CMH;
```

produce *k* tables, where *k* is the number of different combinations of values for the variables A and B. Each table has the values of C down the side and the values of D across the top.

The CMH option gives a stratified statistical analysis of the relationship between C and D, after controlling for A and B. The stratified analysis provides a convenient way to adjust for the possible confounding effects of A and B without being forced to estimate parameters for them. The analysis includes computation of Cochran-Mantel-Haenszel statistics, estimation of the common relative risk (case-control and cohort studies), and Breslow's test for homogeneity of the odds ratios. See the **Summary Statistics** section for details of the stratified analysis.

Note: multi-way tables can generate a great deal of printed output. For example, if the variables A, B, C, D, and E each have ten levels, five-way tables of A*B*C*D*E could generate 4000 or more pages of output.

PROC FREQ Contrasted with Other SAS Procedures

Many other procedures in SAS can collect frequency counts. PROC FREQ is distinguished by its ability to compute chi-square tests and measures of association for two-way and *n*-way tables. Other procedures to consider for counting are the following: TABULATE for more general table layouts, SUMMARY for output data sets, and CHART for bar charts and other graphical representations. PROC CATMOD can be used for general linear model analysis of categorical data.

SPECIFICATIONS

The statements available in PROC FREQ are

PROC FREQ *options*;
 TABLES *requests / options*;
 WEIGHT *variable*;
 BY *variables*;

PROC FREQ Statement

PROC FREQ *options*;

The options that can be used in the PROC FREQ statement are as follows:

DATA=*SASdataset*
    specifies the data set to be used by PROC FREQ. If the DATA=
    option is omitted, FREQ uses the most recently created data set.

Sample size summary The total sample size and the frequency of missing subjects are printed. The EFFECTIVE SAMPLE SIZE is the frequency of nonmissing subjects.

Printed Output

For a one-way table showing the frequency distribution of a single variable, FREQ prints these items:

1. the name of the variable and its values
2. FREQUENCY counts giving the number of subjects that have each value
3. CUMULATIVE FREQUENCY counts, giving the sum of the frequency counts of that value and all other values listed above it in the table (the total number of nonmissing subjects is the last cumulative frequency)
4. percentages, labeled PERCENT, giving the percent of the total number of subjects represented by that value
5. CUMULATIVE PERCENT values, giving the percent of the total number of subjects represented by that value and all others previously listed in the table.

   Two-way tables can be printed either as crosstabulation tables (the default) or as lists (when the LIST option is specified). Each cell of a crosstabulation table contains items 6 through 12:

6. FREQUENCY counts, giving the number of subjects that have the indicated values of the two variables
7. PERCENT, the percentage of the total frequency count represented by that cell
8. ROW PCT, or the row percentage, the percent of the total frequency count for that row represented by the cell
9. COL PCT, or column percent, the percent of the total frequency count for that column represented by the cell
10. if the EXPECTED option is specified, the expected cell frequency under the hypothesis of independence
11. if the DEVIATION option is specified, the deviation of the cell frequency from the expected value
12. if the CELLCHI2 option is specified, the cell's contribution to the total chi-square statistic.
13. if the CHISQ option is specified, the following statistics are printed for the two-way table in each stratum: Pearson chi-square, likelihood ratio chi-square, continuity-adjusted chi-square, Mantel-Haenszel chi-square, Fisher's exact test (for 2 by 2 tables), phi, the contingency coefficient, Cramer's V, the sample size, and the frequency missing. For each test statistic, its degrees of freedom (DF) and its significance probability (PROB) are also printed.
14. if the MEASURES option is specified, the following statistics are printed for the two-way table in each stratum: gamma, Kendall's tau-b, Stuart's tau-c, Somer's D, Pearson's product-moment correlation, Spearman's rank correlation, lambda (symmetric and asymmetric), the uncertainty coefficient (symmetric and asymmetric), the sample size, the frequency missing, and (for 2 by 2 tables) estimates of the relative risk for case-control and cohort studies, together with their confidence intervals.
15. if the CMH option is specified, the following statistics are printed: the total sample size, the total frequency missing, and three Cochran-Mantel-Haenszel summary statistics (the correlation statistic, the ANOVA statistic, and the general association statistic), with corresponding degrees of freedom (DF) and significance probabilities (PROB). For 2 by 2 tables, additional statistics printed are stratum-adjusted estimates (both

Mantel-Haenszel and logit estimates) of the common relative risk for case-control and cohort studies, together with their confidence intervals, and the Breslow-Day test for homogeneity of the odds ratios.

16. if the ALL option is specified, all of the statistics requested by the CHISQ, MEASURES, and CMH options are printed.
17. if two contingency tables can fit on a page, one table above the other, then the tables are printed in that manner. Similarly, a table and its corresponding statistics are printed on the same page, provided that they fit.

EXAMPLES

Evans County Study: Example 1

Data for the following example are from the Evans County cohort study of coronary heart disease. Data for the variable CAT, however, are hypothetical. The data are given in Table 17.7, and used in Examples 17.2 and 17.9 of Kleinbaum, Kupper, and Morgenstern (1982).

The purpose of the analysis is to evaluate the association between serum catecholamine (CAT) and coronary heart disease (CHD) after controlling for AGE and electrocardiogram abnormality (ECG). The summary statistics show that the association is significant ($p = .04$), and that subjects with high serum catecholamine are about 1.7 times more likely to develop coronary heart disease than those subjects with low serum catecholamine.

```
DATA CHD;
    INPUT AGE $ ECG $ CHD $ CAT $ WT;
    CARDS;
<55  0  YES  YES    1
<55  0  YES  NO    17
<55  0  NO   YES    7
<55  0  NO   NO   257
<55  1  YES  YES    3
<55  1  YES  NO     7
<55  1  NO   YES   14
<55  1  NO   NO    52
55+  0  YES  YES    9
55+  0  YES  NO    15
55+  0  NO   YES   30
55+  0  NO   NO   107
55+  1  YES  YES   14
55+  1  YES  NO     5
55+  1  NO   YES   44
55+  1  NO   NO    27
;
PROC FREQ ORDER=DATA;
    WEIGHT WT;
    TABLES AGE*ECG*CAT*CHD/ALL;
    TITLE 'EXAMPLE 17.9 FROM KLEINBAUM, KUPPER, AND MORGENSTERN, P. 353';
```

The NPAR1WAY
Procedure

Operating systems: All

ABSTRACT

The NPAR1WAY procedure performs analysis of variance on ranks and certain rank scores of a response variable across a one-way classification. NPAR1WAY is a nonparametric procedure for testing that the distribution of a variable has the same location parameter across different groups.

INTRODUCTION

Most nonparametric tests are derived by examining the distribution of rank scores of the response variable. The rank scores are simply functions of the ranks of the response variable, where the values are ranked from low to high. Statistics defined as linear combinations of these rank scores are called *linear rank statistics*. The NPAR1WAY procedure calculates these four scores:

- **Wilcoxon scores** are the ranks

$$z_i = R_i$$

and are locally most powerful for location shifts of a logistic distribution.
- **Median scores** are 1 for points above the median, 0 otherwise:

$$z_i = (R_i > (n + 1)/2)$$

and are locally most powerful for double exponential distributions.

83

- **van der Waerden scores** are approximations to the expected values of the order statistics for a normal distribution
  $$z_i = \Phi^{-1}(R_i/(n + 1))$$

  where Φ is the distribution function for the normal distribution. These scores are powerful for normal distributions.
- **Savage scores** are expected values minus 1 of order statistics for the exponential distribution

  $$z_i = \Sigma_{j=1}^{R_i} 1/(n - j + 1) - 1$$

  and are powerful for comparing scale differences in exponential distributions (Hajek 1969, 83). NPAR1WAY subtracts 1 to center the scores around 0.

The statistics computed by PROC NPAR1WAY can also be computed by calculating the rank scores using PROC RANK and analyzing these rank scores with PROC ANOVA. **Table 26.1** shows the correspondence between PROC NPAR1WAY scores and various nonparametric tests.

Table 26.1 Comparison of NPAR1WAY with Nonparametric Tests

NPAR1WAY scores...	correspond to these tests if data are classified in two levels...*	correspond to these tests for a one-way layout or k-sample location test...**
Wilcoxon	Wilcoxon rank sum test Mann-Whitney U test	Kruskal-Wallis test
Median	median test for two samples	K-sample median test (Brown-Mood)
van der Waerden	van der Waerden Test	k-sample van der Waerden test
Savage	Savage test	k-sample Savage test

SPECIFICATIONS

The following statements are used to control NPAR1WAY:

PROC NPAR1WAY *options*;
  VAR *variables*;
  CLASS *variable*;
  BY *variables*;

The CLASS statement is required.

---

* The tests are two-tailed. For a one-tailed test transform the significance probability by p/2 or (1-p/2).
** NPAR1WAY provides a chi-square approximate test.

PROC NPAR1WAY Statement

PROC NPAR1WAY *options*:

The options below can be used in the PROC NPAR1WAY statement:

DATA=*SASdataset*
    names the SAS data set containing the data to be analyzed. If DATA= is omitted, the most recently created SAS data set is used.

These options can be specified in the PROC NPAR1WAY statement. If none is specified, then all five analyses are performed by default.

  ANOVA   requests a standard analysis of variance.

  WILCOXON   requests an analysis of the ranks of the data, or the Wilcoxon scores. For two levels, this is the same as a Wilcoxon rank-sum test. For any number of levels, this is a Kruskal-Wallis test.

  MEDIAN   requests an analysis of the median scores. The median score is 1 for points above the median, 0 otherwise. For two samples, this produces a median test; for any number of levels, this is the Brown-Mood test.

  VW   requests that van der Waerden scores be analyzed. These are approximate normal scores derived by applying the inverse normal distribution function to the fractional ranks:

$$\Phi^{-1}(R_i/(n + 1)) \quad .$$

    For two levels, this is the standard van der Waerden test.

  SAVAGE   requests that Savage scores be analyzed. These are expected order statistics for the exponential minus 1. This test is appropriate for comparing groups of data with exponential distributions.

VAR Statement

VAR *variables*;

This statement names the response or dependent variables to be analyzed. If the VAR statement is omitted, all numeric variables in the data set are analyzed.

CLASS Statement

CLASS *variable*:

The CLASS statement, which is required, names one and only one classification variable.

BY Statement

BY *variables*:

A BY statement can be used with PROC NPAR1WAY to obtain separate analyses on observations in groups defined by the BY variables. When a BY statement appears, the procedure expects the input data set to be sorted in order of the

BY variables. If your input data set is not sorted in ascending order, use the SORT procedure with a similar BY statement to sort the data, or, if appropriate, use the BY statement options NOTSORTED or DESCENDING. For more information, see the discussion of the BY statement in "Statements Used in the PROC Step," in the *SAS User's Guide: Basics*.

DETAILS

Missing Values

If an observation has a missing value for a response variable or the classification variable, that observation is excluded from the analysis.

Limitations

The procedure must have 20*n bytes of memory available to store the data, where n is the number of nonmissing observations.

Resolution of Tied Values

Although the nonparametric tests were developed for continuous distributions, tied values do occur in practice. Ties are handled in all methods by assigning the average score for the different ranks corresponding to the tied values. Adjustments to variance estimates are performed in the manner described by Hajek (1969, Chapter 7).

Printed Output

NPAR1WAY produces the printed output described below.
  If the ANOVA option is specified, NPAR1WAY prints

  1. the traditional ANALYSIS OF VARIANCE table
  2. the effect mean square reported as AMONG MS
  3. the error mean square reported as WITHIN MS.

(These are the same values that would result from using a procedure such as ANOVA or GLM.)
  NPAR1WAY produces a table for each rank score and includes the following for each level in the classification:

  4. the LEVEL
  5. the number of observations in the level (N)
  6. the SUM OF SCORES
  7. the EXPECTED sum of scores UNDER H0, the null hypothesis
  8. STD DEV, the standard deviation estimate of the sum of scores, and
  9. the MEAN SCORE.

For two or more levels, NPAR1WAY prints

  10. a chi-square statistic (CHISQ)
  11. its degrees of freedom (DF)
  12. PROB>CHISQ, the significance probability.

If there are only two levels, NPAR1WAY reports

13. the smallest sum of scores as S
14. the ratio (S-expected)/std as Z, which is approximately normally distributed under the null hypothesis
15. PROB> |Z|, the probability of a greater observed Z value
16. T-TEST APPROX, the significance level for the the t-test approximation.

EXAMPLE

Weight Gains Data

The data are read in with a variable number of observations per record. In this example, NPAR1WAY first performs all five analyses on five levels of the class variable DOSE. Then the two lowest levels are output to a second data set to illustrate the two-sample tests.

```
TITLE 'WEIGHT GAINS WITH GOSSYPOL ADDITIVE';
TITLE3 'HALVERSON AND SHERWOOD - 1932';
DATA G;
   INPUT DOSE N;
   DO I=1 TO N;
      INPUT GAIN @@;
      OUTPUT;
      END;
   CARDS;
 0 16
    228 229 218 216 224 208 235 229 233 219 224 220 232 200 208 232
.04 11
    186 229 220 208 228 198 222 273 216 198 213
.07 12
    179 193 183 180 143 204 114 188 178 134 208 196
.10 17
    130  87 135 116 118 165 151  59 126  64  78  94 150 160 122 110 178
.13 11
    154 130 130 118 118 104 112 134  98 100 104
;
PROC NPAR1WAY;
   CLASS DOSE;
   VAR GAIN;
DATA G2;
   SET G;
   IF DOSE<=.04;
PROC NPAR1WAY;
   CLASS DOSE;
   VAR GAIN;
   TITLE4 'DOSES<=.04';
```

87

2 Differential Equations, Arms Race and Related Models

A.   Differential and Integral Calculus and Arms Race Models

There are many variables such as defence expenditure, increases in military personnel, military threats or pressure, etc. whose rates of change can either increase or decrease the intensity of a given conflict. The rate of change in mathematics is measured by the derivative. Let us discuss very briefly the concept of derivative (closely following Chiang, 1984).

1.   Function

A variable "y" is said to be a function of another variable "x" if for each value of "x" there is a value of "y". Thus $y = x^2$ is a function of x. When "x" takes different values $0, 1, 2, 3...$, x^2 takes the values $0, 1, \overline{4}, 9...$ Whenever we have a function, we can draw a graph corresponding to that function. For the above function the graph will be of the form (Fig. 2.1).

Another example is the profit function:

$$f(Q) = -Q^3 + 59.25Q^2 - 328.5Q - 2000$$

where Q is the level of output. The graph of this function may look as in (Fig. 2.2): For the function in Fig. 2.2, we may be interested in knowing the value of Q, i.e. the output level for which the profit is maximum. For this purpose we can use the concept of derivative. The derivative of the function at a given point (denoted by dy/dt) measures the rate of change of the graph represented by that function at that point. For example, the derivative of $y = x^2$ at $x = 2$ is

Figure 2.1　$y=x^2$

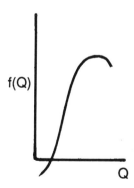

Figure 2.2　Profit Function

$(2x)$. When $x = 2$, this derivative is equal to $2 \times 2 = 4$. Besides the polynomial type function such as $y = x^2$, we can have log functions, trigonometrical functions (sine/cosine), exponential functions, etc. It is not our purpose to show how to take derivatives of different functions. Some of the derivatives are as follows:

$$y = 3x^4 + x^2 + 3$$
$$\frac{dy}{dx} = 3 \times 4x^3 + 2x^1 + 0 - 12x^3 + 2x$$

$$y = \log x$$
$$\frac{dy}{dx} = \frac{1}{x}$$

$$y = e^x$$
$$\frac{dy}{dx} = e^x$$

A calculus text will give a list of derivatives of many functions. For some functions, such as the profit given before, we may be interested in the value of Q for which the total profit is maximum. For this purpose, we have to take the derivative of the profit function and set it equal to zero

$$f(Q) = -Q^3 + 59.25Q^2 - 328.5Q - 2000$$
$$\frac{df}{dQ} = -3Q^2 + (2)(59.25)Q - 328.5 - 0 = 0$$

and then find the value of Q. When such a value (or values) are obtained they should be inserted in the second derivative

$$\frac{d^2f}{dQ^2} = (-3Q)(2) + 118.50$$

and we have to see whether it is negative. If it is negative, then the function is maximum at the value of Q. If it is positive, the function is minimum.

Taking another example, let the function be

$$f(Q) = Q^3 - 12Q^2 + 36Q + 8$$
$$\frac{df}{dQ} = 3Q^2 - 24 + 36 = 0 \quad \text{or} \quad Q^2 - 8Q + 12 = 0$$
$$(Q-2)(Q-6) = 0 \quad \text{or} \quad Q = 2 \text{ or } 6$$

The second derivative $\dfrac{d^2f}{dQ^2} = 2Q - 8$

For Q = 2 the second derivative is negative. As such, the function attains maximum value for Q = 2. For Q = 6, the second derivative is positive, indicating that the function is minimum at Q = 6. The graph of the function is shown below (Fig. 2.3):

So far we have considered functions of single variables. Of course, a function may involve more than one variable. For example, demand for a product may be a function of price and

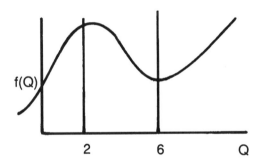

Figure 2.3   Minima and Maxima

advertisement. The same rule applies to the idea of derivatives (called partial derivatives), except that when we take a derivative with respect to one variable, we treat all other variables as constant. For example, if

$$Q = x^2y + 3y^2x$$
$$\frac{\delta Q}{\delta x} = 2xy + 3y^2$$

$$\frac{\delta Q}{\delta y} = x^2 + 6xy$$

To find the value of maximum or minimum of a function of more than one variable (say two variables x,y) we have to equate both the derivatives with respect to x and y to zero and solve their values. To decide whether it is a maximum or minimum we have to apply second order conditions. These concepts are too complex to be treated further in this work.

Differential Equations

In the case of comparative statistics, we assume that the process of adjustment will lead to an equilibrium. In the case of dynamic analysis, the adjustment process is investigated. In economics and other social sciences we are often interested in this process of transformation from one state to another, which is a dynamic system. For this purpose, we can profitably use differential equations which are discussed below.

1. First order linear differential equation

An equation of the form 3X + 4 = 9 is said to be a linear equation from which the value of x can be obtained. Similarly, an equation like

$$\frac{dy}{dt} + a(t)y = b(t) \tag{1}$$

involving the derivative, is known as a differential equation from which the function y(t) can be obtained. If R.H.S of (1) is zero and a(t) is a constant (independent of t) we have a linear homogeneous differential equation. Then equation (1) can be transformed to

$$\frac{dy}{dt} + ay = 0 \quad \text{or} \quad \frac{1}{y}\frac{dy}{dt} = -a \tag{2}$$

or, $y(t) = Ae^{-at}$ which is known as the general solution. (3) when t = 0, y(t) = y(O) = A. So the general solution reduces to a particular solution:
$$y(t) = Y(O)e^{-at}. \tag{4}$$
Obviously, there can be many <u>particular solutions</u> depending on the value of A. In this case we can call it a <u>definite solution</u> because it satisfies the initial condition.

2. Non-homogeneous linear differential equations

In equation (1) when "b" is not equal to zero we have a case of a non-homogeneous equation

$$\frac{dy}{dt} + ay = b \tag{5}$$

The solution of this equation (5) has two parts. One is the complementary function (Y_c) and the other is known as particular integral (Y_p). The non-homogeneous equation is called a complete equation and the homogeneous equation is called the reduced equation.

The complementary function is nothing but the general solution of the homogeneous equation, namely

$$Y_c = Ae^{-at}$$

The particular integral is <u>any</u> particular solution of the complete equation. We can try to find the simplest solution, namely

$$y = k$$

or

$$\frac{dy}{dt} = 0$$

from (5) $ay = b$

$$y = \frac{b}{a}$$

So the general solution of the complete equation is

$$Y(t) = Y_c + Y_p = Ae^{-at} + \frac{b}{a}$$

To get the value of A, we set the initial condition

$$Y(0) = A + \frac{b}{a} \quad \text{or} \quad A = Y(0) - \frac{b}{a}$$

So the definite solution of the original equation is

$$Y(t) = [Y(0) - \frac{b}{a}]e^{-at} + \frac{b}{a}$$

3. Variable coefficient and variable term

So far, we have assumed "a" as a constant. But it can also be a function of time (t). So the differential equation is

$$\frac{dy}{dt} + u(t)Y = W(t) \tag{6}$$

In the homogeneous case $W(t) = 0$

$$\frac{dy}{dt} + u(t)Y = 0$$

93

$$\frac{1}{y}\frac{dy}{dt} = -u(t)$$

So the solution of the equation (6) is

$$Y(t) = A\ Exp\ [-\int u(t)dt]$$

An example: $\frac{dy}{dt} + 4t^2 y = 0$ Here $u = 4t^2$

which gives $\int udt = \int 4t^2\ _{dt} = \frac{4t^3}{3} + C$

$$Y(t) = A\ Exp\ (-t^3)\ Exp\ (-C) = ß\ Exp\ (-t^{3)}.$$

It can be shown that when $W(t) \neq 0$, the general solution will be

$$Y(t) = Exp\ (-\int udt\ (A + \int w\ Exp\ (\int udt)\ dt)$$

An example: $\frac{dy}{dt} + 3t = t$

$$u = 3t,\ W = t,\qquad \int udt = \int 3tdt = \frac{3t^2}{2} + K$$

or $y = Ex\ [(-3t^2/2) + K]\ (A + \int te^{-t}\ dt)$

$$y = (Ae^{-K} + c)\ e^{-t^2} + \tfrac{1}{2}$$

The solution is $y = Be^{-t^2} + \tfrac{1}{2}$

Note: Notice that we are considering first order (only first derivative) and first degree (no power of the derivative and no $\frac{dy}{dt}$ term). This is a linear differential equation.

4.   Exact differential equation

An equation of the form

$$dF(y,t) = \frac{\delta F}{\delta y}\ \cdot\ dy + \frac{\delta F}{dt}\ \cdot\ dt = 0$$

or Mdy + Ndt = 0   where $M = \frac{\delta F}{dy}$

$$N = \frac{\delta F}{dt}$$

is known as an exact differential equation. To test whether a differential equation is exact we test

$$\frac{\delta M}{dt} = \frac{\delta N}{dy}$$

An Example: Let us have a function

$$F(y,t) = y^2 t + K$$

$$dF = 2ytdy + y^2 dt = 0\qquad\text{or}\qquad \frac{dy}{dt} = -\frac{y^2}{2yt}$$

94

is an exact equation. We can check in this case

$$M = 2yt$$
$$\frac{\delta m}{\delta t} = 2y \quad \text{and}$$
$$N = y^2$$
$$\frac{\delta N}{dy} = 2y$$

Hence
$$M = N$$

Let us take an example to show how to solve the exact differential equation

$$2ytdt + y^2dt = 0$$

Here $M = \dfrac{\delta F}{\delta y} = 2yt$

$N = \dfrac{\delta F}{\delta t} = y^2$

Step 1. Let us start with a preliminary result

$$F(y,t) = \quad Mdy + x(t) \quad = \quad 2ytdy + x(t)$$
$$= \quad y^2t + x(t).$$

Step 2. Differentiating both sides

$$\frac{dF(y,t)}{dt} = y^2 + \dot{x}(t)$$

But since $N = \dfrac{\delta F}{dt} = y^2$

$$\dot{x}(t) = 0$$
$$x(t) = K$$

Step 3. In this case $x(t)$ is constant. But it can be a function of "t".

Step 4. Steps 1-3 can be combined to get

$$F(y,t) = y^2t + K.$$

The solution of the exact differential equation should then be

$$F(y,t) = C$$
$$\text{or } y(t)t = C \quad \text{or} \quad y(t) = Ct^{-\frac{1}{2}}$$

5. Nonlinear differential equations of the first order and first degree

$$F(y,t)dy + g(y,t)dt = 0$$
$$\text{or } \frac{dy}{dt} = h(y,t)$$

An Example: $3y^2dy = tdt$

Integrating both sides

$$y^3 + C_1 = \tfrac{1}{2}t^2 + C_2$$

$$y^3 = \tfrac{1}{2}t^2 + C$$
$$y = [(\tfrac{1}{2}t^2 + c)^2]^{1/3}$$

Higher Order Differential Equation

$$\frac{d^ny}{dt^n} + a\frac{d^{n-1}y}{d^{n-1}} + \ldots + a_{n-1}\frac{dy}{dt} + a_ny = b$$

is a linear differential equation of nth order.

A second order equation is
$$y''(t) + a_1y'(t) + a_2y(t) = b$$
The particular solution can be obtained by
$$y(t) = y''(t) = 0, \quad a_2y = b$$
or
$$Y_p = \frac{b}{a_2}$$

Ex:
$$y''(t) + 6y'(t) + 9y(t) = 27$$
$$a_1 = 6$$
$$a_2 = 9$$

$$b = 27 \qquad\qquad a_1^2 = 4a_2, \text{ roots}(r) \text{ will be}$$
$$\text{repeated where } r = -a_1/2 = -3$$

$$Y_p = \frac{27}{9} = 3$$

The complementary function $y_c = A_3e^{rt} + A_4te^{rt}$

$$= A_3e^{-3t} + A_4te^{-3t} + 3$$

From the initial conditions A_3, A_4 can be determined.
In the above equation

$$a_1^2 = 4a_2$$

If $a_1^2 > 4a_2$ than there are distinct but unequal roots of the equation

$$r_1, \ r_2 = \frac{-a_1 \pm \sqrt{a_1^2 - 4a_2}}{2}$$

If $a_1^2 < 4a_2$ than we have complex roots
For example
$$y''(t) + 2y'(t) + 17y = 34 \qquad\qquad y(0) = 0$$
$$y'(0) = 11$$

The particular solution
$$Y_p = \frac{b}{a_2} = \frac{34}{17} = 2$$

Since $a_1^2 < 4a_2$ we have imaginary roots. The complementary function is given by

$$y_c = e^{-t}(A_3\cos 4t + A_4\sin 4t)$$

$$r = \tfrac{1}{2}\sqrt{(4a_2 - 2a_1)} = 4$$

The differential equation theory can be quite complex. We need not discuss any further material. Standard computer programs to solve equations are readily available. Let us now show how this theory can be used in handling conflict resolution problems.

Differential Equations and Arms Control Model

One of the applications of differential equations in conflict analysis is the arms race model. The well-known Richardsonian model states that the change in military expenditure of any country $\underline{i}$ depends on a reaction to the military expenditure of another country $\underline{j}$ restrained by the cost of such an expenditure and aided by an amount reflecting any grievance. In symbols:

$$\dot{M}_i(t) = \alpha_i(t)Mj(t) - \beta_iM_i(t) + g_i(t)$$

$$\dot{M}_j(t) = \alpha_j(t)Mi(t) - \beta_jM_j(t) + g_j(t)$$

The Richardsonian model can be modified in many ways. The rate of change in arms spending may depend upon the difference (gap) between the spending of the two countries rather than the absolute level of one contesting country. Again, the spending depends on the scale of weapons. In the Richardson equation there are three parameters; reaction (α), fatigue (β) and grievance, (g) which are usually positive. If (g) is negative, it implies cooperation.

Of course in reality, the economic cost (β) may face constraints due to resource unavailability. Thus a portion of the desired new stock of weapons can be achieved through a disequilibrium partial adjustment process until and unless increased economic growth leading to higher availability of resources brings the system to Richardsonian equilibrium. Again, the economic constraint can be linked to GNP, unemployment, etc.

The Richardson model is an equilibrium model, not an optimization model. However, the model can be converted to a dynamic optimization and control type model to maximize national utility function (aggregation of individual utility function), which depends on national security and non-military goods. The aggregation process (of utility) and measurement of security are two of many hurdles encountered in building a theoretical model, not to speak of empirical verification of such a model. But this and control theory approaches (with time discounted) lead to meaningful and well-known substitution principles between marginal utility and marginal cost. The utility of any country not only depends on how much it spends on non-defence expenditures but also on how much its opponent spends. Thus the optimal control problem can be transformed to a differential game.

Weapons are acquired either to attack or deter an opponent. Thus stockpiling arms in the Richardson model may be taken in these two different contexts. This type of deterrence - attack model - implies that when a nation attacks, it is motivated to do so because of an anticipated increase in net utility: the sum of utility gains from moving to the expected attack; less the disutilities from countries and other negative outcomes from so moving. Similarly, military technology say, a non-threatening defence system (purely retaliatory second strike weapons backed by reserves) vs. a threatening system (missile) does not affect the security of the opponent, but it can dampen the arms race. Further disaggregation by category of weapons will complicate the Richardsonian equations.

Some other factors which can be integrated into the arms race models are information asymmetry, uncertainty, technology, international tension and terrorism, psychological factors, organization politics and budgeting. Of course, in its utmost generalization, it may contain n nations in an alliance with international economic systems, foreign trade and foreign aid. Considerable theoretical development is possible for developing the background process of decision making by individuals involved in arms procurement, including the behaviour of the leader, information processing, negotiation and mediation, and process of developing.

So far I have not discussed specifically the solution procedure of Richardson's model. This is a first order linear differential equation of the form

$$\frac{dX_i}{dt} = \sum_{j=1}^{n} a_{ij}X_j + b_j \qquad (i = 1, \ldots . n) \qquad (1)$$

In this case $i = 1,2$ where a_{ij} and b_j are all constant. A system of homogeneous linear equations of the form in (1) can be written as a single equation

$$\frac{d^n X}{dt^n} = C_{n-1} \frac{d^{n-1} X}{dt^{(n-1)}} + \ldots + C_o X \qquad (2)$$

The general solution of (2) is also a general solution of (1). Let us consider a two variable case like the Richardson model.

$$\frac{dX_1}{dt} = aX_1 + bX_2 \qquad (3)$$

$$\frac{dX_2}{dt} = CX_1 + dX_2 \qquad (4)$$

Taking the derivative of (3)

$$\frac{d^2 X_1}{dt^2} = a \frac{dX_1}{dt} + b \frac{dX_2}{dt}$$

$$= a \frac{dX_1}{dt} + b(CX_1 + dX_2)$$

or

$$\frac{d^2 X_1}{dt^2} = (a + f) \frac{dX_1}{dt} + (bC-ad)X_1 \qquad (5)$$

which is of the form (2).
The solution of (5) is

$$X_1(t) = C_{11}e^{r1t} + C_{12}e^{r2t}$$

$$X_2(t) = C_{21}e^{r1t} + C_{22}e^{r2t}$$

where C_{11} can be determined from the initial condition; and the r_1 and r_2 are the roots of the quadratic function

$$q^2 - (a+d)q + (ad-bC) = 0$$

98

i.e. $r_1, r_2 = 1/2[(a+d) \pm \sqrt{(a-d)^2 + 4bC}]$

As mentioned before, the Richardson equation is of the following form

$$\frac{dX}{dt} = m_1 y - m_2 X + C_1 \qquad (6)$$

$$\frac{dy}{dt} = m_1 X - n_2 y + C_2$$

when the system is in equilibrium, i.e. $\frac{dX}{dt} = 0$
and $\frac{dy}{dt} = 0$. Setting the equation (6) = 0

$$y = \frac{m_2 X}{m_1} - \frac{C_1}{m_1} \qquad (7)$$

$$y = \frac{n_1 X}{n_2} + \frac{C_2}{n_2}$$

The stability is denoted by the point of intersection of the lines indicated by (7). For this equilibrium to be stable

$$\frac{m_2}{m_1} > \frac{n_1}{n_2}$$

or $\quad M_2 n_2 > m_1 n_1$ as (Rapoport, 1983)

B. **An Example:** A Model of Resolution of Conflict Between India and Pakistan

There has been recently a great increase in the literature of conflict resolution models. More and more often, realities of the world are being taken into account and restrictive assumptions are being relaxed. Testing these models is becoming easier because of the development of new concepts and methods to measure qualitative variables. The scope of these models, however, can be enlarged in at least two respects. First of all, spatial relations of the contending parties, i.e. geopolitical aspects of the conflict, can be considered. For example, when we look at the map of the Indian subcontinent, we find that the geographical boundaries of two other major powers, namely China and Russia, meet the boundaries of India and Pakistan. In considering political relations between India and Pakistan, this factor is of crucial importance. The second factor is the diverse forces that are acting within the contending parties. The rate of economic growth, population growth rates, and internal peace and stability are a few of many factors which greatly influence the foreign relations of a country. This is particularly true in Indo-Pakistani relations.
The case of India and Pakistan offers an excellent field of study to which we can apply the modern game theoretical approaches for analysing a mutual relationship. Here we have two countries which are independent from geographic, economic,

political and social points of view. They can gain much by cooperating or lose much by quarrelling, while the great powers, through cooperation, can act as moderating influences. This study casts some light on these aspects and is intended as a beginning toward a more generalized study to be undertaken in the future.

The emergence of India and Pakistan as two nations in the Indian subcontinent has ushered in a new phenomenon is Asia. Before 1947, they were a single country whose people struggled together for freedom from British rule. When the British decided to leave, the Moslem minority, apprehensive of the Hindu majority, demanded a separate state, which they obtained after a bloodbath, the consequence of religious riots (East Pakistan, a former part of Pakistan, is now Bangladesh). The division of the country resulted in a complete breakdown in the social, economic and political system of the country.

India now has about 850 million people, of which 10% are Moslem. Of Pakistan's 150 million people, there are very few Hindus. The enmity between Hindus and Moslems in India has not ended as a result of the division of the country. These two groups have now become arch enemies, spending millions of rupees in defence preparation. Already they have fought significant wars resulting in loss of lives and resources.

The very existence of these two countries depends on their mutual cooperation and friendship. There are many ways through which this friendship can be brought about. This has to be brought about on a government level, on personal levels, and also through the auspices of other countries. One significant step in the right direction would be in the field of disarmament. This paper throws some light on this aspect. It is not intended to provide an easy solution, since conflict between nations is too complicated a matter to be solved easily. This is just a simple approach to conflict resolution taking into consideration the realities as far as possible.

Following Richardson (1960), we assume that there are three factors related to the arms race: namely, mutual suspicion and mistrust, cost of military expenditure and grievances. Let us consider these factors for India and Pakistan in the context of their relationship and other internal and external variables.

India
So far as India is concerned, there are two fronts to guard, namely, the borders with Pakistan and China. India is suspicious of both these countries. Thus, it can be assumed that the rate of change of its military expenditure will depend upon the military expenditure of Pakistan and China in the previous period. The lag in time period is appropriate since responses are never instantaneous and there is always a time lag in intelligence reports. A time lag of one year is assumed. So we have the following relation:

$$\frac{dM}{dt}_{1t} = kM_{2(t-1)} + nM_{3(t-1)} \tag{1}$$

where

M_{1t} =   military expenditure (rupees in millions) of India for the time period t

$M_{2(t-1)}$ =   military expenditure (rupees in millions) of Pakistan in the time period (t-1)

$M_{3(t-1)}$ =   military expenditure (rupees in millions or an index number) of Communist China in the period (t-1)

The left-hand side of (1) denotes the rate of change of India military expenditure. k and n are positive constants which, following Richardson's terminology, can be called "defence coefficients". It is difficult to obtain data for China's defence expenditure. If they are not available we can try to employ some index numbers or use some proxy variables. This equation (1) represents the mistrust and suspicion on the part of India against Pakistan and China. It is true that mistrust is a qualitative aspect of the state of mind. However, we assume that military expenditure is a satisfactory yardstick for measuring it.

The second factor involved in the arms race is the cost of keeping up the defences. It can be assumed that a significant portion of resources devoted to military efforts is a complete waste, while other military expenditures, such as road building, etc. may have some economic value. It is not the purpose of this paper to identify those items as useful and useless, nor do we want to make any estimate of them at this stage. Secondly, since the investment resources of India are limited, military expenditure implies sacrificing economic development (in terms of increase in the Gross National Product) that would have been achieved if the resources were used for national economic development.

The third factor is the amount of benefit that would have accrued to India if these two countries become friendly and cooperated in the field of international trade. In regard to many commodities, such as jute, tea, textiles, etc., the foreign exchange income of both countries could increase appreciably if they cooperated in production and distribution. These three factors have been combined in the following equation:

$$O_{1t} = a_1 M_{1t} + b_1 Y_{1t} + c_1 T_{1t} \qquad (2)$$

O_{1t} =   represents the cost of defence

Y_{1t} =   Gross National Product of India at the time period t (GNP in short)

T_{1t} =   is the foreign exchange income of India at the time period t

a_1 =   constant showing what percentage of the military expenditure can be treated as waste

b_1 =

the percentage of Indian GNP that could have increased if there were a friendly relationship between the two countries. In the extreme case, b_1 may be taken as the percentage of Indian GNP that could have increased if there is no military spending. Since such a utopian situation is nowhere in sight in the near future, we shall take b_1 as the percentage of GNP that could be increased if the defence expenditure is kept at a "normal" level. We shall not attempt a comprehensive definition of the term "normal" and shall assume that such a figure has been agreed upon.

c_1 =

a constant which shows the percentage of foreign exchange income that could be added with mutual cooperation between these countries.

The third factor related to conflict is grievances. For the sake of simplicity, let us assume that India's grievances against Pakistan consist of two parts: (1) alleged collusion with China, and (2) alleged Pakistani inspired rebellions in tribal areas of northeastern India. Again, we do not want to verify whether these allegations are true or not, but take the grievances as given. These two sources of grievances are assumed to be measurable in monetary terms. Some portion of them — say, military help from China to Pakistan — is measurable. The following equation then represents the third factor:

$$Q_{1t} = d_1 A_{2t}^{c} + e_1 I_{2t} \tag{3}$$

where

Q_{1t} =

is the grievance of India against Pakistan at time period t

A_{2t}^{c} =

military help from China to Pakistan in the time period "t" (rupees in millions)

I_{2t} =

"Help" (assumed to be expressed terms of monetary value) by Pakistan to the tribal rebels in northeastern India (rupees in millions).

d_1 and e_1 are respective weights given by the Indian government to match these threats. These constants can also show what amount of money has to be spent by India to face these dual fronts. The grievance equation involves some qualitative aspects which are assumed to be expressed in quantitative terms. It is easy to identify other "cost" and "grievances," but for the sake of simplicity we assume that all these items can be expressed through the variables we have considered.

Combining the three factors together, we have

$$\frac{dM}{dt}_{1t} = k M_{2(t-1)} + n M_{3(t-1)} - O_{1(t-1)} - Q_{1(t-1)} \tag{4}$$

which states that the rate of change in Indian military expenditure equals the sum total of three factors in the previous period. Substituting the values of $O_{1(t-1)}$ and $Q_{1(t-1)}$ from (2) and (3) respectively into (4) we get

$$\frac{dM_{1t}}{dt} = kM_{2(t-1)} + nM_{3(t-1)} - b_1Y_{1(t-1)}$$
$$-c_1T_{1(t-1)} + d_1A^c_{2(t-1)} + e_1I_{2(t-1)} \quad (5)$$

Let us next make the following simplifying assumptions

$$A^c_{2t} = f_1M_{3t} \quad (6)$$

where f_1 is a constant. This equation states that Chinese help to Pakistan is proportional to Chinese military expenditure.

$$T_{1t} = g_1Y_{1t} \quad (7)$$

where g_1 is a constant. This equation states that India's foreign exchange income is proportional to its GNP.
   The third substitution is

$$I_{2t} = h_1Y_{1t} \quad (8)$$

where h_1 is a constant; it states that the grievances are proportional to GNP in the sense that more grievance means a greater portion of GNP is set aside to meet these grievances.
   Substituting (6), (7), and (8) into (5) we get

$$\frac{dM_{1t}}{dt} = kM_{2(t-1)} + \frac{(n + d_1)A^c_{2(t-1)}}{f_1} - a_1M_{1(t-1)}$$
$$- b_1Y_{1(t-1)} - c_1g_1Y_{1(t-1)} + e_1h_1Y_{1(t-1)} \quad (9)$$

or

$$\frac{dM_{1t}}{dt} = kM_{2(t-1)} + \frac{(n + d_1)A^c_{2(t-1)}}{f_1} - a_1M_{1(t-1)}$$
$$- Y_{1(t-1)}(b_1 + c_{1g1} - e_1h_1) \quad (10)$$

Let us transform this differential equation into its simplified difference equation form as follows:

$$M_{1(t+1)} - M_{1t} = kM_{2(t-1)} + \frac{(n + d_1)A^c_{2(t-1)}}{f_1}$$
$$- aM_{1(t-1)} - (b_1 + c_1g_1 - e_1h_1)Y_{1(t-1)} \quad (11)$$

or,

$$M_{1(t+2)} - M_{1(t+1)} + a_1M_{1t}$$
$$= kM_{2t} + \frac{(n + d_1)A^c_{2t}}{f_1} - (b_1 + c_1g_1 \quad e_1h_1)Y_{1t} \quad (12)$$

Equation (12) is a linear second order difference equation of the form

$$Y_{t+2} + AY_{t+1} + Y_t = F(t) \quad (13)$$

We shall work in terms of the difference equation for the sake of simplicity. The difference equation formulation is realistic since the military expenditure decisions are made in several discrete steps rather than through instantaneous changes. Let us first consider the general solution of the homogeneous equation

$$M_{1(t+2)} - M_{1(t+1)} + a_1 M_{1t} = 0 \qquad (14)$$

The auxiliary equation is

$$m^2 - m + a_1 = 0 \quad \text{where } M_{1t} = m^t \qquad (15)$$

The roots of the equation (15) are

$$m_1 = 1 + \sqrt{1 - 4a_1} \qquad (16)$$

$$m_2 = 1 - \sqrt{1 - 4a_1} \qquad (17)$$

Consider the two cases.

Case 1. $a_1 < 1/4$. The roots m_1 and m_2 are real and unequal. In that case the general solution of equation (14) is

$$M^*_{1t} = \lambda_1 (1 + \sqrt{1 - 4a_1})^t + \lambda_2 (a - \sqrt{1 - 4a_1})^t \qquad (18)$$

where λ_1 and λ_2 are constants to be determined from the initial conditions.

Case 2. When $a_1 > 1/4$, the roots will be unequal but complex conjugate

$$m_1 = r(\cos\theta + i\sin\theta) = a + ib = 1 + \sqrt{1 - 4a_1} \qquad (19)$$
$$m_2 = r(\cos\theta - i\sin\theta) = a - ib = 1 - \sqrt{1 - 4a_1} \qquad (20)$$

where

$$r = \sqrt{a^2 + b^2} \qquad (21)$$
$$\tan\theta = \frac{b}{a} \qquad (22)$$

In our case a = 1 and b will be determined for given value of a_1; for example, if $a_1 = 1/2$, then a = 1 and b = 1 and

$$r = \sqrt{1^2 + 1^2} = \sqrt{2}$$

$$\tan\theta = 1$$

i.e. $\qquad \theta = 45°$

Again, if $a_1 = 3/4$

$$a = 1, \quad b = \sqrt{2}$$

$$r = \sqrt{3}$$

$$\tan\theta = \sqrt{2}$$

$$\theta = \tan^{-1} \sqrt{2} = 55° \text{ (approx.)}$$

In the case of complex roots, the general solution is given by

$$M^*_{1t} = AR^t Cos(t\theta + B) \qquad (23)$$

when $a_1 = 1/2$,

$$M^*_{1t} = A(\sqrt{2})^t Cos\ (\pi t + B) \qquad (24)$$

and where A and B are obtained from the initial conditions.

Let us next find the particular solution of the complete equation (12). Unless we make simplifications in the form of the functions involved in the right-hand side of (12), we shall face serious difficulties. For this purpose, we make the following substitutions:

$$M_{2t} = L_0 + \alpha_2 \beta_2^t \qquad (25)$$

which states that military expenditure of Pakistan[1] can be approximated by a modified exponential curve. It is obvious that military expenditure cannot increase ad infinitum. It has an asymptote (in this case L_0), α_2, which is a negative constant showing the difference of M_{20} and the asymptote, and β_2 which is the rate of growth of military expenditure.

The second substitution is

$$A^c_{2t} = \delta_0 + aSin\frac{\pi t}{2} \qquad (26)$$

which states that China's help to Pakistan can be approximated by a constant amount plus a periodic amount depending on Indo-Pakistani relations and international politics over time.

The third simplification is

$$Y_{1t} = Y_{10}(1 + \alpha_1 t) \qquad (27)$$

which states that the Indian GNP increases by α_1 per cent annually, Y_{10} being the GNP at the initial period, say in 1950.

Substituting (25), (26), and (27) in (12) we get

---

[1] Military Expenditure of India and Pakistan

	World (billion dollars)	India (billion dollars)	Pakistan (billions of dollars)
1980	567	4.2	.8
1981	580	4.9	1.0
1982	615	5.9	1.1
1983	632	6.6	1.6
1984	643	7.3	1.6
1985	663	7.7	1.9

$$M_{1(t+2)} - M_{1(t+1)} + a_1 M_{1t} = kL_0 + k\alpha_2 \beta_2^t$$

$$+ \left(\frac{n}{f_1} + d_1\right)\delta_0 + a\left(\frac{n}{f_1} + d_1\right)\operatorname{Sin}\frac{\pi}{2}t$$

$$- (b_1 + c_1 g_1 - e_1 h_1)Y_{10} - \alpha_1(b_1 + c_1 g_1 - e_1 h_1)t \qquad (28)$$

or equation (12) reduces to

$$M_{1(t+2)} - M_{1(t+1)} + a_1 M_{1t} = A_0 + A_1 \beta_2^t + A_2^t + A_3 \operatorname{Sin}\frac{\pi}{2}t \qquad (29)$$

where

$$A_0 = kL_0 + (n/f_1 + d_1)\delta_0 - (b_1 + c_1 g_1 - e_1 h_1)Y_1^n \qquad (30)$$

$$A_1 = k\alpha_2 \qquad (31)$$

$$A_2 = \alpha_1(b_1 + c_1 g_1 - e_1 h_1) \qquad (32)$$

$$A_3 = a(n/f_1 + d_1) \qquad (33)$$

Thus our job is to solve (29).
Let us attempt a trial solution of (29)

$$M_{1t}^* = B_0 + B_1 \beta_2^t + B_2 t + B_3 \operatorname{Sin}\frac{\pi}{2}t + B_4 \operatorname{Cos}\frac{\pi}{2}t \qquad (30')$$

Putting this value on the L.H.S. of (29) we get

$$M_{1(t+1)}^* = B_0 + B_1 \beta_2^{t+2} + B_2(t+2) + B_3 \operatorname{Sin}\frac{\pi}{2}(t+2) + B_4 \operatorname{Cos}\frac{\pi}{2}(t+2)$$

$$(31')$$

$$- M_{1(t+1)}^* = - B_0 - B_1 \beta_2^{t+1} - B_2(t+1) - B_3 \operatorname{Sin}\frac{\pi}{2}(t+1) - B_4 \operatorname{Cos}\frac{\pi}{2}(t+1)$$

$$(32')$$

$$a_1 M_{1t}^* = a_1 B_0 + a_1 B_1 \beta_2^t + a_1 B_2 t + a_1 B_3 \operatorname{Sin}\frac{\pi}{2}t + a_1 B_4 \operatorname{Cos}\frac{\pi}{2}t \qquad (33')$$

Adding both sides of (31), (32) and (33)

$$M_{1\,t-2)}^* - M_{1\,t+1)}^* + a_1 M_{1t}^* = (a_1 B_0 + 2B_2 - B_2)$$

$$+ \beta_2^t(B_1 \beta_2^2 - B_1 \beta_2 + a_1 B_1) + t(B_2 - B_2 + a_1 B_2)$$

$$+ \operatorname{Sin}\frac{\pi}{2}(B_4 - B_3 + a_1 B_3) - \operatorname{Cos}\frac{\pi}{2}t(B_4 + B_3 - a_1 B_4) \qquad (34)$$

NOTE:

$$\operatorname{Sin}(t+2)\frac{\pi}{2} = \operatorname{Sin}\left(t\frac{\pi}{2} + \pi\right) = -\operatorname{Sin}t\frac{\pi}{2}$$

$$\operatorname{Cos}(t+2)\frac{\pi}{2} = \operatorname{Cos}\left(t\frac{\pi}{2} + \pi\right) = -\operatorname{Cos}t\frac{\pi}{2}$$

$$\text{Sin } (t + 1)\frac{\pi}{2} = \text{Sin } \left(t\frac{\pi}{2} + \frac{\pi}{2} \right) = \text{Cos } t\frac{\pi}{2}$$

$$\text{Cos } (t + 1)\frac{\pi}{2} = \text{Cos } \left(t\frac{\pi}{2} + \frac{\pi}{2} \right) = - \text{Sin } t\frac{\pi}{2}.$$

Making these substitution on the R.H.S. of (31) and (32) we see that the six grigo-metrical terms reduce to

$$\left(\text{Sin } \frac{\pi}{2}t \right)(B_4 - B_3 + a_1 B_3) - \left(\text{Cos } \frac{\pi}{2}t \right)(B_4 + B_3 - a_1 B_4)$$

Comparing (29) and (34) we see that in order for M_{1t}^* to be a solution of (29) we must have

$$A_0 = a_1 B_0 + B_2 \tag{35}$$

$$A_1 = B_1 \beta_2^2 - B_1 \beta_2 + a_1 B_1 \tag{36}$$

$$A_2 = a_1 B_2 \tag{37}$$

$$A_3 = - B_3 + a_1 B_3 + B_4 \tag{38}$$

$$0 = B_4 + B_3 - a_1 B_4 \tag{39}$$

After little simplification

$$B_0 = \frac{a_1 A_0 - A_2}{a_1^2} \tag{35'}$$

$$B_1 = \frac{A_1}{\beta_2^2 - \beta_2 + a_1} \tag{36'}$$

$$B_2 = \frac{A_2}{a_1} \tag{37'}$$

$$B_3 = \frac{A_3(a - 1)}{1 + (a_1 - 1)^2} \tag{38'}$$

$$B_4 = \frac{A_3}{1 + (a_1 - 1)^2} \tag{39'}$$

Substituting the values of A_0, A_1, A_3 from (30)—(33) into (35')—(39') we get

$$B_0 = \left[a_1 k L_0 + a_1 \delta_0 (n/f_1 + d_1) + a_1 Y_1^0 (b_1 + c_1 g_1 - e_1 h_1) - \frac{\delta_1 (b_1 + c_1 g_1 - e_1 h_1)}{2a} \right] \tag{35''}$$

$$B_1 = \frac{k\alpha_2}{\beta_2^2 - \beta_2 + a_1} = \frac{k\alpha_2}{a_1 - \beta_2 (1 - \beta_2)} \tag{36''}$$

$$B_2 = \alpha_1 \frac{(b_1 + c_1 g_1 - e_1 h_1)}{a_1} \tag{37''}$$

$$B_3 = \frac{a(a_1 - 1)(n/f_1 + d_1)}{1 + (a_1 - 1)^2} \tag{38''}$$

$$B_4 = \frac{a(n/f_1 + d_1)}{1 + (a_1 - 1)^2} \tag{39''}$$

107

So when $a_1 < 1/4$, the complete solution is given by

$$M_{1t} = \lambda_1(1 + \sqrt{1 - 4a_1})^t + \lambda_2(1 - \sqrt{1 - 4a_1})^t$$

$$+ B_0 + B_1\beta_1^t + B_2t + B_3 \, \mathrm{Sin}\,\frac{\pi}{2}t + B_4 \, \mathrm{Cos}\,\frac{\pi}{2}t \tag{40}$$

where λ_1 and λ_2 are obtained from initial conditions and the values of B_0, B_1, B_2, B_3 are given above. For example if the values M_{10} and M_{11} are given, then from (40) we get

$$M_{10} = \lambda_1 + \lambda_2 + B_0 + B_1 + B_2 + B_4 \tag{41}$$

$$M_{11} = \lambda_1 + \lambda_2 + (\sqrt{1 - 4a_1})(\lambda_1 - \lambda_2) + B_0 + \beta_1 B_1 + B_2 + B_3 \tag{42}$$

(42) can be written with the help of (41)
or

$$M_{11} = M_{10} + (\sqrt{1 - 4a_1})(\lambda_1 - \lambda_2) + \beta_1 B_1 - B_1 + B_3 - B_4 \tag{43}$$

from (41) and (43)

$$\frac{M_{11} - M_{10}}{\sqrt{1 - 4a_1}} = (\lambda_1 - \lambda_2) + \frac{\beta_1 B_1 - B_1 + B_3 - B_4}{\sqrt{1 - 4a_2}} \tag{44}$$

Adding and subracting (41) and (44)

$$\lambda_1 = \frac{1}{2}M_{10} + \frac{M_{11} - M_{10}}{2\sqrt{1 - 4a_1}} - \frac{1}{2}\left(B_0 + B_1 + B_2 + B_4 - \frac{\beta_1 B_1 - B_1 + B_3 - B_4}{\sqrt{1 - 4a_1}}\right) \tag{45}$$

$$\lambda_2 = \frac{1}{2}M_{10} - \frac{M_{11} - M_{10}}{2\sqrt{1 - 4a_1}} - \frac{1}{2}\left(B_0 + B_1 + B_2 + B_4 - \frac{\beta_1 B_1 - B_1 + B_3 - B_4}{\sqrt{1 - 4a_1}}\right) \tag{46}$$

if $a_1 > 1/4$ then the complete solution is given by

$$M_{1t} = Ar^t \, \mathrm{Cos}\,(t\theta + B) + B_0 + B_1\beta_2^t + B_2^t + B_3 \, \mathrm{Sin}\,\frac{\pi}{2} + B_4 \, \mathrm{Cos}\,\frac{\pi}{2}t \tag{47}$$

where

$$r = \sqrt{a^2 + b^2} \qquad \text{See page 91}$$

$$\theta = \tan^{-1} b/a$$

A and B are constants to be obtained from initial conditions. If as before we take $r = \sqrt{2}$, $\theta = \pi/4$ and assume $A = 1$ and $B = \pi/2$ (without going through the initial conditions) then (47) becomes

$$M_{1t} = (\sqrt{2})^t\left(-\mathrm{Sin}\,\frac{\pi}{4}t\right) + B_0 + B_1\beta_2^t + B_2t + B_3 \, \mathrm{Sin}\,\frac{\pi}{2}t + B_4 \, \mathrm{Cos}\,\frac{\pi}{2}t \tag{48}$$

$$= -2^{t/2} \, \mathrm{Sin}\,\frac{\pi}{4}t + B_0 + B_1\beta_2^t + B_2t + B_3 \, \mathrm{Sin}\,\frac{\pi}{2}t + B_4 \, \mathrm{Cos}\,\frac{\pi}{2}t \tag{48'}$$

In any case (whether a < 1/4 or > 1/4) we can write equations (40) or (48') as

$$M_{1t} = g(t, \beta^t_2, \text{ Sin } \pi t/2, \text{ Cos } \pi t/2, k, L_o, \quad n, \quad f_1, d, \delta_o, \\ b_1, c_1, g_1, e_1, h_1, Y_1, \alpha_2, \alpha_1, a) \qquad (49)$$

In (49) we have explicitly written the constants, since we want to keep track of the constant involved in the above equation. At the end of the paper, we have listed the constants in one place for convenience. We hope to collect data in the future from which these constants can be estimated. Ignoring these constants (49) can be written in short

$$M_{1t} = g(t, \beta^t_2, \text{Sin } \frac{\pi t}{2}, \text{Cos} \frac{\pi t}{2}). \qquad (49a)$$

Let us next consider the question in regard to Pakistan.

Pakistan

The reasoning in this case is similar to that of India with some variation. The "mistrust" equation is given by

$$\frac{dM_{2t}}{dt} = 1M_{1(t-1)} \qquad (50)$$

where 1 is the defence coefficient for Pakistan

When we consider the "cost" equation an additional factor is involved. One of the basic problems in Pakistan was the feud between its two wings, i.e. East Pakistan and West Pakistan. The people in these two wings were as different as can be except for their common religious bond. East Pakistan had 55% of the population of Pakistan. It was mostly agricultural and its per capita income is much lower than that of West Pakistan.

The political power rested with the leaders of West Pakistan. Again, these two wings are separated by a thousand miles of Indian territory. East Pakistan had certain disadvantages to start with. If there is increased defence spending, resources for development will be scarce and the difference between the per capita income of the two wings will increase, leading to interregional dissension. The cost equation is given by*

$$O_{2t} = a_2 M_{2t} + \frac{b_2 Y_{2t}}{P_{2t}} + b' \frac{(Y^W_2 t - Y^E_2 t) + C_2 T_{2t}}{P^W_{2t}} \qquad (51)$$

where M_{2t} = Military expenditure of Pakistan at the time period "t" (millions of rupees)

Y_{2t} = the GNP for Pakistan at the time period "t" (millions of rupees)

Y^W_{2t} = the Gross Regional Product for West Pakistan at the time period "t" (millions of rupees)

P_{2t} = total population of Pakistan (in millions) at the time "t"

P^W_{2t} = total population of West Pakistan (in millions) at the time "t"

P^E_{2t} = total population of East Pakistan (in millions) at the time "t"

T_{2t} = foreign exchange income of Pakistan at the time "t".

*The study was done before the creation of Bangladesh.

a_2, b_2, b'_2, c_2 are constants having a similar meaning as in the case of India.

Thus we have

$$P_{2t} = P_{2t}^W + P_{2t}^E \tag{51'}$$

$$Y_{2t} = Y_{2t}^W + Y_{2t}^E \tag{52}$$

As regards grievances, Pakistan's fixed grievance is the possession of Kashmir which is an Indian state. Pakistan claims it since the majority of its inhabitants are Moslems. The second grievance is variable concerning the alleged repression of Moslems in India. So the grievance equation is given by

$$Q_{2t} = K + R_{1t} \tag{53}$$

where

$$K = \text{grievance for Kashmir}$$

$$R_{1t} = \text{alleged repression of Moslems in India}$$

So the complete equation is

$$\frac{dM_{2t}}{dt} = 1M_{1(t-1)} - 0_{2(t-1)} + Q_{2t} \tag{54}$$

or

$$\frac{dM_{2t}}{dt} = 1M_{1(t-1)} - a_2 M_{2(t-1)} - b_2 \frac{Y_{2(t-1)}}{P_{2(t-1)}}$$
$$- b_2 \left(\frac{Y_{2(t-1)}^W}{P_{2(-1)}^W} - \frac{Y_{2(t-1)}^E}{P_{2(-1)}^E} \right) - C_2 T_{2(t-1)} + K + R_{1t} \tag{55}$$

Reducing the above differential equation to a difference equation we have

$$M_{2(t+2)} - M_{2'(t+1)} + a_2 M_{2t} = 1M_{1t} - b_2 \frac{Y_{2t}}{P_2} - b'_2 \left(\frac{Y_{2t}^W}{P_{2t}^W} - \frac{Y_{2t}^E}{P_{2t}^E} \right)$$
$$- C_2 T_{2t} + K + R_{1t} \tag{56}$$

Note that

$$\frac{Y_{2t}^W}{P_{2t}^W} - \frac{Y_{2t}^E}{P_{2t}^E} = \frac{Y_{2t}^W}{P_{2t}^W} - \frac{Y_{2t} - Y_{2t}^W}{P_{2t} - P_{2t}^W} = \frac{Y_{2t}^W P_{2t} - Y_{2t}^W P_{2t}^W - P_{2t}^W Y_{2t} + P_{2t}^W Y_{2t}^W}{P_{2t}^W (P_{2t} - P_{2t}^W)}$$

$$= \frac{Y_{2t}^W \dfrac{P_{2t}}{P_{2t}^W} - Y_{2t}}{P_{2t} - P_{2t}^W} = \frac{\dfrac{Y_{2t}^W}{r} - Y_{2t}}{P_{2t}(1-r)}$$

(where $r = P_{2t}^W / P_{2t}$)
$$= \frac{Y_{2t}^W - r Y_{2t}}{r(1-r)P_{2t}} = \frac{Y_{2t}^W}{r(1-r)P_{2t}} - \frac{1}{1-r} \frac{Y_{2t}}{P_{2t}} \tag{57}$$

Putting (57) into (56) and working with per capita income

$$y_{2t} = \frac{Y_{2t}}{P_{2t}} \tag{58}$$

$$y_{2t}^W = \frac{Y_{2t}^W}{P_{2t}^W} \tag{59}$$

we get after some simplification

$$M_{2(t+2)} - M_{2(t+1)} + a_2 M_{2t} = 1M_{1t} - Y_{2t}\left(b_2 - \frac{b_2 - b'_2}{1-r}\right)^2$$

$$- (b')^2 \frac{y^w_2 t}{1-r} - C_2 T_{2t} + K + R_{1t} \qquad (60)$$

Again we have the second order non-homogeneous difference equation. To solve it we made the following substitutions in the same manner as we did before.

$$M_{1t} = S_o + \alpha_1 \beta^t_1 + b \sin \frac{\pi}{2} t \qquad (61)$$

which notes that Indian military expenditure is of a modified exponential type plus cyclical variation due to occasional threats from China. S_o is the asymptotic value; β is the rate of growth of military expenditure; is the difference between the asymptotic value and the defence expenditure at $t = o$, and b measures the intensity of cyclical variation.

The second simplification is

$$Y_{2t} = y^o_2(t + x_2 t) \qquad (62)$$

where y^o_2 is the per capita income at $t = 0$, and x_2 is the constant rate of growth of per capital income. The same type of relation is assumed to be true for West Pakistan as given by

$$Y^w_{2t} = y^o_2(1 + x^w_2 t) \qquad (63)$$

Again as before

$$T_{2t} = \phi_2 Y_{2t} \qquad (64)$$

Notice that for the sake of algebraic simplification we have used the per capita income (and not GNP) in explaining foreign exchange income. Finally we have

$$(K + R_{1t}) = Y_{2t} \qquad (65)$$

Making these substitutions in (60) and simplifying (also substitute $1 = k/4$ since the population of India is about four times that of Pakistan), we get

$$M_{2(t+2)} - M_{2(t+1)} + a_2 M_{2t} = \frac{(kS_o + b_2 y^o_2 - c_2 \phi_2 y^o_2 + y^o_2 + \alpha_1 k \beta^t_1)}{4}$$

$$+ \frac{kb}{4} \sin \frac{\pi t}{2} + [b_2 x_2 y^o_2 + \frac{b_2 y^o_2(x_2 - x^w_2)}{1-r} - c_2 \phi_2 y^o_2 x_2 + xy^o_2 x_2]t \qquad (66)$$

We can solve this equation as before and it will be like

$$M_{2t} = (t, \beta^t_2, \sin \frac{\pi t}{2}, \frac{k}{4}, S_o, y^o_2, b_1, c_2, \phi_2, X, \delta_1, \beta_1, b, b_2, r, x_2, x^w_2 \cos \frac{\pi t}{2})^2 \qquad (67)$$

111

At the end of the paper we have given the definition of the constants. Ignoring the constants

$$M_{2t} = (t, \beta^t_1, \sin\frac{\pi t}{2}, \cos\frac{\pi t}{2}) \qquad (68)$$

Equations (49') and (68) give the expression for military expenditures of India and Pakistan, respectively, in terms of other variables and a set of constants. The parameters β_1 and β_2 involved in these two expressions can be termed decision parameters. If, for example, India wishes to change β_1 at a particular point of time, then β_2 will also change throughout M_{2t} in (68) and this value will affect M_{1t} in (49') and consequently β_2 through (49'). It is to be noted here that changes in β values or in the responses of each country will also depend upon cost of defences, etc. In a sense, then, equations (49') and (68) give the response curve for India and Pakistan and each country will try the best "response" via these two equations (Isard and Smith, 1965).

Let us next consider another interesting factor. The military expenditure in each country equals the maximum amount each country can afford plus the foreign aid. So we write

$$M_{1t} = \gamma_1(t, P_{1t})Y_{1t} + A^{US}_{1t} + A_{1t}R \qquad (69)$$

$$M_{2t} = \gamma_2(t, P_{2t})Y_{2t} + A^{US}_{2t} + A^c_{2t} + A^R_{2t} \qquad (70)$$

The equation (69) states that military expenditure of India equals disposable (for defence) GNP plus aid from the USA and the USSR. The case is the same for Pakistan in (70) considering Chinese help. It is to be noted that in talking of "disposable" military expenditure, we take into account population growth and time (a proxy variable for good and bad harvests).

If our goal is to see that at any future time period T, the sum of $M_{1T} + M_{2T}$ becomes minimum, then the problem can be stated in the following fashion: choose the decision parameters β_1 and β_2 at each point of time t such that at the time period T

Total military expenditure = $M_{1T} + M_{2T}$ is minimum subject to:

$$M_{1t} \geq g(t, \beta^t_2, \sin\frac{\pi t}{2}, \cos\frac{\pi t}{2}) \qquad (I)$$

$$M_{2t} \geq f(t, \beta^t_1, \sin\frac{\pi t}{2}, \cos\frac{\pi t}{2}) \qquad (II)$$

$$M_{1t} \leq \gamma_1(t, P_{1t})Y_{1t} + A^{US}_{1t} + AR_{it} \qquad (III)$$

$$M_{2t} \leq \gamma_2(t, P_{2t})Y_{2t} + A^{US}_{2t} + A^R_{2t} + A^c_2 \qquad (IV)$$

In simple language, the growth path of defence expenditure should be such that at each point of time each country will give the "best" response to the other and at the same time keep within its budget. It is interesting to note from (I)–(IV) that if during the time period foreign help from the USA and USSR decreases very much, or if these countries cooperate in striving towards peace in the Indian subcontinent, or if in a particular year excessive population

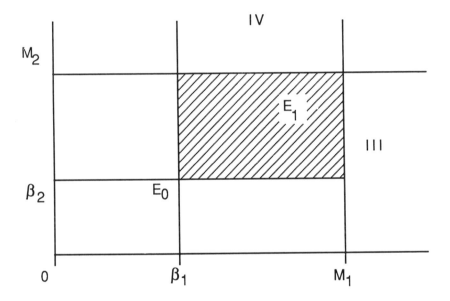

Figure 2.4 Optimum Disarmament Levels

113

or low GNP or both force the governments to slow down defence expenditures, then the value of β_1 and β_2 will be restricted.

We shall not attempt to solve the dynamic programming problem above. It is quite complicated and we do not have information about the value of the constant involved in the response equation. We shall conclude our paper by giving a graphical interpretation of the problem in Fig. 2.4. In Fig. 2.4, defence expenditures are measured along two axes.

For the initial period for any β_1 there will be an M_1 and consequently β_2 and then an M_1. These initial values will be determined through I and II. This (M_{10}, M_{20}) point can lie anywhere above E_0. At this stage, restrictions III and IV apply. So the initial point is restricted in the shaded area. If E_0 is the chosen minimum point, we proceed as before and get another point E_1, and so on. For each set of equilibrium values $(E_0, E_1 \ldots)$ we shall get a terminal value $M_{1T} + M_{2T}$ at the time T. The problem is to choose the set such that $M_{1T} + M_{2T}$ is minimum.

From the discussion above, it is evident that we have made too many assumptions and, in real life, the conflict resolution problem is more complex. In regard to that, it can be pointed out that at this stage I wished merely to present this research as an exercise in the mathematics of conflict resolution. In the future, if satisfactory values of the constants are obtained, a numerical solution will be attempted and the model will be tested. The validity of the assumptions can be judged with reference to Indo-Pakistani relations.

Constants of the Model

INDIA:

K	=	Response coefficient, i.e. rate of the change in defence expenditure of India in unit time to the defence expenditure of Pakistan in the previous period
L_0	=	Asymptotic value for the military expenditure for Pakistan
n	=	Response coefficient for China from India
f_1	=	Ration of military help to Pakistan from China to the total Chinese military expenditure
d_1	=	Response to Pakistan's collusion with China
d_0	=	Fixed military help from China to Pakistan
b_1	=	Percentage of Indian GNP that could have been increased with "normal" military expenditure
c_1	=	Percentage of foreign exchange that could have been increased through cooperation with Pakistan
g_1	=	Ratio of foreign exchange to GNP
e_1	=	Indian response to Pakistan's help to Indian tribal insurgents
h_1	=	Money values of grievances as a ratio to GNP
Y_{10}	=	Initial GNP of India (say in 1950)
d_2^{10}	=	The difference between the asymptotic value of defence expenditure and the initial defence spending by Pakistan
δ_1	=	Growth of GNP per year

          a   =   Intensity of the oscillating part for
                      Chinese help to Pakistan

PAKISTAN:
          1   = $k/4$ = Response coefficient
          S_0 =   Asymptotic value for military expenditure
                      for India
          Y^0_2 =   Per capita income for Pakistan at the
                      initial time period, say in 1950
          C_2 =   Percentage of foreign exchange that could
                      have been increased through cooperation
                      with India
          ϕ_2 =   The ratio of foreign exchange to per capita
                      income
          χ =   Money value of grievances as a ratio to the
                      per capita income
          d_1 =   The difference between the asymptotic of
                      Indian defence expenditure and initial
                      value
          β_1 =   Growth of military expenditure per year for
                      India
          b   =   Intensity of oscillation in the Indian
                      defence expenditure
          b_2 =   Percentage of per capita income that could
                      have been increased by "normal" defence
                      spending in Pakistan
          b'_2 =   Percentage of the difference between West
                      Pakistan and East Pakistan per capita
                      income which could have been decreased
                      through "normal" defence spending
          r   =   The ratio of West Pakistan's population to
                      total Pakistan population
          x_2 =   Percentage growth in per capita income in
                      Pakistan
          x^w_2 =   Percentage growth in per capita income of
                      West Pakistan related to Pakistan's per
                      capita income.

Although the timing of the study is grossly outdated,
the political situation in South Asia has not changed
dramatically. However, in the present configuration of
politics, we need a different type of approach.

C.   Topology

In mathematics, the subject called Topology is very developed.
This is the study of properties of geometric configuration
invariant under transformation of continuous mapping. Since
international relations are based on configuration of
relationships, this has considerable potential for
application. (For details see van Gastel and Paelneck, 1990,
and van Gastel and Paelneck, 1988.)

D.   Catastrophe Theory

The Richardsonian arms race model is given by two equations

$$\frac{dx}{dt} = ay - mx + g \tag{1}$$

$$\frac{dy}{dt} = bx - ny + h \tag{2}$$

Setting $\frac{dx}{dt} = \frac{dy}{dt} = 0$ and solving for x and y, we get the

equilibrium conditions

$$x^* = \frac{ah + gn}{mn - ab}$$

$$y^* = \frac{bg + nh}{mn - ab}$$

For the stability of the system $mn - ab \geq 0$, i.e. $mn > ab$. If $mn < ab$, then it will be unstable. It will move to ever increasing amounts of armament levels or to disarmament depending on the initial disturbance. It is to be pointed out that only the equilibrium system is observed, and not the parameter. Thus we shall only see the sudden change in the system and cannot ascribe it to any "cause". As long as $mn > ab$, small changes in the parameters will lead to small changes in the system. However, if $mn < ab$, even a small change in the parameters will lead to catastrophic change in the system.

Until recently, mathematicians could not model this phenomenon since it violates the fundamental assumption of continuity relations between variables. The discontinuity may appear not only with respect to time, as in the case of Richardsonian problem, but also over space or, for example, in a population where sharp differences of opinion may suddenly emerge as in the case of military action (hawk vs. dove). The catastrophe theory, where small changes in some variables may cause large variations in a dependent variable (in some cases it is natural and interrelated), is presently amenable to rigorous mathematical treatment. The theory is used to give qualitative understanding and global insight. Mathematics is based on three types of structures: order, topological and algebraic. In order, we are interested in such things as proximity or smoothness (as in calculus); and in algebraic structure, we add or subtract, which may not have any sociological meaning. The first two properties will be called qualitative and the third one quantitative.

It is not possible to express laws in the social sciences, such as Boyles' law, quantitatively. But that does not mean that there are no laws. There we use qualitative language, i.e. mathematical terms that are invariant under qualitative changes of scale. Of course, for an experiment, we have to transform the qualitative variables into quantitative terms such as employment, population, etc. and obtain graphs or equations. But the qualitative properties of these graphs or equations can be used for conclusions. Thus we need not specify concrete references to variables to provide qualitative reference to catastrophe models. World Wars I and II are examples where catastrophe theory can explain not only the sudden emergence of war but also the relative continuity of changes in the level of conflict (Rapoport, 1983). World War I was a sudden transition from relative peace but World War II did not exhibit sudden transitions from peace to war to peace.

The mathematical model of catastrophe theory can be explained by taking a polynomial where the constant terms and a term involving X^r ($r \geq 3$) are missing. The following four degree polynomial is such as example:

$$f(x_1, a_1, a_2) = x^4 - a_2 x^2 - a_1 x$$

Here x denotes the level of conflict and a_1, a_2 are central parameters. Rapoport (1983) makes the hypothesis that "a_1" may denote degree of incompatibility of aspiration of European national states before World War I. It is a global measure aggregating the aspirations of many nations. The value of a_2 is low when the alliance structure is loose and vice versa. The transition from no violence to high violence may be due to the fact that alliances were firmed up first and aspirations became increasingly incompatible. The cessation of violence signalled that "a_1", decreased when a_2 remained high. In catastrophe theory the state of the system is always determined by the value of the variable "x" that determines the minimum of "f". For example, if the system is determined by a cubic polynomial

$$f = x^3 - a_1 x$$

the state of the system is determined by

$$\frac{df}{dx} = 0; \quad x^2 - a_1 = 0 \quad \text{or} \quad x^2 = a_1$$

The values of x may be: two real roots but unequal; two real roots but equal; or no real roots. In the first case one is maximum and the other is minimum. If $a_1 < 0$, there is no state in the system as in the case of the Richardsonian arms race.

The second assumption of catastrophe theory states that the changes in the value of central parameters are governed by slow macrodynamics (this is true in the case of gradual historical change) but the trend in the system variable is governed by fast microdynamics (such as adjustment of the system to those changes due to intervention). The third and fourth degree polynomial systems can also be represented graphically and are called fold and cusp. The four and five parameters cases are called Butterfly and Wigwam, respectively. Zeeman (1977) gives an example of the effect that occurs due to changes in the distribution of public opinion on the policy of the government in times of conflict, where the aim of the administration is to maximize public support. Figure 2.5 gives the initial situation. In the passage of time, the situation may change Fig. 2.6, where there are now two local maxima. The problem for the administration is to choose between the two. This may depend on Maxwell Rule, where support is maximum, or Delay Rule, where we change policy in the direction that locally increases support. Due to lack of information, institutions, sociological pressure, inertia, poor history, etc. Delay Rule may be preferable. As the Delay Rule and Hawk's maxima (X_7)

117

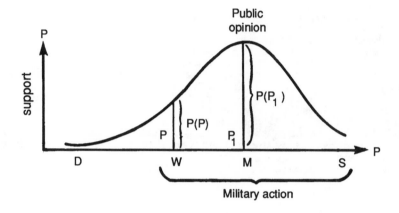

Figure 2.5   Public support for different strategies

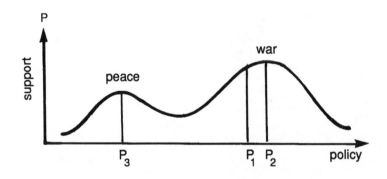

Figure 2.6   Split public support

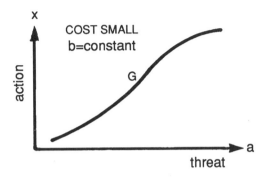

Figure 2.7   Threat-action graph for low cost

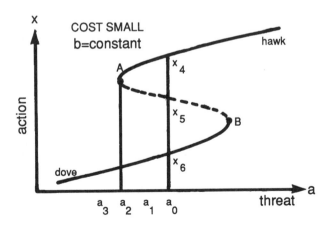

Figure 2.8   Threat-action graph for high cost

119

and minimum (X_8) are followed, an unstable equilibrium X_{10} is generated.

When this local maximum in which the behaviour was locked vanishes, the system jumps to X_{12} catastrophically. It may be hypothesized that public opinion is influenced by threat (a) and cost (b).

When the cost of war is low, the more unified is public opinion; and the level of military action will be higher, the greater the threat (Fig. 2.7). If the cost is high and the threat is moderate, opinion will be split. If the cost is high and the threat is very great, then opinion is unified for strong action. But if the cost is high and the threat is small (e.g. Vietnam), then opinion will be for withdrawal (Fig. 2.8).

There is only one way the transfiguration of Fig. 2.7 takes place to Fig. 2.8.

There are few examples of catastrophe and chaos theory in conflict situations. Obviously, there is great potential for their application to such situations. Since conflict, if not controlled, leads to war, it will be useful to know the parameters of the process and see how to control its application so that there is no war or violence.

E.   Chaos Theory

Strange attractors have appeared in the scientific literature relevant to this subject quite recently. Dissipative systems of differential equations in more than two dimensions can have bounded trajectories whose behaviour does not converge to an equilibrium point nor to a periodic or quasiperiodic orbit. They can be attracted by an object of complicated structure which attracts the neighbouring points but has some inherent instability along it. The flow is essentially aperiodic.

The study of trajectories of differential equations can be simplified thanks to the analysis of the sequence of points of intersection of the trajectory within a given hypersurface (a surface of section). Then we need to study the iterates of points under a given mapping (the Poincaré mapping associated with the flow with respect to the surface of section). The complicated structure of attracting points of a neighbourhood appears much more clear when we analyse the related mapping. Therefore, it seems easier to learn about these attractors using the Poincaré map. We can generally study the attractors of without explicit reference to the flow which initiates them. We note that the Poincaré map cannot be defined on some points and is not differentiable nor even continuous on others. Without dimension reduction we can also use the map "flow acting along a fixed time" $\emptyset_t$.

Since the 1960s there has been an increasing interest (even at an explosive rate), in strange attractors, in their appearance in many applications, and in some attempts at putting order to chaos. However, there is still not even agreement on the definition of an S.A. For applications of Chaos Theory see Garrido (1982).

3 Gaming, Coalition Theory and Simulation

A. Decision Science and Game Theory

In many international conflict situations, the decision maker faces a number of choices. Depending on the occurrence of events in the environment, and in conjunction with the decision he chooses, a payoff or net inflow is generated. Of course, the choice of a particular decision depends on the personality or risk taking behaviour of the decision maker. To explain the situation, let us take a hypothetical example.

A company has received a low-interest industrial loan to enable it to build a manufacturing plant in an economically depressed area. Potential economic and political conditions influence the site selection. As a preliminary study of the situation, ratings have been assigned as outcomes for operating the plant at each site under each of the more likely future conditions (Riggs and West, 1986).

POSSIBLE CONDITIONS

Site	1	2	3	4
NW	0	2	8	20
NE	4	14	12	10
SW	16	6	6	8
SE	4	14	18	6
C	4	14	10	9

The questions that can be asked are:

a. Which site is dominated?
b. White site is preferred according to the maximum principle?
c. Which site is preferred according to the maximax principle?
d. Which site gets a preference when the equal-likelihood principle is applied?
e. When $\alpha = 0.75$, which site has the highest rating by the partial-optimist principle?
f. Which site is preferred according to the regret principle?

A decision is said to be dominated if the payoff of that decision for all possible conditions is equal for less than the corresponding payoff of any other decision. For example, site c is dominated by the NE since the payoffs for NE site are always equal to or greater than the corresponding payoffs for c. So for decision making analysis, we need not consider the strategy c. If the decision maker is adverse to risk, then he will take the maximum principle where he chooses that strategy which gives him the maximum value of the minimum possible. For example, we find the minimum value for each row and choose that strategy for which he gets the maximum of the minimum. In this case SW is chosen since 6 is the maximum, as can be seen from the following table. If the decision maker is a risk taker, she might take a maximax policy where she is expecting the best. For that purpose, we select the maximum of each row and choose that strategy for which we get the maximum of the maximum. In this case we choose NW, and the payoff is 20. When the decision maker is indifferent he assumes the equal probability (.25) for each of the four events and his expected value of the average of the payoff figures in each row equally weighted with .25. On that basis he will choose NE location. If we use Hurwicz criteria when the decision maker places high weight (α) for the good thing to happen (in this case $\alpha = .75$) then we can compute the weighted average (.75) (highest payoff = 20) + .25 (lowest payoff = 0) = 15 for NW location. Then we choose that location for which this weighted average is highest. In this case it is NW.

Another criterion where the relative loss rather than the absolute outcome is considered is when the decision maker chooses the alternative for which the maximum possible opportunity loss is smallest after the fact. For this purpose, we have to construct the regret matrix as shown in the following table. The elements of each column in this table are attained by subtracting each element from the highest value. After the regret matrix is constructed, we get the maximum value of each row showing the greatest regret (opportunity loss) one gets if he makes a particular decision. That strategy which minimized their maximum loss is known as the "minimax regret strategy".

Site	1	2	3	4	Maximin	Maximax	Likelihood	(Hurwicz)
NW	0	2	8	20	0	20 / 14	7.5	15 / 11.5
NE	4	14	12	10	4	14	10 / 8	11.5
SW	16	6	6	8	6	16	8	14.5

Regret Matrix

Site	1	2	3	4	Max
NW	16	12	10	0	16
NE	12	0	6	10	12
SW	0	8	12	12	12
SE	12	10	0	14	14

Of course the problem may be complicated if we have a probability distribution for each condition for each site. The problem will be more realistic if this is a demand stock problem when there may be a probability distribution of demand.

The simple example given before brings us to the subject matter of game theory, which combines substantial generalizations of mathematical economics — namely, equilibrium stability and dynamic optimality.

In a game theory setting there are one or more members of a group involved in a decision process. The members in the group may have cooperative or conflicting goals to optimize; they may have symmetric or asymmetric information structures. The players may have a number of finite discrete strategies or they may have one continuous infinite strategy. When we are considering games of timing in which a player decides the point of time when he will make a move, we have an example of continuous games with infinite strategies. For the sake of simplicity, we can classify games in a number of ways (Sengupta, 1987).

1. A static game is one in which the players choose strategies at a given point of time. Dynamic games, on the other hand, involve taking strategies sequentially over a period of time so as to obtain intertemporal optimality.
2. A game may be determined or probabilistic. In the probabilistic case, random error in the utility function or constraint may exist due to lack of information.
3. Strategic games are those in which the opponent is a rational active player. In contrast, we may have a passive game where the opponent is naive and does not retaliate.
4. Three types of games can be identified. The normal form usually involves two persons whereas the characteristic function form is most useful for more than two persons. Another analytical form of the game is known as the extensive form where there is: (1) a starting point, (2) a payoff function, (3) a set of moves with chance moves, and (4) an information set from each player who knows what information set, but not which vertex or node of that information set, he is in. An extensive form of a game can be represented by a finite tree structure in

the case of a matching pennies game as follows
(Sengupta, 1987):

N = 1.2
Starting point = a.
Set of moves = {a,b,c}, S_o = {0}
Payoff functions (-1, 1), (1, -1), (1, -1), (-1, 1).
Information set

$$S_1 = \{a\} \qquad\qquad S_1(1) = \{a\}$$
$$S_2 = \{b,c\}, \qquad\qquad S_2^1(1) = \{b,c\}$$

Player 1 has the first move in vertex a.
Player 2 selects H (Heads) or T (Tails) not knowing
Player 1's choice. If two choices are alike (HH) or
(TT), Player 2 gets a penny and Player 1 loses one.
Normal form is a simplified case of extensive form where
we have two players having more than one strategy as
follows:

		Player 2		
		Y_1	Y_2	Y_3
	X_1	8	4	6
Player 1	X_2	6	5	7
	X_3	0	3	4

Let us first consider a two person zero sum (or constant sum)
game, a strictly competitive game in which the stakes are a
gain of $8 for Player 1 (for the [X_1, Y_1] strategy
combination) and a loss of $8 for Player 2. (Since we can
change the scale, constant sum is equivalent to zero sum.)
In the above example, the equilibrium position (saddle
point) is (X_2,Y_2) where the payoff is $5. Player 1 may get
less than $5 if he chooses position X_1 when Player 2 chooses
X_2.
Of course, in the case of a non-cooperative pure strategy
game where a player can choose one strategy only, saddle point
may not exist. The following is an example of a two person,
zero sum (constant sum) game where there is no saddle point

		Player 2	
		Y_1	Y_2
Player	X_1	8	6
1	X_2	5	7

However, when we consider mixed strategies where X_i, Y_j
are interpreted as probability (e.g. percentage of time i^{th}
strategy is chosen by player 1 and j^{th} strategy by player 2),
it can be shown in this case that there is a saddle point
solution:

Player 1	(Y_1, Y_2)	(1/4, 3/4)
Player 2	(X_1, X_2)	(1/2, 1/2)

and expected payoff 6 1/2 (loss or gain). When the game is
against the nature which is passive, the outcome agrees with
the discussion of optimum strategy for equal probability,
minimax, maximin, etc. which was noted earlier.

It is possible that in a two person zero sum (non-cooperative) game we may have more than one equilibrium (in the sense that neither player can do better by changing), but the equilibria are equivalent (i.e. payoff pairs are the same) and interchangeable (i.e. they intersect at an equilibrium).

However, when we have two person non-constant sum games, if they have more than one equilibria they are not necessarily equivalent and interchangeable as follows:

		B_1	B_2
Player 2	A_1	2, 2	-100, 100
Player 1	A_2	100, -100	-500, -500

In the payoff matrix, A_1B_2 and A_2B_1 are in "equilibria" from which they cannot move. Moreover, if player 1 chooses A_2, player 2 will choose B_2; A_2B_2 is not an equilibrium and both of them are worse off. Also the two equilibria are neither equivalent nor interchangeable.

This problem does not arise in a non-constant sum game if there is only one equilibrium, as shown in Prisioner's Dilemma.

		C_2	D_2
Player 2	C_1	1, 1	-10, 10
Player 1	D_1	10, -10	1, -1

Here the only equilibrium position is D_1D_2. To each of the players, D is the best strategy, not only from the standpoint of individual rationality, but also from the point of view of collective rationality (if agreement is enforced). This brings us to the discussion of cooperative games where players have the opportunity to coordinate their strategies and abide by enforceable agreements.

Most of the literature in n person (n > 2) game theory is concerned with a cooperative game, where a subset of the players is formed to make a coalition in which the participants formulate strategies such that their collective interest is achieved. They can also make side payments to each other so that they can adjust payments themselves. The allocation or sharing of payoff is called imputation if: (1) the share of a player in the coalition is at least equal to or more than the payoff he/she can get without anybody's help (this must satisfy individual rationality condition); and, (2) total payoff in the coalition is equal to that of a grand coalition when all the players form a grand coalition; this is known as Pareto optimality. There are many solutions of the same game. Many desirable criteria can be developed, such as uniqueness, enforceability, etc. However, the conditions described above - (1) feasibility, (2) individual rationality, and (3) Pareto optimality - are usually the most desirable. In the case of a cartel of, for example, OPEC or farmers in the US, individual rationality criterion is accepted but group rationality criteria is not recognized since this cartel breaks down in many cases.

Some imputations may satisfy a stronger condition of group rationality as described previously. The set of all undesignated inputalities in a game is called the "core".

In any coalition, there are two groups of players - a coalition m of a given size, and N-m, which is not in the coalition. The characteristic function $v(s)$ is the value (in this maximin value) of the minimum guaranteed payoff for each coalition.

Several solutions are available. Let us examine a two person game strategy first suggested by Cournot in a duopoly game.

The total market demand for water is

$$p = 1 - (X_1 + X_2)$$ where X_i is the output for i^{th} producer
$$i = 1,2.$$

There is no cost. Clearly the profit functions are

$$Z_i = X_i(1-X_1-X_2) \qquad i = 1,2.$$

What output will the two producers produce?

(1) In the case of the <u>Cournot solution</u>, player 1 maximizes his own profit,

$$Z_i = X_i(1-X_1-X_2) \qquad i = 1,2$$

setting derivative

$$\frac{Z_i}{X_i} = 0 \quad i = 1,2.$$

The equation of the reaction curves are given by

$$2X_1 + X_2 = 1$$

$$X_1 + 2X_1 = 1$$

The intersection of the two curves will give the equilibrium points. This problem can be easily made dynamic and extended to n players.

(2) Stackelberg Solution

In the above example, player 2 may obey his reaction curve

$$X_2 = \frac{1-X_1}{2}$$

but player 1 may not follow his reaction curve and assumes that player 2 will follow his reaction curve. So the profit function for player 1 is

$$Z_1(X_1, X_2) = X_1(1-X_1-X_2) =$$

$$X_1(1-X_1 - \frac{1-X_1}{2}).$$

Taking

$$\frac{dZ_1}{dX_1} = 0$$ we get $X_1 = 1/2$, $X_2 = 1/4$, $Z_1 = 1/8$ $Z_2 =$

1/16. However, player 2 may not be a follower and player 1 may not know the reaction curve.

(3) Pareto solution

This is a cooperative solution accomplished by choosing the total output $X = X_1 + X_2$ to maximize total profit $Z = Z_1 + Z_2 = X(1-X)$

$$\frac{dZ}{dX} = 0 \quad \text{we get}$$

$X_1 + X_2 = 1/2$ and profit $= 1/4$

(4) Nash Bargaining Solution

Instead of engaging in a price war, two companies, one large and the other small, may agree that the larger of the two buys out the smaller and the only question is what price the buyer will pay. In the case of non-agreement it can be shown that the optimal threat of each player is to pretend that the other supplier does not exist.

So far we have considered static games. But the game may be played over a continuous time period, so that the pure strategies and the payoff are not fixed points but are time paths to optimize inter-temporal payoff functions. The problem can be specified to choose the strategies $U_1(t)$, $U_2(t)$ for the two players, such that

$$\text{Max } J_i \; (U_1, U_2) = L_j((X_1 t), U_1(t), U_2(t))dt$$

$$\text{where} \qquad i = 1,2$$

subject to:

$$\frac{dX}{dt} = f(X_1(t), U_1(t), U_2(t))$$

$$X(0) = X_0$$

Game Theory is a vast field and it is difficult to cover all its aspects. It has many potential applications in conflict situations. I shall now present a study one of such situation.

B.   An Example: A Game Theoretic Approach to Coalition –
      Politics in an Indian State

1. Background of the Conflict

In many Indian states, the conflicts between a multiplicity of political parties' and defection of several led to weak governments and, in some cases, to bloodshed, chaos and immense hardship to the populace. One such state is West Bengal. Like many other underdeveloped areas, it is suffering from high population, low income, rising migration from the rural areas to Calcutta and other cities, chronic unemployment and poor public facilities. But what makes West Bengal and Calcutta unique is their continuous political instability and strife. Unlike other states in India, politics here are not based on personalities or caste, but on political ideology. As its chief asset, the area has an articulated, well-informed and determined (often sentimental) intellectual base which sometimes makes the conflict situation more intense and painful.

After the British left in 1946, the Congress party (which controlled the central government) was left in control with the Communist party as their main opposition. Excluding Kerala, the Communist party was the strongest in West Bengal. In 1966, a splinter group led by Mr Ajoy Mukherjee broke away from Congress and formed a party called Bangla Congress. We shall denote this party by C(B). Members of this party were veteran Congressmen who had no policy differences with the Congress. Their sole complaint was the so-called corrupt, high-handed leadership of the state organization. C(B) vowed to make a coalition with other opposition parties to defeat the Congress in the election. It is to be noted that at the central government level a rift between two factions within the Congress party evolved over the years; one, led by Mrs Indira Gandhi (with more radical views and programmes) was called C(R); the other (with more traditional conservative outlook) was called C(O). Although the West Bengal government was controlled by C(O) leaders, they were still paying allegiance to the Indira Gandhi's party at the centre, i.e. C(R).

In West Bengal, C(B)'s position was very near to that of C(R). Its membership and control of electorate was insignificant compared with that of other opposition parties; its main asset was its leader, Mr Mukherjee — an unquestionably honest, sincere man — a fact acknowledged even by his enemies. The main opposition party with which C(B) could combine was the Communist party (CP). By that time, in line with international developments, this party was divided into two groups, one called CP(M), which was upro-Chinese, and the other CP(I), which was Russian supported. They became arch enemies but they had a common goal to defeat the Congress in association with other opposition parties. CP(M) was without question the strongest opposition party, and enjoyed extensive support among rural areas (except in one district where C(B) had its hold), student communities, and in the urban labour force. Since CP(M) could not join forces with CP(I) and vice versa, there were actually two United Fronts (henceforth to be referred to as U.F.) against the Congress party in spite of C(B)'s effort to form a one unified party. Fourteen parties divided themselves into two groups as shown below.

People's United Left Front (PULF)
1. Communist part of India – CP(I)
2. Bangla Congress, C(B)
3. Praja Socialist, (PS)
4. Bolshevik Party, (BP)
5. Gorkha League, (GL)
6. Forward Block, (F)
7. Lok Sevak Sangha, (LS)

United Left Front (ULF)

1. Communist Party of India – Marxist, CP(M)
2. Forward Block – Marxist, FB(M)
3. Revolutionary Socialist Party, (RSP)
4. Workers Party of India, (WP)
5. Socialist Unity Center, (SUC)

6.   Samuktya Socialist Party, (SSP)
7.   Revolutionary Communist Party, RCP(M)

The birth and growth of the smaller factions and their rationships with the larger parties gives us rich material for game theoretical and conflict resolution studies. In these smaller parties, it is ideology, rather than personality or group interest, that provides the dominant motivational force.

ULF is an extreme left coalition with CP(M) as the leader. The other parties in this coalition have very little strength unless accompanied by CP(M). The consequent gain to PULF is not substantial in terms of seats in the assembly, but would enhance its prestige in the eye of the public, which, as mentioned before, is articulate and sensitive, responding even to a minor change in W. Bengal politics.

PULF has no single leader. CP(I) and C(B) are joint leaders. This coalition is left of the centre. CP(I)'s problem is that although it believes in communist ideology, it cannot move too far to the left, since people will label it CP(M) – an uncomfortable position not only from an ideological viewpoint but also in regard to the preservation of its own independent existence. And CP(I) cannot move far to the right either, since this would mean joining hands with the Congress – a situation it dislikes most, particularly when C(O) leaders dominate the latter. As mentioned before, other members on PULF do not have a serious quarrel with Congress, except in suggesting that the leadership should be changed, i.e. some sort of C(R) should emerge in the state.

At this point, it should be mentioned that at the centre, C(R), with Indira Gandhi as the leader, did not have a majority and had to depend on CP(I) and CP(M) to run her government. Strangely enough, CP(I) and CP(M) did not have alternatives. If they opposed her, C(O), with the support of other rightist parties (which, by the way, do not exist in W. Bengal), would have formed the government, and that would have been the death-knell for the Communists. The situation at that time was volatile. It was difficult to judge the relative strength of C(O) and C(R). The Communists decided that if they went down, it would be better to join with Mrs Gandhi, who in the eyes of Indian people was forward-looking with socialist goals supposedly designed to benefit all.

Let us, then, put the parties in W. Bengal on a scale relative to the Congress party. The further to the left the position of a party is on this scale, the more it inclines towards CP(M). At the most extreme left position is the Communist party (Marxist-Leninist) – CP(ML) – to which we shall come later.

·   ·   ·   ·   ·   ·   ·   ·   ·   ·   ·   ·   ·   ·   ·

CP (M)	WP	RCPI	SUC	RSP	FB(M)	SSP	CP(I)	FB	BP	GL	LS	PS
CP(ML)										C(B)		C

| ULF | PULF |

A general election was held in February 1967. PULF and ULF opposed the Congress party as the common enemy, but in some constituencies they fought against each other. Although

they were united against the Congress, they were far from
united amongst themselves in other respects. Thus, the
Congress came out as the largest single party in the new
assembly but without having captured an absolute majority.
The party lost 29 seats in an assembly of 280 and captured
only 40.97% of the votes as compared with 47.9% in the 1962
election. One significant aspect of the election is the
defeat of the leaders belonging to C(O), so that the party
seemed to be moving towards C(R) of Mrs Gandhi. C(B) was not
unhappy with this situation.

Table 3.1 gives the relative strength of each party after
the election.

Following the victory, a U.F. government with 19 members
was formed with Ajoy Mukherjee of C(B) as the Chief Minister
and Jyoti Basu of CP(M) as the Deputy Chief Minister.
Although the head of the government was from C(B), the two
Communist parties held crucial portfolios such as Finance,
Land and Land Revenue, and Information and Education. Table
3.2 gives the relative strength of ULF and PULF. From these
tables it is seen that excluding the Congress party, CP(M),
had balanced control both in rural and urban areas.
Individually, CP(I) or C(B) was no match for CP(M). Indeed,
in many constituencies people voted for CP(I) – not because
they like its policy, but because they supported the United
Front, in which CP(M) was the most important party.

The U.F. government had an inauspicious start. A new
phenomenon emerged in the political scene of W. Bengal. It
was a movement called the Naxalities, who formed the (Marxist-
Leninist) party, or, in short, CP(M-L). Originating in a
small village in North Bengal bordering Nepal and China, it
gradually spread over large parts of W. Bengal. This extreme
leftist revolutionary movement, composed of students, farmers
and hard-core ultra-leftist CP(M) members, did not believe in
elections and branded CP(M) as revisionist. The Naxalities
started killing politicians, landlords and innocent people.
These incidents were trivalized by the authorities; the Chief
minister, Mr Mukherjee, thought that the situation was just a
limited agrarian struggle, the CP(M) dismissed it as "nothing
extraordinary", and the CP(I) described it "as a limited
problem of agrarian relations and democratic freedom".

At this stage, international communism entered the scene.
The Chinese openly supported CP(M-L) and accused CP(M) and the
U.F. of being the "suppressor[s] of the revolutionary
peasants". In short, the CP(M-L) movement exerted heavy
pressure on CP(M) to come to the extreme left. This was
untenable for CP(M) since it would require a break with the
U.F. and possibly lead to its destruction since the country
itself was not prepared, as CP(M) admitted, "for an armed
revolution". On the other hand, partners in the U.F.
government complained that CP(M) was trying to strengthen its
position through Deputy Chief Minister Mr Basu by
infiltrating both the policy and the administration with its
own people, that CP(M) was trying to annihilate the partners,
and that the CP(M), in collusion with the Naxalities was
responsible for the murders and chaos in the state. The
situation was so serious that the Chief Minister threatened to
resign in October 1967, voicing complaints against some of his
own ministers for creating deliberate troubles in industries,

for inspiring farmers to murder landlords, and for inviting China to bring about a bloody revolution in the State. But the time was not ripe for Mukherjee since the Congress party to whom he could turn was not yet out of the C(O) power. His CP(M) colleagues agreed to behave.

Within a month, however, 16 other PULF members broke away from the party and claimed that they could form the government with the help of the Congress. While the Congress did not want to participate in such an undertaking, they tacitly decided to support such a move. The governor of the State (who has no power except in the case of emergency), acting as the agency of the Central government, asked both sides to show

TABLE 3.1

Party Position After 1967 Election in W. Bengal Assembly

Parties	Total No. of Members	Rural	Urban
Congress	127	80	47
C.P.(M)	43	24	19
Bangla Congress	34	30	4
CP(I)	16	6	10
Forward Bloc	13	9	4
Praja Socialist Party	7	6	1
Samyukta Socialist Party	7	5	2
Revolutionary Socialist Party	6	5	1
Lok Sevak Sangha	5	4	1
Socialist Unity Centre	4	4	–
Gorkha League	2	1	1
Workers Party of India	2	1	1
Forward Bloc (Marxist)	1	1	–
Swantantra	1	1	–
Jana Sangh	1	1	–
Independents	11	10	1
	280	188	92

NOTE: (a) Three Bangla Congress, One Independent, and the Jana Sangh, MLAs joined the Congress Party in June 1967; (b) nine more Bangla Congress MLAs left the party in October 1967 and sat as Bharatya Kranti Dal MLAs.

TABLE 3.2

Relative Strengths of ULF and PULF

Parties	No. of Seats in the Assembly	No. of Ministers
1. P.U.L.F.		
Bangla Congress	34	4
C.P.(I)	16	2
Forward Bloc	13	2
P.S.P.	7	1
Lok Sevak Sangha	5	1
Gorkha League	2	1
Bolshevik Party	--	--
	77	11
2. U.L.F.		
C.P.(M)	43	3
S.S.P.	7	1
R.S.P.	6	1
S.U.C.	4	1
Workers Party	2	1
Forward Bloc (Marxist)	--	--
	63	7
3. Others	13	1

strength in the assembly. Due to some legal difficulties, this could not be done, and the Governor, acting on the advice of the central government, dismissed the U.F. government and declared President's rule. The assembly, however, was not dissolved. Mrs. Gandhi hoped that some sort of coalition could be formed. She was somewhat hesitant to take a drastic step since she was still depending on CP(I) and CP(M) for her government. But the expected coalition did not materialize. President's rule was had by the U.F. and the people of the state at large regarded it as evidence of some sort of a conspiracy by the central government. The U.F. became more united and prepared to contest the Congress again in a new mid-term election in 1969. This time they dealt a heavy blow to the Congress, which obtained only 55 seats. Table 3.3 gives the result of the election.

TABLE 3.3
Result of Mid-Term Election

Parties		No. of Seats
1.	Congress C(R)	55
2.	Bangla Congress C(B)	33
3.	C.P.(I)	30
4.	Forward Block (F.B.) + others	2
5.	Praja Socialist Party (PSP)	5
6.	Lok Sevak Sangha (L.S.S.)	4
7.	Communist Party (Marxist) CP(M)	80
8.	Revolutionary Socialist Party (R.S.P.)	12
9.	Forward Block (Marxist) + Others F.B.(M)	18
10.	Samuyukta Socialist Party	9
11.	Others	26
12.	Independents	6
	TOTAL	230

As a result of these events, a second United Front government was formed. CP(M) was much stronger this time, but it could not form the government by itself or even with its closest allies in ULF, and troubles started again. CP(M) was blamed for the increasing strength of the Naxalite movement, there were inter-party clashes within U.F., and the United Front government became more and more unworkable. The Congress party became a silent spectator. In the centre, under Mrs Gandhi's leadership, C(R) won a sweeping victory at the polls. The Chief minister, Mr Mukherjee of C(B), resigned, and President's rule was proclaimed once again. This time Congress tried to change its image, now blaming CP(M), which, it said, was leading the State to disaster. They did not have the old leaders of C(O) whom C(B) and its allies hated. The ULF partners also blamed C(M) for these misfortunes. In short, PULF slowly moved to the right, the Congress shifted to the left and allies of CP(M) in ULF moved to the right. CP(M) became more and more isolated. It had bitter clashes with CP(M-L) and was in trouble from both left and right.

After the defeat of Pakistan in the Indo-Pakistani War of 1971 and the emergence of Bangladesh, C(R)'s position became such stronger. In the elections of February 1972, it swept the polls in all states including W. Bengal, where, out of 280 seats in the assembly, the People's Democratic alliance of Congress (R) and CP(I) captured 252 seats. C(R)'s share was 216 seats. C(B) merged with C(R). CP(M) alleged fraud and was kept out of the assembly. In spite of formal coalitions, C(R) did not have to depend on CP(I). At this time, law and order situation improved considerably. This was due partly to the popular image of the party created by the then Chief Minister, Mr Ray, and partly to sympathetic considerations extended by the centre toward W. Bengal's need and problems.

I have very briefly given the basic background of conflict in W. Bengal in the 1960s. The whole picture is much more complicated and confused. It can also be viewed in the broader context of the Indian political scene. I have considered only the minimum that is necessary to construct the theoretical structure of the materials in the following two sections.

2.   A Game Theory Interpretation

Following is an example involving the political situation in the Indian State of West Bengal. The brief background given here is necessary in order to understand the structure of the problems.

Following the events just described, the situation in West Bengal became quiet. But the basic problem was not solved. The law and order situation looked better but the Naxalities were merely taking a breather. The probability of the recurrence of past events was high; this led to the formation of a U.F. between ULF and PULF or C(R) with PULF. It is not to be forgotten that CP(M), in their smashing defeat in 1972, polled 41% of the total votes. The only difference is that there now appeared four groups in the scene, namely:

C(R)   CP(M)   PULP   ULF

At this point the structure of PULF/ULF will not be the same as it was in the past, but whatever the consequent shifts, the final position will tend to the above four-party structure. In the whole conflict process, for each party, there were two possible strategies. One was to shift to the left, and other to the right. But these two options did not have the same connotation to each party.

In C(R)'s moving towards the left, the strategy Q_1 meant bringing back old Congressmen who had defected, making active efforts for friendship with Russia and Bangladesh, taking strong positions against the United States and China, supporting North Vietnam, keeping the student movement alive but without violence, and undertaking programmes of economic development. The other alternative, Q_2, signified a move toward the right. It reflected an independent position, without regard for PULF or other parties. Q_2 should not be interpreted as low on socialism and high on capitalism, although it may lead to a friendly relationship with the USA. The political scene changes quickly and such a strategy is entirely possible.

For CP(M) the first strategy, P_1, denotes the position it has taken so far - no alliance with CP(M-L) but maintenance of the same goals within parliamentary democracy, infiltration of the administrative structures of its members, the use of Home portfolios to guide police forces to its advantage, neutrality with the Chinese with mild censure in specific issues like Bangladesh, no compromise with CP(I), and the agitation of students and labourers to keep up a situation of turmoil. In short, looking from the view of ULF partners, it signifies accepting the assistance of the ULF in order to remain in power, encouraging the more radical elements of the ULF to defect to CP(M), keeping up an uncompromising posture toward the USA, expressing strong support for the NLF of Vietnam, and not mentioning the USSR in its support of North Vietnam. The other position is P_2: scaling down its extreme positions, no greed for the Home portfolio, toning down its differences with CP(I), voicing strong denunciation of China and mild criticism of the USSR, and giving up the demand of state autonomy/secession - in short, cooperating with ULF and PULF against C(R) and maintaining a moderate tone while still supporting a radical programme.

In the case of ULF, the first strategy, R_1, will be to move toward CP(M) and R_2 will be towards PULP and C(R). Similarly, for PULF these strategies will be denoted by S_1 and S_2, respectively. It should be mentioned here that the calibration of the preference scale of ULF to move to the left toward CP(M)-or, for the matter of the right - is not the same type as that those of PULF. For example, a given degree of shift by ULF to the left to form a government with CP(M) may not be equivalent to that of PULF moving the same amount to the right to form a government with C(R). This also depends whether C(R) shifts to Q_1 or Q_2. This situation can be shown as follows:

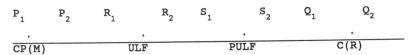

Let us denote a five-point preference scale as follows for each party:

1. Most preferable   Score = +1
2. Preferable   Score = .5
3. Neutral   Score = 0
4. Not preferable   Score = -.5
5. Highly unfavourable   Score = -1

I am fully aware of the weakness of this process, and the risk involved in dealing with a qualitative scale such as this. But this scale is often used in the literature due to the lack of better approaches. It is also assumed that these preferences can be interpreted as the payoff, and that the sum of these for any particular situation is zero. In essence, then, we are dealing with a four-person zero sum game. For this game we have constructed the following payoff Table 3.4,

135

which will be invariant for all situations.

From the payoff matrix it is seen that for the choice $P_1Q_1R_1S_1$, the payoff to CP(M) is +1, indicating that it is the best situation for it. ULF and PULF have moved toward it, and it has not changed its own position. All this happened in spite of the fact that C(R) is interested in moving towards the left. This is a bitter disappointment for C(R). Consequently, its payoff is -1. ULF is happy to have a united government against C(R) but remains insecure since it is afraid that CP(M) may destroy it. PULF is not happy since it could not come out with C(R), which has come toward it, and has been forced to cooperate with strange bedfellows. Similarly, take another choice, $P_1Q_2R_2S_2$. Here, CP(M) is unhappy but not especially so since it knows ULF will be reluctant to do business with C(R), particularly if the latter moves to the right. C(R) is very happy to see that PULF and ULF are moving toward it, in spite of the fact that it did not previously care for them. ULF is unhappy and PULF is indifferent. All other cases can be explained in similar fashion. Suppose now the following coalition situation takes place. The question is: What will be the equilibrium choice situation? It can be explained as follows

TABLE 3.4
Payoff Table for Four-Person Zero Sum Game

CHOICE				PAYOFF			
CP(M)	C(R)	ULF	PULF	CP(M)	C(R)	ULF	PULF
P_1	Q_1	R_1	S_1	+1	-1	+.5	-.5
P_1	Q_1	R_1	S_2	-.5	0	0	.5
P_1	Q_1	R_2	S_1	+.5	0	0	-.5
P_1	Q_2	R_2	S_2	-.5	+1	-.5	0
P_1	Q_2	R_1	S_2	.5	0	-.5	0
P_1	Q_2	R_2	S_1	-.5	+.5	0	0
P_1	Q_1	R_2	S_2	-1	.5	0	.5
P_1	Q_2	R_1	S_1	+1	-1	+.5	-.5
P_2	Q_1	R_1	S_1	+.5	-.5	+.5	-.5
P_2	Q_1	R_1	S_2	+.5	-.5	0	0
P_2	Q_1	R_2	S_1	0	0	.5	-.5
P_2	Q_2	R_1	S_2	-.5	.5	-.5	.5
P_2	Q_2	R_2	S_2	.5	-.5	.5	-.5
P_2	Q_2	R_2	S_1	.5	0	-.5	0
P_2	Q_1	R_2	S_2	-.5	+.5	-.5	+.5
P_2	Q_2	R_1	S_1	+1	-1	.5	-.5

Then the payoff matrix for CP(M) will be given by:

Payoff matrix for CP(M)

	$Q_1R_1S_1$	$Q_1R_1S_1$	$Q_1R_2S_1$	$Q_2R_2S_2$	$Q_2R_1S_2$	$Q_2R_2S_1$	$Q_1R_2S_2$	$Q_2R_1S_1$
P_1	+1	-.5	0	-.5	.5	-.5	-1	+1
P_2^1	.5	+.5	0	-.5	.5	.5	-.5	+1

(ii) Congress vs. others.

The game has a saddle point and the resulting choice is $P_2Q_1R_1S_2$. Although CP(M) expressed a desire to come to an understanding with ULF and PULF, they have moved instead to the right toward C(R), which in turn, moved to the left. The payoff matrix for Congress is given by:

C(R)	$P_1R_1S_1$	$P_1R_1S_2$	$P_2R_1S_1$	$P_2R_2S_1$	$P_1R_2S_1$	$P_1R_2S_2$	$P_2R_1S_2$	$P_2R_2S_2$
Q_1	-1	0	-.5	0	0	.5	-.5	.5
Q_2	-.1	0	-1	0	+.5	+1	-.5	.5

Again, there is a saddle point at $Q_2P_1R_1S_1$. Interestingly enough, this was the situation when Congress (R) was dominated by rightist leaders and ULF and PULF moved rigorously to the left with CP(M). If we consider the coalition between CP(M) and ULF, vs. C(R) and PULF, then the equilibrium situation will be $P_2R_1S_2Q_1$, which means CP(M) has to move to the left and PULF to the right. This is a reasonable potential position for each.

In the future, there may be three contesting parties in the political scene: C(R), CP(M) and others, comprising third group forming coalitions with either of the other two and leading to a similar game theoretical situation. A three-person non-zero sum game may arise with the central government as the fourth party forcing a zero sum game. Until that happened, the four-party situation would persist.

The interesting point is that the two groups, PULF and ULF, are placed in a situation similar to Prisoner's Dilemma. If PULF stands alone and does not cooperate with ULF in supporting CP(M) or C(R), then it will receive severe punishment no matter who wins, but ULF will be rewarded with power in the government and vice versa. If they cooperate in supporting the winning party, both will be rewarded. The payoff matrix in the Prisoner's Dilemma case appears as follows (C - denotes cooperation, D - denotes defection).

PRISONER'S DILEMMA
PULF

		C_2	D_2
	C_1	R,R	S,T
ULF			
	D_1	T,S	P,P

In the tables above, C_1 and C_2 refer to the strategies of ULF and PULF in cooperating in the election or on issues facing the state. The reward corresponding to the strategy is denoted by R. It is assumed, as is generally the case in Prisoner's Dilemma situations, that they are the same. The situation $C_1 D_2$ denotes that ULF cooperates, i.e. takes an independent stand and stands alone in the election, whereas PULF forms a coalition with C(R) and gets more than its parity norm share due to the strategic aspect of the game; then, ULF receives the punishment. The $C_2 D_1$ denotes the opposite situation, where PULF cooperates but ULF defects to CP(M). If they both defect, i.e. if they do not cooperate in taking joint actions, they will receive punishment P. The rewards in this matrix can be measured in terms of the number of seats in the ministry, percentage of popular votes, and such things as the image in the public eye, ideological considerations, etc.

With this framework, if a sufficient number of observations were available regarding the behaviour of PULF and ULF, it would be possible to estimate (following a Markov Chain approach) the probability that they will cooperate in a particular case given their behaviour on previous occasions. Since the time period is too short to generate such data, we cannot make such estimates. However, if we trace back the history of their behaviour on issues rather than focusing on the formulation of election time coalitions, such estimates can be made. Alternatively, we could look at similar coalition politics in other states of India and make some estimates.

In this research, I have tried in a small way to apply some game theoretical concepts to the political events in the state of West Bengal in the past decade. This type of approach, if properly carried out, can effectively explain the behaviour of political parties in a coalition situation in India and in other developing countries. It can also be applied in formulating cooperative procedures to solve intergroup/ interstate problems leading to the efficient utilization of scarce resources for the benefit of all concerned.

3.   CONCLUSION

The situation in India, and West Bengal in particular, has changed significantly in recent years. Particularly with the assassination of the late prime minister Rajiv Gandhi. The Congress party has become friendly with CPI and the rest of PULF has either joined Congress or become non-existent.

CP(M) has not moved toward Congress. It is interesting to note that more recently there has been a decline in the power of both Congress and CPI. Furthermore, the international situation has changed significantly. It is hoped that a more comprehensive model incorporating these new developments will be forthcoming in the future.

C.   Coalition Theory

In many conflict situations, participants form groups or coalitions. That way, they can obtain payoffs which they may not receive if they act individually. The questions which naturally arise in regard to these situations are: which of the possible coalitions will form, are the coalitions stable and what are their payoffs? Following Isard (1967), we may stipulate a number of reasonable prerequisites for a coalition. It should be efficient, meaning there is no other coalition which will give the participant a higher payoff. It should be simple in the sense that the participants can make the necessary computations. The normality principle stipulates equity considerations; strategy property will ensure strategic potential of the coalition.

The possible scenarios can be explained with the help of an example. Suppose there are three participants described by $i=1,2,3$. These participants may be leaders of the political parties controlling w_i votes ($i=1,2,3$). For the sake of simplicity, let us assume $w_1=25$, $w_2=30$, $w_3=45$, which can be termed as the decision weight. The critical weight W^* is defined as a weight which for the coalition is a winning coalition. In this case it is $W^*=51$. Any coalition denoted by C will be a winning coalition if its weight $W(C)>W^*$. In our case, coalitions (1,2), (2,3) and (1,3) are all winning coalitions. It is clear here that no participant has veto power, no two coalitions can form simultaneously, and no single participant can control a decision.

If there is a winning coalition then the payoff (say $10m) has to be divided according to the $Wi/w(C)$ ratio; i.e. the share of demand for each participant in the coalition payoff must be proportional to its relative contribution to that coalition. This is known as the parity-norm principle. For example, the payoff outcome in the (1,2) winning coalition will be (4.54, 5.46, 0.0). However, participant 3 can induce the first participant to form a coalition with him by giving her a higher payoff. Thus (1,3) coalition may be formed with the payoff function (4.54 +, 0, 5.46-). This payoff can be termed as the defection payoff. However, the defection process can go on indefinitely. So from the point of view of the parity-norm principle, the coalition (1,2) may be the cheapest winning coalition.

The coalition is cheapest in the sense that the ith relative contribution $Wi/w(C i)$ yields him a maximum share of $10m, i.e. i^{th} relative contribution is maximum. Of course, the participants may work to form an all-party coalition and divide the payoff equally. But to do so is to ignore the existence of the coalition situation altogether.

The question that remains to be answered is whether it is possible to construct a coalition satisfying both the equity aspect and strategic aspect of the coalition. Isard (1967) calls this a coalition compromise procedure.

In the case of this procedure, there are two phases, namely an intra-coalition phase and an inter-coalition phase. We first construct the intra-coalition compromise $(1,2)$, $(1,3)$ and $(2,3)$ and the corresponding payoff $\pi_{12}=(4.54, 5,46,0)$, $\pi_{13}=(3.56,0,6.44)$, $\pi_{13}=(0.4,6)$ based on the parity-norm principle. We take the coalitions as participants and compute the inter-coalition weights $(i.j. = 1,2,3)$ $W(i,j)=Wij/(W_{12}+W_{13}+W_{23})$ where $Wij=Wi+Wj$. This process gives the payoff $(1.25, 1.50, 2.25)$.

If instead of parity-norm procedure, the the split-the-difference procedure is adopted, then the compromise solution will be $1/3(\pi_{12} + \pi_{13} + \pi_{23}) = (1.35,1.58,2.07)$.

While it may not be possible to form a winning coalition, all winning coalitions are not strategically equivalent. For example, in the present example, the members in the mutually cheapest coalition $(1,2)$ may be considered in relatively stronger positions than other participants. To consider this strategic aspect, we can reconsider the disruptive coalitions d_{13} and d_{23} based on modified parity norm shares in the intra-coalition and the split-the-difference procedure in the inter-coalition stage. The final compromise position will be $1/3(d_{12} + d_{13} + d_{23}) = 1/3(1.51 + 1.82 + 1.67)$. However, just as all winning coalitions are not strategically equivalent, neither are all disruptive coalitions. For example, $(2,3)$ coalitions will not be as disruptive, since 3 can do better by enticing 1 rather than 2. A modified situation may result if there is a series of disruptive coalitions leading to an equilibrium payoff. The situation becomes more complicated when it is extended to n (more than three) participants. This procedure also assumes that:

(1)   social actions are continuous and convex
(2)   preference orderings of the social functions can be represented by continuous utility functions
(3)   the procedures have only touched a few strategic relevants.

There may be other possibilities.

In many countries, both developed or developing (such as in India), coalitions with left and right wing parties have become the norm. It will be very interesting to study the dynamics of these coalitions and the causes for their formations and their breaking up.

D.   Simulation

International conflict is a complex process influenced by the social, economic, political and environmental conditions of the world community as well as those of specific countries. It is burdensome to establish meaningful mathematical relationships between different variables. It is even more laborious to collect data and estimate the parameters of these relationships (equations). To some extent, we are successful in obtaining this goal in the construction of macro econometric model building, in constructing and solving hypothetical examples of real problems and thus obtaining insights about the real problem. This is frequently done in the field of industrial engineering and management. Let us consider as an example an airline scheduling problem.

An airline has 15 flights leaving a airport per day, each with one pilot. The airline has a policy of keeping three reserve pilots on call to replace those who become ill and are scheduled for flights. The probability distribution of a daily number of sick pilots can be calculated. We are asked to estimate the utilization of reserve pilots and also the probability that at least one flight will be cancelled because no pilots are available. This problem can be handled through the Monte-Carlo simulation technique.

Similar models − urban situation models − were used by Forester and his associates at M.I.T. In their experiments, many variables, such as population, employment, housing, transportation and land use, are related to decision and uncontrollable variables. If no new decisions are made, these interrelationships (equations) are used to compute the consequence at a base period. If this consequence or the measure of effectiveness is not satisfactory, then new policy decisions are made, leading to new measures of effectiveness which may or may not be satisfactory. The whole process is repeated until and unless satisfactory results are obtained.

One simulation model we shall discuss is by Bremer (1977). It defines the decision making environment and specifies the ways in which it changes in response to the behaviour of the national decision making units. The national decision making environment is composed of an international system national economic system and national political system. The international system, until recently, is composed of superpowers. The national economic system is composed of consumption (CS), investment and government (FC). When the resources are allocated to the economic sector, the national product or total basic capability (TBC) is generated. Clearly

$$CS = CSP \cdot TBC \cdot CSGR \qquad (1)$$

The total consumption satisfaction depends on the capability (e.g. 100) multiplied by generation rate (e.g. 1.4) or opportunity cost CSGR. CSP is the proportion of natural resources allocated to consumption. Similarly

$$FC = FCP \cdot TBC \cdot FCGR \qquad (2)$$

$$BC = BCP \cdot TBC \cdot BCGR \qquad (3)$$

Similar equations can be written for investment equations.

The restraint of political systems is exercised through the allocation of resources for economic and security needs. In the political arena, equations can be specified to indicate the degrees of authoritarianism, minimum consumption level, etc.

After specifying the national and international framework, Bremer outlines the decision making processes where the first job of the decision maker is to set the goals and make them operational. The next four processes − trading, resource allocation, aid requesting, and aid granting − are means of satisfying the goals. In the end, conflict is generated due to the steps of goal formulation and operation leading to changes in the goal themselves.

For each of the steps Bremer sketches a flow chart similar to those used in computer analysis. For example, the first chart gives the goal formation process of economic growth, and second gives the goal operation flow chart. Once all the flow charts are drawn, they are combined into one system. Then Bremer takes a hypothetical value of the parameters involved in the relationships of the variables in the flow chart and observes their impact on the system.

There are certain advantages to this simulation model, such as:

1. The model can have repeated applications.
2. The model is able to be used even when the information is quite sketchy and its relationship unknown.
3. Data for simulation analysis can be obtained more cheaply than that for a real work system.
4. Analytical models may be impossible to develop.

The difficulties of the simulation models are:

1. They are very costly to construct and validate (e.g. computer time may be very expensive).
2. There is no reliable theory developed in the process.
3. Simulation models give only approximate solutions.

The variables in Bremer's model are:

CSP: proportion of national reserves allocated to consumptions (CS)

BCP: the proportion of national resources devoted to investment (BC)

FCP: the proportion of national resources devoted to the defence sector for the production of FC value

BCGR: Basic capability generation rate; the basic capability value produced by the commitment of one unit of resources (TBC) to the investment sector

CSGR: Consumption satisfaction generation roles; the consumption satisfaction value produced by the commitment of one unit of resources (TBC) to the consumption sector

4 Factor Analysis and Related Methods

A.   Factor Analysis

Although factor analysis is a powerful technique with great flexibility. We shall confine our discussion to only one aspect of this method.

Suppose we have a number of statistical variables ($j = 1,2...n$) for a country. For example, the variables can be the population, employment levels, the number of radios, percentage of literacy, and so on. Assume that the country is designated by $i=1...N$. Then the variables X_{ji} will represent the value of the jth variable in the ith country, and the mean value of the ith variable – for instance, the average number of radios for all countries – can be defined as:

$$\bar{X}_j = \sum_{i=1}^{n} X_{ji}/N \tag{1}$$

The variance of the jth variable is similarly defined as:

$$\sigma_j^2 = \Sigma (X_{ji} - \bar{X}_j)^2/N \tag{2}$$

It is useful to use small letters to denote the deviations:

$$x_{ji} = X_{ji} - \bar{X}_j \tag{3}$$

The equation (2) can be written as:

$$\sigma_j^2 = \Sigma x_{ji}^2/N \tag{4}$$

If we further define

$$Z_{ji} = x_{ji}/\sigma_j \tag{5}$$

(that is, take the standard deviation as the unit of measurement), then the variables Z_{ji}, or Z_j, are called standardized variables $(i=1,\ldots N)$ and $(j=1,\ldots n)$. It is easily seen that

$$\overline{Z}_j = 0$$
$$\sigma_{zj}^2 = 1 \tag{6}$$

That is, the mean and the standard deviation of the standardized variables are 0 and 1, respectively. We also know that the product moment correlation coefficient between the jth and kth variable is defined as

$$r_{jk} = \frac{\Sigma_i (X_{ji} - \overline{X}_j)(X_{ki} - \overline{X}_k)}{\sqrt{\Sigma_i (X_{ji} - \overline{X}_j)^2 \ \Sigma (X_{ki} - \overline{X}_k)^2}} \tag{7}$$

Following the definition of the standardized variable (equation 5), the correlation r_{jk} can be defined as:

$$r_{jk} = \sum_{i=1}^{n} Z_{ji} Z_{ki}/N \tag{8}$$

Let us now concentrate on the variable Z_{ji}, which represents for the ith country the value of the jth variable, say, the number of coups in Burma. This number can be thought of both as characteristic of the jth variable and as due to a unique result of the interplay of a number of factors, that is, demographic F_1, social development F_2, technological development F_3, educational development F_4, and so on. In mathematical notation

$$Z_{ji} = a_{ji}F_{ij} + a_{j2}F_{2i} - \ldots + a_{jm}F_{mi} + a_j U_{ji} \tag{9}$$

gives a mathematical model of the observed variables Z_i. For the sake of simplicity, the relationship is taken in the linear form. If we wish to write the equation for all variables in equation (9), we have

$$Z_1 = a_{11}F_1 + a_{12}F_2 \ldots + a_{1n}F_m + a_1 U_1$$
$$Z_2 = a_{21}F_1 + a_{22}F_2 \ldots + a_{2m}F_m + a_2 U_2$$
$$\vdots$$
$$Z_n = a_{n1}F_1 + a_{n2}F_2 \ldots + a_{nm}F_m + a_n U_n \tag{10}$$

The variable Z_2 may refer to population, Z_3 employment, Z_4 to the number of physicians, etc. Also, we assume without the loss of generality that factors $F_1 \ldots F_m$ are in standard form. That is

$$\overline{F}_i = 0 \tag{11}$$

$$\sigma_{Fi}^2 = 1$$

Notice that in the equation set (10) the subscript i has been omitted to avoid complication in the notation. Strictly speaking, the variable Z_j, F_1, F_2...F_m, U_j should be written as Z_{ji}, F_{1i}, F_{2i},...F_{mi}, U_{ji} (j=1...n). If a factor is present in more than one variable, then it will be called a common factor.

If all the factors are present in all the equations, obviously they should be termed general factors. The coefficients, or a_{ji}'s, are known as factor loadings. The main objective of the factor analysis is to estimate the factor loadings that tell us the value of the variable, say, number of telephones assigned to factor 1 (for example, demographic factors); factor 2 (for example, social development); and so on.

Suppose the factor loadings of some group of variables with a given factor are similar. Then we conclude that the factor represents the given set of variables. Instead of using these variables in a regression, we can use the factor. The methods of estimation of the factor loadings can be varied depending on what types of factor models we are using and whether we have an orthogonal or an oblique system. In the orthogonal system, the factors are independent; that is, technological change and demographic factors are not related.

When the factors are uncorrelated (that is, orthogonal), it can be shown that

$$a_{j1}^2 + a_{j2}^2 + \ldots + a_{jm}^2 + a_j^2 = 1$$

Defining

$$h_j^2 = a_{j1}^2 \ldots a_{jm}^2 \qquad (12)$$

from equation (12) it follows that

$$h_j^2 + a_j^2 = 1 \qquad (13)$$

The communality h_j^2 of a variable measures the amount of variation explained by the factors. The amount that cannot be explained by the factors is a_j^2.

When we have a principal factor model – that is, when there is a unique factor and m common factors, as in equation (10) –the method of <u>principal axes</u> is used to estimate the factor loadings. In the principal factor model, we have

$$Z_j = a_{j1}F_1 + a_{j2}F_2 \ldots + a_{jm}F_m (j = 1 \ldots n) \qquad (14)$$

The principal axes method states that the first factor loading, a_{j1}, is chosen in such a way that

$$V_1 = a_{11}^2 + a_{21}^2 \ldots + a_{n1}^2 \qquad (15)$$

is maximum, subject to

$$r_{jk} = \sum_{i=1}^{m} a_{jp}a_{kp} \ (j,k, = 1 \ldots n) \qquad (16)$$

where r_{jk} are the correlations between the jth and k^{th} variables. This amounts to solving the characteristic equations:

$$(h_1^2 - \lambda)a_{11} + r_{12}a_{21} \ldots r_{1n}a_{n1} = 0$$

$$r_{21}a_{11} + (h_2^2 - \lambda)a_{21} \ldots + r_{2n}a_{n1} = 0 \qquad (17)$$

$$r_{n1}a_{11} + r_{n2}a_{21} \ldots + (h_n^2 - \lambda)a_{n1} = 0$$

where h_j^2 is the communality of the variable j defined before. In solving equations (17) the following processes are involved:

1. Computation of the correlation matrix of the input variables Z_j.
2. Extracting initial and varimax final factor loadings (called factor load matrix) from correlation matrix by solving equation (17).
3. Weights to estimate variables from factors (factor pattern matrix).
5. Correlation between factors and variables (factor structure matrix).
6. Correlation matrix for terminal factors.
7. Factor score for each country for each factor. The factor score of any country with respect to any factor (F_j) – say, employment – shows the importance of that country with respect to that factor.

B.   An Example: Conflict and Development

One conclusion often made in analysing conflict situations in developing countries is that the declining socio-economic conditions, high level of population growth, inequality in the distribution of income, tribal rivalry, etc. lead to the escalation of domestic conflict. One general consensus is that as the standard of living improves, education spreads, news media develop and the number of conflicts declines. In an earlier paper (Chatterji, 1978) I tried to test the hypothesis using a small number of countries and a limited set of variables. The countries selected for this study are the following: 1. Afghanistan, 2. Burma, 3. Ceylon (Sri Lanka), 4. India, 5. Indonesia, 6. Nepal and 7. Pakistan.

This selection was made since a comparable set of data is available. I excluded India from my analysis because of its large size and relatively high degree of development in the social and industrial infrastructure. For these countries, the data for the following variables were collected for the years 1950-65.

A.   Socio-economic Variables
1.   Area
2.   Population
3.   Population Density
4.   Number of Telephones
5.   Number of Telephones per Capita
6.   Radios
7.   Number of Newspapers
8.   Primary School Enrollment
9.   Primary School Enrollment (per 10,000 population)
10. Secondary School Enrollment

11. Secondary School Enrollment (per 10,000 population)
12. Primary and Secondary School Enrollment
13. Primary and Secondary School Enrollment per 10,000 population
14. Primary School Enrollment Divided by Primary and Secondary School Enrollments
15. University Enrollment
16. University Enrollment per 10,000 population
17. All School Enrollment
18. All School Enrollment per 10,000 population
19. Per cent Literate
20. Inhabitants per Physician
21. Physicians per Inhabitant
22. Gross Domestic Product per Capita

B. Political Stability Variables
1. Number of Coups d'Etat
2. Number of Major Constitutional Changes
3. Type of Government (Premier or Not)
4. Effective Executive (Type)
5. Effective Executive (Selection)
6. Degree of Parliamentary Responsibility
7. Changes of Effective Executive
8. Legislative Effectiveness

C. Conflict Variables
1. Assassinations
2. General Strikes
3. Guerilla Warfare
4. Government Crises
5. Purges
6. Riots
7. Revolutions

For each country, we took each of the variables in (C) as the dependent variables and the factor scores of the socio-economic variables as the independent variable and ran regression equations. These equations helped us to make statements regarding the linkages between demographic characteristics, socio-economic structures, technological developments and conflicts in some developing countries.

Let us discuss the regression results of each country separately. The estimated regression equations for Afghanistan are given in Table 4.1. From this table it is seen that the regression coefficient for population is mostly positive and statistically significant. The exceptions are for newspapers and university enrollment where they are negative and insignificant. This implies that in those cases, population cannot be taken as a good predictor. The reason probably is that the literacy factor is important and university education is relatively expensive. To test this, we regressed the number of newspapers variable with income and for literacy. But in so doing we obtained meaningful results for Pakistan, Indonesia and Ceylon only.

When we consider the impact of income, we have for the most part the right signs, but the coefficients are not statistically significant; this indicates that income has not been a crucial factor. The exceptions are university enrollment, as mentioned before, and the number of newspapers, since both of them are responsive to increases in income. The

147

conclusion which emerges from Table 4.1 and other regression results is that population alone has been the driving force and income has had a negligible impact. It appears that there ha been a decline or at best a maintenance of the status quo in the socio-economic infrastructure in Afghanistan.

If we study the regression equations in Table 4.2 for Burma, we find that all the regression coefficients with respect to population have the proper signs and are significant except for newspapers. In that case, population is not a good predictor, but income is, since it is significant. As before, the income regression coefficients for university education and physicians are highly significant. However, the statistical results show that population alone explains 90% of the variability in all the regressions.

In the case of Ceylon (Table 4.3), the regression coefficients for population have the right signs and are significant except for the number of telephones and the number of physicians, where the income variables are significant. In most cases, the income variables are either non-significant or have the wrong signs, indicating that population alone is the basic predicting variable. The same conclusion follows from Table 4.4, which gives the regression equations for Indonesia. The population regression coefficients are significant with the exception of the number of newspapers. Population is the dominating variable, explaining about 93 percent of the variability. The information revealed in Table 4.5 about Nepal is also interesting. Here, income plays a more important role since the socioeconomic conditions in Nepal are much worse and have not changed significantly over time. The regression equations for Pakistan (Table 4.6) support the claim for the population as the dominant variable. Thus, on the basis of regression analysis we conclude that socioeconomic conditions did not change much.

To further substantiate this conclusion we conducted factor analyses for each year for the three sets of variables mentioned before (Table 4.8). For each set, a single factor was extracted. Factors can be termed as demographic-economic, communication, and education, respectively. With the exception of university enrollment (V17), the correlation of the factor with the variables is quite high. For each year and for each country we also obtained the factor scores. They are shown in Table 4.9. It is interesting to note the factor scores of each country over time. They have not changed significantly. Also, note the ranking of the countries, with respect to socio-economic factor scores, with the real situation. Ceylon (Sri Lanka) is at the top, then comes Pakistan. Followed by Indonesia, Afghanistan, and Nepal.

Our next objective was to relate the incidence of conflict with the socioeconomic factor scores for each country. It is of course difficult to precisely define conflict and its measurements, and the difficulty is increased in attempting to monitor it over time. Furthermore, conflict does not follow a continuous time path. In a particular year, the number of conflicts may suddenly jump with no readily apparent reason. So it will not be proper to relate the number of conflicts for each year to socioeconomic structure scores for that year even if such data were available. For

Table 1
THE ESTIMATED REGRESSION EQUATIONS--AFGHANISTAN

Dependent \ Independent Variable	Constant a	Population b_1	Domestic Product[*] b_2	$\bar{R}^2$	F
Number of Telephones	-68.96	0.0019 (0.0053)	2.2818 (0.9820)	0.91	78.58
Number of Radios	-569.87	0.0529 (0.0173)	-2.1240 (3.2185)	0.89	63.82
Number of Newspapers	-67.54	-0.0118 (0.0066)	5.2974 (1.2338)	0.91	73.05
Primary School Enrollment	-1247.64	0.1075 (0.0261)	-0.2359 (4.8512)	0.96	181.08
Secondary School Enrollment	-159.74	0.0142 (0.0034)	-0.3528 (0.6335)	0.95	142.97
University Enrollment	-4.11	-0.00037 (0.0003)	0.2164 (0.0602)	0.90	67.33
Physicians	-102.00	0.0066 (0.0024)	0.7049 (0.4483)	0.96	201.99

[*] Per capita.

Table 2
THE ESTIMATED REGRESSION EQUATIONS--BURMA

Dependent	Constant a	Population b_1	Domestic Product[*] b_2	$\bar{R}^2$	F
Number of Telephones	-528.28	0.0219 (0.0015)	3.3926 (0.5661)	0.96	199.26
Number of Radios	-370.29	0.0156 (0.0015)	1.7727 (0.6026)	0.92	83.20
Number of Newspapers	3.33	-0.0004 (0.0009)	1.8699 (0.3782)	0.64	13.67
Primary School Enrollment	-4197.05	0.1902 (0.0302)	27.6814 (11.8151)	0.82	33.59
Secondary School Enrollment	-1271.83	0.0764 (0.0066)	-0.9879 (2.5653)	0.91	78.44
University Enrollment	-56.85	0.0026 (0.0002)	0.2594 (0.0727)	0.95	148.81
Physicians	-153.76	0.0077 (0.0006)	0.8767 (0.2393)	0.94	123.71

[*] Per capita.

Table 3

THE ESTIMATED REGRESSION EQUATIONS--CEYLON (SRI LANKA)

Dependent Variable	Constant a	Population b_1	Domestic Product* b_2	$\overline{R}^2$	F
Number of Telephones	-1654.45	-0.0334 (0.0285)	6.9370 (2.6784)	0.76	24.05
Number of Radios	-982.13	0.0032 (0.0217)	9.8392 (2.0433)	0.97	275.92
Number of Newspapers	387.70	0.0556 (0.0039)	-4.3348 (0.3690)	0.95	149.15
Primary School Enrollment	-390.45	0.1313 (0.0240)	5.0983 (2.2588)	0.99	661.64
Secondary School Enrollment	-1044.52	0.2028 (0.0190)	-3.0682 (1.8754)	0.99	823.26
University Enrollment	-13.45	0.0077 (0.0006)	-0.4364 (0.0538)	0.98	376.76
Physicians	-46.01	-0.0789 (0.0090)	8.0907 (0.8473)	0.87	49.31

*Per capita.

Table 4

THE ESTIMATED REGRESSION EQUATIONS--INDONESIA

Dependent Variable	Constant a	Population b_1	Domestic Product* b_2	$\overline{R}^2$	F
Number of Telephones	-2936.46	0.0471 (0.0059)	-2.9212 (4.9528)	0.93	92.73
Number of Radios	-169.47	0.0021 (0.0002)	0.6945 (0.1994)	0.97	239.23
Number of Newspapers	108.03	-0.0021 (0.0001)	2.2639 (0.1515)	0.94	112.90
Primary School Enrollment	-13637.10	0.2666 (0.0227)	-23.6252 (18.9440)	0.96	191.98
Secondary School Enrollment	-581.18	-0.0061 (0.0038)	22.4354 (3.1608)	0.88	56.36
University Enrollment	-242.20	0.0033 (0.0001)	-0.0718 (0.0906)	0.995	1479.78
Physicians	-35.47	0.0008 (0.0003)	-0.1637 (0.0222)	0.99	923.48

*Per capita.

Table 5

THE ESTIMATED REGRESSION EQUATIONS--NEPAL

Dependent Variable	Constant a	Population b_1	Domestic Product* b_2	$\bar{R}^2$	F
Number of Newspapers	-50.29	-0.0015 (0.0021)	1.3764 (0.2202)	0.91	78.92
Primary School Enrollment	-472.23	0.0007 (0.0124)	12.3233 (1.2751)	0.97	233.77
Secondary School Enrollment	-64.40	-0.0023 (0.0018)	2.1948 (0.1870)	0.97	278.28
University Enrollment	-16.38	0.0019 (0.0004)	0.0534 (0.0441)	0.91	73.41
Physicians	-36.43	0.0033	0.3695	0.986	507.27

*
Per capita.

Table 6

THE ESTIMATED REGRESSION EQUATIONS--PAKISTAN

Dependent Variable	Constant a	Population b_1	Domestic Product* b_2	$\bar{R}^2$	F
Number of Telephones	-1937.15	0.0190 (0.0060)	13.1568 (0.5933)	0.98	390.28
Number of Radios	-67.57	0.0002 (0.0001)	3.0198 (0.0612)	0.998	3039.78
Number of Newspapers	-151.52	-0.0007 (0.0005)	3.9818 (0.3179)	0.99	1077.01
Primary School Enrollment	-4894.08	0.0859 (0.0251)	27.5768 (15.0759)	0.97	231.12
Secondary School Enrollment	-273.73	-0.0144 (0.0091)	43.1890 (5.4693)	0.98	345.84
University Enrollment	-241.78	0.0016 (0.0009)	3.2534 (0.5269)	0.986	538.02
Physicians	-201.16	0.0031 (0.0008)	0.4876 (0.4578)	0.966	215.46

*
Per capita.

Table 7
FACTOR LOADINGS FOR P-FACTOR ANALYSIS

Country	Demographic-Economic			Communication				Education		
	V4	V22	V23	V8	V7	V6	V20	V10	V12	V17
1. Afghanistan	.9688	.9668	.9596	0.9775	0.8613	0.9367	0.9994	0.9982	0.9991	0.7958
2. Burma	.9310	.9874	.5841	0.6393	0.9709	0.9244	0.9049	0.9419	0.9283	0.9293
3. Ceylon	.9466	.5299	.9925	0.7001	0.9483	0.0704	0.9942	0.7923	0.9830	0.9258
5. Indonesia	.9950	.9556	.8773	0.1589	0.9947	0.9392	0.9913	0.9435	0.6346	0.9917
6. Nepal	.9553	.9864	.9615	0.9934	0.5765	0.9138	0.9335	0.9960	0.9786	0.8444
7. Pakistan	.9989	.9906	.9838	0.9804	0.9886	0.9900	0.9806	0.9469	0.9636	0.9612

Table 8
FACTOR LOADINGS FOR R-FACTOR ANALYSIS

Year	Demographic-Economic			Communication				Education		
	V4	V22	V23	V8	V7	V6	V20	V10	V12	V17
1	0.8986	0.9900	0.9982	0.9997	0.9203	0.9778	0.8783	0.8878	0.9991	0.2009
2	0.8970	0.9847	0.9998					0.8634	0.9895	0.2887
3	0.8929	0.9792	0.9945					0.8529	0.9824	0.4212
4	0.8980	0.9750	0.9830	0.9985	0.9361	0.9701	0.8364	0.8368	0.9958	0.4140
5	0.9021	0.9662	0.9688	0.9972	0.9652	0.9628	0.8251	0.8334	0.9839	0.5067
6	0.9144	0.8592	0.8505	0.9969	0.9718	0.9595	0.8286	0.8482	0.9986	0.4114
7	0.9245	0.9494	0.9397	0.9964	0.9856	0.9543	0.8316	0.8703	0.9956	0.2742
8	0.9346	0.9376	0.9207	0.9971	0.9888	0.9527	0.8304	0.8995	1.0000	0.2177
9	0.9412	0.9214	0.9096	0.9963	0.9886	0.9578	0.8384	0.9187	0.9987	0.2238
10	0.9404	0.9167	0.9334	0.9968	0.9878	0.9602	0.8323	0.9275	0.9714	0.1744
11	0.9384	0.9152	0.9511	0.9991	0.9887	0.9632	0.8006	0.9397	0.9470	0.1897
12	0.9401	0.9102	0.9635	0.9980	0.9888	0.9800	0.7480	0.8873	0.9672	0.1451
13	0.9404	0.9065	0.9771	0.9883	0.9934	0.9844	0.7077	0.8525	0.9783	0.2700
14	0.9398	0.8898	0.9897	0.9680	0.9807	0.9957	0.6866	0.8299	0.9731	0.3003
15	0.9658	0.8384	0.9988	0.9342	0.9677	0.9637	0.6712	0.7781	0.9994	0.3224
16	0.9814	0.7770	0.9977	0.9242	0.9428	0.9894	0.6343	0.7646	0.9837	0.4065
17	0.9892	0.7070	0.9823	0.9094	0.9123	0.9971	0.6066	0.7245	0.9980	0.4367

Table 9

FACTOR SCORES

	Demographic-Economic	Communication	Education
Year 1			
Country 1	-0.701363	-0.655740	-0.490730
Country 2	-0.370894	-0.090063	-0.555839
Country 3	1.976246	2.001543	2.005338
Country 5	-0.308926	-0.249951	-0.705079
Country 6	-0.595920	-0.520038	-0.320853
Country 7	0.000860	-0.985753	0.067160
Year 2			
Country 1	-0.689202		-0.577165
Country 2	-0.377941		-0.520976
Country 3	1.978189		1.938967
Country 5	-0.223986		-0.679975
Country 6	-0.645177		-0.405160
Country 7	-0.041883		0.244307
Year 3			
Country 1	-0.697526		-0.650713
Country 2	-0.391476		-0.416884
Country 3	1.959339		1.898939
Country 5	-0.229359		-0.579123
Country 6	-0.652261		-0.509377
Country 7	0.011282		0.257156
Year 4			
Country 1	-0.714256	-0.650084	-0.688353
Country 2	-0.399966	0.021030	-0.327269
Country 3	1.937742	1.967699	1.904909
Country 5	-0.260297	-0.181612	-0.615534
Country 6	-0.637622	-0.639508	-0.558394
Country 7	0.074399	-0.517625	0.284641
Year 5			
Country 1	-0.748726	-0.650562	-0.820291
Country 2	-0.417494	0.069155	0.218398
Country 3	1.911401	1.951468	1.783560
Country 5	-0.264253	-0.163964	-0.645090
Country 6	-0.614770	-0.681213	-0.708515
Country 7	0.133841	-0.525484	0.171938
Year 6			
Country 1	-0.781441	-0.623220	-0.801560
Country 2	-0.440987	0.093424	0.072075
Country 3	1.885298	1.003502	1.874026
Country 5	-0.263940	-0.158596	-0.592631
Country 6	-0.588157	-0.725007	-0.679488
Country 7	0.189227	-0.530103	0.126875

Table 9 (Continued)

	Demographic-Economic	Communication	Education
Year 7			
Country 1	-0.817043	-0.619772	-0.072973
Country 2	-0.472445	0.106776	-0.058617
Country 3	1.862843	1.928390	1.022066
Country 5	-0.242216	-0.126709	-0.368934
Country 6	-0.561129	-0.771279	-0.667703
Country 7	0.229991	-0.517406	0.046160
Year 8			
Country 1	-0.852923	-0.587272	-0.757149
Country 2	-0.512323	0.115185	-0.157181
Country 3	1.838206	1.923389	1.943784
Country 5	-0.222163	-0.126271	-0.410781
Country 6	-0.517902	-0.815005	-0.657351
Country 7	0.267105	-0.509939	0.032675
Year 9			
Country 1	-0.878360	-0.613045	-0.751068
Country 2	-0.555067	0.129768	-0.201222
Country 3	1.817210	1.894284	1.956466
Country 5	-0.183030	-0.044239	-0.356439
Country 6	-0.489703	-0.888347	-0.654446
Country 7	0.288947	-0.478425	0.006707
Year 10			
Country 1	-0.864949	-0.582994	-0.837597
Country 2	-0.555294	0.139160	-0.152110
Country 3	1.824800	1.893472	1.875102
Country 5	-0.157972	-0.088179	-0.109782
Country 6	-0.520794	-0.899642	-0.731038
Country 7	0.274208	-0.466818	-0.044577
Year 11			
Country 1	-0.863973	-0.527901	-0.867778
Country 2	-0.541718	0.100679	-0.113011
Country 3	1.820593	1.933966	1.826611
Country 5	-0.132960	-0.220938	0.025455
Country 6	-0.571239	-0.872900	-0.772831
Country 7	0.289297	-0.412905	-0.098448
Year 12			
Country 1	-0.879075	-0.553531	-0.792406
Country 2	-0.540112	-0.047124	-0.104871
Country 3	1.811955	1.962408	1.877923
Country 5	-0.111081	-0.249211	-0.220493
Country 6	-0.594237	-0.825028	-0.723482
Country 7	0.312550	-0.287510	-0.036673

Table 9 (Continued)

	Demographic-Economic	Communication	Education
Year 13			
Country 1	-0.882975	-0.465617	-0.779911
Country 2	-0.521304	-0.108137	-0.089140
Country 3	1.805086	1.980479	1.895150
Country 5	-0.081143	-0.189014	-0.365416
Country 6	-0.652848	-0.799513	-0.681685
Country 7	0.333183	-0.373200	0.021001
Year 14			
Country 1	-0.876977	-0.471118	-0.195144
Country 2	-0.511311	-0.314378	-0.058404
Country 3	1.801720	1.943200	1.874898
Country 5	-0.043610	0.039415	-0.398605
Country 6	-0.718491	-0.887861	-0.670895
Country 7	0.348671	-0.309259	0.048149
Year 15			
Country 1	-0.831554	-0.437633	-0.737857
Country 2	-0.732988	-0.330537	-0.032050
Country 3	1.787694	1.917554	1.921625
Country 5	-0.011390	0.081915	-0.608333
Country 6	-0.626023	-0.883470	-0.617434
Country 7	0.414261	-0.347831	0.074046
Year 16			
Country 1	-0.819351	-0.449213	-0.782794
Country 2	-0.932992	-0.485663	-0.000997
Country 3	1.711071	1.907389	1.871592
Country 5	-0.073672	0.163192	-0.566753
Country 6	-0.441466	-0.906998	-0.629560
Country 7	0.556410	-0.228708	0.108510
Year 17			
Country 1	-0.934896	-0.473840	-0.756855
Country 2	-0.922971	-0.592610	0.036060
Country 3	1.666024	1.903011	1.885303
Country 5	-0.168641	0.214168	-0.683019
Country 6	-0.230411	-0.881218	-0.607429
Country 7	0.590895	-0.169504	0.125937

this reason, we have combined (with weights) the data of all the conflict variables listed before into one group. The weights are:

Assassinations	25
General Strikes	5
Guerilla Warfare	10
Government Crisis	5
Purges	5
Riots	15
Revolutions	30
Antigovernment Demonstrations	5
TOTAL	100

Since it is not easy to decide the weights from any objective criteria, we selected the weights subjectively, e.g., giving more weight to conflicts which lead to violence and bloodshed. The higher the value of this index, the more intense is the conflict. Besides socio-economic variables, political stability variables (S) listed before also influence the number of conflicts. The following sets of weights are adopted depending upon the existence or non-existence of some stability characteristics.

Number of Coups d'Etat	If No — 0
	If Yes — 30
Number of Major Constitutional Changes	If No — 0
	If Yes — 25
Premier	If No — 20
	If Yes — 0
Effective Executive (Type)	If (1) — 10
	If (2) — 0
	If (3) — 5
	If (4) — 10
Effective Executive (Selection)	If (2) — 0
	If (3) — 5
Degree of Parliamentary Responsibility	If (0) —(10)
	If (1) — 7
	If (2) — (5)
	If (3) — (0)

Total possible score = 100

Since the number of countries is small, to generate a greater degree of freedom, a pooled time series cross-section analysis approach is adopted. For each country, two time periods, namely 1953-55 and 1957-59, are chosen for the conflict variate (Y). The dates for the corresponding factor score (F) are 1950 and 1954 respectively. A three-year lag was adopted to take into consideration the fact that it takes time for the worsening socio-economic condition to have any impact on conflict. It was also chosen due to the availability of data. The corresponding dates for the political stability (S) variate are 1950-54 and 1955-59. This type of overlapping time period was used due to data availability and also because of the fact that lag effect and current political stability variable affect conflict. On the

156

basis of 12 observations for the variate Y (conflict), F_1 (demographic-economic factor), F_2 (communication factor), F_3 (education factor) and S (political stability), a linear regression equation was computed:

$$Y = 2.0974 + 2.1032\ F_1 - 189.9251\ F_2$$
$$(10.6961) \qquad (88.7831) \qquad\qquad (18)$$
$$- 52.1338\ F_3 - 1.2950\ S$$
$$(85.5544) \qquad (.0501)$$
$$R^2 = .5753$$

It is interesting to note from the above equation that both mass communication and education factor scores have negative signs, implying that higher factor scores will lead to lower conflict. The political stability variate also has negative signs. It implies that when we have a more authoritative dictatorial political structure, the incidence of conflict decreases. The sign of F_1 is positive. This apparently inconsistent result can be explained in the following way. As mentioned before, for all the countries in question, the regression analysis, P-factor analysis, and R-factor analysis all emphasized the importance of population. The income variable was weak. So if we have a high factor score (F_1), this means that for that country population is quite important. From the above equation, it follows that the higher the population factor, the higher will be the conflict. The value of the coefficient of determination (R^2) is not too low considering cross-section observations. The standard errors are given in parenthesis under each coefficient. It is interesting to note
that the political stability variable is highly significant.

Thus, from the results presented earlier, we can tentatively conclude that worsening socio-economic conditions do lead to conflict. It does not, of course, follow that improvements in the quality of life will change the situation. This depends upon the country in question, its value system and also on the nature of the conflict. For example, in western societies, although socio-economic conditions have changed considerably, domestic conflict in terms of crime did not decrease. Another important variable not considered is international intervention.

It is true that our conclusion was based on a small sample and limited number of variables. The objective has been to present a prototype structure of analysis. I hope it will be of some value to more comprehensive studies in the future.

C.   Discriminant Analysis

In many conflict analysis problems, two or more groups are involved. Sometimes, the existence of certain values for a number of predetermined variables indicates that the particular scenarios may lead to a bloody confrontation whereas the existence of other values of the variables may not lead to such an event.

Klecka (1980) gives an example of terrorism where the objective is to determine the elements of the situation that would predict the safe release of hostages. Among the variables that might affect the elements are (1) the number of terrorists, (2) the strength of their support from the local population, (3) whether they belong to an independent group or a larger militant group, (4) the tone of their rhetoric, (5) type and quantity of weapons possessed, etc. If we study the previous incidents during which the authorities refused to accede to the demands of the terrorists, we may be interested in determining (1) how useful variables are in predicting the fate of the hostages, (2) how the variables can be combined in equations to predict the likely outcome, and (3) the accuracy of the derived equation. Take another example, namely, the confrontation between Hindus and Moslems in India. We can get information about the incidents when the confrontation led to riots, as opposed to when they did not. We can collect data for such variables as the number of people in both communities, police presence, number of demonstrations, number of provocations, etc. Based on this information, we can use the discriminant function to predict the riot/non-riot situation when we have the information about the types of variables mentioned before.

The discriminant analysis has been used widely in personnel decision, educational testing, spatial variation of economic activities, voting behaviour, auditing, effects of medical treatments, etc. The discriminant function is applicable when there are more than two groups and the discriminating variables are measured at the interval or ratio scale so that the mean, variance and covariances can be computed. Dependent variables (in this case, riots or nonriots) can be a binary 0/1 or 1/2 variable. The independent and the discriminating variables are collected for each case. The case may refer to individual persons, countries, economies at different points in time, or incidents of previous occurrences. Obviously, the groups are defined in such a way that each case belongs to one and one group only. In the case of religious riots, each Hindu-Moslem confrontation, leading to either riot or non-riot, is a case. Discriminant analysis embraces a number of closely related techniques. The function is so formed as to maximize the separation of groups for two uses, namely, analysis and classification.

The analysis or interpretation phase helps us to study how the groups differ, how well they discriminate and what discriminating variables are most powerful. The classification functions following the initial compositions will help to classify new cases, i.e. whether a particular confrontation will result in a riot or non-riot situation. This technique is related to regression analysis and factor analysis and the usual assumptions of independence of the discriminating variables and normality are needed for statistical testing. The application of the method will be clear with the presentation of the following example.

Suppose we have information about $N_1 = 25$ cases where Hindu-Moslem confrontation led to riots and $N_2 = 30$ where such confrontation did not lead to riots.

Let:
                    Y = 1 if there was a riot
                       = 2 when there was no riot
                    X_1 = percentage of Moslem population in the
                          community
                    X_2 = Number of processions
                    X_3 = Number of police per 1000 population
                    X_4 = Number of incidents with outside agitation
                    X_5 = Number of Hindus–Moslems meeting for
                          reconciliation
                    X_6 = Number of times a representation of the
                          central government visits the community

        Other variables can also be introduced. The study can
start with the computation of a regression equation of the
type

$$Y = a + b_1 X_1 + b_2 X_2 + b_3 X_3 + b_4 X_4 + b_5 X_5$$

and the estimated regression coefficients $b_1 \ldots b_5$ will give
the weights each variable has on the riot variable Y.
Obviously the Y variable is a binomial variable with the
observed mean of the first group = 1 and the observed mean of
the second group = 2. The total sums of the square of Y =
$Np(1-p) = 55(25/55)(30/55)$. The estimated means of the two
groups can be obtained from the estimated regression equation
from which the expected Y values of the two groups can be
computed by plugging the value of X's. On the basis of
analysis of variance information, we can test the null
hypothesis
        $H_0: (\mu_1 = \mu_2)$ against $H_1(\mu_1 \neq \mu_2)$.

by using the 't' statistic

$$t = \frac{\overline{Y}_1 - \overline{Y}_2}{S_p \sqrt{\left(\frac{1}{N_1} + \frac{1}{N_2}\right)}}$$

where

$$S_p^{\,2} = \frac{(N_1 - 1)\, S_1^{\,2} + (N_2 - 1)\, S_2^{\,2}}{N_1 + N_2 - 2}$$

        with $d \cdot f = N_1 + N_2 - 2$
        As we mentioned before, in the discriminant function the
variable Y is a nominal variable (binary 0/1 or 1/2, etc.),
whereas the discriminating variables are interval/ratio
variables. If the variable Y is viewed as the dependent
variable, than it is the same as the regression analysis.
When the values of the discriminating variables are dependent
on the groups then we have a multivariate analysis of
variance. The following symbols can be used for this purpose:
        g = number of groups
        p = number of discriminating variables
        n_i = number of cases in group i
        n = total number of cases over all the groups

159

The assumptions of this technique are:

1) two or more groups $g \geq 2$
2) at least two cases per group $n_i \geq 2$
3) $0 < p < n \cdot 2$
4) discriminating variables are measured in interval scale
5) no discriminating variable may be a linear combination of other discriminating variables
6) covariances of the two groups are equal
7) each group is drawn from a multivariate normal distribution on the discriminating variables.

The mathematical theory of "discriminant function" first developed by Fisher (1936) may prove useful in our analysis. Let there be "p" discriminating variables X_1, X_2 ... X_p for each group $i = 1,2$ consisting of n_i cases. The population means for each group can be expressed as vectors

$$\mu_1 = [\mu_{11}, \mu_{12}, \ldots \mu_{1p}]$$
$$\mu_2 = [\mu_{21}, \mu_{22}, \ldots \mu_{2p}] \qquad \text{and}$$

these sample estimates are

$$\overline{X}_1^{\,1} = [\overline{X}_{11}, \overline{X}_{12} \ldots \overline{X}_{1p}]$$
$$\overline{X}_2^{\,1} = [\overline{X}_{21}, \overline{X}_{22} \ldots \overline{X}_{2p}] \qquad \text{and}$$

the grand mean is given by

$$\overline{X}' = [\overline{X}._1, \overline{X}._2 \ldots \overline{X}._p]$$

In terms of the sample estimates the mean values of the discriminating functions of the two groups are:

$$\overline{L}_1 = A_1 \overline{X}_{11} + A_2 \overline{X}_{12} \ldots + A_p \overline{X}_{1p} = A' \overline{X}_1$$
$$\overline{L}_2 = A_1 \overline{X}_{21} + A_2 \overline{X}_{22} \ldots + A_p \overline{X}_{2p} = A' \overline{X}_2$$

With the grand mean

$$\overline{L} = A_1 \overline{X}._1 + A_2 \overline{X}._2 \ldots + A_p \overline{X}._p = A \overline{X}$$

The difference in the mean value is

$$L_1 - L_2 = A'(\overline{X}_1 - \overline{X}_2).$$

$$V(L_1 - L_2) = V(A'\overline{X}_1) + V(A'\overline{X}_2)$$

$$= A' \frac{\Sigma_1 A}{N_1} + A' \frac{\Sigma_2 A}{N_2}$$

where Σ_1 and Σ_2 are variance and covariance matrices of the two populations. Assuming $\Sigma_1 = \Sigma_2 = \Sigma_{xx}$

$$V(L_1 - L_2) = A' \Sigma'_{xx} A(1/N_1 + 1/N_2).$$

XX' is unknown but it can be estimated by

$$MSw_p = \frac{(N_1 - 1)\ S_{1p}^2}{(N_1 - 1)} + \frac{(N_2 - 1)\ S_{2p}^2}{(N_2 - 1)} \quad \text{for diagonal elements}$$

$$MSw_{pp}' = (N_1 - 1)\ r_{1pp}'\ S_{1p}\ S_{1p}'$$

$$+ \frac{(N_2 - 1)\ r_{2pp'}}{(N_1 - 1)} \cdot \frac{S_{2p}\ S_{2p'}}{(N_2 - 1)} \quad \text{for off diagonal elements}$$

MSw_p and MSw_{pp}' are within mean square sums of square.

With these estimates $V(L_1 - L_2)$ can be estimated as

$$SE^2\ (L_1 - L_2) = A'\ (MSw_p)A(1/N_1 + 1/N_2)$$

Under this model, the square of the two sample 't' statistics is

$$t^2 = \frac{(L_1 - L_2)^2}{L_1 - L_2}$$

The objective of the discriminant function is to choose the parameters $A_1, \ldots \ldots A_p$ in such a way that $L_1 - L_2$ is maximum. Fisher showed that maximizing $L_1 - L_2$ is identical to maximizing t^2.

Although there is no unique solution to the problem, all solutions are proportional to the classical solution

$$A = (\Sigma_{xx})^{-1}\ (X_1 - X_2)$$

Depending upon the specific computer program used, the value of the parameters 'A' will be different. However, they will all be proportional. As such, care should be taken for interpretation. The computation scheme for this function is as follows:

I.

Variables	Group 1 Mean	Group 1 S.D.	Group 2 Mean	Group 2 S.D.	Total M.S. MS_T	Within M.S. MS_W	$\bar{X}_1 - \bar{X}_2$
X_1	.	.	.	.	.	.	.
X_2	.	.	.	.	.	.	.
.							
X_p	.	.	.	.	.	.	.

II. Within sample variance–covariance matrix Σ_{xx}

$$
\begin{array}{c|c}
 & X_1 \ldots\ldots\ldots\ldots\ldots\ldots X_p \\
\hline
X_1 & \\
. & \\
. & \\
. & \Sigma_{xx} \\
. & \\
. & \\
X_p & \\
\end{array}
$$

The coefficients $A = (A_1, A_2, \ldots A_p)$ is computed as $\Sigma_{xx}^{-1}\, (\bar{X}_1 - \bar{X}_2)$.

D.   Cluster Analysis

Conflict arises in clusters along with other variables such as poverty, slums, religious bigotry, illiteracy, economic interests, etc. If we can identify the membership of the cluster and the relationship of the numbers to the cluster, then we may get a perspective on how to reduce the potential for conflict. Identification of clusters and the interpretation of the individuals in these clusters can be accomplished with the help of cluster analysis. The cluster can be identified and examined with respect to variables such as population density, gross national product per capita, educational level, food availability per capita, etc. The cluster may be considered in terms of object; for example, if we consider world leaders, we can put them in a cluster on the basis of their properties. This is the same as putting children in a cluster on the basis of their mental abilities. Cluster analysis is an objective, logical way to group together entities on the basis of similarities and differences. When the entities are variables, the process is called cluster analysis of variables or V-analysis. V-analysis is very similar to factor analysis, which we have discussed. In fact, factor analysis is a sub-set of V-analysis where the objective is factoring. "The factors derived from variables by the process of factoring are often interpreted as underlying the observed variables as if they represent genetic or psychological dispositions of persons. The term cluster analysis was chosen to stress the fact that one can discover the general properties of objects by an objective clustering procedure of grouping variables without imparting conservative underlying dynamics to the properties" (Tryon and Bailey, p. 2).

The process of grouping objects (e.g. leaders) that have similar patterns of characteristics is called cluster analysis of objects or simply O-analysis. This is the field of topology or numerical taxonomy. One type of V-analysis is the formation of "rational composites" out of the variables into a priority content category where the variables correlate positively. Such like-patterned groups are called collinear structures. There is a difference between the rational cluster and the collinear cluster. The procedure of determining the number of clusters is the same as factoring. The process determines the amount of variance (commonality) that we want to account for by the reduced number of composites. This is done to make (1) each cluster as tight, i.e. collinear, as possible; (2) as nearly independent of the others as possible; and (3) able to account for as much general variability as possible. In the case of cluster analysis of objects, the analysis is similar. For each object (leader), profiles, or a set of variables, A, B, C ..., is constructed and objects are grouped in a cluster by grouping them in a class where the "Euclidean distance" between the profile sets is minimum.

E.   Content Analysis

In any conflict situation there are voluminous transactions of information between the contesting parties. There are meetings between leaders, utterances, speeches, etc. Sometimes, the intent of the speeches is not the same message that was delivered. The important thing is how the decision makers detect and assign meaning to inputs within the framework of their own environment. For any leader to respond to another, there will be, first of all, the detection of sensory signals. In addition, we must have some code by means of which to interpret the meaning. The codification of events and the interpretation of the meaning of the stimulus can be achieved through the multivariate procedure of content analysis where the objective is the codification of all events, speeches, etc. and the build-up of a correspondence. Based on this correspondence, judgements are made about the intent of a speech or event (Halsti 1968).

The DISCRIM Procedure

Operating systems: All

F.   Computer Programs

ABSTRACT

The DISCRIM procedure computes linear or quadratic discriminant functions for classifying observations into two or more groups on the basis of one or more numeric variables. The discriminant functions can be stored in an output data set for future use.

INTRODUCTION

For a set of observations containing one or more quantitative variables and a classification variable defining groups of observations, PROC DISCRIM develops a discriminant function to classify each observation into one of the groups. The distribution within each group should be approximately multivariate normal.

The discriminant function, also known as a classification criterion, is determined by a measure of generalized squared distance (Rao 1973). The classification criterion can be based on either the individual within-group covariance

164

matrices or the pooled covariance matrix; it also takes into account the prior probabilities of the groups.

Optionally, DISCRIM tests the homogeneity of the within-group covariance matrices. The results of the test determine whether the classification criterion is based on the within-group covariance matrices or the pooled covariance matrix. This test is not robust against non-normality.

The classification criterion can be applied to a second data set during the same execution of DISCRIM. DISCRIM can also store calibration information in a special SAS data set and apply it to other data sets.

Background

DISCRIM develops a discriminant function or classification criterion using a measure of generalized squared distance assuming that each class has a multivariate normal distribution. The classification criterion is based on either the individual within-group covariance matrices or the pooled covariance matrix; it also takes into account the prior probabilities of the groups. Each observation is placed in the class from which it has the smallest generalized squared distance. DISCRIM can also compute the posterior probability of an observation belonging to each class.

The notation below is used to describe the generalized squared distance:

t a subscript to distinguish the groups

S_t the covariance matrix within group t

$|S_t|$ the determinant of S_t

S the pooled covariance matrix

x a vector containing the variables of an observation

m_t the vector containing means of the variables in the group t

q_t the prior probability for group t.

The generalized squared distance from x to group t is

$$D_t^2(x) = g_1(x, t) + g_2(t)$$

where

$$g_1(x, t) = (x - m_t)'S_t^{-1}(x - m_t) + \log_e |S_t|$$

if the within-group covariance matrices are used, or

$$g_1(x, t) = (x - m_t)'S^{-1}(x - m_t)$$

if the pooled covariance matrix is used; and

$$g_2(t) = -2\log_e(q_t)$$

if the prior probabilities are not all equal, or

$$g_2(t) = 0$$

if the prior probabilities are all equal.

The posterior probability of an observation x belonging to group t is

$$p_t(\mathbf{x}) = \frac{\exp(-0.5D_t{}^2(\mathbf{x}))}{\Sigma_u(\exp(-0.5D_u{}^2(\mathbf{x})))}$$

An observation is classified into group u if setting $t=u$ produces the smallest value of $D_t{}^2(\mathbf{x})$ or the largest value of $p_t(\mathbf{x})$.

SPECIFICATIONS

The following statements are used with DISCRIM:

    PROC DISCRIM *options*;
      CLASS *variable*;
      VAR *variables*;
      ID *variable*;
      PRIORS *probabilities*;
      TESTCLASS *variable*;
      TESTID *variable*;
      BY *variables*;

PROC DISCRIM Statement

PROC DISCRIM *options*;

The options below can appear in the PROC DISCRIM statement:

SIMPLE
S

    prints simple descriptive statistics for all variables.

POOL=YES
POOL=NO
POOL=TEST

    determines whether the pooled or within-group covariance matrix is the basis of the measure of generalized squared distance.

    When POOL=YES appears or when the POOL= option is omitted, the measure of generalized squared distance is based on the pooled covariance matrix.

    When you specify POOL=NO, the measure is based on the individual within-group covariance matrices.

    When you specify POOL=TEST, a likelihood ratio test (Morrison 1976; Kendall and Stuart 1961; Anderson 1958) of the homogeneity of the within-group covariance matrices is made and the result is printed. If the test statistic is significant at the level specified by the SLPOOL= option (below), the within-group matrices are used. Otherwise, the pooled covariance matrix is used.

    The discriminant function coefficients are printed only when the pooled covariance matrix is used.

SLPOOL=*n*

    specifies the significance level for the test of homogeneity. SLPOOL= is used only when POOL=TEST is also specified.

    If POOL=TEST appears but SLPOOL= is omitted, .10 is used as the significance level for the test.

WCOV

    prints the within-group covariance matrices.

WCORR

    prints the within-group correlation matrices.

PCOV
> prints the pooled covariance matrix.

PCORR
> prints the partial correlation matrix based on the pooled covariance matrix.

LIST
> prints the classification results for each observation.

LISTERR
> prints only misclassified observations.

THRESHOLD=*n*
> specifies the minimum acceptable posterior probability for classification. If the posterior probability associated with the smallest distance is less than the THRESHOLD value, the observation is classified into group OTHER.

DATA=*SASdataset*
> names the data set to be used by DISCRIM. If DATA= is omitted, DISCRIM uses the last SAS data set created.

NOSUMMARY
> produces a classification summary of the discriminant model unless NOSUMMARY is specified.

OUT=*SASdataset*
> names the output SAS data set. If you want to create a permanent SAS data set with PROC DISCRIM, you must specify a two-level name (see "SAS Files" in the *SAS User's Guide: Basics* for more information on permanent SAS data sets).

TESTDATA=*SASdataset*
> names a second data set whose observations are to be classified. The variable names in this data set must match those in the DATA= data set.
>
> When TESTDATA= is specified, TESTCLASS and TESTID statements can also be used (see below).

TESTLIST
> lists all observations in the TESTDATA= data set.

TESTLISTERR
> lists only misclassified observations in the TESTDATA= data set.

CLASS Statement

> CLASS *variable*;

The classification *variable* values define the groups for analysis. Class levels are determined by the unformatted values of the class variable. The specified variable can be numeric or character. A CLASS statement must accompany the PROC DISCRIM statement.

VAR Statement

> VAR *variables*;

The VAR statement specifies the quantitative variables to be included in the analysis. If you do not use a VAR statement, the analysis includes all numeric variables not listed in other statements.

167

ID Statement

ID *variable*;

The ID statement is effective only when LIST or LISTERR appears in the PROC DISCRIM statement. When DISCRIM prints the classification results, the ID *variable* is printed for each observation, rather than the observation number.

PRIORS Statement

PRIORS *probabilities*;

You need a PRIORS statement whenever you do not want DISCRIM to assume that the prior probabilities are equal.

If you want to set the prior probabilities proportional to the sample sizes, use:

```
PRIORS PROPORTIONAL;
```

The keyword PROPORTIONAL can be abbreviated PROP.

If you want other than equal or proportional priors, give the prior probability you want for each level of the classification variable. Each class level can be written as a numeric constant, a SAS name, or a quoted string, and it must be followed by an equal sign and a numeric constant between zero and one. For example, to define prior probabilities for each level of GRADE, where GRADE's values are A, B, C, and D, you can use the statement:

```
PRIORS A=.1  B=.3  C=.5  D=.1;
```

If GRADE were numeric, with values of 1, 2, and 3, the PRIORS statement can be:

```
PRIORS 1=.3  2=.6  3=.1;
```

The prior probabilities specified should sum to one.

TESTCLASS Statement

TESTCLASS *variable*;

The TESTCLASS statement names the *variable* in the TESTDATA= data set to use in determining whether an observation in the TESTDATA= data set is misclassified. The TESTCLASS variable should have the same type (character or numeric) and length as the variable given in the CLASS statement. DISCRIM considers an observation misclassified when the TESTCLASS variable's value does not match the group into which the TESTDATA= observation is classified.

TESTID Statement

TESTID *variable*:

When the TESTID statement appears and the TESTLIST or TESTLISTERR options also appear, DISCRIM uses the value of the TESTID variable, instead of the observation number, to identify each observation in the classification results for the TESTDATA= data set. The variable given in the TESTID statement must be in the TESTDATA= data set.

BY Statement

BY *variables*:

A BY statement can be used with PROC DISCRIM to obtain separate analyses on observations in groups defined by the BY variables. When a BY statement appears, the procedure expects the DATA= data set to be sorted in order of the BY variables. If your DATA= data set is not sorted in ascending order, use the SORT procedure with a similar BY statement to sort the data, or, if appropriate, use the BY statement options NOTSORTED or DESCENDING. For more information, see the discussion of the BY statement in "Statements Used in the PROC Step" in the *SAS User's Guide: Basics*.

If TESTDATA= is specified and the TESTDATA= data set does not contain any of the BY variables, then the entire TESTDATA= data set is classified according to the discriminant functions computed in each BY group in the DATA= data set.

If the TESTDATA= data set contains some but not all of the BY variables, or if some BY variables do not have the same type or length in the TESTDATA= data set as in the DATA= data set, then DISCRIM prints an error message and stops.

If all the BY variables appear in the TESTDATA= data set with the same type and length as in the DATA= data set, then each BY group in the TESTDATA= data set is classified by the discriminant function from the corresponding BY group in the DATA= data set. The BY groups in the TESTDATA= data set must be in the same order as in the DATA= data set. If NOTSORTED is specified on the BY statement, there must be exactly the same BY groups in the same order in both data sets. If NOTSORTED is not specified, it is permissible for some BY groups to appear in one data set but not in the other.

DETAILS

Missing Values

Observations with missing values for variables in the analysis are excluded from the development of the classification criterion. When the classification variable's values are missing, the observation is excluded from the development of the classification criterion, but if no other variables in the analysis have missing values for that observation, it is classified and printed with the classification results.

Saving and Using Calibration Information

Calibration information developed by DISCRIM can be saved in a SAS data set by specifying OUT= followed by the data set name in the PROC DISCRIM statement. DISCRIM then creates a specially structured SAS data set of TYPE=DISCAL that contains the calibration information.

To use this calibration information to classify observations in another data set:

- give the calibration data set after DATA= in the PROC DISCRIM statement, and
- give the data set to be classified after TESTDATA= in the PROC DISCRIM statement.

Only the TESTLIST, TESTLISTERR, and THRESHOLD options and the TESTCLASS and TESTID statements are effective in this case.

Here is an example:

```
DATA ORIGINAL;
   INPUT POSITION X1 X2;
   CARDS;
   data lines
PROC DISCRIM OUT=INFO;
   CLASS POSITION;
```

```
DATA CHECK;
    INPUT POSITION X1 X2;
    CARDS;
    second set of data lines
PROC DISCRIM DATA=INFO TESTDATA=CHECK TESTLIST;
    TESTCLASS POSITION;
```

The first DATA step creates the SAS data set ORIGINAL, which DISCRIM uses to develop a classification criterion. Specifying OUT=INFO in the PROC DISCRIM statement causes DISCRIM to store the calibration information in a new data set called INFO. The next DATA step creates the data set CHECK. The second PROC DISCRIM specifies DATA=INFO and TESTDATA=CHECK so that the classification criterion developed earlier is applied to the CHECK data set.

Machine Resources

Core requirements In the following discussion, let n equal the number of observations, c equal the number of class levels, and v equal the number of variables. If POOL=YES, DISCRIM needs core for one covariance matrix. If POOL=NO, DISCRIM needs core for one covariance matrix for each class plus the pooled covariance matrix. Each covariance matrix requires $4v(v + 1)$ bytes. Additional array storage is about $48v + 124c + 4c^2 + 2cv$ bytes.

Time requirements There are three stages in the time requirements of discriminant analysis.

1. Time needed for reading the data and computing covariance matrices is proportional to nv^2. DISCRIM must also look up each class level in the list; the time for this is proportional to c (this is faster if the data are sorted by the CLASS variable). Time for this step is proportional to a value ranging from n to nc.
2. Time for inverting covariance matrices is proportional to v^3 for each covariance matrix.
3. Time for classifying observations is proportional to ncv.

Each stage has a different constant of proportionality.

Printed Output

The printed output from PROC DISCRIM includes:

1. values of the classification variable, FREQUENCY (frequencies), and the PRIOR PROBABILITIES for each group.
2. optionally, SIMPLE descriptive STATISTICS including N (the number of observations), SUM, MEAN, VARIANCE, and STANDARD DEVIATION for each group.
3. optionally, the WITHIN COVARIANCE MATRICES, S_t for each group.
4. optionally, WITHIN CORRELATION COEFFICIENTS (the within-group correlation matrix for each group) and PROB>|R| to test the hypothesis that the population correlation coefficients are zero.
5. optionally, the POOLED COVARIANCE MATRIX, S.
6. optionally, PARTIAL CORRELATION COEFFICIENTS COMPUTED FROM POOLED COVARIANCE MATRIX (the partial correlation matrix based on the pooled covariance matrix) and PROB>|R| to test the hypothesis that the population correlation coefficients are zero.
7. WITHIN COVARIANCE MATRIX INFORMATION including COVARIANCE MATRIX RANK and NATURAL LOG OF DETERMINANT

OF THE COVARIANCE MATRIX for each group (the rank of S_t and $\log_e |S_t|$) and pooled (the rank of S and $\log_e |S|$).

8. optionally, TEST OF HOMOGENEITY OF WITHIN COVARIANCE MATRICES (the results of a chi-square test of homogeneity of the within-group covariance matrices) (Morrison 1976; Kendall and Stuart 1961; Anderson 1958).

9. the PAIRWISE SQUARED GENERALIZED DISTANCES BETWEEN GROUPS.

10. if the pooled covariance matrix is used, the LINEAR DISCRIMINANT FUNCTION

11. optionally, the CLASSIFICATION RESULTS FOR CALIBRATION DATA including OBS, the observation number (if an ID statement is included, the values of the identification variable are printed instead of the observation number), the actual group for the observation, the group into which the developed criterion would classify it, and the POSTERIOR PROBABILITY of its MEMBERSHIP in each group.

12. a CLASSIFICATION SUMMARY FOR CALIBRATION DATA, summary of the performance of the classification criterion.

EXAMPLES

Iris Data: Example 1

The iris data published by Fisher (1936) have been widely used for examples in discriminant analysis and cluster analysis. The sepal length, sepal width, petal length, and petal width were measured in millimeters on fifty iris specimens from each of three species, Iris setosa, I. versicolor, and I. virginica. DISCRIM is used to classify the irises using a quadratic classification function.

```
DATA IRIS;
    TITLE 'FISHER (1936) IRIS DATA';
    INPUT SEPALLEN SEPALWID PETALLEN PETALWID SPEC_NO aa;
    IF SPEC_NO=1 THEN SPECIES='SETOSA    ';
    IF SPEC_NO=2 THEN SPECIES='VERSICOLOR';
    IF SPEC_NO=3 THEN SPECIES='VIRGINICA ';
    DROP SPEC_NO;
    LABEL SEPALLEN=SEPAL LENGTH IN MM.
          SEPALWID=SEPAL WIDTH  IN MM.
          PETALLEN=PETAL LENGTH IN MM.
          PETALWID=PETAL WIDTH  IN MM.;
    CARDS;
50 33 14 02 1 64 28 56 22 3 65 28 46 15 2
67 31 56 24 3 63 28 51 15 3 46 34 14 03 1
69 31 51 23 3 62 22 45 15 2 59 32 48 18 2
46 36 10 02 1 61 30 46 14 2 60 27 51 16 2
65 30 52 20 3 56 25 39 11 2 65 30 55 18 3
58 27 51 19 3 68 32 59 23 3 51 33 17 05 1
57 28 45 13 2 62 34 54 23 3 77 38 67 22 3
63 33 47 16 2 67 33 57 25 3 76 30 66 21 3
49 25 45 17 3 55 35 13 02 1 67 30 52 23 3
70 32 47 14 2 64 32 45 15 2 61 28 40 13 2
48 31 16 02 1 59 30 51 18 3 55 24 38 11 2
63 25 50 19 3 64 32 53 23 3 52 34 14 02 1
49 36 14 01 1 54 30 45 15 2 79 38 64 20 3
44 32 13 02 1 67 33 57 21 3 50 35 16 06 1
58 26 40 12 2 44 30 13 02 1 77 28 67 20 3
63 27 49 18 3 47 32 16 02 1 55 26 44 12 2
50 23 33 10 2 72 32 60 18 3 48 30 14 03 1
51 38 16 02 1 61 30 49 18 3 48 34 19 02 1
```

171

The CLUSTER Procedure

Operating systems: All

ABSTRACT

The CLUSTER procedure hierarchically clusters the observations in a SAS data set using one of eleven methods. The data can be numeric coordinates or distances. CLUSTER creates an output data set from which the TREE procedure can draw a tree diagram or output clusters at a specified level of the tree.

INTRODUCTION

The CLUSTER procedure finds hierarchical clusters of the observations in a SAS data set. The data can be coordinates or distances. If the data are coordinates, CLUSTER computes (possibly squared) Euclidean distances. The clustering methods available are average linkage, the centroid method, complete linkage, density linkage (including Wong's hybrid and kth-nearest-neighbor methods), maximum-likelihood for mixtures of spherical multivariate normal distributions with equal variances but possibly unequal mixing proportions, the flexible-beta method, McQuitty's similarity analysis, the median method, single linkage, two-stage density linkage, and Ward's minimum variance method.

All methods are based on the usual agglomerative hierarchical clustering procedure. Each observation begins in a cluster by itself. The two closest clusters are merged to form a new cluster replacing the two old clusters. Merging of the two closest clusters is repeated until only one cluster is left. The various clustering methods differ in how the distance between two clusters is computed. Each method is described below in **Clustering Methods**.

CLUSTER prints a history of the clustering process, giving statistics useful for estimating the number of clusters in the population from which the data were sampled. CLUSTER also creates an output data set that can be used by the TREE procedure to draw a tree diagram of the cluster hierarchy or to output a partition at any desired level.

Agglomerative hierarchical clustering is discussed in all standard references on cluster analysis, for example, Anderberg (1973), Sneath and Sokal (1973), Hartigan (1975), Everitt (1980), and Spath (1980). An especially good introduction is given by Massart and Kaufman (1983). Anyone considering doing a hierarchical cluster analysis should study the Monte Carlo results of Milligan (1980), Milligan and Cooper (1983), and Cooper and Milligan (1984). Other essential, though more advanced, references on hierarchical clustering include Hartigan (1977, 60-68; 1981), Wong (1982), Wong and Schaak (1982), and Wong and Lane (1983). See Blashfield and Aldenderfer (1978) for a discussion of the confusing terminology in hierarchical cluster analysis.

SPECIFICATIONS

Use the following statements to invoke the CLUSTER procedure:

PROC CLUSTER *options*;
  VAR *variables*;
  ID *variables*;
  COPY *variables*;
  FREQ *variable*;
  RMSSTD *variable*;
  BY *variables*;

Usually, only the VAR statement is needed in addition to the PROC CLUSTER statement.

PROC CLUSTER Statement

PROC CLUSTER *options*:

33. (NORMALIZED) MCQUITTY'S SIMILARITY or MCQ, the distance between the two clusters based on McQuitty's similarity method.

If METHOD=SINGLE, CLUSTER prints:

34. (NORMALIZED) MINIMUM DISTANCE or MIN DIST, the minimum distance between the two clusters.

If you specify the NONORM option along with METHOD=WARD, CLUSTER prints:

35. BETWEEN_CLUSTER SUM OF SQUARES or BSS, the ANOVA sum of squares between the two clusters joined.

If METHOD=TWOSTAGE or DENSITY, CLUSTER prints:

36. the number of MODAL CLUSTERS.

EXAMPLES

Cluster Analysis of Flying Mileages between Ten American Cities: Example 1

The first example clusters ten American cities based on the flying mileages between them. Six clustering methods are shown with corresponding tree diagrams produced by the TREE procedure. The EML method cannot be used because it requires coordinate data. The other omitted methods produce the same clusters, although not the same distances between clusters, as one of the illustrated methods: complete linkage and the flexible-beta method yield the same clusters as Ward's method, McQuitty's similarity analysis produces the same clusters as average linkage, and the median method corresponds to the centroid method.

All of the methods suggest a division of the cities into two clusters along the east-west dimension. There is disagreement, however, about which cluster Denver should belong to. Some of the methods indicate a possible third cluster containing Denver and Houston.

```
TITLE 'CLUSTER ANALYSIS OF FLYING MILEAGES BETWEEN 10 AMERICAN CITIES';

DATA   MILEAGES(TYPE=DISTANCE);
   INPUT  (ATLANTA CHICAGO DENVER HOUSTON LOSANGEL
           MIAMI NEWYORK SANFRAN SEATTLE WASHDC) (5.)
           @56 CITY $15.;
   CARDS;
   0                                              ATLANTA
  587    0                                        CHICAGO
 1212  920    0                                   DENVER
  701  940  879    0                              HOUSTON
 1936 1745  831 1374    0                         LOS ANGELES
  604 1188 1726  968 2339    0                    MIAMI
  748  713 1631 1420 2451 1092    0               NEW YORK
 2139 1858  949 1645  347 2594 2571    0          SAN FRANCISCO
 2182 1737 1021 1891  959 2734 2408  678    0     SEATTLE
  543  597 1494 1220 2300  923  205 2442 2329    0  WASHINGTON
                                                    D.C.
```

174

```
PROC CLUSTER DATA=MILEAGES METHOD=AVERAGE PSEUDO;
   ID CITY;
PROC TREE;

PROC CLUSTER DATA=MILEAGES METHOD=CENTROID PSEUDO;
   ID CITY;
PROC TREE;
PROC CLUSTER DATA=MILEAGES METHOD=DENSITY K=3;
   ID CITY;
PROC TREE;

PROC CLUSTER DATA=MILEAGES METHOD=SINGLE;
   ID CITY;
PROC TREE;

PROC CLUSTER DATA=MILEAGES METHOD=TWOSTAGE K=3;
   ID CITY;
PROC TREE;

PROC CLUSTER DATA=MILEAGES METHOD=WARD PSEUDO;
   ID CITY;
PROC TREE;
```

Principal component analysis, unlike common factor analysis, has none of the above problems if the covariance or correlation matrix is computed correctly from a data set with no missing values. Various methods for missing value correlation may produce negative eigenvalues in principal components, as may severe rounding of the correlations.

Computer Resources

Let:

n = number of observations
v = number of variables
f = number of factors
i = number of iterations during factor extraction
r = number of iterations during factor rotation.

The overall time for a factor analysis is very roughly proportional to iv^3.

The time required to compute the correlation matrix is roughly proportional to nv^2.

The time required for PRIORS=SMC or ASMC is roughly proportional to v^3.
The time required for PRIORS=MAX is roughly proportional to v^2.

The time required to compute eigenvalues is roughly proportional to v^3.

The time required to compute final eigenvectors is roughly proportional to fv^2.

Each iteration in METHOD=PRINIT or ALPHA requires computation of eigenvalues and f eigenvectors.

Each iteration in METHOD=ML or ULS requires computation of eigenvalues and $v - i$ eigenvectors.

The time required for ROTATE=VARIMAX, QUARTIMAX, EQUAMAX, ORTHOMAX, PROMAX, or HK is roughly proportional to rvf^2.

ROTATE=PROCRUSTES takes time roughly proportional to vf^2.

Printed Output

FACTOR's output includes:

1. MEAN and STD DEV (standard deviation) of each variable and the number of OBSERVATIONS if SIMPLE is specified
2. CORRELATIONS if CORR is specified
3. INVERSE CORRELATION MATRIX if ALL is specified
4. PARTIAL CORRELATIONS CONTROLLING ALL OTHER VARIABLES

(negative anti-image correlations) if MSA is specified. If the data are appropriate for the common factor model, the partial correlations should be small.

5. KAISER'S MEASURE OF SAMPLING ADEQUACY (Kaiser 1970; Kaiser and Rice 1974; Cerny and Kaiser 1977) if MSA is specified, both OVER-ALL and for each variable. The MSA is a summary of how small the partial correlations are relative to the ordinary correlations. Values greater than .8 can be considered good. Values less than .5 require remedial action, either by deleting the offending variables or including other variables related to the offenders.

6. PRIOR COMMUNALITY ESTIMATES, unless 1.0s are used or METHOD=IMAGE, HARRIS, PATTERN, or SCORE

7. SQUARED MULTIPLE CORRELATIONS of each variable with all the other variables if METHOD=IMAGE or HARRIS

8. IMAGE COEFFICIENTS if METHOD=IMAGE

9. IMAGE COVARIANCE MATRIX if METHOD=IMAGE

10. PRELIMINARY EIGENVALUES based on the prior communalities if METHOD=PRINIT, ALPHA, ML, or ULS, including the TOTAL and the AVERAGE of the eigenvalues, the DIFFERENCE between successive eigenvalues, the PROPORTION of variation represented, and the CUMULATIVE proportion of variation

11. the number of FACTORS that WILL BE RETAINED unless METHOD=PATTERN or SCORE

12. A SCREE PLOT OF EIGENVALUES if SCREE is specified. The preliminary eigenvalues are used if METHOD=PRINIT, ALPHA, ML, or ULS.

13. the iteration history if METHOD=PRINIT, ALPHA, ML, or ULS, containing the iteration number (ITER); the CRITERION being optimized (Joreskog 1977) and the RIDGE value for the iteration if METHOD=ML or ULS; the maximum CHANGE in any communality estimate; and the COMMUNALITIES

14. SIGNIFICANCE TESTS if METHOD=ML, including CHI-SQUARED, DF, and PROB>CHI**2 for H0: NO COMMON FACTORS and H0: the factors retained ARE SUFFICIENT to explain the correlations. The variables should have an approximate multivariate normal distribution for the probability levels to be valid. Lawley and Maxwell (1921) suggest that the number of observations should exceed the number of variables by 50 or more although Geweke and Singleton (1980) claim that as few as ten observations are adequate with five variables and one common factor. Certain regularity conditions must also be satisfied for the χ^2 test to be valid (Geweke and Singleton 1980), but in practice these conditions usually are satisfied. The notation PROB>CHI**2 means "the probability under the null hypothesis of obtaining a greater χ^2 statistic than that observed."

15. AKAIKE'S INFORMATION CRITERION if METHOD=ML. Akaike's information criterion (AIC) (Akaike 1973; Akaike 1974) is a general criterion for estimating the best number of parameters to include in a model when maximum-likelihood estimation is used. The number of factors that yields the smallest value of AIC is considered best. AIC, like the chi-square test, tends to include factors that are statistically significant but inconsequential for practical purposes.

16. SCHWARZ'S BAYESIAN CRITERION if METHOD=ML. Schwarz's Bayesian criterion (SBC) (Schwarz 1978) is another criterion, similar to AIC, for determining the best number of parameters. The number of factors that yields the smallest value of SBC is considered best. SBC

seems to be less inclined to include trivial factors than either AIC or the chi-square test.

17. SQUARED CANONICAL CORRELATIONS if METHOD=ML. These are the same as the squared multiple correlations for predicting each factor from the variables.
18. COEFFICIENT ALPHA FOR EACH FACTOR if METHOD=ALPHA
19. EIGENVECTORS if EIGENVECTORS or ALL is specified, unless METHOD=PATTERN or SCORE
20. EIGENVALUES OF THE (WEIGHTED) (REDUCED) (IMAGE) CORRELATION or COVARIANCE MATRIX, unless METHOD=PATTERN or SCORE. Included are the TOTAL and the AVERAGE of the eigenvalues, the DIFFERENCE between successive eigenvalues, the PROPORTION of variation represented, and the CUMULATIVE proportion of variation.
21. the FACTOR PATTERN, which is equal to both the matrix of standardized regression coefficients for predicting variables from common factors and the matrix of correlations between variables and common factors, since the extracted factors are uncorrelated
22. VARIANCE EXPLAINED BY EACH FACTOR, both WEIGHTED and UNWEIGHTED if variable weights are used.
23. FINAL COMMUNALITY ESTIMATES, including the TOTAL communality; or FINAL COMMUNALITY ESTIMATES AND VARIABLE WEIGHTS, including the TOTAL communality, both WEIGHTED and UNWEIGHTED, if variable weights are used. Final communality estimates are the squared multiple correlations for predicting the variables from the estimated factors and can be obtained by taking the sum of squares of each row of the factor pattern, or a weighted sum of squares if variable weights are used.
24. RESIDUAL CORRELATIONS WITH UNIQUENESS ON THE DIAGONAL if RESIDUAL or ALL is specified
25. ROOT-MEAN-SQUARE OFF-DIAGONAL RESIDUALS, both OVER-ALL and for each variable, if RESIDUAL or ALL is specified
26. PARTIAL CORRELATIONS CONTROLLING FACTORS if RESIDUAL or ALL is specified
27. ROOT-MEAN-SQUARE OFF-DIAGONAL PARTIALS, both OVER-ALL and for each variable, if RESIDUAL or ALL is specified
28. a PLOT OF the FACTOR PATTERN for unrotated factors if PREPLOT is specified; the number of plots is determined by NPLOT=
29. VARIABLE WEIGHTS FOR ROTATION if NORM=WEIGHT is specified
30. FACTOR WEIGHTS FOR ROTATION if HKPOWER= is specified
31. ORTHOGONAL TRANSFORMATION MATRIX if an orthogonal rotation is requested
32. ROTATED FACTOR PATTERN if an orthogonal rotation is requested
33. VARIANCE EXPLAINED BY EACH FACTOR after rotation. If an orthogonal rotation is requested and if variable weights are used, both weighted and unweighted values are given.
34. TARGET MATRIX FOR PROCRUSTEAN TRANSFORMATION if ROTATE=PROCRUSTES or PROMAX
35. the PROCRUSTEAN TRANSFORMATION MATRIX if ROTATE=PROCRUSTES or PROMAX
36. the (NORMALIZED) OBLIQUE TRANSFORMATION MATRIX if an oblique rotation is requested, which for ROTATE=PROMAX is the product of the prerotation and the Procrustean rotation
37. INTER-FACTOR CORRELATIONS if an oblique rotation is requested
38. ROTATED FACTOR PATTERN (STD REG COEFS) if an oblique rotation is

requested. giving standardized regression coefficients for predicting the variables from the factors

39. REFERENCE AXIS CORRELATIONS if an oblique rotation is requested. These are the partial correlations between the primary factors when all factors other than the two being correlated are partialled out.

40. the REFERENCE STRUCTURE (SEMIPARTIAL CORRELATIONS) if an oblique rotation is requested. The reference structure is the matrix of semipartial correlations (Kerlinger and Pedhazur 1973) between variables and common factors, removing from each common factor the effects of other common factors. If the common factors are uncorrelated, the reference structure is equal to the factor pattern.

41. VARIANCE EXPLAINED BY EACH FACTOR ELIMINATING the effects of all OTHER FACTORS if an oblique rotation is requested. Both WEIGHTED and UNWEIGHTED values are given if variable weights are used. These variances are equal to the (weighted) sum of the squared elements of the reference structure corresponding to each factor.

42. FACTOR STRUCTURE (CORRELATIONS) if an oblique rotation is requested. The (primary) factor structure is the matrix of correlations between variables and common factors. If the common factors are uncorrelated, the factor structure is equal to the factor pattern.

43. VARIANCE EXPLAINED BY EACH FACTOR IGNORING the effects of all OTHER FACTORS if an oblique rotation is requested. Both WEIGHTED and UNWEIGHTED values are given if variable weights are used. These variances are equal to the (weighted) sum of the squared elements of the factor structure corresponding to each factor.

44. FINAL COMMUNALITY ESTIMATES for the rotated factors if ROTATE= is specified. The estimates should equal the unrotated communalities.

45. SQUARED MULTIPLE CORRELATIONS OF THE VARIABLES WITH EACH FACTOR if SCORE or ALL is specified, except for unrotated principal components

46. STANDARDIZED SCORING COEFFICIENTS if SCORE or ALL is specified

47. PLOTs OF the FACTOR PATTERN for rotated factors if PLOT is specified and an orthogonal rotation is requested. The number of plots is determined by NPLOT=

48. PLOTs OF the REFERENCE STRUCTURE for rotated factors if PLOT is specified and an oblique rotation is requested. The number of plots is determined by NPLOT=. Included are the REFERENCE AXIS CORRELATION and the ANGLE between the reference axes for each pair of factors plotted.

If ROTATE=PROMAX is used, the output includes results for both the prerotation and the Procrustean rotation.

EXAMPLES

Principal Component Analysis: Example 1

The data in the example below are five socio-economic variables for twelve census tracts in the Los Angeles Standard Metropolitan Statistical Area as given by Harman (1976).

The first analysis is a principal component analysis. Simple descriptive statistics and correlations are also printed.

```
DATA SOCECON;
    TITLE 'FIVE SOCIO-ECONOMIC VARIABLES';
```

INPUT POP SCHOOL EMPLOY SERVICES HOUSE;
CARDS;

5700	12.8	2500	270	25000
1000	10.9	600	10	10000
3400	8.8	1000	10	9000
3800	13.6	1700	140	25000
4000	12.8	1600	140	25000
8200	8.3	2600	60	12000
1200	11.4	400	10	16000
3100	11.5	3300	60	14000
9900	12.5	3400	180	18000
3600	13.7	3600	390	25000
9600	9.6	3300	80	12000
3400	11.4	4000	100	13000

;

PROC FACTOR DATA=SOCECON SIMPLE CORR;
TITLE3 'PRINCIPAL COMPONENT ANALYSIS';

There are two large eigenvalues, 2.873314 and 1.796660, which together account for 93.4% of the standardized variance. Thus the first two principal components provide an adequate summary of the data for most purposes. Three components, explaining 97.7% of the variation, should be sufficient for almost any application. FACTOR retains two components on the basis of the eigenvalues-greater-than-one rule since the third eigenvalue is only 0.214837.

The first component has large positive loadings for all five variables. The correlation with SERVICES (0.93239) is especially high. The second component is a contrast of POP (0.80642) and EMPLOY (0.72605) against SCHOOL (−0.54476) and HOUSE (−0.55818), with a very small loading on SERVICES (−0.10431).

The final communality estimates show that all the variables are well accounted for by two components, with final communality estimates ranging from 0.880236 for SERVICES to 0.987826 for POP.

Output 17.1 Principal Component Analysis: PROC FACTOR

Principal Factor Analysis: Example 2

The next example is a principal factor analysis using squared multiple correlations for the prior communality estimates (PRIORS=SMC). Kaiser's measure of sampling adequacy (MSA) is requested. A SCREE plot of the eigenvalues is printed. The RESIDUAL correlations and partial correlations are computed. The PREPLOT option plots the unrotated factor pattern.

Specifying ROTATE=PROMAX produces an orthogonal varimax prerotation followed by an oblique rotation. The REORDER option reorders the variables according to their largest factor loadings. The SCORE option requests scoring coefficients. The PLOT procedure produces a plot of the reference structure.

An OUTSTAT= data set is created by FACTOR and printed.

```
PROC FACTOR DATA=SOCECON PRIORS=SMC MSA SCREE RESIDUAL PREPLOT
            ROTATE=PROMAX REORDER PLOT
            OUTSTAT=FACT_ALL;
   TITLE3 'PRINCIPAL FACTOR ANALYSIS WITH PROMAX ROTATION';

PROC PRINT;
   TITLE3 'FACTOR OUTPUT DATA SET';
```

If the data are appropriate for the common factor model, the partial correlations controlling the other variables should be small compared to the original correlations. The partial correlation between SCHOOL and HOUSE, for example, is .64, slightly less than the original correlation of .86. The partial correlation between POP and SCHOOL is −.54, which is much larger than the original correlation and an indication of trouble. Kaiser's MSA is a summary, for each variable and for all variables together, of how much smaller the partial correlations are than the original correlations. Values of .8 or .9 are considered good while MSAs below .5 are unacceptable. POP, SCHOOL, and EMPLOY have very poor MSAs. Only SERVICES has a good MSA. The overall MSA of .57 is sufficiently poor that additional variables should be included in the analysis to better define the common

181

5 Econometric Models and Rational Expectations

A.   Econometric Models

A number of techniques are presently available for regional forecasting. The first may be termed the regional history approach. In this approach, we look into the economic, social and political history of a region and identify the general pattern of its responses in the past when faced with new forces of change. If exogenous changes in the future can be foreseen, then the region's responses can be predicted on the basis of past experience. It is true that this method is quite subjective and qualitative; but such a historical study, together with a quantitative analysis, can lead to more valid conclusions than will either method alone.

A more quantitative form of the historical study may be termed the "regional economic development approach". This method emphasizes such concepts as capital-output ratio, savings-income ratio, population growth, resource and factor availability, levels of investment, allocation of resources, productivity changes, and other economic and demographic indexes pertaining to the economic development of a region. Mathematical formulations involving these indexes can be developed, and conditions for an optimum growth path can be determined (Chakroborty, 1959). Such models appear more and more often in the literature, but most of them exist on the national level. There are few attempts to develop what can be termed regional and interregional growth models. The best of such models is that of Rahman; Sakashita's (1967) effort in this respect should also be mentioned. If such a regional and interregional growth theory can be developed, it can be integrated with the input-output analysis discussed in the next chapter. This will be a major contribution to regional science theory. Without this integration and synthesis, such growth models will remain theories rather than tools of developmental planning, despite their mathematical elegance and sophistication.

Another potentially significant avenue of research in which there has been little work is the regional econometric model. An econometric model tries to relate several variables of an economy, such as GNP, consumption, investment, export and import, by means of a system of regression equations. The variables are classified into two types: endogenous and exogenous. An endogenous variable is one that, if changed, can affect the whole system and that in turn is affected itself. For example, consumption is an endogenous variable that can affect GNP and other variables in an economic system and then can in turn be itself affected. On the other hand, the exogenous variable can affect the system without itself being affected; an example is the investment variable.

An example of a simple macroeconomic model can be given as follows: Endogenous variables (all in real terms)

1.	Consumption	C
2.	Gross private domestic investment	I
3.	Disposable personal income	Y
4.	Business gross product	X_b
5.	Labor income in business	W_b
6.	Property income	P
7.	Corporate saving	S_c

The exogenous variables (in real terms)

1.	Government purchases	G
2.	Government wage bill	W_g
3.	Personal taxes	T_p
4.	Business taxes	T_b
5.	Depreciation	D

The static model is:
1. Consumption: $C = \alpha Y + \beta$
   Consumption depends on personal income investment.
2. Investment: $I = \delta X_b + \epsilon$
   Investment depends on business gross product.
3. Labor: $W_b = \gamma X_b + n$
   Labor income depends on the business gross product.
4. Corporate saving: $S_b = \theta P + \lambda$
   Corporate savings depends on property income since property income corporate profit corporate saving.
5. GNP = expenditure: $X_b + W_g = C + I + G$
6. GNP = income: $X + W_g = Y + T_p + S_c + T_b + D$

7. Income distribution: $P + W_b + W_g = Y + T_p + S_c$
   Property income is defined as residual.
   Slopes: $(\alpha, \beta, \gamma, \theta)$ have positive signs and < 1

There are seven endogenous variables and seven equations.

If we start with a system of linear equation interrelating all the endogenous, exogenous, and lagged variables, we can, in general, solve for each of the endogenous variables in terms of predetermined (exogenous and lagged endogenous) variables alone. This form of equation is known as a reduced-form equation. For example, the reduced-form equation of X_b:

$$X_b = (\overset{b}{g} - W_g) + \alpha W_g - \alpha t_p - \delta(1 - \theta)(T_b + D) + U,$$

where $\qquad M = 1 - \delta - a[1 - \theta(1 - \gamma)].$
$\qquad\qquad U = \beta + \epsilon - \alpha\gamma + \alpha\theta$.

For real GNP the reduced-form equation is
$$X_b + W_g = (g - W_g) + (\alpha + \delta)W_g - \alpha t_p - \alpha(1 - \theta)(t_b + d) + U,$$

where M is a positive multiplier.

Although the regression relationships are formulated on the basis of macroeconomic theory, the "usual procedure is to develop an aggregative model from a more global and less closely reasoned argument" (Klein, 1965). The coefficients of the regression equations are estimated from time-series data, using such models as single-stage least square, two-stage least square, limited information, and maximum likelihood methods. In recent years national econometric models have been increasingly available since the publication of the Klein-Goldberger model (1955). There also are econometric models in the field of regional science. The work of Maki and Tu (1962) cannot be termed an econometric model, although their growth model for rural areas development is an important contribution to regional science. It is identical to a national model except that a smaller area has been substituted for a nation. The same is true for Niedercorn and Kain's model, which is "used first in an attempt to describe the structure of metropolitan development, and later is used to evaluate changes in spatial structure of large urban complexes" (Niedercorn and Kain, 1963). This model is definitely an outstanding contribution to the field of urban complex analysis; but, as mentioned before, this model has few spatial characteristics. The article by Ichimura (1966) is a significant contribution in this field; for more recent work, see Glickman (1978) and Brown et al. (1978).

Some Examples of Regional Econometric Modelling

A regional growth model, unlike a national model, should take into account sociological and political variables such as age structure, sex ratios, migration characteristics and political opinions, since these are very important factors on the regional level. The model can be made an intraregional one that will predict economic activity in subareas of a region as well. Generally, areas within a region (for example, the towns in Calcutta's metropolitan region) are not uniform with respect to economic and other activities. Some areas are so-called bedroom communities in which people live but do not work; others are industrial areas specializing in certain industries; still others are business districts, and so on. Some subareas contain a concentration of people whose demographic, cultural and political outlook may be quite different from that of those in nearby areas. The central city influences these subareas with varying degrees of intensity through different types of transportation, and social and political interactions. In short, a dichotomy is suggested, with the central city and the rest of the metropolitan district as distinct units. Then an intraregional model may be constructed, taking into consideration the influence of the central city on meaningful subareas in the metropolitan districts. This model can be used for projection purposes for these subareas, for the central city, and, consequently, for the whole region.

This model will take into account the fact that growth in any area depends on the location of that area with respect to the central city, the type of people living in that area, the type of activities pursued, the history of development of that area, and many other characteristics that depend on the distance of the subarea from the centre city. Again, most growth models are based on either time-series or cross-section data. There have been few efforts to combine the two to obtain more reliable estimates, although this can be done with little trouble. For example, in the case of the central city (e.g. Calcutta) a time-series procedure can be used, whereas the cross-sectional data (for this case, of towns) may be used to estimate the growth of the subareas. Then they can be combined to obtain better estimates for the region as a whole. This will avoid difficulty caused by the absence of data about the subareas on a time-series basis.

Some models I will use as illustrations of my premise are:

1. Industrial region (Calcutta) in a developing country (India).
2. Highly urbanized (Philadelphia) area in a developed country (United States).
3. Depressed area (Nova Scotia) in a developed country (Nova Scotia).
4. Agricultural region (North Atlantic Region) in a developed country (North Atlantic region, United States).
5. Econometric models for disarmament.
6. Global modelling of food, energy and conflict.

1. Industrial Region in a Developing Country: Calcutta Industrial Region

The greatest difficult in constructing regional econometric models is the unavailability of data. In the case of the United States, even if we were to take the states (or a combination of states) or the standard metropolitan statistical areas (SMSAs) as the areal units, data regarding income, consumption or investment are difficult to obtain for a time series of years. Until adequate data is available, research must be limited to partial studies. Instead of studying the whole economy, for example, we can focus on the one most important industry or all the manufacturing industries for which reliable data is usually available on a time-series basis. This method will be particularly useful in studying industrial regions in an underdeveloped country. Many such countries have a few basic manufacturing industries that account for a considerable proportion of the total economic activity of a region. Other activities are closely linked to these industries. If a satisfactory model can be constructed for these major sectors, then the projection for the total economy can be made by means of base theory or other more refined techniques.

The Calcutta Industrial Region (CIR) includes Calcutta City and 34 adjoining urban centres. It covers a major portion of the Calcutta Metropolitan District as defined by the Calcutta Metropolitan Planning organization. The towns lie on both sides of the Hooghly River. Administratively, 22 towns belong to the district of 24-Paraganas, all lying to the east of the Hooghly. Eleven towns belong to the district of Hooghly and two to the district of Howrah; all 13 of these towns are on the western side of the Hooghly River. Most of the towns grew with the development of the jute industry in this region. The CIR covers an area of 164 square miles and had a population of nearly 15 million in 1991.

Starting primarily as a jute-manufacturing region, the CIR was until recently one of the leading centres of business and economic activity in India. Since India gained independence in 1947, however, its importance has declined, although it still holds a leading position in the country in terms of international trade, bank deposits, corporate headquarters and the like.

The region, however, once a prosperous centre of economic activity, now faces serious problems. After the partition of India, millions of refugees poured into this congested region, which already suffered from various other problems. With its chronic unemployment and refugee problems, this region has become a nightmare for the troubled state of West Bengal. One Calcutta household in every four has one or more unemployed persons: at least 20% of the labour force is unemployed. Paradoxically, unemployment is severe among the educated. Nearly 8% of the illiterate labour force is unemployed (illiterates constitute a significant percentage of the CIR labour force). A large percentage of both high school and college graduates belonging to the labour force are unemployed. Perhaps even more serious are the environmental conditions, notably poor housing and inadequate transportation. Finally, it is noteworthy that single individuals form more than one-half of all households.

For determining the economic development of such a depressed region, regional econometric models can be effectively used. However, the data requirement precludes the development of such a comprehensive model. Alternatively, we can construct a partial model of a dominant industry (in this case, the jute industry) and project the global economic condition on the basis of the prospects of this industry.

Jute is a soft fibre derived from the leaves of jute plants. It can replace hard fibres in more uses than any other soft fibre. The principal use of jute is in manufacturing the fabrics from which jute bags, used for packaging, are made. Jute fabric is also a component of many other industrial and commercial products.

Jute is grown in only a small portion of the world, in four Indian states (West Bengal, Bihar, Orissa and Assam) and

186

Bangladesh. Before World War II, Bengal accounted for 2.25 million acres out of a world total of 2.70 million acres of jute. Most of this territory was in East Bengal, which is now part of Bangladesh. Ironically, almost all the jute mills in undivided India were in the CIR. Therefore, after the partitioning of the country, India was left with the jute mills in the CIR without any supply of raw jute; Pakistan, with an abundance of raw jute, found itself with no mills.

To feed the ready market for raw jute, rice fields were increasingly used for jute cultivation in the state of West Bengal. This transition was very rapid in the agricultural districts of Hooghly, Howrah and 24-Paraganas surrounding the CIR, where transportation costs were low. Neighbouring states like Assam and Bihar also began cultivating jute, although they are at a disadvantage because of the high transport cost. As result, of the total of 4,965,000 acres under jute cultivation in the world, India's share was 43%, Pakistan's 40%, and the rest of the world's share was 17%.

Despite the upward trend in the area under jute cultivation, there have been fluctuations in the past. The most important determining factor has been the demand for jute goods in the world market. Any change in the world market has affected the output of jute mills, which in turn has influenced the decision whether to cultivate jute or rice. The prices of raw jute and rice and the cost of production have also played important parts. Other factors, no less significant in determining the acreage, are the importation of raw jute from Pakistan, the purchase of raw jute by the mills, the stock of raw jute in the mills, and the area under cultivation of mesta (a substitute crop).

Any change in the level of these exogenous factors will affect the endogenous acreage variables, which again will influence production of jute goods. The major purpose of this model is to estimate the degree of change in the endogenous variables related to the jute industry in the CIR following a stipulated change in the level of exogenous variables. I have used an econometric model of the Jute industry to project the economic condition of the state; see Chatterji (1966) for details.

2. <u>Highly Urbanized Area in a Developed Country:</u>
<u>Philadelphia Standard Metropolitan Statistical Area</u>

The Philadelphia standard metropolitan statistical area (henceforth known as Phila SMSA) consists of eight counties or districts. Five of these counties-namely Philadelphia, Chester, Montgomery, Delaware and Bucks-are in the state of Pennsylvania; the remaining three counties-Gloucester, Burlington and Camden-are in the state of New Jersey. Each of these counties consists of a number of townships or municipalities. These townships make up the lowest levels of administrative area in the Phila SMSA. These subregional areal units have unique economic structures and spatial interrelationships. The intra-areal differentiation was developed for various social, economic and political reasons, including the forces of regional economic history.

The importance of political factors can be realized from the fact that Gloucester, Burlington and Camden counties are within the boundary of the State of New Jersey and, as such, are governed by different tax laws and other public policies. The pattern of public expenditure and planning objectives in these areas may be quite different, despite their linkage with Philadelphia through spatial interaction. Other areas in the Phila SMSA are favourably located in the eastern megalopolis of the United States and have a definite comparative advantage for transport cost-orientated industries.

Some areas within the Philadelphia SMSA are close enough to good transportation networks such as highways and waterways that movement to and from the city of Philadelphia is both quick and economical. Some areas are specifically reserved for residential purposes, with severe zoning restrictions. The people in these areas work in Philadelphia, so that what is happening in the city is extremely important to them. Finally, some areas in the Phila SMSA are dependent to a large extent on defence and space contracts; thus any cut in these expenditures by the federal government is bound to affect the economy of these areas.

When we consider the city of Philadelphia in particular, the problem becomes more complicated; such factors as intra-city transportation, housing conditions, distribution of population by different ethnic and economic classes, demographic features,
zoning restrictions, labour force participation and the availability of social and health benefits become important variables to be considered in our model.

This data emphasizes the importance of intraregional differences within the Phila SMSA, and demonstrates that any effort to construct a global growth model (such as the input-output model) that ignores these differences is sure to lead to inconsistent and inaccurate projections. Besides, a micro approach to projection will be extremely useful for planning purposes with respect to such civic amenities as water supply, drainage, and the like in a township or county. For a more detailed statement of the model to project regional economic conditions involving econometric defence expenditure, see Chatterji (1982).

3.   Depressed Area in a Developed Country: Nova Scotia, Canada

In recent years there has emerged a new form of underdevelopment in the midst of the affluence of highly industrial countries, manifested by pockets of poverty that cannot compete against other areas because of locational or other disadvantages.

The province of Nova Scotia in Canada is a good example. It was once a prosperous area, but now it can definitely be termed a declining region, in which per capita income is far below the national average. Much of the income generated in the region is the result of central and provincial subsidies. The problem in this case is to identify a set of policy variables and to determine their levels so that the values of some target variables can be achieved. This has to be done by

188

taking into consideration the rate of growth of the economy in Nova Scotia, its interindustry connections, and its relation to the rest of the world.

This model will be somewhat different from the normal econometric type of model, wherein short-run cyclical functions are of prime importance. In contrast, this can be termed a planning model, where the objective is to find the values of instrument variables that would maximize the welfare function or attain some targets. For this purpose, given the dimension of some target variables, the required value of the instrument variables and intermediate variables through which the instrument variables will act to achieve the targets has to be discovered. For such a model, see Czamanski and Chatterji (1967).

4.   Agricultural Region in a Developed Country: North Atlantic Region in the United States

Most of the techniques of regional science have been devised to attack the problems of an industrial region, particularly for a Western country. If we want to apply them to agricultural countries or agricultural regions, they must be properly modified so that new techniques for agricultural regional planning can be developed. Such factors as quality of the soil, pattern of ownership, fertilizers, irrigation facilities, market size, transportation network, weather conditions, and so on become quite important.

The case of an agricultural region in the midst of a highly urbanized region, as in the North Atlantic region of the United States, presents an interesting problem. The North Atlantic region of the United States is unique in at least one sense. Agriculture is becoming less important in this area, and there is a tendency for subregional specialization; for example, dairy products in New England, poultry in Delaware and Maryland, and so on. On the other hand, the region is becoming more and more urbanized. Although agriculture still occupies a considerable amount of land, it is competing with the ever-growing demand of the expanding urban centres for new housing, industry, highways, roads, recreational facilities and other urban amenities. To the farmer, the spreading urban centres present a vast market with immense purchasing power. He therefore faces the dilemma of whether to sell the land as real estate or use it for agricultural purposes.

The spread of urbanization poses a serious problem not only to agriculturists but also to the urbanized areas themselves. When the empty spaces between cities are filled, the problems of housing, transportation and other urban amenities will be greatly increased. The problem here is to project agricultural economic activity and land use in the face of increasing urbanization and competition against highly efficient agricultural regions in other parts of the country. The North Atlantic region includes the following states:

1.   Maine
2.   Vermont
3.   New Hampshire
4.   Massachusetts

5. Rhode Island
6. Connecticut
7. New York
8. Pennsylvania
9. New Jersey
10. Delaware
11. Maryland (including Washington, DC)
12. Virginia
13. West Virginia

To discern the impact of urbanization on agricultural activities, land use, population, etc., I proposed a model structure with the following submodels.

1. Population submodel
2. Supply submodel
3. Land use submodel

The structure of the models will be found in Chatterji (1982).

5.   Econometric Models for Disarmament

Although it is grossly outdated, I shall discuss Professor Suits's econometric method for disarmament. As a first step, a 32 equation system characterizing the economy of the United States is constructed (Suits, 1963). From the equations, Suits estimates the response of particular economic magnitudes, such as the gross national product; consumption expenditure; unemployment insurance benefits; tax receipts both on the federal, state and local level; employment, etc. from a change of $1 billion in the indicated government activity. Then, following the READ model (Economic Impacts of Disarmament, US Arms Control and Disarmament Agency, Economic Series I, Publication 2, Jan. 1962) Suits considers a net reduction of expenditure of $32 billion divided between $10.4 billion in wages and salaries and $21.6 billion in purchases from private industry. By using the responses (as measured by multipliers), he obtains the full economic implications of the programme (Table).

For example, from column 1 of his Table 1, (see Suits, 1963) it can be seen that with no alternative markets provided for released resources, the decline in gross national product is 50% larger than the expenditure cutback. Federal tax receipts would decline drastically, but much less than the expenditure reduction, leaving the federal government with a $20 billion annual surplus. Suits concludes that "without any offset programs the problem of adjustment to disarmament, at its worst, is only a half or a third that of the annual problem of absorption of a growing labor force".

Then the author proposes a tax reduction programme involving a $20 billion reduction in federal income taxes – along with a minor $300 million increase in state and local expenditures. The net impact after this offset programme is shown in column 3 of his Table 2 (see Suits, 1963). For this programme, for example, the net decline of the GNP is $11 billion, which is the order of magnitude of the drop that can occur from one quarter to the next in a mild postwar recession. The same is true about the unemployment figure of 2.7 million. As seen from the last column of Table 2, the second offset programme, which plans personal income tax reductions by only $13.2 billion and a transfer payment of $10 billion to state and local governments, stimulates consumption somewhat less and employment somewhat more than the first programme. The rise in unemployment would be only about one quarter as serious as in the absence of offsets. Professor Suits concludes "that adequate economic adjustment to disarmament can be made though with some friction. The problems to be encountered are qualitatively the same and quantitatively much smaller than the problems of daily adjustments in a growing economy."

Obviously the data presented here are grossly outdated. For a more recent study see Klein and Gronicki (1991) and Adams and Behrman (1991).

The article by Professor Suits opens a new direction in peace research. But in many respects his analysis can be improved. His econometric model does not seem to have been constructed specifically for estimating the impact of disarmament, where the number of variables is small. Although it is a highly aggregative model, variables related to major industries likely to be affected by disarmament, such as aerospace, shipbuilding, ordnance, etc., could have been included. Monetary and financial variables have also been excluded.

The method of estimation of the regression coefficients can now be greatly improved, utilizing the advanced methods presently available in econometric literature. Since the R^2 values and the standard error of the regression coefficients are not given, it is difficult to judge the reliability of the estimates. If a simulation study of the model had been presented, the stability of the model could have been tested. The multiplier obtained from the equation system does not take into account interindustry relationships which are taken into account by the matrix multiplier of the regional input-output models. Suits's model offers no way of estimating regional impacts. For this purpose a regional econometric model can be constructed. If time series data for regions are not available, cross-sectional data can be utilized for this purpose. Since Suits is dealing on the national level, his offset programme becomes more realistic than that of Isard and Schooler. But the effect of a policy decision takes time to materialize and this time lag has not been taken into account in the model. Nor has he discussed all of the implications of a major tax cut. The model would have been more accurate if he had considered other offset programmes, such as foreign aid, in addition to a tax cut. However, his article remains a significant contribution to peace research.

6.   Global Modelling of Food, Energy, Health Care and Conflict

It is clear that, due to a variety of reasons, there exists a serious imbalance in the standard of living between the majority of the people living in the Third World Countries and a small minority living in the industrialized developed world. The most significant aspect of this underdevelopment is the lack of food and health care. It is true that high population growth, low levels of agricultural technology, lack of water and sanitation, poor social and political organization, and primitive distribution networks led to this unfortunate situation. What should be noted is that in this age of high technology and biotechnology, increasing the productivity of the soil and finding the best seed is not a primary problem. The main bottleneck is the politics of development both domestically and internationally – how to take the food and health care to people who need them. Fortunately, development of the poorer countries is now seen in the context of self-interest of the rich countries. It will be helpful if we can identify the relationship between the different variables associated with health care and food, estimate the parameters and use the relationship for the projection of future scenarios. Here I intend to sketch out the parameters of such a series of relationships. Before I present such parameters, I will discuss a number of contextual issues.

It is true that agricultural production in any country is very much influenced by the economic factors governing the country. Thus it will be appropriate to build individual country models and link them with international trade. In this work, however, we present a more global view in the sense that we argue that the developing countries in the world can be grouped in such a way so that the agricultural and health situations are seen to be similar. The relationship between the variables for those countries can be estimated using the data for the countries in that group (Figure 1 shows the listing of countries) (Chatterji, 1986).

Total food production, of course, depends upon the total amount of cultivated land in a country, as well as upon the fertility of the soil, amount of irrigation, rainfall, and labour and capital. Ownership structures also greatly influence the incidence of hunger. In many countries, while the landless labourers till the soil, they do not obtain the fruits of their labour; instead, the absentee landlord gets of the profit. The analysis of hunger must also consider the distribution and marketing of inputs. Another important factor is the use of energy, both conventional and non-conventional (bio-moss). Rural-urban migration resulting in increased demand for agricultural goods by urban dwellers and international demand for food and cash crops play an important part in determining the level and type of agricultural production. A schematic relationship of these factors is given in Fig. 5.1. If we are interested in formulating relationships on the basis of these graphs, they can be discussed within the framework of supply, demand, income and price.

Economic expansion and technological progress in highly industrialized countries have brought about a spectacular increase in the standard of living, but at the same time have created the worst environmental problems in human history. The problems of housing, transportation, water and electric supply have been acute; and water pollution, air pollution, and solid and liquid waste disposal have made the situation worse. The gravity of the situation in the United States, United Kingdom, Western Europe, USSR and Japan is too well-known to have to be emphasized here. Most of these countries, however, have realized the magnitude of the problem and have started taking precautionary steps to correct the condition. To do this adequately would require maximum investment and a modification of the socio-cultural outlook of the country.

The nature of the urbanization process has assumed a different aspect due to the sudden increase in the price of energy. Migration patterns are going to change, and new patterns of urbanization will emerge. The question that arises from this is whether this movement has any relevance for the developing countries. I think it does. Let me discuss the process with reference to one developing country, namely, India.

The strategy of economic development in India seems to lie in modernizing the agricultural sector. In this process of modernization, a substantial proportion of the agricultural population in the country has to leave and go somewhere else, and there is no place to go except to the urban areas. It has been widely accepted that the rural population of India is comparatively non-migratory, because socio-cultural features of Indian society have acted as barriers in this respect. However, this thesis is disputed by demographics, the persuasiveness of which makes one doubt whether the conditions of near perfect immobility ever existed. It is quite possible that the great dominance of the village over the residential desires of the average Indian citizen has been greatly exaggerated and that deficient statistics have perpetuated this bit of misinformation. Whatever the reason in the past, rural to urban migration associated with industrialization is a worldwide phenomenon, and there is no reason why this should not happen in India. In fact, with villagers becoming progressively more orientated toward the new urbanized economy, and with migration channels firmly established, the nation seems to be ready to enter a phase of unprecedented urbanization assisted by the family system and culture rather than hindered by them. So it will be useful to try to identify the nature of the social, economic, political and environmental implications of this new phenomenon and then to devise plans accordingly.

Again, for many years to come, India will remain basically an agricultural country, although its agricultural structure and relations to other sectors of the economy will change dramatically. To assess the true nature of this change and use this for the overall development of the country, it is necessary to identify different agricultural regions and to study their linkages with urban regions. A regional approach to planning will also be beneficial for conflict resolution of interdependent states and in sensitive border areas.

In studying Indian urban problems, we very often neglect the socio-cultural aspects e.g. crime, mental health, discrimination, noise, etc. – and assume that they are the exclusive property of highly industrialized countries. This is, of course, not true.

Food production, agriculture, poverty and starvation are very much related to the process of urbanization. If we look at the developmental pattern in the Third World, we see that

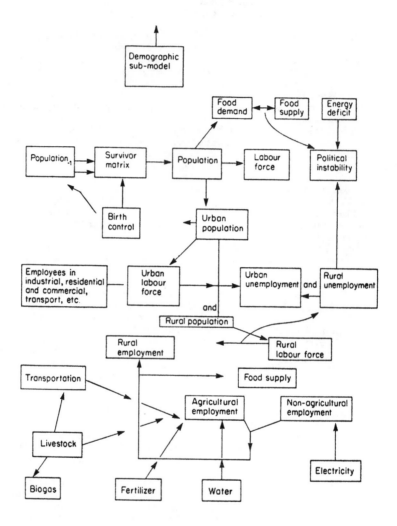

Figure 5.1   Demographic-agricultural sub-model

a proportionate amount of resources are being devoted to the urban population and services devoted to it. Since the power structure in these countries is in the hands of the urban elite, very little is left over for real agricultural development, and the agricultural poor are flocking to the urban centres for non-existent opportunities.

The major problem of health care in the developing countries is malnutrition; almost all diseases in those regions have their roots in this fact. Health care planning in these problems is thus a developmental rather than a medical problem. Whatever money is being spent in health care is being used to build expensive hospitals and to acquire high-technology treatments in order to meet the demand of a few urban residents who have the power and money to afford them. Similarly, doctors and nurses are reluctant to go to the rural areas and prefer to remain in the urban areas, even if they remain unemployed there. The rural areas lack economic and social superstructures (housing, transportation, recreational facilities, etc.). Thus, any model of a health care development plan should be expressed through this developmental approach.

A Prototype Model of Food, Energy and Health

In the framework to be discussed below, we shall only be concerned with countries (Chatterji, 1986). For each country the time reference point is a year for which reasonable data are available. The years 1970 to 1980 will be chosen.

a.   Demographic and Agricultural Subsystems – Let us concentrate for the present on the developing countries (low income). For each country in this group, we locate the demographic submodel given in Equation 1.

Total population at any time is the sum of urban and rural population

$$P(t) = P^u(t) + P^R(t) \tag{1}$$

The rural population in a given period is determined by the sum of a) the population in the previous period plus the increase due to natural growth, and b) migration from the rural areas to the rest of the world (mostly urban areas in the same country); i.e.

$$P_t^R = N_t^R + M_{t-1}^{R \to u} \tag{2}$$

For the rural areas the population in the age-sex cohort N_t is obtained by multiplying the cohort in the previous year by the average survivor probability matrix. So,

$$N(t) = \lambda P_{t-1} \tag{3}$$

Where λ is given as follows:

a square matrix of order equal to the number of age-sex cohorts. The elements of the matrix are (1) probabilities of survival of different age-sex cohorts, (d_i^m or d_i^f and (2) age specific birth rates, (b_i^m, b_i^f).

$$d_i = \text{the probability that an individual selected at random from the } i^{th} \text{ age-sex group will survive another unit of time}$$

$$b_i = \text{the age-specific fertility rates in the } i^{th} \text{ child-bearing group}$$

When the symbol (m,f) is given, it means that the variables refer to the age-sex cohort dimension. Once the cohort population in each age-sex classification is obtained, the total population due only to natural increases can be obtained by summing all the elements in that column, i.e.

$$N'(t) = \delta N(t) \quad \text{where } \delta \text{ is a row sector} \quad (4)$$

(1, 1,...1), and as mentioned before, $N_{(t)}$ is the population in the age-sex cohort column.

The population in the urban area is the sum of the migration from the rural areas and the natural growth of the urban areas.

$$P_t^u = N_t^u + M_t^{R \to u} \tag{5}$$

The urban population is assumed to increase in a fixed proportion, i.e.

$$N_t^u = (1+w) \, N_{t-1}^u \tag{6}$$

where "w" is the rate of growth in the urban population. Instead of taking w as a fixed number, we must assume that it can change, depending upon the expenditures on education, birth control, and other factors which reduce the birth rate. It is difficult to estimate a migration function. It can be taken as

$$M_{(t)} = a + b_1 \, U^R + b_2 \, W^R/W^u + b_3 \, E_t^u \tag{7}$$

which states that the migration is a function of rural unemployment, the ratio of rural wages to urban wages, and the employment level in the urban area. A structural equation of the type (7) will be estimated by the cross section of countries in each group in a given year.

When the population of the urban and rural areas are estimated, the labour force in each area can be obtained by multiplying the labour force participation R^u and R^R, i.e.

$$L^R = R^R \times P^R \tag{8}$$
$$L^u = R^u \times P^c \tag{9}$$

When the labour force in each area is known, the unemployment level in each area will be obtained by computing the difference between available employment and the labour force, i.e.

$$U^R = L^R - E^R \tag{10}$$
$$U^U = L^U - E^U \tag{11}$$

Total rural employment will be determined by the agriculture output

$$E^R = R_1 \, Q^A \tag{12}$$

R_1 need not be a fixed parameter. It can be chosen depending upon the anticipated change in the agricultural development. The total agricultural output is composed of cash crops like coffee, tea, jute, etc., and non-cash crops (mainly food):

$$Q^A = Q^{AF} + Q^{AC} \qquad (13)$$

$$\uparrow \qquad \uparrow$$

Foodcrop   Cash

The total food production is a function of the total number of workers, (E^R) total amount of animal energy input (A), fertilizers (f), water (W), pesticides (P) and irrigated land (IL).

$$Q^A = f(E^R, A, F, W, P, IL) \qquad (14)$$

The production of cash crops is determined by its export level

$$Q^{AC} = f(Ex^{AC}) \qquad (15)$$

Once these are determined, the total amount of crops is estimated from (13).

Once the agricultural food production and the population known, the surplus or deficit (export/import) of food can be obtained, i.e.

$$I^F = Q^{AF} - P \cdot C_F \qquad (16)$$

Depending upon the world price of oil, the total availability of these inputs can be determined as:

$$F = f(P_o) \qquad (17)$$
$$W = f(P_o, P_E) \qquad (18)$$
$$P = f(P_o) \qquad (19)$$

where C_F is the per capita minimum food consumption, and P is the total population. Depending upon this minimum amount and protein content, the life expectancy and the death rates will be affected. This again will influence the population growth.

The central focus of this model will be food production. Food production depends very much on oil-based fertilizer, rainfall, electricity, oil-driven water irrigation and pesticides. Through an agricultural production function of the sort outlined in (14), it may be possible to find out how differential levels of these inputs and food production will be determined.

It should be noted that the form of the equations presented above is overly simplified. The explicit form of these equations has not been written for that reason. It is not necessary that the form and the parameters in the equation be estimated econometrically. On the basis of past data and the opinions of experts, we shall find out how much the demand for fertilizer will decline, if the price of oil increases, say, 10% (the numbers will be approximate). The relation between food production and oil price is also not direct. It may be necessary to estimate this equation on the basis of reduced form. It is true that for all countries in all groups we do not have time series data. However, for a single country in a group, it is possible to get that type of data. In that situation, we shall estimate the value of the parameter on the basis of these data and use it for the whole group. If more extensive data are available, we shall use a more sophisticated production function (Cobb-Douglas, C.E.S., etc).

The demand for energy (mostly oil) in rural transportation and for kerosene in lighting can be estimated on the basis of total production, i.e.

$$O_{T+L}^R = f(P) \qquad (20)$$

When the oil requirements for fertilizer, pesticide, etc. are added to this, it will give the total requirement for energy on the part of the rural sector, i.e.

$$O^R = O_{T+L}^R + O_F^R \qquad (21)$$

where the demand for energy for food production is obtained through Equation (13).

If the price of oil becomes very high, cow manure, (M^c), the quantity of which depends upon the number of livestock, (A), replaces fertilizer

$$M^c = f(A) \qquad (22)$$

$$M^c = \underset{\uparrow}{M^{CF}} + \underset{\uparrow}{M^{CC}} \qquad (23)$$
$$\text{fertl} \quad \text{cooking}$$

More cow manure applied to fertilizer means that less will be available for biogas production, and the usage of firewood for cooking will increase,

$$M^{CF} = f(P_o, Q^t) \qquad (24)$$

$$M^{CC} = f(P^R, P_o) \qquad (25)$$

$$FW = f(P^R, M^{CC}) \qquad (26)$$

Equation (24) notes that the amount of cow manure needed for fertilizer depends on the price of oil and total agricultural production. Equation (25) states that total cow manure needed for cooking will depend upon the price of oil and rural population, and Equation (26) states that the firewood demand will be a function of rural population and the availability of cow manure for cooking. The biogas production (M^g) depends inversely on cow manure used for cooking.

$$M^g = f(M^{CC}) \qquad (27)$$

It should be pointed out again that estimation of structural equations will be made by using the cross-section observations of the countries (wherever applicable) in a group. When no econometric estimation procedures are needed, for each country in the group, the demand will be separately computed and added for all the countries. Due to an increased population or higher standard of living, the consumption of energy in the rural areas will increase. This increase, wherever possible, has to be bridged by electricity produced from thermal power (TH), nuclear energy (NE) and solar energy (SO). The energy demand must be equal to supply. Defining O^U as the demand for energy in the urban area

$$\underset{\uparrow}{O_s} + \underset{\uparrow}{O_{imp}} = O^R + O^U \qquad (28)$$
$$\text{Domestic} \quad \text{Imports}$$
$$\text{Supply}$$

The demographic and agricultural subsystem is shown in Fig. 5.1. This subsystem is linked to urban and industrial complexes and the rest of the world system through migration, energy, import, food import, etc.

    b.   <u>Urban and Industrial Systems</u> – When we consider the case of urban areas, the employment in the non-agricultural production sectors can be divided into a number of groups:

        1.   Manufacturing
        2.   Wholesale and retail trade
        3.   Finance, insurance, real estate

4.   Services
5.   Government

Data for individual countries in the group for a given year (1970 or 1980) will constitute the basis for the estimation of the employment in each sector with such variables as population and income. For example,

E_m = employment in manufacturing = $f(V_m)$ (29)

is a function of value added in manufacturing.

Total employment in wholesale and retail trade

E_{WR} = $F(P, PI)$ (30)

is a function of population and per capita income.

E_s =   Employment in services is a function of total population (P) and per capita income   (31)
(PI) = $f(P, PI)$

When the equations for individual sectors have thus been estimated, the total employment figure can be obtained by summing up the individual sectoral employment. What we are suggesting here is that for the organized industrial sector, a Klein-Goldberger type econometric model can be constructed and estimated on the basis of individual countries. Alternatively, for each country, an input-output model can be constructed to estimate the levels of endogenous variables. Since a considerable amount of literature exists with respect to the econometric model, we are not detailing the fine structure of each equation in the system.

A macroeconomic model of this type for a developing country should consider a number of special factors. For example, the input-output model should consider the small-scale industries. The input of energy should be specifically considered in both the production function and the demand function. Once the industrial output of the countries in question is determined, the need for different sources of energy can be computed. That will give us the amount of energy needed for industrial goods.

In urban residential areas, the major form of energy consumed is electric and is devoted to lighting as well as some air conditioning. The electricity demand can be estimated on the basis of urban population land income.

$$ELEC = f(P^U, PI)   (32)$$

There is almost no need for energy for heating purposes. Some amount of coal and gas is used for cooking. This again can be based on population and income. In the estimation of the electricity demand, the price of electricity can be used in addition to population and income. The demand for the commercial sector can also be based on income and population.

In the case of urban transportation, the main sources are gas (petrol), electricity (commuter trains), and coal (locomotives). The consumption of gas can be based on the number of cars, which again depends on population and per capita income. The demand for inter-urban road transport can be estimated on the basis of road mileage and the number of trucks. The demand for intra-urban trailway transportation can be based on urban population and the mileage between cities, in those countries where such transportation exists.

When the total demand of energy types for transformation sources is estimated, they can be added to residential, commercial and industrial demand quantities to give us the total urban demand of energy, O^U. When these demands are added to the rural demand, we shall attain the total demand for each country for different types of energy sources. When the country's demands are summed up, we obtain the figures for all the developing countries.

So far we have discussed the demand side only. The supply of energy sources in the developing countries can come from the following resources.

1. Oil and gas
2. Coal
3. Thermal electricity
4. Nuclear power
5. Firewood
6. Solar power
7. Biogas and other non-traditional sources
8. Hydroelectric power
9. Others

Assuming that enough coal is available and that the demand for electricity can be met from hydroelectric and nuclear power, the extra need for oil will have to come from oil imports. This will put a strain on foreign exchange and increase international debt. It will compete with the need for food imports. In the absence of a sufficient quantity of food to meet minimum requirements, political violence might result. Another potential source of conflict is the fact that usually one or two energy-producing regions of a country feed the rest of it. If there is not enough development in the energy-producing regions, interregional conflicts may break out. So side by side with the demand and supply model for energy, there is also a need for developing a conflict submodel. How scarcity of food and energy sources can lead to this conflict can be formalized through a factor analysis structure. In this structure, we can collect large numbers of socio-economic and political variables with respect to each country and factor analyse the correlation matrix. For details of such a model see Chatterji (1983).

Estimation of Econometric Models

Econometrics is the application of probability and statistics to the measurement of economic relations. These relations are based on sound judgement, economic theory and institutional arrangements. Since social, political and economic variables are interrelated, the methodology of econometrics can be extended to measure and estimate relations in economics, politics and sociology.

Roughly speaking, there are two classes of correlated variables which are correlated. The dependent or the endogenous variables are those which affect the system and in turn are affected. For example, consumption is an endogenous variable. If consumption changes, it affects GNP, wages and salaries, disposable income, and, in turn, the consumption in the next period if affected. Though variables such as taxes, war, famine and rainfall can affect the system, they are, in turn, not affected by it. We can collect data from these variables, e.g. sales (Y) and advertisement (X). The data can be shown in terms of a time series where the value of the variables Y_t, X_t (in a two variable formulation) for the years t = 1960, 61...can be collected. It can also be cross-section data where the data for, say, 50 companies at a given point of time (i.e. 1980) can be collected for Y_s, X_s (S = 1, 2...50). Or it can be a pooled time series, cross-section data, where the data for 50 companies for two years (1980 and 1981) are collected. After the data are obtained, the next step is to plot the data in a scatter diagram, either in the original scale or in logarithmic or other scales, to decide whether a definite pattern (say, linear) exists. Obviously, even if there may be a linear relation in the population (when all possible values of Y and X are available), the points in the sample scatter diagram will not fall on a straight line since there will be sampling error (our data is a sample from the population) and measurement error. The object is to fit a straight line (to obtain equation of the form $Y_i = a + bx_i$) so that the line passes through the scatter in such a way that the sum of squared differences of the expected value Y_i (obtained by plugging the observed value of X_i when "a" and "b" are known) and the observed value Y_i, i.e.

$$\sum_{i=1}^{n} (Y_i - \hat{Y}_i)^2$$

is minimized. Obviously the location of the line depends on the value of "a" (intercept) and "b" (slope). The method of least square states that if the objective is to minimize the residual sum of square

$$\sum_{i=1}^{n} (Y_i - \hat{Y}_i)^2$$

The best estimate of 'a' and 'b' are given by

$$a = \overline{Y} - b\overline{X} \qquad (1)$$

$$b = \frac{\sum_{i=1}^{n} (X_i - \overline{X})(Y_i - \overline{Y})}{\sum_{i=1}^{n} (X_i - \overline{X})^2} = r \cdot Sy/Sx \qquad (2)$$

$$= \frac{S.P(X\ Y)}{S.S.(x)}$$

where $r = \dfrac{\sum (X - \overline{X})(Y - \overline{Y})}{\sqrt{\sum (X - \overline{X})^2\ \sum (Y-\overline{Y})^2}}$ = correlation coefficient and where $\bar{Y}$ and $\bar{X}$ are the sample means and S.P(X,Y) and S.S(x) are corrected (deviation from the mean) sums of product of X and Y are corrected (deviation from the mean) sums of product of x respectively.

The equation of line is then:

$$Y_i = a + bx_i + e_i \qquad (i=1,2,...n) \qquad (3)$$

where a, b are parameters and e_i are random errors (measurement + sampling error) distributed normally with E(e) = 0 and V(e) = σ^2. At this time, two points should be made. First, (2), known as the sample regression coefficient of Y on x, is a sample relation. If the population values are known, an equation of the form $Y_i = \alpha + \beta x_i + e_i$ (i=1,2,...N) could have been obtained where a and b in equation (1) and (2) are estimates of α and β. Secondly, the method of least square assumes that the variable "X" is a fixed non-stochastic variable (like rainfall, time, etc.) with no error. If this is not the case (which is usually true for variables such as consumption, income, wages and salary, etc.), then the slope "b" will be biased and will be less in absolute value. In order to avoid this problem, we can use other advanced methods of estimation.

Using (1) and (2) by calculator or by SAS (Statistical Analysis System as in Example (1), we can compute the regression equation say,

$$Y = 19.8 + 4.1x \qquad r^2 = .7630$$
$$(1.18) \qquad D.W = 1.78$$

To decide whether this is a good equation to predict the future value of "Y" when the value of "x" is given, we must see whether the slope b = 4.1 has the correct sign. In this case, it is positive, since the higher the value of x (advertisement), the higher the value of "Y". The second step is to test whether r^2 = .7630 (in this case) is high. For the sake of simplicity, in the case of time series data (as in Example 1), any r^2 over .60 will be termed as high. In the case of cross-section data r^2 = .45 to .60 is considered high. The third step is to test, where the standard error of the slope b, S_b where

$$S_b^2 = \frac{\Sigma (Y_i - \hat{Y}_i)^2 / n-2}{\Sigma (X - \bar{X})^2} = \frac{\text{Residual M.S.}}{\text{S.S. (X)}}$$

is small. Using normal distribution, we can say that the standard error is small when the regression coefficient "b" (slope) is more than three times the standard error (S_b). We conclude that the "slope" cannot vary significantly from sample to sample and that the population regression coefficient (slope) cannot be equal to zero. X is a good predictor of Y. For a more sophisticated test, when the number of observations is small, we can use the "t" distribution. A good equation implies that when we know the value of the independent variable X for a future time period, the value of "Y" can be predicted with confidence. Although we have considered the linear regression, the relationship can be quadratic, cubic or double log, or semi-log scale, if the scatter diagram implies that such a transformational is necessary.

Example 1

The following tables gives the data for sales and advertising
for an organization called Datacom. Compute the regression
equation of sales and advertisement.

Answer:

```
DATA       PAGE 311;
INPUT           YEAR      SALES       ADVERT;
LS=LOG10 (SALES);
LA=LOG10 (ADVERT)'
CARDS;
1981  37    4.5
1982  48    6.5
1983  45    3.5
1984  36    3.0
1985  25    2.5
1986  55    8.5
1987  63    7.5

PROC        PLOT  DATA=PAGE311;
            PLOT  LS*LA;
TITLE       "PLOT  OF  LOG(10)  OF  SALES  VS.  LOG(10)  OF
            ADVERTISING";
PROC        PLOT  DATA=PAGE311;
            PLOT  SALES*ADVERT;
TITLE       "PLOT OF SALES VS. ADVERTISING";
PROC        REG   DATA=PAGE311;
            MODEL SALES=ADVERT/P    R    DW;
TITLE       "REGRESSION ON SALES=ADVERTISING";
PROC        REG   DATA=PAGE311;
            MODEL LS=LA/P    R    DW;
TITLE       "REGRESSION ON LOG OF SALES=LOG OF ADVERTISING";
```

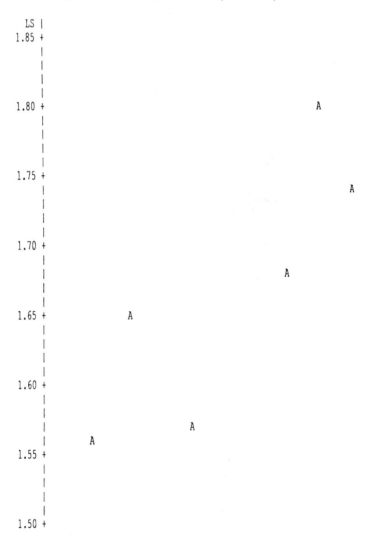

PLOT OF LS*LA   LEGEND: A = 1 OBS, B = 2 OBS, ETC.

```
       PLOT OF SALES*ADVERT    LEGEND: A = 1 OBS, B = 2 OBS, ETC.

SALES |
      |
      |
      |
      |
   63 +                                        A
   62 +
   61 +
   60 +
   59 +
   58 +
   57 +
   56 +
   55 +                                                 A
   54 +
   53 +
   52 +
   51 +
   50 +
   49 +
   48 +                            A
   47 +
   46 +
   45 +        A
   44 +
   43 +
   42 +
   41 +
   40 +
   39 +
   38 +
   37 +            A
   36 +    A
   35 +
```

DEP VARIABLE: SALES

ANALYSIS OF VARIANCE

SOURCE	DF	SUM OF SQUARES	MEAN SQUARE	F VALUE	PROB>F
MODEL	1	742.30789	742.30789	16.099	0.0102
ERROR	5	230.54925	46.10985011		
C TOTAL	6	972.85714			

ROOT MSE	6.790423	R-SQUARE	0.7630	
DEP MEAN	44.14286	ADJ R-SQ	0.7156	
C.V.	15.38284			

PARAMETER ESTIMATES

VARIABLE	DF	PARAMETER ESTIMATE	STANDARD ERROR	T FOR H0: PARAMETER=0	PROB > |T|
INTERCEP	1	19.88222698	6.56869555	3.027	0.0292
ADVERT	1	4.71734475	1.17571601	4.012	0.0102

OBS	ACTUAL	PREDICT VALUE	STD ERR PREDICT	RESIDUAL	STD ERR RESIDUAL
1	37.0000	41.1103	2.6755	-4.1103	6.2411
2	48.0000	50.5450	3.0221	-2.5450	6.0809
3	45.0000	36.3929	3.2122	8.6071	5.9826
4	36.0000	34.0343	3.5965	1.9657	5.7598
5	25.0000	31.6756	4.0302	-6.6756	5.4651
6	55.0000	59.9797	4.7081	-4.9797	4.8932
7	63.0000	55.2623	3.7772	7.7377	5.6429

OBS	STUDENT RESIDUAL	-2 -1 0 1 2	COOK'S D
1	-0.6586	| *| |	0.040
2	-0.4185	| | |	0.022
3	1.4387	| |** |	0.298
4	0.3413	| | |	0.023
5	-1.2215	| **| |	0.406
6	-1.0177	| **| |	0.479
7	1.3712	| |** |	0.421

DEP VARIABLE: LS

ANALYSIS OF VARIANCE

SOURCE	DF	SUM OF SQUARES	MEAN SQUARE	F VALUE	PROB>F
MODEL	1	0.08305932	0.08305932	17.277	0.0089
ERROR	5	0.02403785	0.004807571		
C TOTAL	6	0.10709717			

ROOT MSE	0.06933665	R-SQUARE	0.7756	
DEP MEAN	1.628086	ADJ R-SQ	0.7307	
C.V.	4.258783			

PARAMETER ESTIMATES

VARIABLE	DF	PARAMETER ESTIMATE	STANDARD ERROR	T FOR H0: PARAMETER=0	PROB > |T|
INTERCEP	1	1.24731269	0.09528318	13.091	0.0001
LA	1	0.56835028	0.13673659	4.157	0.0089

OBS	ACTUAL	PREDICT VALUE	STD ERR PREDICT	RESIDUAL	STD ERR RESIDUAL
1	1.5682	1.6186	0.0263	-0.0504	0.0642
2	1.6812	1.7093	0.0327	-0.0281	0.0611
3	1.6532	1.5565	0.0314	0.0967	0.0618
4	1.5563	1.5185	0.0372	0.0378	0.0585
5	1.3979	1.4735	0.0455	-0.0755	0.0523
6	1.7404	1.7755	0.0441	-0.0352	0.0535
7	1.7993	1.7447	0.0384	0.0547	0.0577

OBS	STUDENT RESIDUAL	-2 -1 0 1 2	COOK'S D
1	-0.7851	| *| |	0.052
2	-0.4594	| | |	0.030
3	1.5633	| |*** |	0.314
4	0.6462	| |* |	0.084
5	-1.4439	| **| |	0.788
6	-0.6577	| *| |	0.147
7	0.9471	| |* |	0.198

Multiple Regression Equations

So far we have considered regression analysis with one independent non-stochastic variable X and shown how the method of least square can be used to estimate the parameters "a" and "b" and make some statistical tests. If X is not a non-stochastic variable (which is usually the case), then the regression coefficient "b" is biased. The analysis can be extended to multiple regression case where "Y" (say, demand), the dependent variable, may be a function of x_1 (price) and x_2 (advertisement)

$$Y_i = a + b_1 X_{1i} + b_2 X_{2i} \qquad (i=1,\ldots n) \quad (1)$$

Using the method of least square and similar equations as discussed in the previous section, the estimates of the parameters a, b_1, b_2 can be obtained. Of course, the relationship between the variables may be other than linear. In Example 2, the relationship is in logarithmic form. In that example, I have shown how the parameters can be estimated by using SAS (Statistical Analysis System) computer program. If the three criteria cited in the previous section are satisfied, then we can call it a good equation which can be used for projection purposes. We want to emphasize that the variables (particularly the independent variables) can be linear, quadratic, cubic, log or lag (one, two...year), or moving average (average of the last few years). Some of these variables such as war or famine, can be "dummy" (0/1). If for a particular time period there is a war, this variable will take the value 1 or 0 otherwise.

Obviously the variables x_1 and x_2 should not be related to avoid the problem of multicollinearity. If they are related, then the second variable will not provide new information. To avoid multicollinearity, we should first compute the correlation coefficient as mentioned in the previous section and judge whether the correlation is too high. If it is, we should take out some variables. Furthermore, in applying ordinary least square (OLS) method and testing of hypothesis, the successive values of "Y_i" or the residuals $e_i = Y_i - a - b x_i$ should not be related. Whether this is the case or not can be observed by looking at Durbin-Watson statistics (as in Examples 2 and 3). Roughly speaking, when the statistic is near 2, no autocorrelation exists.

Another problem which arises in the case of parameter estimation is the question of identification. For example, consider the demand curve $Y = a + bx$ (Y denotes demand and x denotes price). We assume that the effect of all other variables in the demand curve have been held constant. This will enable us to conclude that if there is a change in demand (movement in the demand curve) it is only due to the change in price. Enough information, e.g. the presence of other variables such as "weather" in the demand function, help us to identify the demand function so that the changes in demand due to changes in price are not confused with the changes in the demand due to shifts in demand curve such as taste, technology, etc. When a satisfactory regression equation has been estimated, avoiding multicollinearity, autocorrelation, and the problem of identification, it can be used for prediction and statistical testing whether the regression coefficients in the population (ß) are zero individually, i.e. H_o ($\beta_i=0$) or $H_o(\beta_1=.. = \beta_p=0)$ or pairwise equal, i.e.

$$H_o(\beta_1 = \beta_2)$$

where β_1 .... β_p are population regression coefficients with p independent variables.

In Example 2, if we are interested in testing whether the real price has any effect on sales, we can compute

$$t = \frac{b-0}{S_b} \qquad \text{degrees of freedom} = n=1 = 6$$

$$= 4.0$$

In the case, "t" is statistically significant (standard error of "b" is small) so we conclude that the population regression coefficient "ß" cannot be zero, i.e. price has effect on demand. If the null hypothesis is $H_o(\beta_1 = .03)$ then the relevant statistics will be

$$t = \frac{b - .03}{S_b} \qquad \text{d.f.} = n-1$$

Example 2

The following table relative to per capita consumption of sugar (Q), price of sugar (P) and the wholesale price index (Z) in a country during the years 1927-40. Fit a demand function of the following type and interpret the constants.

$$Q = A \left(\frac{P}{Z}\right)^{(b1)} e^{-(b2)t}$$

Year	Per Capita Consumption (in lbs)	Average Price ¢ /16	Index Number
t	Q	P	Z
1927	7.4	16.4	145
1928	8.2	15.3	142
1929	8.3	14.6	122
1930	7.1	14.3	97
1931	6.2	16.9	93
1932	6.3	15.8	88
1933	6.2	14.9	89
1934	6.5	14.4	90
1935	6.5	14.0	91
1936	7.2	10.7	101
1937	7.1	12.3	96
1938	6.5	17.3	101
1939	5.9	18.0	123

```
DATA   PAGE314;
INPUT    T    Q    P    Z;
         M=P/Z;
         U=T*0.43429;
         LQ=LOG10(Q);
         N=LOG10(M);
CARDS;
1927       7.4       16.4       145
1928       8.2       15.3       142
1929       8.3       14.6       122
1930       7.1       14.3        97
1931       6.2       16.9        93
1932       6.3       15.8        88
1933       6.2       14.9        89
1934       6.5       14.4        90
1935       6.5       14.0        91
1936       7.2       10.7       101
1937       7.1       12.3        96
1938       6.5       17.3       101
1939       5.9       18.0       123
;
PROC   PLOT    DATA=PAGE314;
       PLOT    Q*T ;
TITLE  "PLOT   OF   Q   VS.   T";
PROC   PLOT    DATA=PAGE314;
       PLOT    Q*N;
TITLE  "PLOT   OF   Q   VS.   N";
PROC   REG  DATA=PAGE314;
       MODEL  LQ=N U/P  R  DW;
TITLE  "REGRESSION   ON   LOG   OF   Q=N";
```

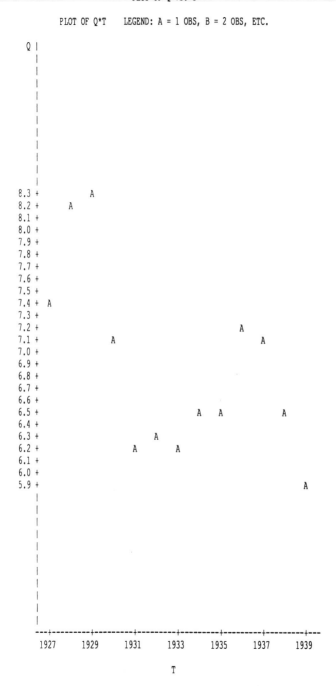

PLOT OF Q*T   LEGEND: A = 1 OBS, B = 2 OBS, ETC.

PLOT OF Q*N   LEGEND: A = 1 OBS, B = 2 OBS, ETC.

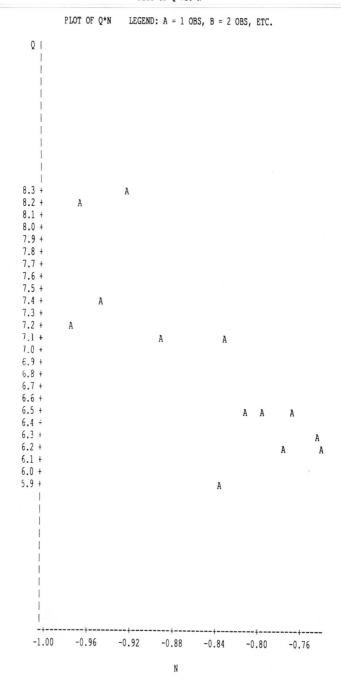

REGRESSION ON LOG OF Q = N

DEP VARIABLE: LQ

ANALYSIS OF VARIANCE

SOURCE	DF	SUM OF SQUARES	MEAN SQUARE	F VALUE	PROB>F
MODEL	2	0.02058304	0.01029152	19.137	0.0004
ERROR	10	0.005377845	0.000537785		
C TOTAL	12	0.02596089			

ROOT MSE	0.02319018	R-SQUARE	0.7928	
DEP MEAN	0.835053	ADJ R-SQ	0.7514	
C.V.	2.777091			

PARAMETER ESTIMATES

VARIABLE	DF	PARAMETER ESTIMATE	STANDARD ERROR	T FOR H0: PARAMETER=0	PROB > |T|
INTERCEP	1	9.49892582	3.50067205	2.713	0.0218
N	1	-0.38166527	0.08291828	-4.603	0.0010
U	1	-0.01070544	0.004144467	-2.583	0.0273

OBS	ACTUAL	PREDICT VALUE	STD ERR PREDICT	RESIDUAL	STD ERR RESIDUAL
1	0.8692	0.9010	0.0132	-0.0318	0.0191
2	0.9138	0.9044	0.0130	.0093751	0.0192
3	0.9191	0.8824	0.0103	0.0367	0.0208
4	0.8513	0.8432	.0087283	.0080862	0.0215
5	0.7924	0.8039	0.0123	-0.0115	0.0197
6	0.7993	0.8012	0.0111	-.001859	0.0204
7	0.7924	0.8081	.0086916	-0.0158	0.0215
8	0.8129	0.8110	.0076073	.0019086	0.0219
9	0.8129	0.8129	.0074965	5.7E-05	0.0219
10	0.8573	0.8700	0.0148	-0.0127	0.0179
11	0.8513	0.8339	0.0111	0.0174	0.0203
12	0.8129	0.7811	0.0115	0.0318	0.0202
13	0.7709	0.8025	0.0124	-0.0317	0.0196

| | STUDENT | | | COOK'S |
| OBS | RESIDUAL | -2 -1 0 1 2 | | D |

OBS	STUDENT RESIDUAL	-2 -1 0 1 2	COOK'S D
6	-0.0913	| | |	0.001
7	-0.7327	| *| |	0.029
8	0.0871	| | |	0.000
9	.0025908	| | |	0.000
10	-0.7105	| *| |	0.114
11	0.8539	| |* |	0.073
12	1.5774	| |*** |	0.268
13	-1.6150	| ***| |	0.344

SUM OF RESIDUALS   6.80012E-14
SUM OF SQUARED RESIDUALS   0.005377845
PREDICTED RESID SS (PRESS)   0.009858608

DURBIN-WATSON D   1.776
(FOR NUMBER OF OBS.)   13
1ST ORDER AUTOCORRELATION   -0.076

Example 3

In order to evaluate the effectiveness of a special energy-saving package in new home construction, a builders' association developed the following data regarding annual energy costs, the square footage of the residence, and whether or not the energy-saving package has been installed:

Square Footage (1000 sq. ft.)	Insulation Package	Annual Energy Costs ($100s)
1.5	Standard	9
2.0	Standard	12
2.2	Energy saving	14
1.8	Standard	11
2.4	Standard	12
2.8	Energy saving	19
2.0	Standard	12
2.4	Energy saving	14
1.9	Energy saving	11
3.0	Energy saving	18
2.1	Standard	13
2.8	Energy saving	17

Use just the data involving the square footage and the annual energy cost to develop an estimated regression function to predict annual energy cost, given the square footage.

Did the function developed above provide a good fit to the observed data? Explain.

In order to incorporate the effect of using the special energy-saving package the builders defined the following dummy variable:

$$x_2 = 1 \text{ if the energy-saving package was used}$$
$$x_2 = 0 \text{ if the standard package was used}$$

With this variable the following regression function was proposed:

$$E(y) = B_0 + B_1 x_1 + B_2 x_2$$

where

$$x_1 = \text{square footage (1000 sq. ft.)}$$
$$y = \text{annual cost ($100s)}$$

In the regression function proposed above, what is the physical interpretation of B_2?

Answer

```
DATA PAGE318;
INPUT   SQ_FT   DUMMY   ENERGY;
CARDS;
1.5      0       9
2.0      0       12
2.2      1       14
1.8      0       11
2.4      0       12
2.8      1       19
2.0      0       12
2.4      1       14
1.9      1       11
3.0      1       18
2.1      0       13
2.8      1       17
;
PROC   PRINT DATA=PAGE318;
TITLE "PRINTOUT OF THE ENERGY DATA";
PROC   PLOT DATA = PAGE318;
       PLOT ENERGY*SQ_FT;
TITLE "PLOT OF ENERGY VS. SQUARE FOOT";
PROC   PLOT DATA = PAGE318;
       PLOT ENERGY*DUMMY;
TITLE "PLOT OF ENERGY VS. INSULATION PACKAGE";
PROC   REG DATA = PAGE318;
       MODEL ENERGY = SQ_FT/P R DW;
TITLE "REGRESSION ON ENRGY = SQUARE FOOT";
PROC   REG DATA = PAGE318;
       MODEL ENERGY = DUMMY/P R DW;
TITLE "REGRESSION ON ENERGY = INSULATION PACKAGE";
```

PRINTOUT OF THE ENERGY DATA

OBS	SQ_FT	DUMMY	ENERGY
1	1.5	0	9
2	2.0	0	12
3	2.2	1	14
4	1.8	0	11
5	2.4	0	12
6	2.8	1	19
7	2.0	0	12
8	2.4	1	14
9	1.9	1	11
10	3.0	1	18
11	2.1	0	13
12	2.8	1	17

216

PLOT OF ENERGY VS. SQUARE FOOT

PLOT OF ENERGY*SQ_FT   LEGEND: A = 1 OBS, B = 2 OBS, ETC.

```
ENERGY |
       |
       |
       |
    19 +                                        A
       |
       |
       |
    18 +                                              A
       |
       |
       |
    17 +                                        A
       |
       |
       |
    16 +
       |
       |
       |
    15 +
       |
       |
       |
    14 +                      A        A
       |
       |
       |
    13 +                  A
       |
       |
       |
    12 +              B            A
       |
       |
       |
    11 +       A   A
```

217

PLOT OF ENERGY*DUMMY   LEGEND: A = 1 OBS, B = 2 OBS, ETC.

```
ENERGY |
       |
       |
       |
    19 +                                                                A
       |
       |
       |
    18 +                                                                A
       |
       |
       |
    17 +                                                                A
       |
       |
       |
    16 +
       |
       |
       |
    15 +
       |
       |
       |
    14 +                                                                B
       |
       |
       |
    13 +A
       |
       |
       |
    12 +C
       |
       |
       |
    11 +A
```

DEP VARIABLE: ENERGY

ANALYSIS OF VARIANCE

SOURCE	DF	SUM OF SQUARES	MEAN SQUARE	F VALUE	PROB>F
MODEL	1	91.55502038	91.55502038	79.996	0.0001
ERROR	10	11.44497962	1.14449796		
C TOTAL	11	103.00000			

ROOT MSE	1.069812	R-SQUARE	0.8889
DEP MEAN	13.5	ADJ R-SQ	0.8778
C.V.	7.924534		

PARAMETER ESTIMATES

VARIABLE	DF	PARAMETER ESTIMATE	STANDARD ERROR	T FOR H0: PARAMETER=0	PROB > |T|
INTERCEP	1	-0.80214894	1.62861986	-0.493	0.6330
SQ_FT	1	6.38014079	0.71334019	8.944	0.0001

OBS	ACTUAL	PREDICT VALUE	STD ERR PREDICT	RESIDUAL	STD ERR RESIDUAL
1	9.0000	8.7681	0.6126	0.2319	0.8771
2	12.0000	11.9581	0.3537	0.0419	1.0097
3	14.0000	13.2342	0.3103	0.7658	1.0238
4	11.0000	10.6821	0.4412	0.3179	0.9746
5	12.0000	14.5102	0.3288	-2.5102	1.0180
6	19.0000	17.0622	0.5040	1.9378	0.9437
7	12.0000	11.9581	0.3537	0.0419	1.0097
8	14.0000	14.5102	0.3288	-0.5102	1.0180
9	11.0000	11.3201	0.3934	-0.3201	0.9948
10	18.0000	18.3383	0.6229	-0.3383	0.8698
11	13.0000	12.5961	0.3249	0.4039	1.0193
12	17.0000	17.0622	0.5040	-0.0622	0.9437

OBS	STUDENT RESIDUAL	-2 -1 0 1 2	COOK'S D
8	-0.5012	| *| |	0.013
9	-0.3218	| | |	0.008
10	-0.3889	| | |	0.039
11	0.3962	| | |	0.008
12	-0.0660	| | |	0.001

SUM OF RESIDUALS   -4.37428E-14
SUM OF SQUARED RESIDUALS   11.44498
PREDICTED RESID SS (PRESS)   15.7771

DURBIN-WATSON D   2.905
(FOR NUMBER OF OBS.)   12
1ST ORDER AUTOCORRELATION -0.455

DEP VARIABLE: ENERGY

ANALYSIS OF VARIANCE

SOURCE	DF	SUM OF SQUARES	MEAN SQUARE	F VALUE	PROB>F
MODEL	1	48.00000000	48.00000000	8.727	0.0144
ERROR	10	55.00000000	5.50000000		
C TOTAL	11	103.00000			

ROOT MSE	2.345208	R-SQUARE	0.4660	
DEP MEAN	13.5	ADJ R-SQ	0.4126	
C.V.	17.37191			

PARAMETER ESTIMATES

VARIABLE	DF	PARAMETER ESTIMATE	STANDARD ERROR	T FOR H0: PARAMETER=0	PROB > |T|
INTERCEP	1	11.50000000	0.95742711	12.011	0.0001
DUMMY	1	4.00000000	1.35400640	2.954	0.0144

OBS	ACTUAL	PREDICT VALUE	STD ERR PREDICT	RESIDUAL	STD ERR RESIDUAL
1	9.0000	11.5000	0.9574	-2.5000	2.1409
2	12.0000	11.5000	0.9574	0.5000	2.1409
3	14.0000	15.5000	0.9574	-1.5000	2.1409
4	11.0000	11.5000	0.9574	-0.5000	2.1409
5	12.0000	11.5000	0.9574	0.5000	2.1409
6	19.0000	15.5000	0.9574	3.5000	2.1409
7	12.0000	11.5000	0.9574	0.5000	2.1409
8	14.0000	15.5000	0.9574	-1.5000	2.1409
9	11.0000	15.5000	0.9574	-4.5000	2.1409
10	18.0000	15.5000	0.9574	2.5000	2.1409
11	13.0000	11.5000	0.9574	1.5000	2.1409
12	17.0000	15.5000	0.9574	1.5000	2.1409

OBS	STUDENT RESIDUAL	-2 -1 0 1 2	COOK'S D
8	-0.7006	| *| |	0.049
9	-2.1019	| ****| |	0.442
10	1.1677	| |** |	0.136
11	0.7006	| |* |	0.049
12	0.7006	| |* |	0.049

SUM OF RESIDUALS   7.99361E-15
SUM OF SQUARED RESIDUALS   55
PREDICTED RESID SS (PRESS)   79.2

DURBIN-WATSON D   1.745
(FOR NUMBER OF OBS.)   12
1ST ORDER AUTOCORRELATION 0.050

Similarly, if we want to test whether the first independent variable in Example 2 has more effect than the second variable, i.e. H_o $(\beta_1 = \beta_2)$, then the relevant test will be

$$t = \frac{b_1 - b_2}{S(b_1 - b_2)} \qquad d.f. = n_1 + n_2 - 2$$

If the null hypothesis is that all the variables are zero in the population $H_o(\beta_1 = \beta_2 = .. = \beta_k = 0)$, then it will require an Analysis of Variance Test, testing whether error variance in (Example 2) (computer output) is significantly bigger/smaller than the mean square due to regression.

In symbolic notation, if the dependent variable Y_i in the i^{ts} observation is a linear function of $R(j=1...k)$ explanatory variation $x_{i1}, x_{i2}...x_{ik}$ plus a random error $E_i(i \neq j)$ in the population which are normally distributed with $E(E_i) = 0$ and $V(E_i) = \sigma^2$ and E_i are independent, i.e. $E(E_i, E_j) = \sigma^2$ then we have (assuming variables are measured from the mean i, $(E(x) = E(Y) = 0, \alpha = 0)$

$$Y_1 = \beta_1 x_{11} + \beta_2 x_{12} ... + \beta_k x_{1k} + e_1$$

$$Y_2 = \beta_1 x_{21} + \beta_2 x_{22} ... + \beta_k x_{2k} + e_2$$

$$.$$
$$.$$
$$.$$

$$Y_n = \beta_1 x_{n1} + \beta_2 x_{n2} ... + \beta_k x_{nk} + e_k$$

In matrix notation

$$Y = X\beta + E$$

where

$$Y = \begin{bmatrix} Y_1 \\ Y_2 \\ \vdots \\ Y_n \end{bmatrix} \quad n \times 1$$

$$X = \begin{pmatrix} x_{11} & x_{12} \cdots & x_{1k} \\ \cdot & & \\ \cdot & & \\ x_{n1} & x_{n2} \cdots & x_{nk} \end{pmatrix} \quad n \times k$$

$$\beta = \begin{bmatrix} \beta_1 \\ \beta_2 \\ \vdots \\ \beta_k \end{bmatrix} \quad k \times 1$$

$$E = \begin{bmatrix} e_1 \\ e_2 \\ \vdots \\ e_n \end{bmatrix} \quad n \times 1$$

and $COV(E) = E(ee')$

$$
\begin{pmatrix}
\sigma^2 & 0 & \cdots & 0 \\
0 & \sigma^2 & \cdots & 0 \\
\cdot & & & \\
\cdot & & & \\
\cdot & & & \\
0 & \cdots\cdots & & \sigma^2
\end{pmatrix}
= \sigma^2 I_n \text{ where } I_{n \times n} \text{ is an identity matrix}
$$

The least square estimate gives
$$ b = (X'X)^{-1} Y $$
such that

$$
\begin{aligned}
E(b) &= \beta + (X'X)^{-1} X'E(E) = \beta \\
CoV(b) &= E(b-E(b)) \ (b-E(b)') \\
&= (X'X)^{-1} \sigma^2
\end{aligned}
$$

So far we have assumed that the random errors e_i (j=i...n) in the observation are distributed normally with $E(e_i) = 0$ and $E(e_i, e_j) = \sigma^2$ and they are independent. However, if the random errors are not independent, then the OLS (ordinary least square) method will be biased. In that case, $E(E'E) = V\sigma^2$ where V exists and it is not an identity matrix. If the successive residuals (errors e_j) are positively correlated

$$ e_i = a_{i-1} \ e_{i-1} + U_i $$

the statistic

$$ d = \sum_{i=1}^{n-1} (e_{i+1} - e_i)^2 / e_i^2 $$

can be used as a Durbin-Watson statistic to test whether there is any serial correlation. Again, if there is multicollinearity problem, i.e. some column vectors are linearly dependent, exactly or nearly so, then the diagonals of the matrix X'X will be either zero or very large, making OLS estimates nearly useless. In that case, prior information about the regression coefficients can be introduced through Bayesian methods or other techniques. In the extreme situation where we have a distributed lag situation

$$ Y_t = \alpha + \Sigma \beta_{jt} \ X_{t-j} - e_t $$

accuracy of the estimates b_j of β_j will be very low since explanatory variables will be highly correlated. Some restrictions can be imposed on β_i. One such restriction is $\beta_j = \lambda^j \beta_o$

subtracting Y_{t-1} from the above equation will give

$$ Y_t = \lambda Y_{t-1} + (1 - \lambda) \ \alpha + B \ X_t + (e_t - \lambda e_{t-1}) $$

giving a lagged dependent variable and non-fixed explanatory variable. This is known as the KOYCK transformation.

Simultaneous Equation Models

So far we have discussed estimations of a single equation with the help of the method of least squares which gives a biased estimate of the regression coefficient b's. However, the relations in the social sciences are jointly determined by a system of interdependent equations rather than individually, one by one. We shall rename the dependent variables in the interdependent equations as endogenous variables. They influence the system but in turn are themselves affected. Variables such as consumption, wages, gross national product, etc. are endogenous. Variables such as investment, tax rate, weather, war, famine, etc. are exogenous variables which affect the system but in turn are not affected themselves, at least not in the short run. Predetermined variables are those which include the exogenous variables and the lagged endogenous variables. We can write the system of G linear simultaneous stochastic equations with K predetermined variables as (closely following Chow, 1983)

$$\beta_{11} Y_{t1} + \beta_{12} Y_{t2} \cdots + \beta_{1G} Y_{tG} + r_{11} X_{t1} \cdots r_{1k} X_{tk} = \Sigma_{t1}$$

$$\beta_{21} Y_{t1} + \beta_{22} Y_{t2} \cdots + \beta_{2G} Y_{tG} + r_{21} X_{t1} \cdots r_{2k} X_{tk} = \Sigma_{t2}$$

$$\cdots\cdots\cdots\cdots\cdots\cdots\cdots\cdots\cdots\cdots\cdots\cdots\cdots\cdots\cdots$$

$$\beta_{G1} Y_{t1} + \beta_{G2} Y_{t2} \cdots + \beta_{GG} Y_{tG} + r_{G1} X_{t1} \cdots + r_{Gk} X_{tk} = \Sigma_{tG}$$

where β_{ij} = coefficient of jth endogenous variables in the ith structural equation. r_{ij} = coefficient of jth predetermined variable in i^{th} structural equation. $\beta_{ij} = -1$ to make Y_{ti} become the variable on the left-hand side in the ith equation. $\Sigma_{t1}, \Sigma_{t2} \ldots \Sigma_{tG}$ are assumed to be serially independent G variate normal with mean zero and covariance matrix $\Sigma = (\sigma_{ij})$. Denoting Y_t as the column vector $(Y_{t1} \ldots Y_{tG})$; X_t as the column vector consisting of $X_{t1}, X_{t2} \ldots X_{tk}$ and Σ_t as the column vector consisting of $\Sigma_{t1}, \Sigma_{t2} \ldots \Sigma_{tG}$, we write in matrix notation

$$BY_t + \Gamma X_t = \Sigma_t \quad \text{or}$$

$$Y_t = -B^{-1} \Gamma X_t + B^{-1} \Sigma_t = \pi X_t + v_t$$

which is known as the reduced form equation. In the above equation

$\pi = -B^{-1}\Gamma$ is the matrix of reduced form coefficients.

$v_t = B^{-1}\Sigma$ as the residual vector such that $E(v) = 0$

and $E_{vv'} = B^{-1}\Sigma B^{-1'} = \Omega$, so the parameters of the structural equations consist of three matrices (B, Γ, Σ) where of the reduced form, two parameters (π, Ω) where $\pi = -B^{-1}.\Gamma, \Omega = B^{-1} \Sigma.$ $(B^{-1})'$ (we assume B^{-1} exists).

There are two problems associated with the simultaneous equation system. One is the problem of identification. Can we estimate the structural parameters (B, Γ, Σ) from π and Ω? Econometricians have developed rules of identification. Crudely speaking, the rule is that the number of equations must be equal to the number of endogenous variables. The second point is the method of estimation. The OLS method will give inconsistent estimates, since, if we regress Y_{t1} on Y_{t2}, X_{t1} and X_{t2}, all the residuals will be correlated with Y_{t2} in the simultaneous equation system. To avoid this problem, econometricians have developed more advanced methods. These are the applications of principles of least squares, maximum likelihood and instrument variables. These estimates can be of two types: (1) full information when the entire system is specified and estimated simultaneously, and (2) limited information where a subset of equations is specified and

estimated. Some of the methods are:
1. Two stage least square
2. Three stage least square
3. Method of limited information maximum
4. K-class estimator
5. Method of full-information maximum likelihood (FIML)
6. Method of instrumental variables
7. FIML with autoregressive variables

So far we have discussed linear equations. However, in many economic problems the appropriate relations may be non-linear, for example, the following type

$$Y_t = \beta_1 \, e^{\beta_2 \, X_t} + \Sigma_t$$

In this equation, the function is nonlinear both in X and parameter β_1 and β_2. To solve such problems, some of the following methods can be used:
(1) Method of GLS or minimum distance
(2) Nonlinear regression
(3) Method of maximum likelihood
(4) Numerical method of maximization
(5) FIML for nonlinear simultaneous equations
(6) Method of instrumental variables
(7) Nonlinear two-stage and three-stage variables
(8) Dynamic nonlinear equations

At this stage, a distinction should be made between a simultaneous equation model discussed before and a dynamic model. A useful dynamic model is the autoregressive model

$$Y_t = a_1 \, Y_{t-1} + a_2 \, Y_{t-2} \ldots + a_p \, Y_{t-p} + \Sigma_t \text{ (order p)}$$

Another model is the moving-average model

$$Y_t = \Sigma_t + b_1 \, \Sigma_{t-1} + \ldots + b_q \, \Sigma_{t-q} \text{ (order q)}$$

Combining the two types of influences of the past on Y_t, one can form an autoregressive moving average (ARMA)

$$T_t = A_1 \, Y_{t-1} + \ldots + A_p \, Y_{t-p} + \Sigma_t + B_1 \, \Sigma_{t-1} \ldots + B_2 \, \Sigma_{t-q}$$

where A and B are matrices.

Dynamic properties of the time series generated by these models and estimating them have been widely discussed in the literature. One very useful method of estimation of the ARMA model is the Box-Jenkins method (called ARMA autoregressive integrated moving average process).

The econometric model helps us to predict the macro variable such as the demand for cars. Alternatively, we may be interested in predicting the probability of a family buying a car. Such a determination can be made by Probit or Logit analysis. We can use the maximum likelihood method to estimate the parameters of multinomial logit models.

In the case of simultaneous models, we assume that the coefficients "B" remain the same as the past sample prediction period. This may not be the case for good prediction. For this purpose, we can use the models of time-varying coefficients.

$$Y_t = X_t \beta_t + \Sigma_t \qquad\qquad (t = 1, \ldots T)$$

$$\beta_t = N\beta_{t-1} + r_t \qquad\qquad (t = 1, \ldots T)$$

Maximum likelihood method for the estimation of such a model in linear or nonlinear form can be developed. It is remarkable that econometricians not only developed large-scale econometric models for many countries, but used extensively the different methods of estimation often using the super computer. Even the software required for performing the complicated estimation procedures are now available in microcomputers.

B.   Rational Expectations

In many situations, the behaviour of economic agents depends on what they think the value of certain economic variables will be. In deciding the amount of economic capital investment, the business manager will have to form estimates of future projects, reserve and costs for such an investment. One hypothesis of adaptative expectation specifies

$$Y_t^e - Y_{t-1}^e = \beta\,(Y_{t-1} - Y_{t-1}^e)$$

where Y_t is the economic variable, and Y^e is its expected value on the basis of information available up to the period t-1. This hypothesis states that the expectation change from period (t-1) to t by a fraction of the discrepancy between actual observation at t-1 to t. In the case of conflict management, the expected result of a policy may not be the same as the observed situation and this adaptive process may be helpful in deciding a plan at an optimum decision.

C.   An Example:   Econometric Analysis to Forecasting in
      International Relations**

      Nazli Choucri

1.Introduction[*]
      The apparent neglect of quantitative methodology in
political analysis can be explained partly by the absence of
a common paradigm or frame of reference for political inquiry
and partly by the lack of experience with experimental
analysis of empirical data. The absence of general theory
poses considerable difficulties for analysis and for
specifying the nature of expected relationships or outcomes.
For example, without a good theory of war, it is difficult to
explain, account for, and predict wars among nations as well
as to forecast the probable range of casualties, the extent or
duration of violence, geographical scope, and so forth. And
the absence of sufficient experience with quantitative
analysis poses equally numerous difficulties bearing upon our
ability to go beyond purely descriptive modes of inquiry. For
example, without sound analytical and computational tools it
is difficult to develop empirical models, or simulations, or
forecasts of such dynamics.
      This paper examines some key issues and difficulties
encountered in the course of applying econometric analysis to
forecasting in international relations. We will note the
problems involved and the solutions adopted, and indicate the
consequences of faulty analysis, analytical bias or
measurement error.
      Our substantive investigations are addressed to the long-
range causes of international conflict. Our objective, during
the past several years, has been to develop systematic
procedures for isolating the determinants of international
violence. The general approach we have employed is one common
to any econometrician concerned with the analysis of time
series data, or any statistician examining the properties of
small samples (Deusenberry, 1965; 1969). But our applications
of these methods are not common in political analysis.
Economists, for example, appear to know much more about the
nature of market systems, business cycles, inflation, etc.
than political analysts know about conflict and warfare, arms
races, lateral pressure or international alignments.[1]
      In the course of our inquiries we have developed a
partial theory of the dynamics in question, translated this
theory into a model from which structural equations were
developed, and then estimated the unknown parameters. The
purpose of this enterprise was to investigate the implications
of alternative parameter estimates upon the behaviour of the
system as a whole. Experimenting with "high" and "low"
coefficients, and comparing these with base-line parameters
and system outputs provided us with reliable means of looking
into alternative outcomes and alternative futures.
      It is not our objective here to question the nature of
causality, or to dispute the assumptions underlying the social
and behavioral sciences. Others have done this elsewhere
(Blalock and Blalock, 1968; Ando, Fisher and Simon, 1963).

Nor is it our intent to deliver an introductory lecture on the algorithms upon which elementary statistical methods are based. Rather, our purpose is to make explicit the critical problems inherent in econometric analysis and the ways we have sought to resolve them.[2] Toward this end we discuss (1) our model of international conflict dynamics developed within the context of the general linear model in regression analysis; (2) methodological implications of alternative perspectives upon causality; (3) some key statistics and common problems in causal inference; (4) simultaneous estimation and the problem of identifiability; (5) serial correlation and time dependent corrections; (6) the use of instrumental variables and generalized least squares; (7) system change and breakpoint analysis; and finally (8) procedures employed for simulation, forecasting and policy analysis and some practical illustrations.

2. A Model of International Conflict: Extensions of the General Linear Model

In recent studies of international behaviour we have argued that the roots of conflict and warfare can be found in the basic attributes and characteristics of nations and that the most critical variables in this regard are population, resources and technology. We have then attempted to specify the intervening sequences between these three sets of variables, on the one hand, and conflict and warfare, on the other. On the basis of empirical and historical analysis, we suggest that the chain of developments relating population, resources and technology to violence appears to be the following.

A combination of population and developing technology places rapidly increasing demands upon resources, often resulting in internally generated pressures. The greater this pressure, the higher will be the likelihood of extending national activities outside territorial boundaries. We have termed this tendency to extend behaviour outside national boundaries lateral pressure. To the extent that two or more countries with high capability and high pressure tendency (and high lateral pressure) extend their interests and psycho-political borders outward, there is a strong probability that eventually the two opposing spheres of interest will intersect. The more intense the intersection, the greater will be the likelihood that competition will assume military proportions. When this happens, we may expect competition to be transformed into conflict and perhaps an arms race or cold war. At a more general level of abstraction, provocation will be the final act that can be viewed as the stimulus for large-scale conflict or violence. But an act will be considered provocation only in a situation which has already been characterized by high lateral pressure, intersections among spheres of influence, armament tensions and competitions, and an increasing level of prevailing conflict.

Major wars, we have argued, often emerge through a two-step process: in terms of internally generated pressure (which can be traced to population dynamics, resource needs and constraints, and technological development) and in terms of

reciprocal comparison, rivalry and conflict, on a number of salient capability and behaviour dimensions. Each process tends to be closely related to the other, and each, to a surprising degree, can be accounted for by relatively non-manipulable variables (or variables that are controllable only at high costs). And it is
these variables, we hypothesize, that provide the long-range roots of conflict and warfare.

The first step in the transition from a general theoretical statement to a model capable of sustaining the empirical test is to identify the variables to be explained. These will eventually serve as the outputs of the model. The second is to specify those effects that contribute to outcome variables by developing equations designed to explain the behaviour of each of the dependent variables.

Those explanatory variables that are thought to contribute to our understanding of the outcomes in question can be other dependent variables (lagged or unlagged) or they may be variables that are exogenous and not to be explained by the model. For policy purposes it is important to select at least some explanatory variables that are manipulable by the policy-maker. For obvious reasons, it would not be useful to select only variables that are all "givens" or variables that are manipulable at very high costs unless, of course, one's objectives were to test for the extent to which non-manipulables dominate system behaviour.

Our theoretical statement can thus be transformed into graphic relationships, as noted in Figure 1. These relationships can then be translated into structural equations, the parameters of which could then be estimated in the context of the general linear model. This particular model pertains to the pre-World War I period, 1870-1914.

The general linear model in econometric and causal modelling is a conceptual mechanism to determine the values of variables when quantitative data are supplied (Johnston, 1972, 121-76; Christ, 1966, 243-98). This mechanism includes a set of equations, their functional form, and an accompanying set of specifications and restrictions. We combine observed data, specifications of a model, and the laws of probability to obtain estimates of unknown parameters. Related procedures are suggested by others (Fennessey, 1968; Rao and Miller, 1971).

This basic linear model is of the following form:

$$Y = X\beta + u,$$

where
Y represents a vector of observations of the dependent or endogenous variable;
X represents the matrix of independent variables (explanatory, predetermined and exogenous);
β is the vector of coefficients to be estimated from empirical data; and u represents the vector of error or disturbance terms, each of which is composed of three errors (a) error due to a linear approximation of the "true" functional form, (b) error resulting from erroneously included or left out variables, and (c) random noise.

The general linear form can be extended to the case of m independent variables and n equations, while the assumption that each dependent variable can be expressed as a linear function of the independent or exogenous variables (linear in the parameters only; the variables can be nonlinear functions of other variables). It is also assumed that empirical observations are generated by a stochastic mechanism. In the case of the linear model, ordinary least squares provides the best linear unbiased estimates of the parameters only if the following assumptions or a priori constraints are not seriously violated: (1) that the disturbance terms (u) are random variables, with zero mean and homogeneous variance; (2) that the disturbances are uncorrelated over time; and (3) that the exogenous variables are not correlated with the disturbances.

The model we have developed is more complex than the general linear case. Some of the complexity is due to (a) the nature of the dynamics being modelled, (b) the procedures we have employed to correct for significant departures from the assumptions underlying an ordinary least squares solution of the general linear model, and (c) the use of simultaneous equation estimators to obtain unbiased coefficients of feedback systems. The resultant system of equations is presented in Table I.

The entire analysis was undertaken on TROLL/1, an interactive computer system developed at the Massachusetts Institute of Technology for the analysis of econometric models and complex systems. We have employed (a) a logarithmic transformation on one of the key endogenous variables (colonial area) in order to approximate the underlying theoretical relationship more closely, and (b) an interactive term combining the effects of population and technology (defined as population times national income) in order to obtain some measure of their multiplicative impact. In addition, we have used generalized least squares, transforming the independent variables according to the structure of the serial correlation in the disturbances, in conjunction with two stage least squares (a limited information maximum likelihood estimator), so as to incorporate a time dependent correction as well as simultaneous effects in the final estimates of the parameters.[3]

It is important to appreciate that the parameters of an equation cannot be estimated purely on the basis of empirical data, no matter how complete, reliable or extensive these may be.[4] The role of data is as follows: Information is useful for identification purposes only if it can serve to distinguish among structural equations. Observational data alone cannot perform this necessary step in model building, although analysis of one set of data can provide clues for specification of the next set. Nonetheless, only in conjunction with a priori restrictions and specifications can empirical data be put to good usage (Coombs, 1964). But the most basic issue of all in making the transition from a theoretical statement to a formal model is specification of causal ordering.

3. Directional Relations and Causal Inference

In the most general sense, "causation" refers to hierarchies of influences or effects, most readily characterized by asymmetrical relations within a specified system. Causation, however, is not necessarily implied by a particular time sequence – a consideration that is commonly neglected in systematic social and political inquiry. Because of this simple, but almost self-evident point, it is important to adopt alternative criteria for the specification of causal relations. In a persuasive argument, Herbert Simon suggests that causal orderings are determined by the appearance of non-zero coefficients in a system of equations. The _a priori_ specification of zero coefficients thus raises the issue of identifiability (Fisher, 1966). "For complete identifiability of a structure those restraints must preclude the existence in the same model of a different equivalent structure, that is (in linear models), a different set of equations whose members are linear combinations of the original equations" (Ando, Fisher, and Simon, 1963, 23). Causation is therefore closely related to identifiability and the requirements of identifiability, by necessity, impose certain constraints on the process of model building.

The causal question gives rise to a related set of philosophical and empirical problems (Orcutt, 1952). The long- standing debate among social scientists regarding causal perspectives upon the "real" world – whether it be essentially hierarchical, or recursive or whether it be essentially non-recursive, or simultaneous – is one that can be resolved through a combination of these two positions, namely that the overall framework or system of relations (or equations) in the structure under consideration may basically be recursive (thus negating simultaneous relations at a macro level), but that small components (or blocks) thereof may be non-recursive (thus allowing for feedback relations within a localized context). In terms of applied analysis, this debate has one important effect: How one perceives the structure one seeks to model (whether it be basically recursive or non-recursive) dictates the kind of estimation procedure employed, and the ways in which "reality" is represented in a system of equations designed to approximate the dynamics under consideration. We have adopted the non-recursive view of causality while recognizing that in the longer run greater understanding of the dynamics in question may be obtained through expansion of our model and use of a block-recursive approach.

In both operational and philosophical terms, the issue of causation thus involves (1) asymmetrics of relations, (2) the necessity for zero coefficients in some equations, (3) the distinction between endogenous and exogenous variables, (4) specification of causal ordering, (5) specification of direct and indirect effects and (6) assumptions underlying the structure of the disturbance term in each equation. The general linear model provides the intellectual tools to structure reality and to think about directional influences, but our analysis goes far beyond to causal modelling, simultaneous estimation, simulation and policy analysis.

232

4.   Causal Inference: Some Key Statistics and Common
      Problems

      The two most common criteria for evaluating the
performance of a model are (1) how well the specified
equations fit known data, and (2) what the outputs of the
model are and why.   Examining the patterns of errors (or
residuals) therefore becomes an important aspect of model
building.
      The variance of the coefficient estimate indicates the
precision of the coefficient as derived from empirical data.
The statistical significance of a parameter is inferred from
the magnitude of the t statistic, and the significance of
several parameters is inferred from the F ratio.   In a
regression equation, the value of F measures the joint
significance of the parameter estimates.   The summary
statistic, R^2, refers to the amount of variance in the
dependent variable explained by the independent variables (and
the associated stochastic mechanism).   A very high R^2 may
imply an identity or a trivial regression equation, while a
low R^2 does not necessarily indicate an invalid equation.[5]
Other summary statistics are needed before an educated
judgement is drawn, such as the standard errors around the
parameters.   In practical applications, however, these
statistics are often subject to bias in the parameters.[6]
When the disturbances are serially correlated, the variances
and standed errors will be deflated, producing inflated t, F,
and R^2 statistics, leading to possible erroneous inferences.
Correcting for serial correlation amounts to a crucial aspect
of causal modelling, thus highlighting the importance of the
Durbin-Watson statistic.
      The Durbin-Watson statistic, otherwise known as the d
statistic, is a test of the significance of serial correlation
in a first order autoregressive process:

$$d = \frac{\sum_{t=2}^{n} (u_t - u_{t-1})^2}{\sum_{t=1}^{n} u_t^2}$$

where u represents the error values (which are both positive
and negative, with an assumed mean of zero).   The d statistic
will tend to be small for positively autocorrelated error
terms and large for errors that are negatively autocorrelated.
Durbin and Watson have worked out upper and lower bounds of
the statistic, with an area of uncertainty inbetween.   As a
rule of thumb, a d statistic of 2.0 ($\pm$0.2) indicates the
absence of serial correlation in the disturbances.   It is also
important to note that the statistic is not applicable in
cases with lagged endogenous variables - since the test was
developed for non-stochastic vectors of explanatory variables
(Durbin and Waston, 1950; 1951).
      The Durbin-Watson statistic is no longer valid when there
is a coincidence of lagged endogenous variables and
autocorrelated disturbances.   In that case, the statistic is

asymptotically biased upward toward 2.0 and no longer tests for autocorrelation. Thus, a non-significant d statistic does not preclude the possibility that ordinary least squares estimates are inconsistent when there are lagged endogenous variables in the equation. In the case of simultaneous systems, the same problem exists for the system endogenous variables. We must replace both system and lagged endogenous variables through the use of instrumental variables.

A common difficulty in statistical analysis is high collinearity among the explanatory variables. But we cannot rule out the use of a particular variable or the estimation of a particular equation simply because of multicollinarity. Other problems might also arise (Rao and Miller, 1971, 48). High intercorrelations result in the loss of precision, but the exclusion of a theoretically relevant variable on those grounds might exacerbate serial correlation in the disturbances.[7] Further, multicollinearity affects the precision of coefficient estimates rather than their values.

By far the most serious problem in data analysis and parameter estimation involves measurement error. It is customary to equate measurement error with faulty data or erroneous quantitative measures. While such problems are undoubtedly the source of much distortion in both analysis and results, it is important to broaden the conventional definition in at least two ways. First, specific estimates of the error in quantitative measures may be obtained from the measures themselves and incorporated as confidence intervals around the basic data for purposes of modifying the results according to the degree, magnitude and direction of cumulated error.[8]

The second extension of measurement error thinking lies in the structure of the underlying equation itself. Measurement error may be attributed to cases where the magnitude of the disturbance of the error term raises serious questions concerning the validity of the equation and the viability of the resulting specification. Ideally, the most desirable situation is one in which (1) errors in the quantitative measures are known to be negligible and (2) the disturbance term is small and exhibits no discernible trend of either positive or negative serial correlation. In practice, however, neither of these conditions may hold: the extent of fault in the data is often not known, and the disturbance term exhibits significant serial correlation, especially in trend analysis of time series data (Blalock, 1965). The methods employed to minimize the effects of serial correlation are discussed briefly.

5.   Simultaneous   Inference   and   the   Problem   of
       Identifiability

When there is mutual dependence among the endogenous variables, simultaneous estimation of the parameters is called for (Christ, 1960). This set of procedures is more complex than standard regression analysis. Estimation in the classical regression mode involves one dependent variable and several independent ones. In the simultaneous case there are several jointly dependent variables. This situation generates an identification problem. This means that even if infinite data were available from which the reduced form of the parameters could be derived exactly, the values of the coefficients cannot be estimated without some a priori theoretical restriction upon the number of exogenous and endogenous variables in each equation.

The addition of a priori restrictions to identify an equation is useful only if the same restrictions are not employed to identify other equations as well. However, additional a priori information is generally in the form of linear inequalities for the coefficients to be estimated. Inequalities of this nature add to the efficiency of the estimates but do not assist in the identification of a particular equation. Furthermore, if a model is not identifiable, manipulating the equations or the order of constituent variables will not assure identifications: either a model is identifiable or it is not.

The problem of identifiability is thus closely related to theory and method and is central to any model building effort. An equation is identifiable when a combination of a priori and observational information allows for a distinction between the parameters of the equation and those of other equations. By extension, a model is identifiable if each equation represents a distinct set of relationships. The problem is one of having sufficient a priori information to distinguish among equations. A certain minimum is necessary. Beyond that, any added information may be put to use. In just identified equations there is exactly one way to obtain the "true" equation from the reduced form. In overidentified cases there is more than one way. In an underidentified situation, where a priori information is insufficient to provide a discriminating service, there is no way in which the "true" equation may be recovered or distinguished from others in the same functional form. The model we have developed through experimentation and alternative specification is an overidentified set of equations: there is more than one way of retrieving the reduced form of each original equation. In practical terms, the problem is generally one of choosing among the various alternatives involving an overidentified equation or model.

It must also be noted that the standard statistical theorems developed for the case in which the explanatory variables are treated as if they were fixed in repeated sampling cannot be used when there are lagged endogenous variables. Furthermore, the coincidence of lagged endogenous variables and autocorrelated disturbances inflates the t statistic and may signal erroneous inferences. Marked departures from the assumptions underlying the general linear model produce biased parameter estimates, often necessitating equally marked departures from standard regression procedures. The practical implications of serial correlation in simultaneous systems for parameter estimation are sometimes overwhelming.

6. Serial Correlation and Time Dependent Correction

Because the structure of the serial correlation in the disturbances is often unclear - if it were known then the solution to the problem would be simply to adjust the parameter estimates accordingly - we are confronted with the necessity of estimating the nature of the autocorrelation parameter empirically and identifying the underlying stochastic process. This involved: (a) isolating the systematic component of the disturbances, and (b) adjusting the independent variables so as to develop consistent estimates of the parameters.

Aitken (1935) had demonstrated that the Generalized Least Squares estimator produces an unbiased estimate of the error variance when disturbances are autocorrelated. But the estimate is not the "true" rho. However, it does have a known statistical distribution and in small samples it is consistent (Hibbs, 1974; Goldberger, 1965). Our objective is to identify the theoretical structure of the time dependent parameter, and determine its statistical properties.

Four disturbance structures have properties which are tractable and well-known: (1) first order autoregressive process (where each error term (u_t) depends only upon its previous value (u_{t-1}) plus a random component (e_t) (2) second order autoregressive structures (where u_t) depends upon u_{t-1} and u_{t-2}, plus a random component (e_t); (3) first order moving average (where the disturbances depend only upon a series of temporally adjacent, independently distributed, random variables; and hence all the disturbances prior to u_{t-1} do not contribute to generating u_t); and (4) second order moving averages (where, for the same reason, the autocorrelation of u_t is effectively zero with all terms beyond u_{t-2}):

(1) $u_t = p_1 u_{t-1} + e_t$
(2) $u_t = p_1 u_{t-1} + p_2 u_{t-2} + e_t$
(3) $u_t = e_t - p_1 e_{t-1}$
(4) $u_t = e_t - p_1 e_{t-1} - p_2 e_{t-2}$

where u_t represents the disturbance and e_t represents the random component. In the "real" world, higher order structures are probably operative, but their statistical tractability amounts to a major computational problem, and it is not always clear that the benefits accrued by computational complexity are greater than the costs incurred.[10]

We seek to identify the structure of serial correlation parameters so as to obtain unbiased general least squares (GLS) estimates of the parameter values and their statistical variance and other attributes. A critical aspect of GLS involves a careful analysis of the residuals. There are at least two ways in which this can be done. The first way involves retrieving the residuals from regression analysis and then correlating the first $t/5$ terms with the initial value of the residual, generating empirical values. A correlogram analysis is then undertaken comparing "theoretical" values (which would be expected from a particular autoregressive structure) to the empirical ones. The second way, applicable only for autoregressive processes, involves regressing the residuals (u_t) upon their previous values (u_{t-1} for AUTO1 and u_{t-1}, u_{t-2}, for AUTO2,) and observing the statistical significance of the two equations and the value of the Durbin-Watson statistics.

These two procedures are not so clear cut as they might appear. In applied analysis, for example, it is often difficult to distinguish moving average processes from autoregressive processes that dampen off sharply (Hibbs, 1974, 51; Hannan, 1960). There are also difficulties in determining whether the discrepancy between the theoretical autocorrelation parameter and its empirical counterpart is significant rather than attributable to noise. Conventional statistics of goodness of fit are generally employed to differentiate significance from noise. Identifying the structure of serial correlation and making appropriate adjustments amount to an important aspect of our investigations.

7. Instrumental Variables and Generalized Least Squares

As noted earlier, ordinary least squares yields inconsistent parameter estimates in dynamic models with lagged endogenous variables and serial correlation in the error term. The OLS residuals are no longer the "true" underlying disturbances in that Y_{t-1} has a tendency to co-opt the systematic component of the disturbances.[11] This results in an upward bias for the coefficient of the lagged endogenous variable and a downward bias for the other exogenous or explanatory variables, frequently leading to erroneous inferences. This was a particularly serious problem in our investigations since determining the effects of the previous year's military allocations upon the next year's budget amounted to an important aspect of our research. For this reason we must find ways of compensating for expected distortions.

One important assumption of Least Squares is that the errors are uncorrelated with the co-terms and uncorrelated with each other.[12] To meet this assumption instrumental variables —which are assumed to be uncorrelated with the error but highly correlated with the original co-terms - are created. The constructed variables, which may be linear combinations of the original terms, are therefore assumed to be uncorrelated with the disturbances, and can thus be used to estimate the coefficients of the original equations. The original data and not the constructed terms is used to calculate the residuals (Eisner and Pindyck, 1972).

Instrumental variables can be thought of as two stage least squares estimators in which not all the predetermined variables need to be used. Rules for a good instrument include (a) those which must be observed to yield a consistent estimator and (b) rules designed to improve efficiency while maintaining consistency. For an equation

$$Y_t = Y_{t-1} + \Sigma X_t + u_t$$

Two stage least squares is consistent because it replaces Y_{t-1} with Z_t, with certain properties for a consistent estimator. These are: (a) Z_t is a linear combination of the predetermined variables: this is necessary so that Z_t will, in the probability limit, be uncorrelated with the disturbances, $u_{1...n}$; (b) Y_{t-1} and Z_t must be linearly independent: this occurs if there are enough predetermined variables used in the first stage (in order to assure that the matrix inverted at the second stage will be non-singular); (c) Z_t must include, as part of its instrument list, all of the predetermined variables in the system, and (d) the same list of instruments must be used in the first stage (or the original equation), otherwise there is no assurance that all the elements of Z_t will be independent of the error term.[13] The equation thus becomes

$$Y_t = Z_t + \Sigma X_t + u_t$$

Z_t replaces the lagged endogenous variables Yt-1, and ΣX_t still represents the remaining exogenous variables. System endogenous variables are treated similarly to the lagged term Y_{t-1}.

Good instruments must have the following properties: (a) they must be predetermined, uncorrelated asymptotically with the disturbances (and a lagged endogenous variable cannot be treated as exogenous), (b) there must be no simultaneous feedback loops connecting the equations to be estimated with the equations explaining the potential instrument (c) the disturbances with the equation to be estimated must not be correlated with the explanatory variable. Predetermined variables are instrumental because of the above three conditions. In short: A good instrument must propel the endogenous variable in the equations to be estimated.[14] The instruments we have employed are listed in Table 1.

The question remains: Is the time dependent correction to be made before or after the second stage instrumental variable substitution?[15] In the analysis reported below we have followed the algorithms implemented in TROLL by undertaking generalized least squares first, then the instrumental variable substitution. But we have tested empirically for the differences that are yielded when the reverse procedure is employed; that is, first the instrumental variable substitution and then generalized least squares, and have found no significant differences for the model in Table 1. Several rounds of generalized least squares rarely produce theoretically meaningful results. For this reason, if an initial use of GLS does not appear to correct for serial correlation adequately, respecification is definitely called for.

Two stage least squares thus "purges" the correlation between the independent variables and the error term, so that a least squares estimate can be performed from the reduced form equation (Hibbs, 1974; Rao and Miller, 1971). The first stage is (a) to regress Y_{t-1} upon the instrumental variables, and (b) replace Y_{t-1} by the created counterpart (Z_t). If the instrument is a good one, all variables are uncorrelated with the disturbance term. This method yields consistent estimates of the parameters for the lagged endogenous variable, and for the parameters of the exogenous variables. The residuals obtained are now the "true" residuals and can be used for correlogram analysis. The next step (c) is to use the consistent estimates of the second stage and the original data to form estimates of the original disturbances (these disturbances are consistent since they are deduced from consistent parameter estimates). The following step (d) is to analyse the residuals for time dependent structure, then (e) generate the Generalized Least Squares estimates, which is one method for generating parameter estimates in the presence of significant serial correlation. SLS is thus an instrumental variable substitution technique since it generates Z_t which are independent of the errors. When employed in conjunction with Generalized Least Squares, we can correct for serial correlation as well as take into account the simultaneities and interdependencies in the dynamics modelled, with the problems mentioned above.

In sum, one correction for the coincidence of lagged endogenous variables and serial correlation involves a two stage instrumental variable substitution and the use of generalized least squares. If we treat lagged endogenous variables as endogenous, then a consistent estimate of the equation can be obtained using an instrumental variable estimator with current and lagged exogenous variables as instruments, provided the system has a sufficient number of exogenous variables. This estimator is robust against all forms of autocorrelation in the disturbances, but not against serial correlation in the explanatory variables. In this case, it becomes necessary to estimate the structure of the disturbances, and then confront the problem of sequencing with respect to generalized least squares and two stage least squares, as noted above.

8.   System Change and Breakpoint Analysis

The occurrence of breakpoints and problems relating to the estimation of system change and prediction beyond the break are central issues in model building and forecasting. Sharp shifts in dynamics may signify discontinuities in some underlying empirical realities (but they may well be quite natural regularities of other empirical realities). Often breakpoints indicate incompleteness of theoretical specification.

We can think of breakpoints either as sharp changes in slope, or as nonlinearities. Some shifts may signify discontinuities which may be directly included in the equation as dummy variables (as we have done when defining changes in rivalling Powers). Econometricians use similar procedures (Thiel, 1970). The incorporation of a break directly in the analysis increases the fit between historical and estimated data and between historical and simulated dynamics.

In some instances the break results from quantitative changes. In others it results from qualitative changes. There are as yet no known methods whereby the particular points at which a significant shift has occurred may be identified precisely (other than costly and complicated iterative procedures). For this reason, the best alternative is to plot the data, then to hypothesize the occurrence of a break based on empirical observation and to test for its statistical significance. The Chow test is still the most appropriate significance test for breakpoints. Quasi-experimental techniques for coping with such problems provide additional perspectives upon these issues but they are cumbersome and complicated (Chow, 1960; Campbell and Stanley, 1966).

The Chow test, modified recently by Fisher, involves the comparison of a set of coefficients with those of another array of which it is a subset, as follows. The least squares regression for an equation with k variables is applied to the first set of observations (sub-period of m observations) and the residual sum of squares (u'u) computed. A least squares regression is fitted again to the entire sample (n observations) and the new residual sum of squares (u'$_i$u$_i$) computed. The test of the null hypothesis that the m observations obey the same relations as the n observations is provided[16] by an F statistic with (m, n - k) degrees of freedom:

$$F = \frac{(u'u - u'_i u_i)/m}{(u'_i u_i)/(n - k)}$$

We have inquired into the statistical significance of differences among two sets of regressions, one yielding coefficients for the period as a whole, the other for a particular sub-period. Cases where a significant difference emerged provided important clues into system change or transformation. Phase shifts can be identified with systematic breaks. But breaks which are more in the nature of non-linearities may not always be identified as such. The result is simply a "bad" fit which cannot be attributed to an underlying break, but rather to nonlinearities which are not specified in the functional form of the equation. A search for breakpoints also assists in identifying poor specification or areas of misspecification.

In sum, the analysis of residuals and identification of breakpoints becomes, much like sensitivity analysis, a critical aspect of the research enterprise.[17]

9.   Simulation, Forecasting and Policy Analysis

The next step in this analysis is to develop viable simulations of the system as a whole and observe their behaviour under various conditions. This is done in two stages: the key relationships are simulated equation by equation (by employing historical values at each iteration in place of calculated endogenous variables), and then the entire system is simulated in simultaneous mode (by employing calculated values for all endogenous variables). A successful (single equation) forecast increases the probability of a valid simulation: a successful[18] simulation almost certainly implies a successful forecast. A forecast (of a single equation) is conducted independently of the other equations and its solution depends primarily upon the existence of historical values for the endogenous variable period by period. A simulation involves the entire system of equations, solving for the jointly dependent variables without recourse to their historical observations. A completely self-contained structure is operative in a simulation, thus allowing for a fairly controlled method of varying parameters and observing the implications for the system as a whole (Naylor, Wertz and Wonnacott, 1968).

The TROLL facilities, upon which our simulation of the system of simultaneous equations was undertaken, calculate values of the jointly endogenous variables in the model over a period of time for which exogenous data are available, or for any sub-period therein. For simulation four types of information are required: the structure of the model itself, initial historical (or known) values for the endogenous variables, and constant files (coefficients and parameters which have been estimated earlier).

The model we have examined is a simultaneous system with as many endogenous variables as equations. Initial values are required only for the exogenous variables, all inclusive of lags and leads. Values for the constants must be supplied, but if their numerical values are specified in the model, they are taken as such and incorporated with the other pertinent information.

A dynamic simulation proceeds as follows. For a given model in which Y and Z are endogenous variables, and A, B, X are exogenous variables:

$$Y_t = a_1 + b_{11} A_t + b_{12} Z_{t-1} + u_1$$
$$Z_t = a_2 + b_{21} X_t + b_{22} B_t + u_2$$

In the first period, Y_t and Z_t are calculated using exogenous values for A_t, B_t, and X_t, and an exogenous starting value for the endogenous variable Z_{t-1}. In the second period, $(t + 1)$, Y_{t+1} and Z_{t+1} are computed using exogenous values for A_{t+1}, B_{t+1}, and X_{t+1} and the simulated endogenous value for Z_t from the previous period. Historical values for the endogenous variables are no longer employed. This procedure then continues, calculating the endogenous variables from their simulated values during the previous period and the current values of the exogenous variables. It must be noted that at each step subsequent to the initial t, historical values for the exogenous variable must be provided.

The solution for a variable at any given period is a function of a series of iterations in which all the equations in the block are solved and iteration values of the endogenous variables produced. Convergence criteria are established by default (or changed by the investigator) and identify the point at which the iteration has reached a solution. Sometimes it is necessary to relax the convergence criteria in order to obtain a solution. A common procedure for checking the performance of the simulation when convergence is attained is to examine the summary statistics, particularly percentage error, and compare the simulated values of the endogenous[19] variables with the actual, or known, historical values.

There are several sources of error in a simulation: first, the disturbance in period t may not be accurately forecasted; second, there may be errors when estimating the parameters from observed samples (errors arising during the sampling period or measurement error); and third, there may be

errors in forecasting the exogenous and lagged endogenous
variables for period t.[20]

The basic procedure for undertaking simulation
experiments is to resimulate the model with different inputs
(or sets of information) from those used in the base
simulation. Changes in parametric values, in estimated
coefficients, in endogenous variables, or in exogenous files
may be made. To compare the results we note the discrepancies
between empirical data output for the initial simulation and
that for the modified simulation. For policy purposes it is
necessary to modify the coefficients of key variables and then
observe the effects upon the simulated output. This is done
by changing coefficients one by one and obtaining the
simulated output after each modification. Only in this way is
it possible to identify the effects of policy changes upon the
entire simulation. This procedure assumes that changes in one
coefficient will not lead to counterbalancing changes in
others.

10. Simulation, Forecasting and Policy Analysis: The
     British Case

By way of providing some empirical reference to the above
discussion we draw upon recent investigations of the British
case, 1870-1914. Table II presents summary statistics of the
mean values of the historical data, the simulated series, and
the forecasted series, and the percentage error and Root Mean
Square errors of the forecasted and simulated series for each
of the dependent variables in the system of simultaneous
equations depicted in Table I and, in diagram form, in Figure
1. These summary statistics provide useful insights into the
structure of the dynamic system modelled. Space limitations
prevent an extensive commentary upon the political
significance of these results. Some brief observations may be
in order concerning the quantitative findings and their "real
world" implications.

In terms of colonial expansion, both the simulation and
the forecast of British territorial acquisitions were
remarkably successful in capturing the trend, although they
failed to replicate occasional outlying points.

In general, the simulations of military expenditures in
the Great Power systems were quite successful. The British
simulation ran slightly lower than the real-world expenditure
levels during the 1870s. In the earlier years of this period,
Britain fought the Ashanti Wars and was involved in other
colonial conflicts, but in many respects the period was
characterized by an 1874 declaration from the Throne of
friendly relations with all Powers. Another peak in 1903
(post Boer War expenditures) was again not captured, but the
simulation was generally extremely close to actual spending.

Although the mean values for the simulation and forecasts
of intersecting spheres of influence were close to the mean
historical values, the percentage errors--calculated over the
entire period--were considerable. Percentage errors take into
account each deviation from the mean in a calculation of the
overall percentage. Since the metrics involved were of small
magnitudes--covering the range of the interaction scale from

1 to 30 -- any increment of deviation makes a greater impact
on the percentage error calculations than similar increments
in the cases where the metric itself involves large numbers--
such as military expenditures in monetary values or colonial
area in thousands of square miles.

The actual discrepancy or error between the historical
alliance commitments and the simulated or forecasted
commitments was small.   But, because of the nature of the
metric involved--low values and variance in the alliance
commitment series--these minor discrepancies in absolute terms
become major ones in percentage terms. In such cases, we can
only observe these two sets of statistics and draw the
appropriate inferences.   Since the actual error between
historical and simulated alliance commitments was very small,
we find it reasonable to conclude that our simulation of these
dynamics captured much of the underlying processes.

A similar assessment may be made with respect to the
results of the simulation of prevailing levels of
international violence: there was a high level of congruence
between the actual level of violence--as measured by scaled
interaction data--and the simulation and forecast of these
levels. The actual error between simulation and forecast, on
the one hand, and real-world data, on the other, was
negligible, but the percentage errors was considerable.
Again, much as in the cases of the intersection and alliance
variables, this outcome is due to the nature of the metrics
involved.

A successful simulation model should do more than enhance
our understanding of the dynamics of a system and the
interdependence among its components. Once such a model is
developed and its parameters estimated from empirical data--
the values being robust and the coefficients statistically
significant--we must still address ourselves to the "so what?"
query. By allowing us to raise questions of a "what if" or
"if ... the ... " nature, a viable simulation should identify
critical intervention points where policy changes (alterations
in coefficients) will yield specific future outcomes.

By modifying the parameters in each equation and
observing the changes in the behaviour of the dependent
variables, it is possible to draw inferences concerning "real-
world" equivalences and expected behaviours. Although even a
summary discussion of our policy analysis for the British case
cannot be presented here, let it suffice to add that the
entire system was much more sensitive to upward swings in the
dynamics under consideration than it was to downward swings.
In other words, the dynamics in question were imbedded,
seemingly, in explosive tendencies which surfaced with any
slight upward changes in key parameters, whereas the system
did not respond as dramatically to counterbalancing downward
changes in the same parameters (Choucri and North, 1974).

Such findings bear witness to the complexities of
decision making and indicate the counter-intuitive tendencies
and behavioural characteristics of many large social systems.
This type of experimental application of econometric analysis
to political inquiry provides a methodology for assessing both
theory and the outcomes of conventional regression analysis
(including departures therefrom) and also a basis for

experimenting with various alterative policy formulations. Overall, these partial and, in some instances, non-obvious outcomes of an "if ... then ... " nature serve as further tests of a model and accompanying equations. Political scientists must now investigate the full range of political problems to which econometric analysis and forecasting might be put to use. Unless the issues raised in the earlier sections of this paper are given sufficient attention, it is unlikely that the exercise described in the last sections will be undertaken with any degree of validity. And, at this stage in the development of quantitative methodology, the issues of theory, method and procedure assume paramount importance.

Table 1

International Conflict Processes:
System of Equations for Simultaneous Estimation

col-area	$= \alpha_1 + \beta_1$ h-pop/h-area $+ \beta_2$ nat-inc/h-pop $+ \beta_3$ trade/pop $+ \beta_4$ mil-exp $+ u_1$
intersections	$= \alpha_2 + \beta_5$ col-area $+ \beta_6$ mil-exp $+ \beta_7$ versus*non-allies' col-area $+ \beta_8$ viol-beh $+ \beta_9$ viol-others $+ u_2$
mil-exp	$= \alpha_3 + \beta_{10}$ mil-exp$_{t-1}$ $+ \beta_{11}$ versus*non-allies' mil-exp $+ \beta_{12}$ intersections $+ \beta_{13}$ col-area $+ \beta_{14}$ h-pop*nat-inc $+ u_3$
alliances	$= \alpha_4 + \beta_{15}$ mil-exp $+ \beta_{16}$ intersections $+ \beta_{17}$ versus*non-allies' mil-exp $+ \beta_{18}$ h-pop*nat-inc $+ u_4$
viol-beh	$= \alpha_5 + \beta_{19}$ intersections $+ \beta_{20}$ mil-exp $+ \beta_{21}$ versus*non-allies' mil-exp $+ \beta_{22}$ alliances $+ \beta_{23}$ viol-others $+ u_5$
and	the co-terms for β_4, β_5, β_6, β_8, β_{12}, β_{13}, β_{15}, β_{16}, β_{19}, β_{20}, β_{22}, are endogenous variables, β_{10} is a lagged endogenous variable, and the co-terms for the other explanatory variables are exogenous,
col-area	= colonial area in thousand square miles
h-pop	= home population in thousand
h-area	= home area in thousand square miles
nat-inc	= national income in thousand U.S. dollars at standardized prices (1901–1910 = 100)
trade	= imports plus exports in thousand U.S. dollars at standardized prices (1901–1910 = 100)
mil-exp	= military expenditures (army and navy allocations) in thousand U.S. dollars at standardized prices (1901–1910 = 100)
versus*non-allies	= dummy variable representing dyadic relationship: 1 when two states are not allied formally, 0 if they are
intersections	= scaled variable (from 1 to 30) denoting intensity of intersections among spheres of influence
alliances	= number of alliance commitments
viol-beh	= scaled variable (from 1 to 30) denoting the highest peak on the scale recorded for each year, and representing the behavior of the actor *toward* other states
viol-others	= scaled variable (from 1 to 30) denoting the highest peak on the scale recorded for each year and representing the behavior of other states *toward* the actor state
h-pop*nat-inc	= multiplicative variable representing interactive effect of population (in thousands) and national income (in thousand U.S. dollars standardized to U.S. dollars, 1901–1910 = 100)
$\alpha_1 \ldots \alpha_5$	= constant or intercept term
$u_1 \ldots u_5$	= error or disturbance term

instrumental variable list: volume of iron and steel production, volume of pig iron, government expenditures, merchant marine tonnage, military expenditures of non-allies, colonial area of non-allies, population density, population times national income, national income per capita, trade per capita, intersections$_{t-1}$, violence behavior$_{t-1}$, violence of others, alliance committments$_{t-1}$, wheat production, coal output.

Table II
Some Comparative Statistics: Historical Data, Simulation, and Forecasting
The British Case

Variable	Historical Mean	Simulated Mean	Mean of % Error: Simulation	RMs of %Error: Simulation	Forecasted Mean	Mean of % Error: Forecast	RMS of % Error: Forecast
Lateral Pressure (Colonial Area: sq. mi.)	10,968,400	10,919,900	-0.206	3.354	10,920,400	-0.204	3.308
Intersections (level: Scale 1–30)	12.969	12.896	73.917	211.261	12.988	72.705	264.524
Military Expenditures (U. S. $)	212,392,000	211,742,000	1.563	24.396	211,856,000	0.934	27.762
Alliance Commitments (number)	1.568	1.578	-15.627	27.270	1.581	-11.645	34.829
Violence Behavior (level: Scale 1–30)	20.364	20.419	67.101	276.158	20.364	70.664	307.747

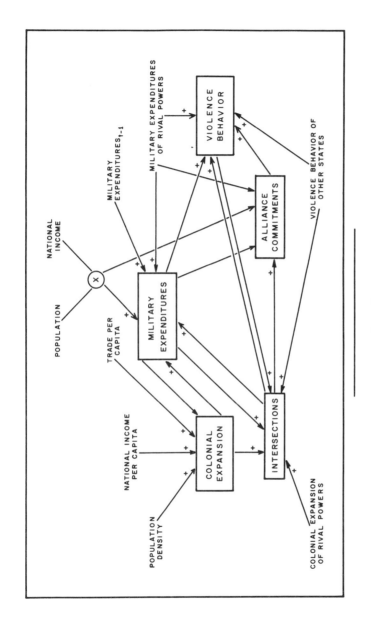

FIGURE 1

International Conflict Processes: The Dynamics Of Complex Systems

247

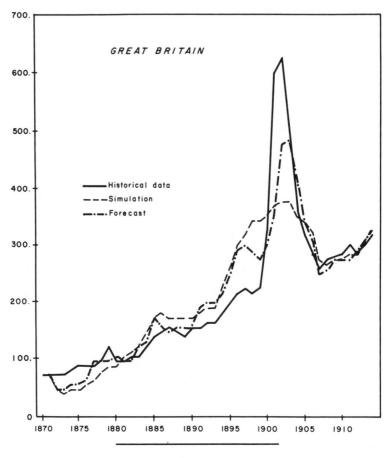

FIGURE 2
Military Expenditures in Millions of U.S. Dollars, 1870–1914

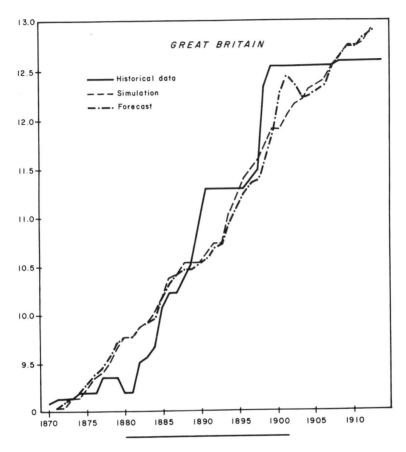

FIGURE 3
Lateral Pressure: Colonial Area
in Millions of Square Miles

A.C. Aitken. "On Least Squares and Linear Combination of Observations," Proceedings of the Royal Society of Edinburgh, 55, 1935.

R.L. Anderson. "Distribution of the Serial Correlation Coefficient," Annals of Mathematical Statistics, 13, 1942.

Albert Ando, Franklin Fisher, and Herbert A. Simon. "Essays on the Structure of Social Science," M.I.T. Press, 1963.

H.M. Blalock. "Some Implications of Random Measurement Error for Causal Inferences," The American Journal of Sociology, 81, 1965.

Hubert M. Blalock and Ann B. Blalock. "Methodology in Social Research, McGraw-Hill, 1968.

Donald T. Campbell and Julian C. Stanley (eds.). "Experimental and Quasi-Experimental Designs for Research," Rand McNally, 1966.

Nazli Choucri and Robert C. North. "Nations in Conflict: Population, Expansion, and War," W.H. Freeman, 1974.

Gregory C. Chow. "Tests of Inequality Between Sets of Coefficients in Two Linear Regressions," Econometrica, 27, 1960.

Carl F. Christ. "Econometric Models and Methods," John Wiley & Sons, 1966.
"Simultaneous Equation Estimation: Any Verdict Yet? Econometrica, 28, 1960.

Clyde H. Coombs. "A Theory of Data," John Wiley & Sons, 1964.

James S. Deusenberry, et al. (eds). "The Brookings-SSRC Quarterly Econometric Model of the United States," Rand McNally, 1965.

J. Durbin and G.S. Watson. "Testing for Serial Correlation in Least Squares Regression," II Biometrika, 38, 1958.
"Testing for Serial Correlation in Least Squares Regression," I Biometrika, 37, 1950.

Mark Eisner and Robert Pindyck. "A Generalized Approach to Estimation as Implemented in the TROLL/1 System," N.B.E.R. Computer Research Center, 1972.

Ray Fair. "The Estimation of Simultaneous Equation Models with Lagged Endogenous Variables and First Order Serially Correlated Errors," Econometrica, 38, 1970.

James Fennessey. "The General Linear Model: A New Perspective on Some Familiar Topics," American Journal of Sociology, 74, 1968.

Franklin M. Fisher. "Simultaneous Estimation: The State of the Art," Working paper, Department of Economics, M.I.T., 1970a.
"Tests of Inequality Between Sets of Coefficients in Two Linear Regressions: An Expository Note," Econometric, 38, 1970b.
"The Identification Problem in Econometrics," McGraw-Hill, 1966.
"Dynamic Structure and Estimation in Economy-Wide Econometric Models," In Deusenberry, et al., 1965.
"Generalization of the Rank and Order Conditions for Identifiable," Econometrica, 27, 1959.

Arthur S. Goldberger. "Econometric Theory," John Wiley & Sons, 1965.

E.J. Hannan. "Time series analysis," Methuen, 1960.

Douglas A. Hibbs, Jr. "Problems of Statistical Estimation and Causal Inference in Dynamic Time Series Regression Models," (In) H.L. Costner, Sociological Methodology: 1973-1974. Jossey-Bass, 1974.
"Mass Political Violence," John Wiley and Sons. 1973.

J. Johnston. "Econometric Methods," McGraw-Hill, 1972.

L. Klein. "Whither Econometrics?" Journal of the American Statistical Association, 66, 1971.

Gerald H. Kramer. "Short-Term Fluctuations in U.S. Voting Behavior, 1896-1964," Cowles Foundation Paper 344, 1971.

Edwin Kuh and John R. Meyer. "How Extraneous are Extraneous Estimates?" Review of Economics and Statistics, 39, 1957.

T.H. Naylor, K. Wertz and Thomas Wonnacott. "Some Methods for Evaluating the Effects of Economic Policies Using Simulation Experiments," Review of the International Statistical Institute, 36, 1968.

Guy H. Orcutt. "Actions, Consequences, and Causal Relations," Review of Economics and Statistics, 34, 1952.

Guy H. Orcutt and Herbert S. Winokur, Jr. "First Order Autoregression: Inference, Estimation, and Prediction," Econometrica, 37, 1969.

Potluri Rao and Zvi Griliches. "Small Sample Properties of Several Two-Stage Regression Methods in the Context of Auto-Correlated Errors," Journal of American Statistical Association, 64, 1969.

251

Potluri Rao and Roger LeRoy Miller. "Applied Econometrics," Wadsworth, 1971.

William A. Schink and John Chieu. "A Simulation Study of Effects of Multicollinearity and Autocorrelation on Estimates of Parameters," Journal of Financial and Quantitative Analysis, 1, 1966.

Henri Theil. "On Estimation of Relationships Involving Qualitative Variables," American Journal of Sociology, 76, 1970.

TROLL/1 User's Guide. N.B.E.R. Computer Research Center, 1972.

Kenneth N. Wallis. "Lagged Dependent Variables and Serially Correlated Errors," Review of Economics and Statistics, 49, 1967.

*.I am particularly grateful to Hayward Alker for critical comments and suggestions at every stage of these investigations. I am also grateful to Douglas Hibbs, Michael Levitt, Amy Leiss, Michael Milhalka and Scott Ross for helpful comments and suggestions on an earlier version of this paper, and to Raisa Deber and Thomas Robinson for editorial commentary. For Shane, Alexis Serri and Walt Maling of the TROLL Project. For research assistance I would like to thank Raisa Deber, again, and Taizo Yakushiji. This paper draws upon Chapters 2, 12, 19, and Appendix B of Nazli Choucri and Robert C. North, <u>Nations in Conflict: Population, Expansion and War (1974)</u>.

Notes

1.Dynamic modelling, which is current in econometric analysis, can be used for political inquiry to provide (a) an aid to understanding political dynamics, (b) a tool for simulation and forecasting political behaviour, and outcomes, and (c) a guide to the choice of public policy. The crucial test of a model lies in its internal and statistical validity. Its prime usefulness is to make forecasts and compare the forecasts with actual historical values as a means of understanding how systems behave. For a survey of the development of econometrics as a field of inquiry see Lawrence R. Klein, "Whither Econometrics?", Journal of the <u>American Statistical Association</u>, 66, June 1971, 415-421. For an instructive application of econometric analysis to political inquiry see Gerald H. Kramer, "Short-Term Fluctuations in U.S. Voting Behavior, 1896-1964," Cowles Foundation Paper No. 344 (New Haven: Cowles Foundation for Research in Economics at Yale University, 1971).

2.Although the broad lines of our investigations are common in econometric analysis, we have found that applied econometrics is not always consonant with econometric theory. In many cases, we have also found that the problems confronting us – such as the coincidence of lagged endogenous variables and serial correlation in the disturbances – are raised in econometric texts as critical problems, but rarely are sufficient guidelines or practical directions provided to assist in resolving such issues. For this reason our approach has been highly exploratory, and the solutions we have adopted amounted to practical applications of theoretical arguments. Since there are, as yet, no clear-cut solutions to problems such as these, much of what we have done is both controversial and experimental.

3.The dynamic elements in a model are usually generated by lagged relationship, by first (or higher order) derivatives, by employing endogenous variables as explanatory and by introducing random shock variables. These considerations are important in drawing inferences about the structure of the system of equations in question and about the ability of the system to predict both behaviour of the model and the behaviour of outcome variables. In the course of our investigations we have employed each of these procedures for approximating dynamic systems. Here we note only the most effective approaches (Fisher, 1965). Dynamic models can be constructed by employing explicit functions of time, by linear approximations, by exponential functions, quadratic trends, first and higher order differences, distributed lags and spectral analysis. The result is a system of equations in the correct form whose parameters are subject to probability error associated with the inference procedure used. We solve the estimation equation of the model in order to obtain an estimate of the reduced form. An earlier version of this analysis was undertaken with the use of rates of change variables on both sides of the equations. In that case, we have found that the resulting parameter estimates were surprisingly fragile throughout.

4.The necessity of a priori specifications, endemic to the question of causality, is predicated on two considerations. First, these specifications must allow the investigator to develop a particular system of equations, and to identify the dependent and independent variables, and the nature of their relationships. This initial specification in itself constitutes an operational statement of theory, however vague, inarticulate, or implicit it may be. Second, a priori information is necessary for the distinction of one equation from another. Information of this nature generally constitutes restrictions of the coefficients of the variables (where some are set at zero) and on the nature of the random or disturbance term. Without the specification of zero coefficients for some variables in each equation there is no way to distinguish one equation from another. See Franklin M. Fisher, The Identification Problem in Econometrics (New York: McGraw-Hill Book Company, 1966), Ch. 1 and 2.

5.The smaller the variance of a parameter estimate, the less sensitive the estimate will be to errors in the independent variables. Furthermore, the smaller the correlation among the independent variables, the higher will be the precision of the regression estimates. However, computational precision does not necessarily guarantee that the most theoretically precise estimation procedure has been used (see Rao and Miller, 1971, 24).

6.The "bias" of a parameter estimate is the difference between the mean value of the distribution of the estimate and its "true" parameter value. Bias may also result from the omission of relevant variables in the equation. But this will not increase the variance of the estimates of the coefficients, nor does the introduction of superfluous variables severely impede the precision of the estimate. Although no statistical tool is a substitute for good theory, some errors are likely to have greater consequences for robust inferences than others. For example, regression coefficients with the wrong sign indicate most likely that some misspecification has taken place, or that the variables are not appropriately defined, or that we are mistaken about the "right" sign, or that there is an interactive effect which has not been taken into account. It is often difficult to identify the "real" reason for a "wrong" sign (Rao and Miller, 1971, 27-35). "Precision" seeks the minimum variance estimate, regardless of bias. As a summary statistic, the mean square error provides importance to bias and to precision:

$$MSE(B) = V(B) + [Bias (b)]2$$

When the estimated equation is the "true" equation, ordinary least squares provides the minimum variance unbiased estimate.

7. The precision of the parameter estimate depends upon the serial correlation parameter as well as upon the process generating the independent variables. Ordinary least squares is still unbiased in the presence of serial correlation, but it does not have minimum variance. If we can identify the structure and value of the autocorrelation parameter, then by an appropriate transformation of the variables we can use ordinary least squares to provide minimum variance estimates. This is appropriate only in the single equation case where simultaneous effects are not thought to operate. When the dependent variables in the equation are also serially correlated, then the bias depends also on the parameters that generated their serial correlation. And when the variance in the error term is not constant, ordinary least squares does not produce the best linear unbiased estimates (Schink and Chieu, 1966). We have attempted to attain high precision (by seeking sharp and robust parameter estimates) and minimize bias (by respecifying each equation to account explicitly for the effects of separate independent variables.)

8. The conventional use of measurement error may thus be viewed in the context of confidence intervals, the problem being defined in terms of the absence of vital information rather than the presence of known error in the quantitative measures.

9. The two necessary conditions for identifiability are the order and rank conditions. For the order condition to hold, there must be at least M - 1 independent restrictions in an equation where M is the number of endogenous variables. This is clearly an exclusion restriction. The rank condition stipulates that at least one non-vanishing determinant of the order M - 1 can be formed from the ordinary least square structure of an equation, corresponding to the variables excluded by a priori specification from the equation (Fisher, 1966, 39-42, 60-62; 1959, 431-47; Hibbs, 1973, App. III).

10. Econometricians have focused primarily upon first order autoregressive structures (due to the ease of computation) and as a result a general tendency to assume that the world is of a first order autoregressive nature pervades much of the econometric literature. In our investigations, however, we have rarely encountered an AUTO1 structure. As AUTO2 often appears to be a suitable trade-off between complexity and accuracy (Rao and Griliches, 1969; Orcutt and Winokur, 1969).

11. See Rao and Miller, 1971, Chapter 7. The true error does not depend on the value of the independent variables, but the residuals do. Residuals, therefore, reflect the properties of the independent variables as well as the errors and the effects of omitted variables. If errors are homoscedastic and random, the residual corresponding to a particular value of the

255

independent variables has a statistical distribution with zero mean and homogeneous variables. Se Christ, 1966, 394-395, Goldberger, 1964, 232-235, and Johnston, 1972, 208-242.

12. In cases where collinearity among the instrumental variables is high, principal component transformation produces a new set of variables which are orthogonal linear combinations of the original variables. The new variables are so ordered so that each variable explains as much of the remaining variance of the original variables as possible. In such cases it is possible to use a smaller number of variables while still accounting for a major fraction of the variance explained by the original equation. We employed a principal components solution only when it was not possible to create instruments in any other way due to excessive collinearity among the instruments.

13. Lagged endogenous variables must not be treated as exogenous, particularly since the number of predetermined variables cannot exceed the sample size (this is an absolute limit). For purposes of quantitative analysis, the number of degrees of freedom lost is a critical consideration, as is meeting the order and rank conditions of identifiability, both of which are restrictions upon the specifications of the equation.

14. The choice of instruments is theoretically intuitive. A predetermined list can be refined in two ways: (a) through the use of principal components, a method which reduces multicollinearity since the components are mutually orthogonal, and principal components summarize the information in the list of instruments; and (b) through structurally ordered instrumental variables, by first establishing a list of preference ordering of instruments relative to a particular explanatory term, and then regressing the endogenous variable on the instruments in differing combinations to determine whether an instrument further down the list has an effect or whether its contribution is simply using up a degree of freedom; the constructed elements of Y_t, together with the elements of Z_t are then employed as instrumental variables in constructing Y_t. See Rao and Miller, 1971, and Eisner and Pindyck, 1972.

15. There are differences in views concerning this ordering, and hence the residuals to be employed when undertaking an instrumental variable substitution. When combining time dependent corrections (generalized least squares), and instrumental variables (two stage least squares), it is not intuitively obvious which residuals, and at which stage, should be used in calculating the relevant statistics for evaluating the parameters at the final stage. On the one hand it is argued that, when generalized least squares and instrumental variables are combined, that transformed residuals should be calculated without the substitution. On the other hand, it is maintained that substitution should first take place, and then the time dependent corrections be performed. In the latter case, the proper asymptotic variance-covariance matrix must contain the instrumental variable substitution. In the former it does not. (Hibbs, 1974; Wallis, 1967; Eisner and Pindyck, 1972; Fair, 1970).

16. In our analysis we have compared the residuals generated by the regression of the n observations with those of the m observations (given k number of variables) and it becomes clear that in instances where the deviations are great the F test picks these and registers as statistically significant, thereby rejecting the null hypothesis (Fisher, 1970b; Johnston, 1972, 206-207).

17. For purposes of experimentation and increasing our understanding of the model we have developed, we found it desirable to identify and test for breakpoints (using the Chow test) in cases where the coefficients were estimated with and without the uses of instrumental variables. We found, generally, that there were no significant differences in terms of the results obtained with and without the use of instrumental variable substitution.

18. Econometricians generally talk of forecasting when the endogenous variable in each equation is replaced by historical values at each point, and simulation when the coefficients, the exogenous variables and the error terms together with the jointly dependent variables are employed to generate an artificial replication of the entire system. This replication is commonly referred to as simulation. In looser parlance, we often talk of forecasting as simulation beyond the existing data which was used to estimate the coefficients initially. Clearly, that is not the usage intended in this paper.

19. If the object is short-term forecasts, multicollinearity need not necessarily be a drawback. If some of the explanatory variables are multicollinear, the prediction interval obtained will be large. By eliminating some collinear variables one can reduce prediction interval for a given value of the included independent variables. But the actual outcome will be indifferent to the extent of collinearity while sophisticated ones will not. Both will make similar forecasts and the errors will be very similar (Kuh and Meyer, 1957).

20. The root mean square of the error (RMS) is the most important summary statistic in indicating how well the simulated model tracks empirical observations:

$$\text{RMS errors} = \sqrt{\frac{\sum_{i=1}^{n} (A_i - P_i)^2}{n}}$$

**Reprinted from the PAPERS of the Peace Science Society (International), Volume 21, 1973, by permission of the editor.

Getting Correlations Using PROC CORR

You can use the SAS procedure CORR to get correlation coefficients.

What does correlation show? Correlation analysis is used to measure the strength of the relationship between two variables.

When two variables are positively correlated, observations that have high values of one variable also tend to have high values of the other. For example, height and weight are correlated. Although there are exceptions, generally a low height value and a low weight value tend to be found in the same individual.

When two variables are not correlated, there is no apparent linear relationship between the values of one and the values of the other.

When two variables are negatively correlated, high values of one variable tend to be associated with low values of the other variable. For example, bond prices tend to rise when the interest rate falls.

Correlation coefficients range from −1 to 1. A correlation coefficient close to 1 means that the two variables are positively correlated; a correlation coefficient near zero means there is little correlation between the values of the two variables; and a correlation coefficient close to −1 means that the variables are negatively correlated.

How to use PROC CORR To get correlation coefficients (Pearson product-moment) for all the numeric variables in the most recently created SAS data set, use the PROC CORR statement alone:

PROC CORR;

The SYSNLIN Procedure

ABSTRACT

The SYSNLIN procedure estimates parameters in a simultaneous system of nonlinear equations. Available estimation methods include:

- nonlinear ordinary least squares (OLS)
- nonlinear seemingly unrelated regression (SUR)
- nonlinear iterated seemingly unrelated regression (ITSUR)
- nonlinear two-stage least squares (N2SLS)
- nonlinear three-stage least squares (N3SLS)
- nonlinear iterated three-stage least squares (IT3SLS).

INTRODUCTION

PROC SYSNLIN combines the solution methods for nonlinear regression (as implemented in PROC NLIN) with the specialized estimation techniques for simultaneous systems (as used in PROC SYSREG).

Before you invoke SYSNLIN, you must specify the model in the MODEL procedure. In PROC MODEL, parameters are identified and given starting values, the other variables are declared, and the equations are specified. For example, to fit the model

$$y = ae^{bx} + error$$

you can specify:

```
PROC MODEL;
   PARAMETERS A B;
   ENDOGENOUS Y;
   EXOGENOUS X;
   Y = A*EXP(B*X);
PROC SYSNLIN;
```

VARIABLE	N	MEAN	STD DEV	SUM	MINIMUM	MAXIMUM
AGE	19	13.3157895	1.4926722	253.00000	11.0000000	16.000000
HEIGHT	19	61.9473684	5.1905222	1177.00000	51.0000000	72.000000
WEIGHT	19	99.8421053	22.8187622	1897.00000	50.0000000	150.000000

PEARSON CORRELATION COEFFICIENTS / PROB > |R| UNDER HO:RHO=0 / N = 19

	AGE	HEIGHT	WEIGHT
AGE	1.00000	0.81254	0.74042
	0.0000	0.0001	0.0003
HEIGHT	0.81254	1.00000	0.87800
	0.0001	0.0000	0.0001
WEIGHT	0.74042	0.87800	1.00000
	0.0003	0.0001	0.0000

figure 10-1

To get correlation coefficients for another data set, use DATA= in the PROC CORR statement:

PROC CORR DATA = LASTYR;

To get correlation coefficients for some, but not all, of tne numeric variables in the data set, list the variables you want in a VAR statement:

PROC CORR;
VAR HEIGHT WEIGHT;

Getting subset   You can get correlation coefficients for subsets of your data with PROC CORR
correlations   and a BY statement. For example, say you wanted to get correlations first for the females and then for the males. You would use a BY statement with PROC CORR:

PROC CORR;
  BY SEX;

Remember that before you can use a BY statement with a SAS procedure, the data set must already be sorted in the order of the variables in the BY statement. So you may need to use PROC SORT before you get correlations:

PROC SORT;
  BY SEX;
PROC CORR;
  BY SEX;

How PROC CORR   When PROC CORR calculates the correlation coefficient for two variables, it
handles missing values   leaves out any observation that has a missing value for either of the two variables.

260

5.   The system of equations can be considered to be stacked
      into one weighted regression. The sum-of-squared error
      mean squared error and degrees of freedom for error from
      this regression are reported. These can be compared for
      different models if the S matrix is fixed.

EXAMPLES

OLS Single Nonlinear Equation: Example 1

This example illustrates the SYSNLIN procedure for nonlinear
ordinary least squares (OLS). There is only one endogenous
variable: population. The model is a logistic growth curve for
the population of the United States.

```
         TITLE LOGISTIC GROWTH CURVE MODEL OF U.S. POPULATION
         DATA USPOP:        INPUT POP 6.3 @@;
             RETAIN YEAR 1780:        YEAR=YEAR+10
             CARDS:
3929   5308   7239   9638   12866   17069   23191   31433   39818   30155
62947    75994    91972    105710    122775    131669    151325    179323
203211
.      .      .
.      .      .
```

```
PROC PRINT:
PROC MODEL:
      PARMS A 500 B 4.8 C -.02:
      ENDOGENOUS POP
      EXOGENOUS YEAR:
      x=YEAR-1790
      POP-A/(1 - EXP (B-C*X)
PROC SYSNLIN OLS ITPRINT:
```

LOGISTIC GROWTH CURVE MODEL OF U.S. POPULATION

OBS	POP	YEAR
1	3.929	1790
2	5.308	1800
3	7.239	1810
4	9.638	1820
5	12.866	1830
6	17.089	1840
7	23.191	1850
8	31.443	1860
9	30.818	1870
10	30.155	1880
11	62.947	1890
12	70.994	1900
13	91.972	1910
14	105.770	1920
15	122.775	1930
16	131.669	1940
17	161.325	1950
18	179.323	1960
19	203.211	1970
20		1980
21		1990
22		2000

6 Input-Output and Programming

A. Input-Output Models

There are several important models and techniques by which regional impacts can be estimated as a result of the changes in the level of major governmental programs. Some of the important methods are:
1. Econometric models (discussed in the previous chapter)
2. Economic base type analyses and their extensions
3. Regional and interregional input-output method

In the case of base studies, the activities in individual regions are divided into two groups, namely basic or export activities and non-basic or services activities. It is postulated that the total employment in any region is determined by employment in the basic activities. So if employment in the basic industries for the future is known, then total employment can be estimated. In the same manner we can have

$$E_t = E_D + E_{ND} \qquad (1)$$

where

E_t = total employment
E_D = employment in the defence industries
E_{ND} = employment in the non-defence industries

From (1)

$$E_t = (1 + E_{ND}/E_D) \; E_D \qquad (2)$$

Assuming

$$\frac{E_{ND}}{E_D} = a = \text{constant}$$

We have,

$$E_t = (1 + a)E_D \qquad (3)$$

If employment in the defence industries after disarmament can be estimated, the change in total employment can also be projected from equation (3). So, as a first step, it is a good idea to calculate E_{NS}/E_D as a measure of vulnerability to disarmament (for similar measures of different states in the United States, see Emile Benoit [1, p. 46]). Although a defence cut will affect all sectors of the economy, the major brunt of the shift-over will have to be borne by the four industries, namely aerospace, shipbuilding, ordinance and electronics. But aggregate demand is still the key variable to analyse. Micro-analysis is important but must be set within the proper aggregative framework.

The base model, is simple but has serious drawbacks. Though some significant improvements and its reformulation have been made, it remains far from satisfactory.

Regional and interregional input-output models, on the other hand, are based on sound methodology. Unlike base models, they use a matrix instead of a single number as the multiplier. We have

$$X = (1 - a)^{-1}F \qquad (4)$$

where X denotes output vector, F denotes vector of final demand, and "a" is the input-output matrix. The matrix multiplier takes into account inter-industry dependence. The government sector is included as a part of the final demand sectors in F. So if there is disarmament, the government purchases of goods and services will change and with the new final demand, the output figure X can be estimated from (4). Also, a region, "human multipliers" are important; these can be taken into account by including household sectors in the structural matrix.

The regional input-output models of Isard and Schooler (1964) could have been utilized to estimate **direct and indirect** changes in export, import, wages and salaries, gross regional product, employment, etc. of a region as a result of change in the final demand due to say disarmament.

For example, let us define,

$$a_{mi} = \frac{T_{mi}}{X_i}$$

as the average number of workers required for one unit's worth of output where T_{mi} denotes the total number of persons employed in the ith sector and X_i is the total output of the ith sector. Then the <u>direct and indirect</u> labour requirement per unit of output is

$$\sum_{i=1}^{n} a_{mi} \ a_{ij} \qquad\qquad (5)$$

where a_{ij} is the coefficient in the inverse matrix $(1-a)^{-1}$. Equation (5) will give the employment multipliers. If there is a drop in the defence purchase, say from shipbuilding industries, these multipliers will help us to estimate the loss of employment in all sectors both directly and indirectly. The construction of a regional input—output model is an expensive and difficult job, so, whenever possible, alternative methods should be devised to reduce the complexity of the job involved.

Use of Input—output Analysis in Disarmament Analysis

It is to be noted that the statistical figures given here are grossly outdated. However, the objective here is to give the possible format of an analysis.

One of the most important problems facing mankind today is the immense disparity between the levels of income and consequently in the standard of living amongst the people in different parts of the world. What is more disheartening is that the growth rate of income of the poor countries is consistently far below the rates of economically advanced countries. The causes of this backwardness are many. Natural environments, climatic conditions, unequal distribution of world resources and population, historical development of the social and cultural backgrounds of different countries, religious factors, and a host of other social, economic and political factors are responsible for the low standard of living in most parts of the world. Cooperation between countries is needed to raise the poor millions from their utter state of starvation, disease and destruction. The most important effort in this respect could be channelling massive investment for productive purposes to the poor countries.

Although the underdeveloped areas of the world contain more than two-thirds of the world's population, they produce as little as one-seventh of the world's gross output of goods and services. As a result of this low level of income and high propensity to consume, they have little to save for investment. Thus, for their economic development, they are heavily dependent on the developed countries, which can greatly accelerate the low rate of growth through aid, loans and investments.

It is estimated that the annual expenditure of human effort and resources devoted to preparation for war, even as early as 1964, was between $100 and $120 billion, which is nearly the national income of the underdeveloped countries. Of the $1400 billion in 1964 gross national product (henceforth to be termed G.N.P.) of the world, $1205 billion is produced in the developed countries including W. Europe (excepting Spain, Portugal, Greece and Turkey), the United States, Canada, Japan, the USSR and other socialist countries, and $195 billion in the rest of the world. Of the $120 billion worldwide military expenditure, $102 billion is assumed to be incurred by the developed countries. The United States accounts for more than one-third, the USSR a little less than one-third, and the rest of the world spends the remaining third. In 1990 the total military expenditure of the world has been estimated about 1 tr. US dollar.

In the case of possible disarmament, this substantial amount could be diverted towards the economic development of the underdeveloped countries. This transfer, besides alleviating mutual suspicion and distrust among nations, could make human existence a good deal more pleasant and meaningful.

The term disarmament "implies a major reduction in national military capabilities in national hands such that it renders war impossible". Following Benoit, we can distinguish three major types of disarmament: unilateral or one-sided; bilateral, involving two major parties; and multilateral, which proposes a supranational authority to inspect national compliance with agreed reduction of the forces in all nations. Although general complete disarmament should be our target, we have to approach this goal by successive cutbacks in arms production agreed upon by all nations concerned. This will leave unchanged the relative capabilities of the military strength of the contending parties but will reduce defence expenditures drastically.

Disarmament, whether complete or partial, is highly desirable, but it has many social, political and economic implications. This is particularly true of those countries such as the United States and the USSR whose economies to a large extent are dependent on the defence industries. The United States government spent, in 1964, more than $40 billion for the maintenance of military establishments and for arms purchases. This amount is less than 10% of the G.N.P. of the United States, but it exceeded by several billion dollars the combined net annual investment in manufacturing, service industries, transportation and agriculture (Benoit, 1963). With the prospect of disarmament followed by reductions in defence expenditure, it will be necessary for the economy to reallocate, to other civilian purposes, labour, plant, and physical resources that now serve directly or indirectly the demands of military establishments (Chatterji, 1991). This transition from war industries to civilian industries is not expected to be smooth and it will take time. Economists are presently engaged in finding out the means of adjustment necessary to minimize the economic hardships (in the form of unemployment and loss of income) to the economy of the United States. It had been demonstrated (Benoit, 1963) that the likely effects on American industry that might have resulted from a total elimination of the defence programme in the 1960s in the absence of compensating or offsetting programmes would have been: (1) a sharp curtailment of demand for the goods of some of the major growth areas of American industry, particularly the electrical and electronics and aerospace equipment manufacturers; (2) a major reduction in the level of research and development performed by American industry -- possibly one-half or more; and (3) a major decline in the employment of engineers and scientists--possibly up to one-fourth of the current 300,000 employed by industry. Another important aspect of disarmament if its regional impact. In the United States, the defence industries are concentrated in some specific states and regions. So a reduction in the military expenditure will greatly affect the economy of these regions and regional adjustments will be called for. There is also the need for changing the monetary and fiscal policies. For example, debt retirement and monetary expansion as offsets to reduced expenditure may be considered. Although disarmament will improve the balance-of-payment situation of the advanced countries, for the underdeveloped countries this would mean the loss of foreign exchange income.

Social scientists in the United States and abroad are presently investigating all these implications on the national, regional and local levels as a result of assumed cutbacks of defence expenditure due to disarmament. The effectiveness of different offset programmes such as lower levels of business and personal taxation, retirement of national debt, public works construction, regional resource development, urban renewal and slum clearance, subsidization of research and education, provision of more adequate medical facilities, and intensified foreign aid, etc. are all being considered. Some excellent impact studies on both the national and regional level, and studies relating efficient utilization of the resources released due to disarmament for the economic development of the poor regions of the world, are presently available. The objective of this paper is to discuss critically some such studies and suggest some improvements. We shall be primarily concerned with foreign aid programmes and emphasize papers by Leontief (1965), Leontief and Duchin (1983), Isard and Schooler (1964), and Suits (1963).

LEONTIEF'S ANALYSIS (1965)

Leontief considers the possibility of a planned increase in capital transfers from the developed countries to the underdeveloped countries as a consequence of a cut in military expenditures due to disarmament. This raises two important questions: (1) how much additional investment the underdeveloped countries would require so as to bring their growth rate to the same level as that of the developed areas; (2) if the source of this additional income is the capital transfers from the developed countries, how large would these transfers have to be?

To answer these questions, Leontief proposes a simple dynamic model based on capital-output and savings-income ratios. This model, together with the assumptions involved, is given in Section 1 of the Appendix. He classifies all the countries of the world as either developed or underdeveloped, the economies of which are completely closed except for the transfer of capital. The growth path of the underdeveloped countries is given by equation (9) of Section 1 of the Appendix.

It is assumed that the annual growth rate of the developed areas is 4% and of the underdeveloped areas is 2% at the base year 1959, and that the aggregate investment levels in the two areas are $229 billion and $15 billion per year respectively. Regarding the prospects of disarmament three possible future states are concerned:

State A. No Disarmament.
Countries continue to spend the same proportion of their gross national products on defence as they do presently, namely 8.465% and 9.231% for the developed and underdeveloped countries respectively.

State B. Complete Disarmament (increase social consumption).
Countries devote one-half of State A military expenditures to increased social consumption (health, education, welfare, space exploration, etc.) and the rest to investment and consumption, according to the ratio of domestically financed investment to consumption under State A in the base year 1959.

State C.   Complete   Disarmament   (no   increased   social consumption).
Countries devote all military expenditures to investment and consumption according to the ratio of domestically financed investment to consumption under State A in the base year.

Regarding the transfer of capital, three alternatives are postulated.   In Table 1 of Leontief article.   (Leontief, 1964).

(a) Columns 1, 2, and 5 are based on assumed increase to $4 billion per year.

(b) Columns 3 and 6 are based on assumed increase to $15 billion per year.

(c) Columns 4 and 7 are based on an assumed increase to $25 billion per year.

The Leontief model projects the growth rates of both the developed and underdeveloped countries for the year 1969 based on these various alternatives.

From column 1 of his Table 1 [Page 161] it is seen that in the case of no disarmament of growth of income of underdeveloped countries is very slow, from 2.0% to 2.1%. But their share of world G.N.P. decreases from 13.8% to 11.7%. Columns 3 and 4 show the effects of increased foreign aid. With a foreign aid total of $15 billion per year, the growth rate of the underdeveloped countries will increase from 2.1% to 3.5% without affecting the growth rate of the developed countries by a significant amount.   Column 4 shows that foreign aid amounting to $25 billion per year will increase the growth rate of the underdeveloped countries to 5%, while cutting the growth rate of the developed countries by .1%.   It is seen from columns 6 and 7 under State C (where it is postulated that none of the resources released from defence is put to social consumption) that a capital transfer around $20 billion per year will equate the growth rates of the two groups of countries.   Since the figure of initial investment of $15 billion per year for the underdeveloped countries and the assumed initial growth rates of 4% and 2% may not be accurate, Leontief made extensive calculations based on $18 billion and $22 billion investment per year, and growth rates of 6% and 2% respectively for the two groups of countries. The results are similar to those shown in his table.   In conclusion he states, "that regardless of which initial assumptions one chooses to accept, one reaches the conclusion that 'break-even point' between the rates of growth of economic expansion for the two groups of countries would not occur until the underdeveloped countries had raised their average annual growth rate to about 4.3% at the minimum. To make this possible within the ten-year period of the projection, the level of their productive investment would have to more than double in the first year. If foreign aid from developed countries were to provide the substance of this rise in investment, it would require an increase of capital transfers during the first year of at least 500% under the most favorable of conditions."

The growth model suggested by Leontief is a significant contribution to peace research. However, let us consider how far this model is applicable in the development process of the poor regions of the world. Growth models were largely formulated for the industrially advanced countries for which the rigorous restrictive assumptions of the models can at least partly be justified. This may not be true for the poor countries. Leontief's growth model, like most other growth models, assumes the constancy of the capital output ratio "b_2" over time. For highly developed countries this assumption can be partly justified. If we are to assume that "b_2" remains constant over time, it becomes necessary to explain factors responsible for its stability. Four such important factors seem to be relevant: (1) the trend of the rate of interest through time, (2) the type of production functions and relation to the law of diminishing returns, (3) the change in technology, and (4) external economies and the nature of changes in the composition of output. From a historical study of the economies of the advanced countries, it can be seen that interest rates have fallen absolutely over the last 70-80 years and that there are no data to contradict the assumption of diminishing returns, particularly for a raw-material or agriculture-orientated economy. These two factors should contribute to a secular upward tendency in the capital-output ratios. On the other hand, "day to day routine innovations are of capital-saving variety and that these, together with particular external economies, provide the necessary counteracting force to a declining rate of interest and diminishing returns and thus producing a constant capital-output ratio."

This analysis is not valid for the underdeveloped countries, since they operate with different levels of technology. With the same relative quantities of labour and capital the output in the developed countries is expected to be more than that of the later countries. In the poor countries the major capital-deepening innovations will be necessary before the minor, routine capital-saving innovations. So at the initial state of development "b_2" will be higher, and when the countries are fairly industrialized, it will begin to fall. In the economic development of the underdeveloped countries, we are interested in changing the structure of the economy. But if we start with a constant value of "b_2" obtained from historical data, we are planning a structure of the future economy which is similar to what it is now. The same is true in regard to the assumption of constancy of the average propensity to save (and hence the marginal propensity to save). As income increases, the distribution of income changes and as society in the poor regions transforms from a feudal structure to an industrial one, the saving-income ratio is bound to be different.

This growth model, though simple, is highly aggregative. The grouping of the countries as either developed or underdeveloped is grossly oversimplified. In reality, the constituent countries in the "underdeveloped" class are in different stages of economic growth and have completely different economic, social and political backgrounds. So the assumption of a single capital-output ratio and a single saving-income ratio for all the countries combined is not tenable. Only one type of product has been assumed, namely total income, and the commodity composition of the total product is ignored. This implies that the system does not undergo any structural change, so that the proportions in which different commodities are produced remain the same — an assumption difficult to justify in the case of economic growth of the underdeveloped countries. Like other growth models, in real terms, the effects of price changes are not analysed. But prices are important factors in those countries. In most poor areas suffering from excessive population growth, labour is a very important factor for any analysis of an economic problem. To increase the per capita income, we have to increase the supply of capital relative to that of labour so that more labour will be released and employed, thus increasing the total and per capita output. But in Leontief's model, labour is completely absent.

Usually, there is a time lag between investment and increase in productive capacity. This maturity lag of capital may differ amongst countries and also between different sectors in one country. This model has not taken into account any such considerations. The question of depreciation has not been mentioned and capital goods are assumed to have an infinite life-span. It has also been assumed that the economies of both groups of countries are running on full capacity. The internal structure of the economies, their interindustrial deliveries, production functions, and monetary and fiscal positions are all ignored. It is assumed that the economies of the two groups of countries are completely closed except for the transfer of capital. But imports and exports are important sectors, and, in the case of disarmament, the export of raw materials by the poor countries to the developed countries may decrease.

Another crucial assumption made by Leontief is that capital alone can change the rate of growth of the poor countries. However, various factors limit the effectiveness of capital transferred to the less developed countries. In these countries, there may be (1) a shortage of entrepreneurs who are willing and able to organize new ventures; (2) a lack of well-conceived projects from an economic and engineering point of view; (3) a shortage of trained labour, supervisors, plant managers and other technical stuff; (4) a lot of time required for the formulation of projects, for conducting engineering and economic surveys and for the actual implementation of projects with the help of aid funds; (5) difficulty in maintaining a proper balance between the pattern of investment and outputs in various sectors of the economy; (6) government policies to reduce business incentives; and (7) social conditions restricting labour mobility, domestic savings and investment.

There are conflicting opinions as to whether or not capital can be regarded as the key determinant of the rate of economic growth. Moses Abramovitz has noted that capital played a relatively unimportant part in raising per capita output in the United States during 1870-1953. The same is found to be true Norwegian data during 1900-50 by Odd Aukrust.

Further, modern technology is difficult to transfer from the country where it developed to another country. It originates from skills, entrepreneurship, and improved methods of social and economic organization which must ultimately be domestic achievements of the poor countries. Transfer of foreign capital, however massive it may be, cannot solve this technological problem.

Leontief's model is on a total basis. But since one of the major problems in the poor countries is population explosion, it will be useful if the growth model is designed on a per capita basis. However, it can be shown that for this model the rate of growth of per capita income is equal to the rate of growth of the total income minus the rate of growth of population.

It has been pointed out that it is not enough that the growth rates of the two groups of countries become equal. To fill the enormous gap between the rich and poor countries the growth rate in the poor countries should be a multiple of that of rich countries. On the other hand, what is desirable may not be feasible. Rosenstein-Rodan calculates that the less developed countries could absorb annual capital, including private foreign investment, of $5.7 billion during 1961-71 and $4.7 billion during 1971-76 [27]. This is much lower than the hypothetical capital transfer in the case of disarmament as postulated by Leontief. Millikan and Rostow have put the annual requirement at $5 billion. The estimates prepared by the United Nations' experts is $10 billion (UN expert study, 1951). Compared with these estimates, Leontief's proposed schemes appear to be too optimistic.

Other questions to be decided are: whether the aid should be for consumption or investment or to remove economic bottlenecks, whether it will be in the form of loans or grants, and whether there would be any pressures to "Buy American". The argument that aid should not be given to increase consumption is not valid in all circumstances. In many cases, foreign aid in the form of food grain supplies under the P.L. 480 programmes has sustained economic development by releasing foreign exchange to import capital goods.

Another problem of no small importance is whether the people in the developed countries can be persuaded by economic arguments, political realities, or humanitarian considerations to sacrifice part of their wealth for the sake of humanity at large. It has been found by the University of Michigan Survey Research Center that expanded foreign aid has the least popular support for national defence savings.

Lastly, the 10-year period assumed by Leontief is too short for the capital transfers to be effective since the infrastructure of the economy of the underdeveloped countries, namely transportation, educational, medical and social services, and housing, takes time to develop. So the problem involves a long-term planning programme covering four to five decades, and for this purpose a programming model is preferable to a growth model.

In Section 2 of the Appendix such a programming model has been presented. Here the problem is to find the optimum combination of the incomes of the two groups of countries at each point of time in the future, such that the total income of the world at the time period T is maximized under certain restrictions. The first constraint is that the total savings available to the two groups of countries from domestic sources plus the transfers of capital from the rich countries to the poor countries equals the total investment. The second is definitional-assuming no capital disinvestment; the third concerns the limitations on disparity of income; and the last is on the amount of capital transferred to the poor regions. The problem has also been presented by graphic representation in Fig. 6.1 of the Appendix.

One of the important problems facing those involved in the utilization of foreign aid is the decision regarding the amount of foreign aid to be given to each sector of the economy of the recipient country such that a certain pattern of employment structure in each sector can be maintained. Equation (12) of Section 3 in the Appendix gives a simple method of such sectoral allocation of foreign aid.

Another important problem is the discovery of what proportion of investment (consisting of domestic resources and foreign aid) should be utilized in the investment goods producing sectors such that the rate of growth of income is maximalized. To answer this question, we have integrated the Leontief model with the Mahalanobis bi-sector model. This is shown in Section 4 of the Appendix.

We do not claim that these modifications made to the Leontief model are either original or spectacular. What is emphasized is that improved models can be developed employing the Leontief model as the base by introducing more realistic assumptions and relaxing the restrictive conditions. However, we can safely conclude that the article by Leontief is a significant contribution in peace research literature and that it has opened up a new direction for disarmament analysis.

ISARD AND SCHOOLER (1964)

In this study, the authors argue that since the defence industries are concentrated in few states and in a number of specific regions of the United States, any cutback of the defence expenditure will be bound to have regional impacts. The following regions are chosen for estimating the regional impacts of cuts in defence expenditure:

1. The Los Angeles-Long Beach Metropolitan area
2. The San Francisco-Oakland Metropolitan area
3. The State of California
4. The St Louis Metropolitan area
5. Kalamazoo Country, Michigan
6. The Philadelphia Metropolitan area

In each area, the impacts are examined in terms of relatively fine industry detail with the help of a regional input-out model. In the face of a 10% reduction of defence expenditure, the authors estimate the loss of employment in each sector and consider several offset programmes to compensate for this loss. Column 1 of their Table 2 gives the decrease in employment in all sectors of the economy of the Los Angeles-Long Beach Metropolitan area as a consequence of a 10% cut in the defence expenditure. The increase in employment by different offset programmes is given in columns 2-10. All of these figures are estimated by using a regional input-output model. An offset programme or a combination of offset programmes is deemed to be most efficient if it can make highest compensation for loss of income due to disarmament. This type of analysis is made for all other regions mentioned before.

The gist of their conclusion is that no particular area will be hurt by cuts in defence demand if:

a.   an equal quantity of new demand were generated;
b.   a share of it were directed to each local area proportional to the cutback of defence demand in those areas; and
c.   the difficulties of reconverting facilities and manpower to the new demand could be suddenly and costlessly overcome.

It cannot be denied that the regional impacts of disarmament are significant and that they call for regional policy decisions. But the types of offsetting programmes suggested by the authors are difficult to implement due to political and legal difficulties. Some of them, such as mass housing construction, are self-contradictory. However, the authors are quite aware of these difficulties when they say:

"We have examined only a few extreme programs. It is very unlikely that one and only one of these (or other) extreme programs will be found suitable for any local economy. Rather, some combination of programs is likely to be found most appropriate. Moreover, since there is considerable diversity among local areas--diversity in such characteristics as mineral resources, labor skills, capital stock, ethnic background, political and cultural institutions and in military contracts and expenditures per capita, we can expect considerable variation in the combinations of the offset programs most suitable for the many different local economies of the United States" (p. 43).

TABLE 1: Changes in Employment by Sector for Combinations of a 10% Reduction in Military Expenditures and an Offset Program (1958 man years)

	Exports to India (except food) (1)	Exports (except military) (2)	Business Investment (3)	Personal Consumption (4)	Public Services Construction (5)	Residential Construction (6)	Maintenance Construction (7)	Government (non-military) (8)
1 Transportation Equipment and Ordnance	− 47,647.8	− 67,733.1	− 64,632.3	− 74,645.3	− 77,326.2	− 78,456.7	− 78,521.3	− 77,164.7
2 Instruments and Allied Products	+ 1,841.1	− 807.5	− 290.7	− 2,680.9	− 1,808.8	− 3,294.6	− 3,294.6	− 3,133.1
3 Electrical Machinery	− 4,812.7	+ 1,272.7	− 3,843.7	− 16,699.1	− 18,443.3	− 17,829.6	− 16,440.7	− 19,735.3
4 Apparel and Textile Mill Products	+ 15,277.9	+ 13,436.8	+ 193.8	− 18,475.6	− 1,647.3	− 452.2	− 1,453.5	− 646.0
5 Leather Products	+ 258.4	− 646.0	+ 96.9	− 2,584.0	− 581.4	− 516.8	− 549.1	− 258.4
6 Fuel and Power	+ 3,165.4	+ 2,034.9	+ 1,841.1	+ 4,489.7	+ 516.8	− 3,423.8	− 3,003.9	− 1,550.4
7 Machinery (except electrical)	+ 36,563.6	+ 18,927.8	+ 39,083.0	− 2,325.6	− 193.8	− 2,713.2	− 2,616.3	− 1,970.3
8 Food and Kindred Products	+ 2,422.5	+ 10,368.3	− 1,033.6	+ 14,373.5	− 1,711.9	− 807.5	− 1,065.9	+ 96.9
9 Miscellaneous Manufacturing Industries	+ 387.6	+ 1,292.0	+ 646.0	+ 2,519.4	− 355.3	− 290.7	− 258.4	+ 872.1
10 Rubber and Rubber Products	+ 3,779.1	+ 2,131.8	+ 1,292.0	+ 646.0	− 484.5	− 226.1	− 323.0	+ 258.4
11 Primary Metals	+ 7,590.5	+ 4,263.6	+ 13,501.4	+ 7,461.3	− 2,293.3	− 3,294.6	− 516.8	− 8,914.8
12 Chemicals and Allied Products	+ 17,183.6	+ 11,401.9	+ 0	+ 1,679.6	− 1,388.9	− 1,098.2	− 2,680.9	− 1,292.0
13 Non-Metallic Minerals and Products	+ 4,651.2	+ 1,615.0	+ 8,882.5	+ 419.9	− 24,386.5	− 15,342.5	− 10,077.6	+ 1,195.1
14 Fabricated Metal Products	+ 4,618.9	+ 2,422.5	+ 14,115.1	− 3,165.4	− 4,134.4	− 4,168.7	− 7,816.6	− 5,426.4
15 Paper and Allied Products	+ 3,423.8	+ 2,551.7	+ 193.8	+ 969.0	− 193.8	− 419.9	− 452.2	− 646.0
16 Lumber and Wood Products	+ 2,325.6	+ 1,098.2	+ 10,626.7	+ 1,582.7	− 1,098.2	− 32,041.6	− 10,594.4	− 1,518.7
17 Trade	+ 50,969.4	+ 23,837.4	+ 41,279.6	+ 75,969.6	− 9,496.2	− 33,818.1	− 31,492.5	− 2,067.2
18 Service and Finance	+ 7,978.1	+ 11,401.9	+ 3,908.3	+ 101,131.3	− 8,785.6	− 2,616.3	− 6,233.9	+ 281,397.6
19 Transportation	+ 37,048.1	+ 14,276.6	+ 5,361.8	+ 6,330.8	− 11,208.1	− 5,943.2	− 1,873.4	+ 1,970.3
20 Construction	− 4,328.2	− 4,328.2	+ 63,211.1	− 4,328.2	+ 137,662.6	+ 113,825.2	+ 104,329.0	− 4,328.2
Net Increase in Business Employment	+ 145,866.8	+ 37,564.9	+ 137,856.4	+ 119,025.5	+ 96,803.1	+ 95,704.9	+ 56,040.5	+ 156,816.5
Civilian Employees Released by the Department of Defense	− 63,857.1	− 63,857.1	− 63,857.1	− 63,857.1	− 63,857.1	− 63,857.1	− 63,857.1	− 63,857.1
Net Change*	+ 82,009.7	− 26,292.2	+ 73,999.3	+ 55,168.4	+ 32,946.0	+ 31,847.8	− 7,816.6	+ 92,959.4

Source: Leontief and Hoffenberg, op. cit., p. 53

* These figures do not include the release of men in uniform

273

TABLE 2: Markets for California Products. Total Employment Linked to Final Demand Sectors by Industrial Sector: Los Angeles-Long Beach Metropolitan Area, 1959 (Employment in thousands)

From: Industrial Sector	To: Final Demand Sectors							Total
	1 X_P	2 X_G	3 C	4 I_B	5 I_H	6 G_C	7 G_I	
1 Primary Metals	13.1	6.4	2.1	3.0	.7	.2	.7	26.2
2 Fabricated Metals	29.4	18.9	7.9	3.0	3.6	.6	1.8	65.2
3 Non-Electrical Machinery	41.9	6.3	.8	11.2	.3	0	.5	61.0
4 Electrical Machinery	33.2	59.9	3.8	15.1	.3	.1	.6	113.0
5 Transportation Equipment	48.0	131.1	13.4	6.7	.8	.3	.4	200.7
6 Instruments and Ordnance	12.5	27.5	.7	.5	0	.1	.1	41.4
7 Stone, Clay and Glass	16.2	.4	2.9	.7	1.1	.3	.4	22.0
8 Lumber Products	3.0	2.3	1.9	.4	.5	.1	.2	8.4
9 Furniture	12.8	.6	8.8	2.4	.4	.3	.7	26.0
10 Misc. Manufacturers	11.5	.3	3.1	.3	.4	0	.2	15.8
11 Apparel	34.9	1.8	10.9	.2	.2	.1	.1	48.2
12 Textile-Leather	5.1	.2	4.1	0	.1	0	0	9.5
13 Paper	10.3	.2	2.8	.2	.1	.1	0	13.7
14 Printing	16.5	1.0	18.0	.8	1.2	.5	.4	38.4
15 Chemicals	13.1	1.3	7.8	.3	.4	.2	.2	23.3
16 Petroleum	8.9	2.2	6.4	.5	.4	.2	.2	18.8
17 Rubber	13.8	4.7	1.6	2.2	1.0	0	.4	23.7
18 Foods and Beverages	17.5	1.2	37.7	.3	.4	.5	.2	57.8
19 Agriculture, Forestry, Fisheries, and Mining	17.2	1.8	26.3	.6	.7	.4	.3	47.3
20 Contract Construction	0	.5	.0	51.0	81.3	0	31.1	163.9
21 Transportation, Communication, and Public Utilities	62.6	11.9	62.0	2.8	2.6	4.8	.9	147.6
22 Wholesale Trade	46.2	12.1	78.4	8.6	11.0	1.2	4.2	161.7
23 Retail Trade	45.9	3.8	361.0	5.3	7.2	4.1	2.7	429.9
24 Finance, Insurance, and Real Estate	28.0	4.3	62.5	7.3	28.1	.2	1.1	131.5
25 Services	77.5	12.4	355.9	7.1	16.7	5.2	1.4	476.2
Government	0	21.2	0	0	0	253.0	3.6	277.8
Total Employment	619.1	334.3	1,080.8	130.5	159.5	272.5	52.4	2,649.0

Source: *Markets ... op. cit.*, p. 52–53.

TABLE 3: Los Angeles-Long Beach Metropolitan Area: Employment Effects, by Industrial Category, of Cutback in Military Expenditures and Selected Offset Programs

	Employment Decrease: 10% Cutback	Employment Increases								
Industrial Sectors		Consumption Program A	Consumption Program B	Investment Housing: Program A	Investment Housing: Program B	Business Investment Program A	Business Investment Program B	Government Investment Program A	Government Investment Program B	Combination of Program B Situations
	(1)	(2)	(3)	(4)	(5)	(6)	(7)	(8)	(9)	(10)
1 Primary Metals	576	22	44	122	140	695	744	763	797	431
2 Fabricated Metals	1,701	82	162	625	720	695	744	1,963	2,050	919
3 Non-Electrical Machinery	567	8	15	52	60	2,595	2,778	545	569	855
4 Electrical Machinery	5,391	38	74	52	60	3,499	3,745	654	683	1,140
5 Transportation Equipment	11,799	133	261	139	160	1,552	1,662	436	456	635
6 Instruments and Ordnance	2,475	8	15	0	0	116	124	109	114	63
7 Stone, Clay, and Glass	36	31	61	191	220	162	174	436	456	228
8 Lumber Products	207	19	38	87	100	93	99	218	228	116
9 Furniture	54	88	174	69	80	556	595	763	797	411
10 Miscellaneous Manufactures	27	30	59	69	80	70	74	218	228	110
11 Apparel	162	107	210	35	40	46	50	109	114	104
12 Textile-Leather	18	40	78	17	20	0	0	0	0	25
13 Paper	18	28	55	17	20	46	50	0	0	31
14 Printing	90	179	353	208	240	185	198	436	456	312
15 Chemicals	117	78	153	69	80	70	74	218	228	134
16 Petroleum	198	64	126	69	80	116	124	218	228	139
17 Rubber	423	16	31	174	200	510	546	436	456	308
18 Foods and Beverages	108	371	729	69	80	70	74	218	228	278
19 Agriculture, Forest, Fish and Mining	162	259	509	122	140	139	149	327	342	285
20 Contract Construction	45	0	0	14,122	16,260	11,817	12,648	33,918	35,420	16,082
21 Transportation, Communications and Public Utilities	1,071	648	1,275	452	520	649	694	982	1,025	879
22 Wholesale Trade	1,089	772	1,519	1,911	2,200	1,993	2,133	4,581	4,783	2,659
23 Retail Trade	342	6,966	1,251	1,440	1,228	1,314	2,945	3,075	2,945	3,199
24 Finance, Insurance, and Real Estate	387	608	1,196	4,881	5,620	1,691	1,810	1,200	1,253	2,470
25 Services	1,116	3,503	6,890	2,901	3,340	1,645	1,761	1,527	1,594	3,396
26 Government (civilian)	1,908	2,454	4,827	0	0	0	0	3,296	4,100	2,232
27 Government (military)*	1,908	0	0	0	0	0	0	0	0	0
Total	31,995	13,127	25,820	27,704	31,900	30,238	32,364	57,146	59,680	37,441

* Military personnel (government) assumed roughly equal to civilian personnel. See Statistical Abstract, p. 252, California row.

275

TABLE 4: San Francisco-Oakland Metropolitan Area: Employment Effects by Industrial Category of Cutback in Military Expenditures and Selected Offset Programs

Industrial Sectors	Employ-ment Decrease: 10% Cutback	Employment Increases	
		Consump-tion Program A	Consump-tion Program B
	(1)	(2)	(3)
1 Primary Metals	45	5	7
2 Fabricated Metals	189	19	27
3 Non-Electrical Machinery	225	1	1
4 Electrical Machinery	238	7	9
5 Transportation Equipment	783	21	29
6 Instruments and Ordnance	45	1	1
7 Stone, Clay, and Glass	18	16	21
8 Lumber Products	0	7	9
9 Furniture	9	16	23
10 Miscellaneous Manufactures	27	5	7
11 Apparel	27	23	32
12 Textile-Leather	9	5	7
13 Paper	9	11	15
14 Printing	171	111	153
15 Chemicals	63	12	16
16 Petroleum	81	45	62
17 Rubber	9	4	5
18 Foods and Beverages	207	175	241
19 Agriculture, Forest, Fish, and Mining	54	140	193
20 Contract Construction	153	0	0
21 Transportation, Communications, and Public Utilities	342	411	568
22 Wholesale Trade	225	384	531
23 Retail Trade	63	1,408	1,946
24 Finance, Insurance and Real Estate	36	229	316
25 Services	162	1,448	2,001
26 Government (civilian)	5,265	1,282	1,771
27 Government (military)		0	0
Total	8,455	5,786	7,991

TABLE 5: State of California: Employment Effects by Industrial Category of Cutback in Military Expenditures and Selected Offset Programs

Industrial Sectors	Employment Decrease: 10% Cutback	Consumption Program A	Consumption Program B	Investment Housing: Program A	Investment Housing: Program B	Business Investment Program A	Business Investment Program B	Government Investment Program A	Government Investment Program B	Combination of Program B Situations
	(1)	(2)	(3)	(4)	(5)	(6)	(7)	(8)	(9)	(10)
1 Primary Metals	1,251	101	197	511	505	1,292	1,550	2,034	2,354	1,152
2 Fabricated Metals	2,268	220	429	1,146	1,131	1,180	1,417	3,639	4,212	1,797
3 Non-Electrical Machinery	1,044	21	42	106	104	5,389	6,469	1,284	1,487	2,026
4 Electrical Machinery	6,570	68	132	123	122	5,211	6,255	1,605	1,858	2,092
5 Transportation Equipment	19,098	207	403	212	209	2,272	2,726	963	1,115	1,113
6 Instruments and Ordnance	4,878	18	36	18	17	401	481	321	372	227
7 Stone, Clay and Glass	90	222	433	476	470	445	535	1,391	1,611	762
8 Lumber Products	369	182	355	970	957	713	855	2,676	3,097	1,316
9 Furniture	108	189	369	229	226	1,448	1,737	1,605	1,858	1,048
10 Miscellaneous Manufactures	81	66	129	123	122	111	134	535	619	251
11 Apparel	279	310	605	106	104	89	107	321	372	297
12 Textile-Leather	54	74	144	35	35	22	27	0	0	52
13 Paper	63	114	223	247	244	200	241	963	1,115	455
14 Printing	333	471	919	353	348	468	561	642	743	643
15 Chemicals	261	174	338	176	174	200	241	428	496	312
16 Petroleum	351	152	297	176	174	290	347	428	496	328
17 Rubber	576	33	64	264	261	690	829	749	867	505
18 Foods and Beverages	477	1,082	2,107	335	331	245	294	749	867	899
19 Agriculture, Forest, Fish and Mining	1,080	2,415	471	987	974	1,891	1,069	2,462	2,849	1,341
20 Contract Construction	531	0	0	33,726	33,286	21,134	25,367	88,086	101,961	40,154
21 Transportation, Communications and Public Utilities	2,430	2,147	4,183	1,657	1,636	1,648	1,978	3,425	3,964	2,940
22 Wholesale Trade	2,196	2,068	4,029	4,390	4,333	3,585	4,304	11,452	13,256	6,481
23 Retail Trade	819	8,474	16,511	3,350	3,306	2,472	2,967	8,455	9,787	8,143
24 Finance, Insurance, and Real Estate	621	1,398	2,723	10,402	10,266	3,140	3,769	2,997	3,469	5,056
25 Services	2,160	7,356	14,334	7,405	7,308	3,697	4,437	2,355	2,726	7,201
26 Government (civilian)	14,103	6,418	12,504	0	0	0	0	14,235	16,477	7,245
27 Government (military)*	14,103	0	0	0	0	0	0	0	0	0
Total	76,194	33,980	61,977	67,523	66,643	57,234	68,697	153,800	178,028	93,836

* Military personnel (government) assumed roughly equal to civilian personnel; see Statistical Abstract, 1962, p. 252, California row.

TABLE 6: St. Louis Metropolitan Area: Gross Output, Income and Employment Effects by Industrial Category of Cutback in Military Expenditures and Selected Programs

| Sector | Prime Military Contract Awards (1) | 10% Cutback Program | | | Consumption Program | | | Gross Output Decreases: $25.6M Cut in Aircraft (8) |
		Gross Output Decreases (2)	Income Decrease (3)	Employment Decrease (4)	Gross Output Increases (5)	Income Increase (6)	Employment Increase (7)	
1 Food and Kindred Products	$2,719,835	$1,825,719	$263,933	52.95	$3,728,206	$538,964	108.12	$1,347,317
2 Textiles and Apparel	555,920	292,275	93,565	30.69	469,916	150,432	49.34	188,465
3 Lumber and Furniture	807,197	247,138	86,302	23.97	248,422	86,750	24.10	145,785
4 Paper and Allied Products	56,352	265,208	69,622	17.50	374,448	98,300	24.71	162,529
5 Printing and Publishing	1,428,649	575,334	257,347	51.78	623,139	278,730	56.08	246,098
6 Chemicals	1,275,349	260,999	66,066	11.48	134,016	33,923	5.90	109,018
7 Products of Petroleum and Coal	2,890,891	868,644	67,283	10.42	996,806	77,210	11.96	484,105
8 Leather and Leather Products	939,715	122,283	46,414	11.13	35,105	13,325	3.19	21,660
9 Iron and Steel	219,010	740,266	261,495	46.64	164,655	58,163	10.37	748,535
10 Non-Ferrous Metals	12,770	81,078	21,662	3.73	31,070	8,301	1.43	50,874
11 Plumbing and Heating Supplies, Fabricated Structural Metal Products	1,545,040	493,866	176,044	53.83	357,716	127,512	38.99	261,742
12 Machinery (except electrical)	1,785,166	411,382	126,788	36.20	267,225	82,359	23.52	158,663
13 Motors and Generators; radios; Other Electrical Machinery	2,638,103	412,088	180,568	42.45	104,184	45,651	10.73	157,716
14 Motor Vehicles	2,354,228	734,078	121,356	14.68	930,982	153,908	18.62	349,458
15 Other Transportation Equipment	193,530,773	19,760,578	6,544,328	1,264.68	24,560	8,134	1.57	26,139,952
16 Miscellaneous Manufactures	17,369,096	2,482,611	927,494	168.82	1,165,712	435,505	79.27	516,007
17 Coal; Gas; Electrical Power; Water	635,624	754,919	192,876	50.58	1,098,731	280,717	73.61	553,285
18 Railroad Transportation		343,499	134,929	23.0	370,574	145,564	24.83	265,505
19 Other Transportation	87,500	556,905	240,929	62.93	1,036,134	448,253	117.08	461,498
20 Trade	2,355,962	2,868,208	1,753,060	570.77	5,913,562	3,614,393	1,176.80	2,277,123
21 Communications	10,300	336,198	149,261	33.62	619,480	275,029	61.95	284,938
22 Finance; Insurance; Rentals		2,840,598	957,392	144.87	6,141,001	2,069,757	313.19	2,373,135
23 Business and Personal Services	17,456,267	3,209,336	1,835,015	333.77	3,014,333	1,723,517	313.49	1,149,686
24 Medical, Educational, Non-Profit Organizations	1,452,432	691,733	531,768	154.26	1,298,867	998,501	289.65	469,665
25 Undistributed		822,563	294,997	42.77	1,428,444	512,286	74.28	587,286
26 Eating and Drinking Places		767,629	267,582	79.83	1,898,010	661,614	197.39	684,220
27 Capital Construction, Maintenance	3,905,284	1,133,128	453,661	62.32	1,111,535	445,016	61.13	668,986
28 Households		1,869,828	159,133	50.61	14,988,572	395,135	125.67	15,083,691
29 Local Government		833,151	588,949	170.80	1,728,110	1,221,591	354.26	727,950
Total	$256,032,015	$61,581,242	$16,869,819	3,621.09	$50,303,515	$14,988,540	3,651.23	$56,671,892

TABLE 7: Kalamazoo County: Gross Output Effects by Industrial Category of Cutback in Military Expenditures and Selected Offset Programs

		Prime Military Contract Awards	Gross Output Decrease: 10% Cutback	Gross Output Increases		
				Consumption Program A	Consumption Program B	Foreign Aid Program
		(1)	(2)	(3)	(4)	(5)
1	Food and Kindred Products	$	$5,698	$38,341	$11,010	$15,221
2	Textile Products and Apparel		100	609	175	10,175
3	Lumber and Lumber Products	82,865	8,854	811	233	1,387
4	Paper and Paper Products (board)	504,864	54,390	3,854	1,107	37,251
5	Paper and Paper Products (coated)	43,433	4,666	811	233	106,312
6	Printing and Publishing (book, etc.)		13,301	25,560	7,340	3,023
7	Printing and Publishing (commercial)		327	1,420	408	510
8	Printing and Publishing (engraving)		1,002	406	117	569
9	Chemicals, Pharmaceuticals, and Petroleum Products	218,396	25,072	15,012	4,311	304,272
10	Rubber Products		20	0	0	10,720
11	Stone, Clay, and Glass Products		142	609	175	241
12	Primary Metals (manufacturing)		365	2,029	583	801
13	Primary Metals (foundry)		1,402	203	58	5,674
14	Fabricated Metals Products	65,793	7,341	406	117	14,013
15	Non-Electrical Machinery (metal working)	87,628	9,484	203	58	29,230
16	Non-Electrical Machinery (construction)	419,317	43,091	2,840	816	46,902
17	Electrical Machinery and Equipment	292,500	29,270	0	0	17,571
18	Transportation Equipment	678,124	74,187	24,343	6,990	142,768
19	Professional, Scientific, and Other Instruments		0	0	0	4,949
20	Miscellaneous Manufacturing	10,457	2,128	4,869	1,398	41,686
21	Military Products	86,263	8,626	0	0	0
22	Non-Metallic Mining Products		1	0	0	35
23	Agricultural Products		2,379	16,026	4,602	41,606
24	Transportation and Warehousing		5,427	22,923	6,582	5,997
25	Wholesale Trade	112,796	28,979	67,958	19,514	9,375
26	Retail Trade		45,980	309,362	88,834	37,789
27	Utilities		9,323	43,615	12,524	7,854
28	Finance, Banking, and Insurance		21,651	128,208	36,815	17,075
29	Real Estate and Rentals		29,244	119,282	34,252	14,190
30	Personal, Business, Professional, and Repair Services	3,222,746	373,340	273,455	78,523	32,884
31	Communications		5,142	17,446	5,010	2,217
32	Construction		0	0	0	0
33	Local Government		15,209	56,598	16,252	13,792
34	Households (Income)		385,579	574,094	164,853	292,782
	Totals	$5,825,182	$1,211,450	$1,751,293	$502,890	$1,268,871

APPENDIX

Section 1

LEONTIEF'S GROWTH MODEL

The following set of aggregative variables is used to describe the state of the two groups of economies at any particular time (t):

Name of the Variables	Developed	Underdeveloped
1. Gross national product (domestically produced)	$Y_1(t)$	$Y_2(t)$
2. Productive Investment (total)	$I_1(t)$	$I_2(t)$
3. Capital transfer from developed to underdeveloped areas	$H(t)$	
4. Growth rate of the domestically produced gross national product $\dfrac{\dot{Y}(t)}{Y(t)}$	$r_1(t)$	$r_2(t)$

Assumptions: The following is a statement of the basic assumptions implicit in the symbolic representation of the model below.

(1) The Capital Transfers (H) from developed countries to the underdeveloped countries during any period of time are a fixed proportion of the gross national product of the developed countries. (See equation 5.)

(2) The Capital-Output Ratios (b_1, b_2) of each group remain constant over time. (See equations 2 and 7.)

(3) Productive Investment in:

(a) Developed Countries (I_1) is a fixed proportion of the gross national product in those countries during the period of time. (Equation 1)

(b) Underdeveloped Countries (I_2) is the sum of

   (1) International Investment (which equals a fixed proportion of the gross national product in those countries during the period of time (Equation 6) and

   (2) External Investment (which equals the capital transfers from developed countries).

Equations of the Model

(A) Developed Areas: The following theoretical relationships are used to derive and to solve the equations describing the growth of the developed areas.

Saving Function

$$I_1(t) = i_1 Y_1(t) \tag{1}$$

i represents the fraction of the GNP allocated to investment.

Acceleration Relationships

$$Y(t) = \frac{I_1(t)}{b_1} \qquad (2)$$

b_1 is the capital coefficient (capital-output ratio) describing the amount of capital required per additional unit of annual GNP. Growth rate equation, obtained from (1) and (2)

$$\dot{Y}_1(t) - i_1 \frac{Y_1(t)}{b_1} = 0 \qquad (3)$$

Exponential growth function obtained by solving (3)

$$Y_1(t) = Y_1(0)e^{\lambda_1 t}, \quad \lambda_1 = i_1/b_1 \qquad (4)$$

Where $Y_1(0)$ represents the level of the GNP in the base year, 0, and λ_1 its growth rate, which remains constant as long as I_1 and b_1 are fixed.

The amount transferred from the developed areas to the underdeveloped areas is assumed to constitute a fixed fraction, h, of the GNP of the capital-exporting countries. Thus, the following transfer relationship, which is derived from equation (4) above, implies that $H(t)$, the amount transferred, will grow exponentially at the same rate as the developed areas' GNP.

Transfer Relationship

$$H(t) = hY_1(t) = hY_1(0)e^{\lambda_{1,t}} \qquad (5)$$

(B) Underdeveloped Areas: The following theoretical relationships are used to derive and to solve the equations describing the growth of the underdeveloped areas. The productive investment in the underdeveloped areas is being supported from two sources: the saved fraction, i_2, of their gross national product, $Y_2(t)$, and the capital imports, $H(t)$:

Investment Function

$$I_2(t) = i_2 Y_2(t) + H(t) = i_2 Y_2(t) + hY_1(0)e^{\lambda_1 t} \qquad (6)$$

Acceleration Relationship

$$\dot{Y}_2(t) = \frac{I_2(t)}{b_2} \qquad (7)$$

b_2 is the capital coefficient describing the amount of capital required per additional unit of annual GNP.

Growth Rate Equation, derived from (6) and (7)

$$\frac{\dot{Y}_2(t)}{b_2} - \frac{i_2 Y_2(t)}{b_2} - h\,\frac{Y_1(0)}{b_2}e^{\lambda_{1t}} = 0 \qquad (8)$$

if

$$\lambda_2 = \frac{i_2}{b_2} \neq \lambda_1 = \frac{i_1}{b_1}$$

Growth function, is obtained solving the differential equation (8):

$$Y_2(t) = \frac{[Y_2(0) + H(0)\,e^{\lambda_{2t}}]}{b_2\,(\lambda_1 - \lambda_2)}$$

$$-\frac{H(0)}{b_2\,(\lambda_1 - \lambda_2)}\,e^{\lambda_{1t}} \qquad (9)$$

Where

$$\lambda_2 = i_2/b_2$$

Section 2

REFORMULATION OF LEONTIEF'S MODEL TO A PROGRAMMING PROBLEM

Let $Y_1(t)$ and $Y_2(t)$ be the domestically produced gross national products of the developed countries and underdeveloped countries respectively. Then the total gross national product of the world in any year t can be written as:

$$Y(t) = Y_1(t) + Y_2(t) \qquad (1)$$

Assuming consumption in any year depends on the gross national product in that year and investment to have a gestation lag of one year in each area we have

$$C_1(t) = c_1 Y_1(t) \qquad (2)$$

$$C_2(t) = c_2 Y_2(t) \qquad (3)$$

$$b_1\{Y_1(t+1) - Y_1(t)\} = I_1(t) \qquad (4)$$

$$b_2\{Y_2(t+1) - Y_2(t)\} = I_2(t) \qquad (5)$$

where $C_1(t)$ and $C_2(t)$ stand for consumption in two areas and c_1 and c_2 are the rates of consumption in the two areas respectively. As before, $I_1(t)$, $I_2(t)$ are investment, b_1 and b_2 the capital coefficients in the two areas respectively.
Again, we have the savings function

$$I_1(t) = i_1 Y_1(t) \qquad (6)$$

$$I_2(t) = i_2 Y_2(t) + H(t) \qquad (7)$$

where i_2 and i_2 represent the fraction of the gross national product saved the allotted to investment in the two areas and $H(t)$ is the transfer of capital from the developed areas to the underdeveloped areas.

Then the total world GNP is
$$Y(t) = Y_1(t) + Y_2(t)$$

$$= C_1(t) + C_2(t) + I_1(t) + I_2(t) - H(t) \qquad (8)$$

combining equation (8) with the equations (2)–(7), we have after simplifications
$$Y(t) = c_1 Y_1(t) + c_2 Y_2(t) + b_1\{Y_1(t+1) - Y_1(t)\}$$

$$+ b_2\{Y_2(t+1) - Y_2(t)\} - H(t) \qquad (9)$$

Remembering that
$$i_1 = 1 - c_1$$
and
$$i_2 = 1 - c_2$$

Equation (9) can be written as
$$Y(t) = (1-i_1)Y_1(t) + (1-i_2)Y_2(t)$$

$$+ b_1\{Y_1(t+1) - Y_1(t)\}$$

$$+ b_2\{Y_2(t+1) - Y_2(t)\} - H(t) \qquad (10)$$

Simplifying
$$b_1\{Y_1(t+1) - Y_1(t)\} + b_2\{Y_2(t+1) - Y_2(t)\}$$

$$= i_1 Y_1(t) + i_2 Y_2(t) + H(t) \qquad (11)$$

The left-hand side of (11) represents total investment and the right-hand side represents the sum of savings in the developed country, savings in the underdeveloped country and the transfer of capital from the developed countries to the underdeveloped countries.

Remembering that
$$H(t) = hY_1(0)e^{\lambda_{1t}} \qquad (12)$$
where $\lambda_1 = i_1/b_1$

Equation (11) can be written as
$$b_1\{Y_1(t+1) - Y_1(t)\} + b_2 \{Y_2(t+1) - Y_2(t)\}$$

$$= i_1 Y_1(t) + i_2 Y_2(t) + hY_1(0)e^{\lambda_{1t}} \qquad (13)$$

It is assumed that the coefficients i_1, i_2, b_1 and b_2 are positive. In reality i_1 and i_2, will lie between 0 and 1 and b_1, b_2 are each likely to be greater than unity. Since the economy of the developed country is generally more productive than that of the underdeveloped countries, let us assume that b_1 is less than b_2.

Replacing $e^{\lambda_{1t}}$ by $1 + \lambda_1^t$ we have from equation

$$b_1\{Y_1(t+1) - Y_1(t)\} + b_2 \{Y_2(t+1) - Y_2(t)\}$$

$$= i_1 Y_1(t) + i_2 Y_2(t) + hY_1(0)(1 + \lambda_1{}^t) \qquad (14)$$

Three types of constraints can be imposed on equation (14)
(a) In the developed countries, total investment equals total available domestic saving, and in the undeveloped areas total investment equals total available domestic savings plus the capital transfer from the developed areas.

In other words, there cannot be any net consumption of capital disinvestment. These constraints may be written as
(i) $Y_1(t+1) \geq Y_1(t)$, and (ii) $Y_2(t+1) \geq Y_2(t)$ (15)
(b) The next constraints may be political constraints which are expressed in the following form:

$$(i) \quad \frac{Y_2(t+1)}{Y_1(t+1)} \geq p_1, \text{ and (ii) } \frac{Y_1(t+1)}{Y_2(+1)} \geq P_2 \qquad (16)$$

where
$$0 < p_1 < 1, \; p_2 > 0$$

The first constraint states that the total gross national product in the underdeveloped areas should not be allowed to fall below a fixed portion of the total gross national product of the developed countries. At present the GNP of the underdeveloped countries is one-sixth that of the developed countries as estimated by Leontief. The second constraint states that from all available evidence about the economic growth of the developed and underdeveloped countries, even assuming massive foreign aid, it is expected that in the near future the GNP of the developed countries will always be greater than the GNP of the underdeveloped countries by a constant multiple. For example, in the next ten years, the GNP of the developed countries can be assumed to be at least five times greater than the GNP of the underdeveloped countries.

The above restraints can also be expressed in terms of per capita basis rather than on total basis, taking into consideration the unequal rate of population growth. In that case p_1 and p_2 will change every year. For the sake of simplicity, we keep p_1 and p_2 unchanged over time.
(c) The third constraint can be on $H(t)$, which is the transfer of capital from the developed countries to the underdeveloped countries. For political and psychological reasons the transfers of capital in the form of foreign aid may be restricted to amounts approved by the governments in the developed areas, so we have
$$H(t) \leq F(t)$$
or
$$hY_1(t) \leq F(t)$$

or
$$Y_1(t) \leq \frac{F(t)}{h} \qquad (17)$$

where the value of $F(t)$ in each year is determined by the governments in the developed countries.

B.   Programming

Linear programming technique helps us choose the level of a given activity in a region at which the income generated by pursuing the activity at this level is maximum, subject to resource restrictions. Consider, for example, a region with two activities and four resources. The amount of input required per unit level of each activity is as follows:

		Act 1	Act 2	Resource Limitation
1.	Water	a_{11}	a_{12}	P_1
2.	Land	a_{21}	a_{22}	P_2
3.	Labour	a_{31}	a_{32}	P_3
4.	Capital	a_{41}	a_{42}	P_4

Let X_1 stand for the level of activity number 1 and X_2 for the level of activity number 2. Let C_1 and C_2 be the amount of income generated by unit level of activities 1 and 2, respectively, so that total income is

$$Y_1 = C_1X + C_2X_2$$

The problem is to find the value of X_1 and X_2 such that Y is maximum subject to the restrictions:

$$a_{11}X_1 + a_{12}X_2 \leq P_1,$$
$$a_{21}X_1 + a_{22}X_2 \leq P_2,$$
$$a_{31}X_1 + a_{32}X_2 \leq P_3,$$
$$a_{41}X_1 + a_{42}X_2 \leq P_4.$$

When we have two activities. This linear programming problem can be solved graphically. However, when the number of activities is greater than two, then obviously the problem cannot be solved by graphical methods. Instead, we have to use the simplex method (Dorfman, Samuelson and Solow, 1958). The linear programming model can be extended to the interregional case (Stevens, 1959). The symbolic representation is just a straightforward extension of the single-region case except that we must take into account the question of transport cost between two regions. This is a powerful tool, and it is extensively used in regional planning problems.

The Leontief model can be reduced to a programming model as follows:

The problem is to

$$\text{Maximize: } Y_t = Y_1(t) + Y_2(t)$$
$$= \text{Total World GNP}$$

subject to the conditions given in the equations (14)-(17). The problem can be well described by the following graphic representation.

Let Y_1 and Y_2 be represented by two axes in Figure 1. The gross national products in the base year $Y_1(0)$ and $Y(0)$ of the two areas are represented by the point P_o in Figure 6.1. The GNP for the year 1 will be given by a position $[Y_1(1), Y_2(1)]$ lying on a straight line D_1 whose equation is given by (14) putting $t = 0$. That equation can be written as

$$b_1\{Y_1(1) - Y_1(0)\} + b_2\{Y_2(1) - Y_2(0)\} = i_1 \cdot Y_1(0) + i_2 Y_2(0) + hY_1(0)$$

or

$$b_1 Y_1(1) + b_2 Y_2(1) = Y_1(0)\{b_1 + i_1 + h\} + Y_2(0)\{b_2 + i_2\}$$

or

$$Y_2(1) = -\frac{b_1 Y_1(1)}{a_2} + \frac{Y_1(0)}{b_2}\{b_1 + i_1 + h\} + \frac{Y_2(0)}{b_2}\{b_2 + i_2\}$$

Remembering that[2]

$$\lambda_1 = \frac{i_1}{b_1} \quad \text{and} \quad \lambda_2 = \frac{i_2}{b_2}$$

we have;

$$Y_2(1) = -\frac{b_1}{b_2} Y_1 + Y_1(0) \cdot \frac{b_1}{b_2}(1 + \lambda_1 + \frac{h}{b_1}) + Y_2(0)(1 + \lambda_2)$$

putting

$$\frac{b_1}{b_2} = m$$

$$Y_2(1) = -mY_1(1) + mY_1(0)(1 + \lambda_1 + \frac{h}{b_1}) + Y_2(0)(1 + \lambda_2)$$

Constraints (15) and (16) apply, feasible points can lie only on the line segment PQ. Next, if the constraint (17) is imposed, feasible points are restricted to PZ. Thus the optimum income combination point will lie somewhere in PZ. The position of that point may be found out by some other method (Rahman [24, p. 31].

A similar frontier D_2 is defined when a specific position $[Y_1(1), Y_2(1)]$ has been chosen on D_1 and so on. The problem is to choose $[Y_1(t+1), Y_2(t+1)]$, $t = 0, 1, 2,...T - 1$ so as to maximize $Y(T) = Y_1(T) + Y_2(T)$. Here we shall not discuss how to solve this problem. The interested reader is referred to Rahman's article. The objective of this analysis was only to show how Leontief's model may be reformulated as a programming model.

In this connection, one important point may be emphasized. The constraint represented by equation (17) is equivalent to putting a constraint on $Y_1(t)$, which is the GNP of the developed countries. This means that we are constraining the consumption expenditure $C_1(t)$ and investment $I_1(t)$ of the developed countries. This is so because Leontief's formulation related capital transfer to the GNP of the developed countries, which in turn is comprised of consumption and investment. But constraining the GNP may not be desirable. To avoid this difficulty we can treat H(t) as the transfer of existing capital stock since it is in no way related to $Y_1(t)$. But in that case it will change the existing capital stock and thus change the capital-output ratio b_1 which has been assumed to be constant over time. In any case, if we do not relate H(t) to Y(t), any other restriction on H(t) will change position of the frontier line D_1 to D_1^* and the effective line segment will be P^*Q^* in Figure 1. Here the level of the line is reduced but the number of feasible points is increased.

As stated before, the dichotomy of the countries as either developed or underdeveloped is highly simplified and it may be more realistic to group the helping countries in "m" classes and the countries helped in "n" classes. In that case, it may be interesting to find out the optimal growth of world income taking into consideration internal structure of each country's economy (by means of capital-output and saving-income ratios) and the pattern of international transfers of capital through foreign aid. This may be theoretically possible but will be difficult to implement in practice. Besides, as inherent in all growth models, the validity of the assumptions (such as the fixity of the capital-output ratios and savings income ratios) may be seriously questioned. The data presented here are grossly outdated. For more recent studies, see Leontief and Duchin (1983).

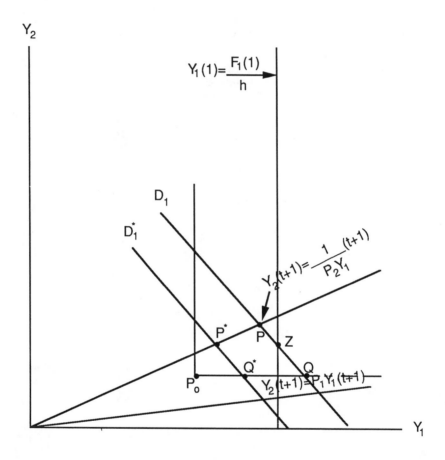

Figure 6.1 A Programming Interpretation

7 Graph Theory and Markov Chain

A. Graph Theory

The international relations of the non-aligned countries are intimately related to superpower rivalry and the fact of the cold war. For the last few years, a drastic change has taken place in the superpower relationship. The lessening of tension between the US and USSR and the political transformation of Eastern Europe will have a major impact on regional conflicts and peace. One such trouble spot is South Asia where India, as a leader of non-aligned countries, is entangled with Pakistan in continuous conflict. Since India's independence in 1947, they have fought three major wars. India also has border disputes and had fought a major war with China. She has less than friendly relationship with bordering countries such as Bangladesh, Nepal and Sri Lanka. The external relationship of India is dictated by at least three factors: (1) the international situation, particularly the superpower relationship; (2) the internal situation which includes economic conditions, pressure groups, religious riots, food situation and changes in the government; and (3) bilateral relations such as border disputes, sharing of river water, etc.

The objective of this study will be to investigate the prospects of peace between India and Pakistan as a result of changing superpower relations. In this exploratory study, the internal factors and bilateral relations need not be considered. The measurement of the relationship of peace and war, and its intensity, can be dealt with by an analytical method called graph theory. Before I discuss how graph theory can be applied for this purpose, I shall give a brief introduction to the theory itself.

Brief Introduction to Graph Theory

A graph is a finite collection of objects of called points. The connection between some of the points is called a line. Thus (p,q) will denote the line connecting the points p and q. When we want to distinguish (p,q) from (q,p) we speak of a directed graph, in which p and q are known as adjacent points. A path between p and q is a sequence of lines (p, a), (a, b) .... (c, d), (d, q). If p = q then the path is called a cycle. A graph is connected if there is path between any two points.

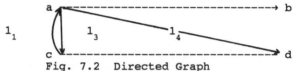

Fig. 7.1 A Graph

1. 4 points, 5 lines --- (b, a), (a, c), (c, d), (d, a), and (c, b).
2. cycle (a, d), (d, c), (c, a).
3. line is an abstract object, no intersection of ad and bc.

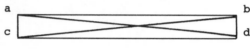

Fig. 7.2 Directed Graph

In Fig. 7.2 -
(a, c) and (c, a) are different lines. The lines are (a, b), (a, c), (c, a), (a, d), (d, c). The segment (d, a) is not a line.

There is a path from d to each other point, but no path from b to d.

Signed Graph

A graph is a signed graph when the lines are labelled either positive or negative. The path or cycle of a signed curve is the same as that of an ordinary graph when the signs are ignored.

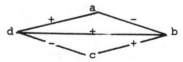

Fig. 7.3 Signed Graph

Cycle: A cycle of a graph is a collection of lines like P_1 $P_2, P_2 P_3, \ldots P_{n-1} P_n, P_n P_1$. The length of a cycle is the number of lines in it. The sign of a cycle is the product of the signs of its lines. If the sign of the cycle is negative, it is unbalanced.

<u>Isomorphic</u>

G and G' are isomorphic if it is possible to label the points in G by (a, b, ... c, ... r) and G' by (a', b', ... c', ...r') in such a way that the line (p, q) is on G if only line (p', q') is on G'

Fig. 7.4 Isomorphic Graphs

<u>Balance</u>

A signed graph is balanced, if and only if, all of its cycles are positive.

The graphs in Fig. 7.5 are designated as balanced or unbalanced.

favourable   : +

unfavourable   : −

no line   : neutral

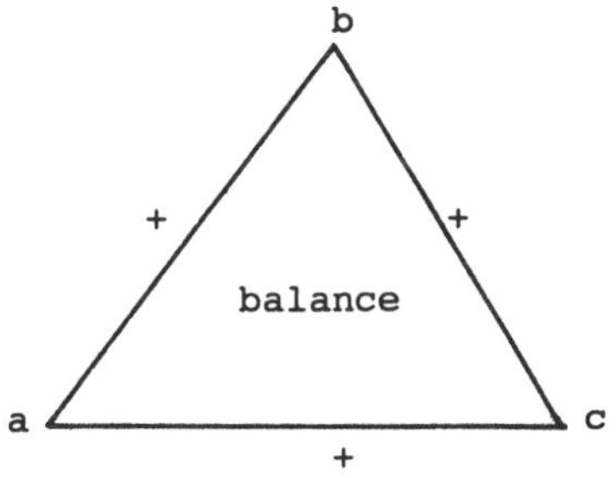

(i)
Fig. 7.5 Balanced Graph

In (iii) in Fig. 7.5 a likes b, but a, b dislike c.

Each graph has a single cycle and the cycle in Fig. 7.5 is balanced if every cycle in it is positive. That a graph is balanced implies that the set of all points in the graph can be portioned into two adjacent sets A and B so that every positive line connects two points in the same set and every negative line connects two points from different sets.

A graph is said to be a complete graph with p points where every pair of distinct points are adjacent, i.e. they are joined by a line. A graph may have different <u>components</u>. A component need not be complete. A clique of a graph G is defined as a maximal complete subgraph (L), i.e. it will not be complete if any other point of the graph G is included. A cut point of a graph is a point where removal increases the number of components. A <u>line or lines</u> whose removal increases the number of components.

<u>Application of Graph Theory to Indo-Pakistani Conflict</u>

I propose to apply graph theory to characterize the regional peace and conflict situation in South Asia. There is theoretical and empirical justification for the statement that a balanced graph has greater stability than an unbalanced

291

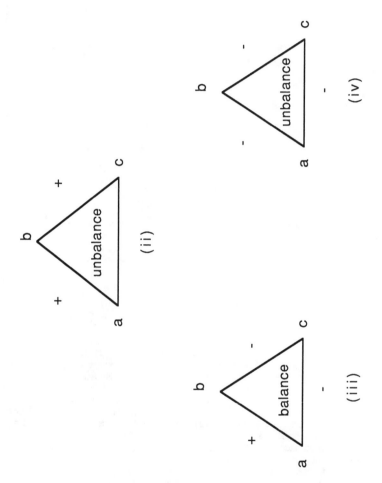

Figure 7.5 (Continued)

graph. If the graph is not balanced, then there will be changes in the graph so that the structure can be balanced. I shall investigate whether this balance existed in the international relationship of India's political history vis-à-vis Pakistan and other major countries throughout the time period after independence in 1947. For the purpose of exploratory research I shall consider only the following countries which will be the points in the graph: 1. India 2. Pakistan 3. USA 4. USSR 5. China

The period 1950-90 will be divided into 8 five-year periods. For each five-year period we shall prepare a detailed chronological history of India's external relations. Further, on the basis of very detailed major events data, I shall determine whether in the aggregate the relationship between a pair of countries, i.e. India and Pakistan, India and U.S., etc. were positive or negative. No major data collection will be involved. In the data bank and the attached references, such events data are available. Subjective weights and scores will be attached to each item on the basis of this information. I shall then draw the structure of the graph and determine its stability based on whether it is balanced or not. The length and sign of the line of the graph will be determined by the intensity and nature (positive or negative) of the relationship defined by the weighted aggregate events. It may be possible to hypothesize the reasons for the imbalance. The structural changes in the graph will be correlated with the corresponding changes of the US-USSR graph. The usefulness of this approach lies in the fact that if we anticipate any significant change in US-USSR relations, it can be used to predict India-Pakistan relations, and consequently, the prospect for peace in the region.

One problem is how to measure the magnitude of intensity between points. Of course we can use numbers like 0,1, - 1,1/2, -1/2, etc.; but that has to be subjective. Secondly, the actual relationship can be expressed differently and has nothing to do with the event. Again, the underlying bond, say between the US and Great Britain, may be very strong, but temporarily there may be friction. Of course, a careful study of the subsystem, i.e. internal affairs of a country, may very much influence the overall system; nevertheless, the graph theory, if accompanied with empirical observations, may shed useful insights into the inter-relationships between nations.

Although events data are available in various publications such as data banks and books, it will take time to organize them so that they can be used readily for the construction of graphs. The expected significance of this study is its analytical orientation. Although extensive materials are available for India-Pakistan relations, this study will provide a mathematical structure and present the framework for other countries simultaneously. Also, it will provide us with the ability to forecast future relationships on the basis of changing relationships of other countries.

Only very elementary properties of graph theory have been presented. The use of other properties of the graph to make the study more realistic will be investigated. My long-term goal will be to conduct a similar graph theory study of the internal situations of India and Pakistan and to integrate it with the proposed research.   I also intend to conduct a comprehensive study involving major countries of the world. To show how international trade influences peace, I shall construct international trade matrices over time and correlate them with the corresponding international graphs of peace and conflict.

It is not possible for me exhaustively to consider all events related to each pair of the countries listed above. Such a study involving more countries will be attempted later. Some of the events will be as follow:

Nehru Era

1.   1947-50

After the independence and partition of the Indian subcontinent in 1947, Jawaharlal Nehru became the first Prime Minister of India.   This was a difficult time.   The relations between India and other countries should be judged against this confused situation. After the Second World War, with the break of wartime alliances and the Soviet thrust into Eastern Europe, deep anti-communist sentiment rose among western allies and the United States.

The USA expected that India would be its crusader for anti-communism in Europe and Asia, but this did not happen. Consequently, the relationship between the USA and India was not quite positive.   John Foster Dulles said that in India, Soviet communism exercised a strong influence through the Interim government.   Nehru was thought to be an agent of the USSR.   Dean Acheson, the Secretary of State of that time, described Nehru as "one of the most difficult men with whom I have ever had to deal".   The events at the UN following the outbreak of the Korean War also indicated a negative relationship between the US and India.   India viewed the Korean War as a local Asian war rather than "premeditated aggression by the communist power for world conquest", as by the US.   India abstained on a UN resolution of a unified UN command and strengthened her efforts to admit China into the UN.

2.   1956-60

I.   Fall 1956
A.   Korean War
B.   Indo-China Crisis
C.   Bandung Conference
D.   Summit meeting in Geneva
E.   Suez episode
F.   Soviet Intervention in Hungary
Suez crises, India and US jointly played an important role in withdrawal of troops from Egypt.
Hungary revolt --→ India and US came nearer.

294

Signing of Indo-American Agreement in August 1956 for food supply.
II. Security Council resolution against India (January 26, 1957). USA supported it.
III. Impact of Bagdad (CENTO) treaty and its relation to India. Eisenhower doctrine January 5, 1957. July 1958, US Marines to Lebanon.
IV. The impact of the SEATO and the crisis in the Far East.
Support of rebels in Indonesia.
Pro-American installation in Laos and Vietnam.
V. Indo-American differences about disarmament, stopping nuclear tests.
VI. Internal development
foreign aid and US investments
Indus Canal water dispute 1959 settled
Tibetan Revolt
President Eisenhower's visit to India
P.L. 480 signing
Convertibility to dollar
1958 -- Tax Concession
1959 -- Two Treaties favourable to US business
USA tried to help the canal dispute
August 1959 ... dispute of Indus water settled
Tibetan revolt 1959
1956 --- Hungary incident
October 1959 --- Chinese intrusions
more loan P.L. 480
1960 - Eisenhower's visit
Indo-China animosity --- good India-US relations

I. Indo-Soviet relation
A. Five principles of Peaceful coexistence
B. Death of Stalin, March 1953
continuous process of libertization
20th party congress in February 1956
All went well except the murder of Hungarian Prime Minister Nagy in 1958.
Visit of Nehru in June 1955
Bulganian and Kruschev in 1955
Steel plant in Bhakara
Racial discrimination in South Africa
Admission of China to UN
1955-56 good agricultural output - aid to India
Change of attitude about India's leaders to Britain
II. Hungary-Suez and Indo-Soviet relation
Condemnation of aggression by Britain and France on Egypt by Nehru within 24 hours
But took several weeks to criticize USSR for Hungary
India ----→ negative vote for USSR in the UN
III. Kashmir Question and Indo-Soviet relations
January 24, 1957 USSR support for India vetoed UN resolution, twice vetoed against CENTO group.

    IV.   Indo-Soviet cooperation to keep Middle East free
           from cold war. Nehru did not see any USSR threat
           in the Middle East. USSR appreciation -- afraid
           of US force.
           India was afraid of US and CENTO support to
           Pakistan.
           Support of USSR peace proposal by Nehru
    V.   Disarmament and Indo-Soviet relations in the
           matter of disarmament, especially in their
           attitude to suspension of nuclear tests, and also
           in the matter of elimination of foreign bases
           unanimity of attitudes between USSR and India
    January 1957
    VI   Visits of Soviet delegates to India and exchange
           cultural delegation
    VI   Soviet Economic Aid to India (1957-59)
           Impact on steel and petroleum
    VII   Expansion of Trade
    VIII   March 1956
           Stalin' death
           liberalization
    IX   Hungary
           India's attitude
    X   India-China clash
           USSR ---→ neutral
           significant
    XI   May 1, 1960 U-2 plane "over reaction by" ---
           India

Indo-British

1.   Suez October 1956
2.   Queen visit to India
3.   Question about Britain's attitude
4.   British nuclear exp. April 1957
5.   Britain future to give loans
6.   July 1958
      India's support for Iraqi coup did not satisfy Britain
      Race riots in Britain. August 30 - September 7
      South Africa ←--- Soft British attitude
                         UN Res. November 1959
           ←--- Soft British attitude towards martial law
           in Pakistan
      Duke of Ediburgh ←--- 1959 visit
      Warming up with USSR and USA

China-India

1.   1954 -- good days of Chou En-lai's visit
2.   Symptoms of cold war
3.   Minor dispute in U.P. 1956
4.   Kalimpong -- Spy centre against China
5.   Nehru's mediation for Tibet
6.   Mao against reform in Tibet
7.   China's five-year plan
8.   Exchange of delegation 1957
9.   President Radhakrisnan's visit to China

10. China's Road to Tibet through Indian Territory
11. India supports China in UN September 1957
12. Expansion of India-China trade January 2, 1958
    Chou En-lai's visit February 19, 1958
13. Withdrawal of Chinese from Korea

Pakistan

1. Kashmir
2. Kashmir in Security Council 1957
3. Jaring report
4. Graham report

Canal Water

1. Suhrawady threat
2. India's reply
3. Pakistan accepts world bank proposal
4. Pakistan repudiate 1948 water argument
5. General Ayub 1958, Oct.
6. World Bank Compromise April 1959 signed September 1960

I have given some examples of the type of data I shall collect. For each item of data, subjective interpretation will be given on whether it is negative, or positive; and on the strength of the relationship. The resulting graphs will be studied, and how the US – USSR graph affects India-Pakistan graph will be investigated.

B.   Markov Chain

Conflict situations between nations change depending upon the internal and international situation. Sometimes there is an extremely bad situation which can change to a better situation. We can classify the different states on the basis of actual incidence. Suppose they are very bad, bad, neutral, good and very good. For a sufficiently long period of time we can compute the probabilities (relative frequencies) of the system changing from one state to another. On the basis of these probabilities, we can construct a transition matrix of the following type

From/to

$$P = \begin{array}{c|ccccc} & S_1 & S_2 & S_3 & S_4 & S_5 \\ \hline S_1 & P_{11} & P_{12} & & & P_{15} \\ S_2 & & & & & \\ S_3 & & & & & \\ S_4 & & & & & \\ S_5 & P_{51} & & & & P_{55} \end{array}$$

297

In the case of a finite Markov Chain, we have a number of states in which the probability of entering a state depends only on the last state occupied. States in. the Markov Chain are said to form an ergodic set when every state can be reached from every other state and which cannot be left once it is entered. In the following transition matrix we have a single ergodic set "a" consisting of the three first states.

$$
\begin{bmatrix}
1 & 0 & 0 & 0 & 0 & 0 \\
0 & 1 & 0 & 0 & 0 & 0 \\
0 & 0 & 1 & 0 & 0 & 0 \\
0 & 0 & 0 & 0 & 1/2 & 1/2 \\
1/4 & 1/4 & 0 & 0 & 0 & 1/2 \\
1/4 & 0 & 1/4 & 0 & 1/2 & 0
\end{bmatrix}
$$

An absorbing State is one which one entered and never left. An absorbing chain is one where all of whose ergodic states are absorbing, i.e. it has at least one absorbing state such that it can be reached from every state. The example above is not an absorbing chain. A regular chain is an ergodic chain that is not cyclic, i.e. can be entered at all times. Once we have a regular Markov chain, we can find out, if the initial probabilities of the system to remain in the different states are $\pi = (P_1 \ldots P_n)$, the resulting equilibrium probabilities after n iterations. This will be πp^n where p is the transition probability matrix. We can also find out the mean passage time and variance of the system passing through different states.

The objective in conflict management is to move the system away from the absorbing state of intensive conflict to the absorbing state of peace. Of course, this may not always be possible. In the second preferable position we may want to keep the system in specific states for a certain number of times and determine what intervention is necessary to move the transition matrix in that direction. Alternatively, if we desire to get a different transition matrix than the one we start, what needs to be done to achieve the goal? Let us now present an example of an application of graph theory.

C.   An Example: Introduction Under Conditions of Crisis:
      Application of Graph Theory to International Relations
      by Patrick Doreian.   Papers, Peace Research Society,
      Vol. XI, 1968.   (Reprinted with the permission of the
      editor.)

      Formal techniques are frequently criticized for being
either false or irrelevant; false because their use rests upon
invalid assumptions and irrelevant because their rigidity
entails leaving out most of the phenomena they are intended to
deal with.   In particular, these criticisms have been made of
graph theory, mainly because of its conceptual simplicity. As
any theoretical endeavour involves making simplifying
assumptions, it is necessary to decide whether the assumptions
made in the application of graph theory are peculiar to that
approach, and whether they are justified.
      One justification for the use of graph theory is that it
provides a ready means of handling a particular definition of
structure. A structure is defined as a set of units and the
relations between these units.   This clearly is not an alien
way of defining structure and can be applied to many different
phenomena.   In order to apply graph theory to problems of
relational structure the units can be treated as points, and
the relations as lines between the points.
      Graph theory has been used primarily in the analysis of
interpersonal relations. In most of the work that has been
done, the relations have been considered as all or nothing
entities. Furthermore, these relations were unsigned and the
matrix corresponding to a graph had only 0's and 1's as
entries.   These two limitations need to be overcome although
in practice the difficulties involved are considerable. Some
of the relations considered (e.g. friendship) clearly have
properties of intensity.   In order to deal with this the
notion of valued graphs can be employed. Valued graphs are
graphs where each arc has a valuation attached to it.   In
order to deal with relations which are intrinsically positive
or negative, signed graphs can be employed. The possible
entries for the matrix corresponding to a signed graph are −1,
0 and 1. Finally graphs having both signed and valued lines
can be used, but the problems involved in these graphs are too
complex to be dealt with in this paper.
      Given that graph theory appears to be fruitful in
analysing structure, it is not meaningless to enquire whether
graph theory could be employed in the analysis of
international relations.   This is not to say that analyses
made at the personal or societal level are to be transferred
without change to international relations.   In the course of
this paper I propose to apply signed graphs to the crises of
the Middle East and valued graphs to data generated by a
simulation of the Vietnam situation.   In so doing, I hope to
be able to indicate the assumptions that appear necessary for
such analyses to proceed and to demonstrate that the changes
of falseness and irrelevance, while not being groundless, do
not have sufficient force to rule out the application of graph
theory to international relations.

1.1   The Theory of Balance

The theory of balance for signed graphs was proposed by Cartwright and Harary[1] as a generalization of Heider's theory of balance.[2]   In his analysis of balance among cognitive units, Heider distinguishes between two types of relation, namely sentiment, L, and unit formation, U. The former refers simply to the evaluation of something. "Naive psychology is fairly certain about the meaning of the sentence 'p likes o'."[3]   This sentiment relation is intrinsically positive or negative.   The unit formation relation holds between two objects when they are perceived as belonging together in a specially close way.   Of the possible unit forming characteristics, Heider lists similarity, causality and ownership.   The unit formation relation used in this paper will, however, be "belongs to" in the set theoretic sense.

Balance is defined in terms of particular combinations of four relations: L, L, U and U.   There is some difficulty in interpreting U as it could be taken as either the negation of U or as its complement.   However, because of the particular type of U relation used here, this ambiguity may be ignored in this paper. A balanced state exists in a dyad if the relation between the two units is alike in all respects.   A triad is balanced if all these relations are positive or if two are negative and one is positive.   In other words, balance obtains when there is an even number of negative relations.

The p-o-x triad considered by Heider can be thought of in terms of graph theory as a 3-cycle.   Starting from this, Cartwright and Harary were able to generalize the notion of balance to larger structures. An n-cycle is balanced if there is an even number of negative arcs and a graph is balanced if all of its cycles are balanced.   This definition of balance is used to give an index ß, of balance, namely the ratio of the number of balanced cycles to the total number of cycles.[4] The index has a range from 0 (complete imbalance) to 1 (balance).   An alternative measure of balance has been defined as the minimum number of sign changes needed for a graph to reach a state of balance.[5]

Using the language of graph theory, Cartwright and Harary were able to establish various results that probably would not have been established without recourse to formal techniques. Not least of these is the structure theorem: a signed graph is balanced if and only if there exists a bipartition of its point-set such that all intra-class arcs are positive and all inter-class arcs are negative.

Having defined balance, Heider claimed that a state of imbalance generates stress and consequently there is a tendency towards balance.   Whether the instability of imbalance is definitional or empirically established is not clear.   However, for Harary, it is a hypothesis that "a balanced structure has greater stability than one which is not balanced.   If a given structure is not balanced there will be a tendency to modify the structural bonds in order to achieve balance."[6]

1.2   Harary's Analysis of the 1956 Middle East Crisis

Harary presented an analysis of the Middle East crisis of 1956 in terms of graph theory, and in particular of balance

theory.[7]   Using graph theory it is necessary, given our
definition of structure, to determine what the units are and
what the relations between them are.   In applying a particular
theory it is necessary also to delineate the conditions under
which the theory could be expected to apply.   Both of these
issues are largely ignored by Harary.   By considering them, it
is possible to demonstrate that balance theory is of greater
relevance to international relations than a reading of
Harary's article would suggest.

1.2.1   The units involved in the crisis

The nations considered by Harary were Egypt (E), other
Arab states (A), Great Britain (B), France (F), Israel (I),
India (D), the USA (U), and the USSR (R).   As well as this
system of units four subsystems were also dealt with:
{B,I,F,E}, {E,U,A}, {U,B,D} and {B,R,A}.   No criteria are
given whereby these units are selected.   Certainly such an
analysis should consider the units immediately involved, and
the situation studied should not be torn apart by an arbitrary
and irrelevant selection of the nations to be considered.
Furthermore, the units can also be selected in accordance with
the theory.   The latter point is particularly important as it
is one thing to suggest that the balance hypothesis is
applicable to the system of nations made up in the Arab States
and Israel, and it is another thing to suggest that it applies
to a system, say, comprising these nations together with those
of the Warsaw Pact and NATO.   Balance theory is an "other
things equal" theory and for the larger system there are more
exogenous variables that need to be considered.
     In particular, the procedure of taking all the Arab
states (other than Egypt) and grouping them together into one
unit violates both of the principles of selection.   It ignores
completely schisms within the Arab world, which means that he
is prone to studying a non-existent system.   For example,
Harary would appear to be ignoring the reality of the Baghdad
Pact and its effect on the Arab world.   Iraq, under the regime
of pro-British Nuri-es Said, signed a pact with Turkey in 1955
which was endorsed by Britain, with Pakistan and Iran joining
later that year.   However, other Arab nations were pursuing a
neutralist policy and in response to the Baghdad Pact, Nasser
concluded pacts with Saudi Arabia and Syria.
     In both nations there were regimes hostile to the Baghdad
Pact, the former particularly for fear of Hashemite Iraq
winning hegemony over the Arab world.   Jordan did not join the
Baghdad Pact because, according to her foreign minister,
"Turkey is an ally of Israel and an Arab proverb says the
friend of my enemy is my enemy".   It may well be that Harary's
treatment of the Arab nations as one unit fits Western
perceptions of the Near East, but by doing so he ignores
phenomena crucial to his analysis.
(It appears that during the 1950s the Western powers
misperceived the situation in the Middle East.   The whole area
was considered by them as yet another theatre for acting out
the Cold War.   This was apparent in Dulles' treaty making
obsession.   All offers of aid were tied to conditions of
alignment to the West.   Neutralist policies on the part of
some Arab states were taken as indications of Communist

aspirations. The fact that local issues were dominant in Arab politics was simply not recognized).

1.2.2 Criteria for evaluating relations between nations

Harary provides no explicit criteria to indicate how he decides whether a link between two nations is positive or negative. In practice, he seems to operate with a variety of differing criteria, with the result that relations between different pairs of units appear to mean different things.

The relation between America and Russia is claimed to be negative, presumably because, in the polarized world of the mid-1950s with East-West differences being emphasized, this was the political reality. By the same token the relation between Britain and America should be positive. Yet because the Eisenhower administration condemned British (and French) military activity, this relation is shown as negative. In his concluding remarks Harary does say that a distinction should be made between long-term and short-term relations. Nevertheless, the fact remains that they do remain confused in his analysis, when to keep them separate would be more in accord with the situation studied and for greater theoretical value.

India is included in the system Harary analyses and two particular relations involving her need to be considered more closely. The link between India and America is initially taken to be negative, but in the final graph, in a time series of graphs, this link is taken to be positive. This change appears to be due to the warm reception given to the US stand by the Indian press and public. Again this seems to show confusion between long and short-term relations. It also confuses the relation between two governments and between one nation's government and the public of another. The link between India and Israel is shown by Harary to be null yet India (or, before 1947, many of her political figures) opposed the creation of the state of Israel and also refused to recognize Israel. In Harary's terms, then, one could expect this bond to be negative. The DE link could also be interpreted as positive in view of Nasser's move towards closer relations with Nehru and Tito in following a neutralist policy. Other links are questionable and clearly, considerable care needs to be taken when deciding whether a bond between two nations is positive or negative. Further, with the possibility of there being more than one signed relation between a pair of nations, such bonds should not be necessarily collapsed into one. The possibility that the sign of a relation may not be decidable in positive and negative terms should not be overlooked either.

1.2.3 Balance in 1956

Let us now consider the state of affairs (allegedly stable) before the crisis which, in Harary's terms, is shown in Fig. 1.

This graph is clearly balanced and the fact that it moved from balance to imbalance so quickly, then moved in and out of balance, and finally reached a state of imbalance (in Harary's analysis) casts doubt upon the hypotheses that (i) balanced states are stable and (ii) imbalanced states tend towards balanced states. Further, if the situation shown in Fig. 1 is really imbalanced and by Harary's admission stable, it is again difficult to continue to accept the balance hypotheses. However, because Harary's selection of units is, as indicated, somewhat arbitrary and because he collapses and confuses different types of relations, one would not expect such a graph to behave in accord once with the balance hypothesis.

By the structure theorem the graph of Fig. 1 can be partitioned, and one of the coalitions is {D,I,R}. Harary observes that these nations form a coalition solely because they have common enemies. One feels that Israel should belong to a coalition separate from India and Russia. Now if the link between India and Israel is negative and Fig. 1 incorrect, then the graph is in fact imbalanced. However, given the nature of this imbalance (i.e. an all-negative triangle) this is a convenient point to introduce the distinction between balance and a generalization of balance, namely clustering.[8]

Whereas a graph is defined as balanced if none of the cycles has an odd number of negative lines, a graph is clusterable if none of its cycles has one negative line. In particular the all negative 3-cycle is imbalanced under the definition of balance but is clusterable under the definition of clustering. The effect of modifying the definition of balance in this way is that in the structure theorem there can be more than two classes of points such that all intra-class arcs are positive and all inter-class arcs are negative.[9] The graph of Fig. 1 with a negative line from D to I (and also from R to I) is clusterable and Israel is now in a coalition separate from Russia and India.

One of the measures of balance, namely that of the minimum number of sign changes needed to create a state of balance in a graph, is of limited value. This is demonstrated by considering the final situation reached by the system of nations in Harary's analysis. This is shown in Fig. 2.

This is imbalanced and the only way in which a single change of sign can give a balanced structure is through the negative US-USSR link becoming positive. In the mid-1950s this link was one that was most unlikely to change. The need to have valuations on the arcs has frequently been pointed out and this is another instance of the same. However, no satisfactory definition of balance has yet been proposed for a valued graph. In attempting to predict changes in a system like this it would be possible to postulate that strong links (regardless of sign) constrain the weaker links. This could be no more than a hesitant first step which would have to take into account the possible interaction between structures, and still leaves the problem of defining the degree of balance unsolved.[10]

1.2.4   Perceptions

It is clearly possible to make the distinction between the objective situation and the manner in which it is perceived by particular actors. Harary does this but again it is crucial that the analysis deals with a perceived situation and not what we allege is the perceived situation. At first sight it appears more likely that the actors' perceptions will be balanced."[11]

While most of the evidence for balance theory comes from social psychological experiments it is not valid to argue from this to balance in larger structures. If balance theory applies in <u>larger structures then</u> its applicability does not rest upon the same assumptions.

However, an analysis of the perception of the various actors can proceed from those assumptions.

Harary suggests that because (i) the US in condemning Britain was seen as a friend and (ii) the other Arab states were not seen as letting Egypt down, Nasser was able to arrive at the balanced perception shown in Fig. 3.

However, this graph may be misleading in that it confuses different types of relational structure and also has lines that are missing. For example, if Nasser perceives a negative relation between U and R then his perception is no longer balanced. If we seek to analyse perceptions it is necessary that we know which relations are defined by the actors as important. Thus, if foreign support against Israel is of overwhelming importance the links will be defined differently than where imperialism or reaction are the important issues.

1.3   Relations Between Slates

1.3.1   Indicators of dyadic relations

In order for an analysis to be made in terms of signed graphs it is necessary that the relations between nations can he regarded as being intrinsically positive or negative. Harary's confounding of different types of relation may stem from the difficulty of establishing any one indicator. Many commentators talk of friendly relations between nations, and national leaders talk of their brothers and allies, but indicators of these relations appear hard to obtain. Diplomatic interactions seem to be of little value. Apart from the economic factors involved in the establishment of diplomatic relations, it would appear that little meaning can be given to them in terms of positivity.[12] Many objections can also be made against the use of trade, and particularly volume of trade, as an indicator of positive or negative relations. Such variables seem to be dependent upon the relation between nations and this dependence does not rest solely on one aspect of the relation. It would be preferable if a more direct indicator for the relation could be found.

In order to obtain something approaching a systematic procedure for deciding what the relations between nations are, I shall use Heider's pox triad in the way he developed it, rather than the graph theoretical form. Both p and o will refer to nation states and will refer to some property,

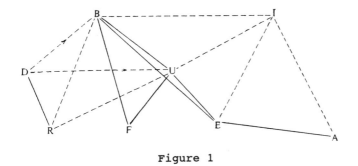

Figure 1

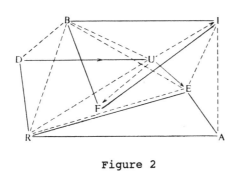

Figure 2

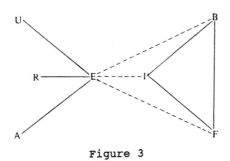

Figure 3

policy, or posture that a nation can have or adopt. The unit
formation relation will be taken as "belongs to" and will only
apply between x and one nation in a given triad. As a working
hypothesis each such triad is assumed to be balanced with
respect to itself. However, a particular pair of nations may
be involved in more than one triad and there is no assumption
that two such triads are mutually consistent. As an example
of the use of the pox triad, consider the triad constructed
from Syria (p), Jordan (o) and reaction (x). The relation is
not taken simply as "likes" in Heider's sense, but as a
positive relation in the terms used by the nation itself.
p L x
o ∈ n(x) [n(x) denotes the class of reactionary Arab states]
p → L O

     In terms of the relation between two nations this schema
may well be redundant as a statement of hostility is enough to
characterize the relation. However, in terms of defining a
structure for one relation it is necessary to know clearly
what the relation is defined over, namely the entity x in the
schema.
     Clearly this analysis is ignoring, to a considerable
extent, the whole controversy over whether or not 'nation' is
a fruitful concept. In talking of a particular nation I am
referring to the governing elite. It can also be argued that
legally constituted entities are not and cannot act as
behavioural units as the current conceptualization demands
they should.   In response to this it is arguable that in
crisis situations such entities are more likely to act as
behavioural units. A further difficulty is that it may not be
possible to characterize relations between nations as being
unequivocally positive or negative. In a large system of
nations this seems to be the case because of the presence of
many exogenous variables. However, in a small system of
nations with dominant issues, fewer and clearer relations may
be assumed. In the case of the Middle East I am talking of
the existence of Israel, imperialism and reaction, and
leadership of the Arab world as being dominant issues.[13]
Thus the ceteris paribus caveat has more validity as the other
factors being held constant are not so important. Clearly if
this approach were to be extended to larger networks this
caveat needs to be looked at very closely and it may be that
balance is insignificant in larger systems of nations.[14]

The 1967 Mid-East Crises
     Reaction and revolution are issues that divide the Arab
world. The extent of the divisions and their intensity vary
from period to period. "By the end of 1963 the Arab world had
never been more divided. Syria was engaged in a cold war with
Egypt and Iraq; her relations with the capitalist Lebanon were
far from cordial and she was hostile to Jordan and Morocco.
Egypt and Saudi Arabia were in military conflict in the Yemen,
each giving more or less open aid to the opposing sides in the
civil war."[15]   Rodinson points out that the countries of
Maghreb were also divided.   "But Israel stirred, and all
quarrels were forgotten." Furthermore Howard and Hunter claim

that for the two years up to the beginning of 1966, "the Arab world was able to put up a remarkable show of unity and moderation".[16] Clearly the relations between the nations are changing in sign and intensity, and in order to examine these changes in a given period more closely, the events leading up to the June war will be considered. In particular the relevance of balance theory will be examined. Instead of a hypothesis claiming that all systems tend to balance, we will consider a modified version that systems tend towards balance under conditions of crisis. In view of the framework we are operating with, namely that there are different structures for different issues, this hypothesis could entail at least two possibilities. One is that each of the different structures change so that they are congruent with each other and the other is that the units involved collapse the separate structures by emphasizing some relations and ignoring others.

1.4.1   Intra-Arab relations over reaction

One of the events that helped to disrupt the unity that Howard and Hunter describe was the proposal by King Feisal of Saudi Arabia to create an Islamic Alliance which he claimed would emphasize the spiritual bonds of Islam. As Rodinson points out, the political implications of the Alliance were not lost on the other Arab nations. With differing versions of Islam represented, at least one of which is considered by the orthodox to be heretical, and with different stances with regard to the place of religion,[17] the religious terms in which the Alliance was couched could be taken as a cover for a political alliance to counter social revolution in the Arab world. Nasser denounced this alliance and the regime that came to power in Syria in February of 1966 also attacked the alliance, calling for an alternative grouping of Egypt, Syria, Iraq and Algeria to counter it.

The propaganda issuing from Radio Damascus and directed against the Islami Alliance (and Jordan in particular) is of the same order as that directed against Israel. Radio Damascus has called more than once for a revolution against Hussein and has continually denounced him. In fact, Syria (and also Egypt) argue that the conservative, reactionary regimes of Jordan and Saudi Arabia need to be overthrown and destroyed before Israel can be dealt with.

Egypt and Saudi Arabia's conflict is revealed in and partially stems from the war in the Yemen. In 1966 Egypt made at least three bombing raids against Saudi Arabia. One of these was on January 27th and on February 9th Saudi Arabia responded by closing all Egyptian banks, to which Egypt reacted by seizing Saudi property in Egypt. Egypt also refused permission for planes supplying US arms to Jordan to use Egyptian airfields, accusing Jordan of wanting the arms for a Jordanian plot in the Yemen. On February 18th, Jordan severed diplomatic relations with the Yemen.

Using the issue of conservatism in conjunction with the p-o-x triad, or more directly using the statements of the regimes, the following signed graph shown in Fig. 4, can be constructed.[18]

However, not all Arab states can be so readily identified with either of these coalitions. The Yemen can be included in the "revolutionary Arab" coalition, through her alliance with Egypt and the orientation of Salal's regime. Tunisia can be included in the "conservative Arab" coalition through her participation in the Islamic Alliance. The rest of the Arab states remain (or appear to remain) neutral over this. Fig. 4 could be incorporated into Fig. 5. Although Fig. 5 is balanced under the definition of balance, this would lead to the neutral Arabs being included in either of the two other (antagonistic) coalitions. Clearly this would not be in accord with the situation described. The graph is also clusterable. Under the definition of clustering the structure theorem predicts at least two coalitions. The clustering does not lead to the inclusion of the neutral Arabs in either of the two other coalitions.

For a balanced incomplete structure a bipartition for each component of the graph is predicted by the structure theorem.[19] Combining these bipartitions to form one for the whole graph is irrelevant as any such bipartition is arbitrary and we do not know in advance which bipartitions, if any, are useful. However, the conditions for the existence of many components are likely to disappear as a crisis develops. Missing links in the structure are likely to appear and the number of components will diminish. The ambiguity in the structure, reflected by a multiplicity of potential bipartitions, is reduced in a crisis situation indicating that graph theory is more applicable under these circumstances.

The nations of the Maghreb have all joined the Arab League and have been drawn into Arab affairs. The ties do not seem to be all that close however. Tunisia has taken a moderate line over Israel and in particular President Bourgiba went so far as to suggest in 1965 an acceptance of the reality of Israel. This brought forth vigorous attacks on him. This, together with his support of the Islamic Alliance and his leanings towards the West leads him to be indicted along with other Conservative leaders. Nasser in his May Day speech of 1967 claimed, "Brothers, the battle we are fighting is not an easy one. It is a big battle headed by America. Actually we are not fighting Faisal, Hussein, the Shah or the imbecile Bourgiba. They are all tools in the hands of the United States."

1.4.2   Israel-Arab relations

As far as each individual Arab nation is concerned, the link between herself and Israel is unequivocally negative and mutually so. This requires no documentation here, but an interesting question is the extent to which these negative links are perceived by other Arab nations. Rodinson implies that the issue over Israel dominates all others ("Israel stirred and all quarrels were forgotten") and that relations defined over other issues change in accordance with this one or disappear into the background. As far as Israel was concerned she was faced in early June by a united and hostile Arab world (c.f. Eban's UN speech on 19th June 1967) and it is this balanced configuration that might have been expected.

308

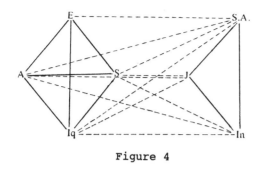

Figure 4

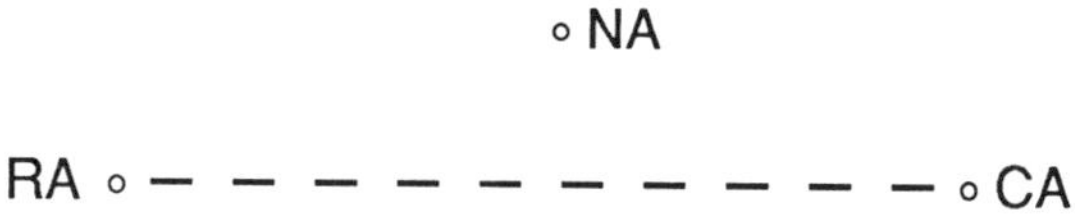

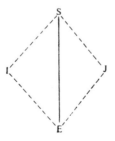

∘ NA

RA ∘ — — — — — — — — — — ∘ CA

Figure 5

Figure 6

However, by keeping the different relational structures separate, it is possible to look at this more closely. Consider the links between Egypt, Syria and Jordan with regard to reaction and the links between Egypt, Syria and Israel. Suppose, for the moment, that these also characterize the relations between these nations and that by combining them we have the structure of Fig. 6.[20]

As far as Jordan is concerned the link between herself and Israel is negative, in which case Fig. 6 is imbalanced. Suppose now that we consider the perceptions of either Egypt or Syria. If they recognize this negative link between Jordan and Israel they have imbalanced cognitions. Balance could be achieved in a variety of ways,[21] and it would appear that the resolution of this imbalance was to define the link between Israel and Jordan as positive. Both have broadcast on their respective radios accusations of a conspiratorial alliance between Jordan and Israel (together with the US) to overthrow the programme of Arab social revolution. As late as 22nd May, 1967, Nasser claimed, "It (the Islamic Alliance) is an imperialist alliance, and this means it sides with Zionism because Zionism is the main ally of imperialism ... we cannot co-ordinate our plans with Islamic Alliance members because it would mean giving our plans to the Jews and Israel."

One could argue that objectively the situation was as in Fig. 7(a), which is imbalanced while Syria perceived it as in Fig. 7(b), which is balanced and that Israel saw it still differently as in Fig. 7(c), which is also balanced.

Of the North African Arab Nations only Algeria has pursued an intransigent anti-Israel policy. Morocco and Tunisia pursued a far less radical policy. Furthermore, Nasser's alleged attempts to gain hegemony over the Arab world do not appeal to Bourguiba either. One of Bourguiba's stated reasons for boycotting the conference of Arab Leaders of States in Casablanca 1965 was Egypt's attempt to establish this hegemony. Diplomatic relations were broken off by Tunisia in October 1966. However, Tunisia offered support and offered aid in the June War, which led immediately after the war to the re-establishment of diplomatic relations which was done in terms of mutual friendship and solidarity. In this instance the relation defined with respect to Israel appears to have dominated other relations defined over the issues of reaction and hegemony over the Arab world.

The presence of refugees from Palestine were in political terms a constant source of friction between Israel and the Arab states. Israel was adamant in refusing to readmit refugees and for the Arabs their presence was a reminder of past injustices. The Arab countries did not resettle these refugees for economic and political, but mainly political, reasons. In 1964, the Arab League established the Palestine Liberation Organization (PLO) and authorized it to create a Liberation Army (PLA). Shukiary, the leader of the PLO, was preparing for the war of liberation. "We will continue guerrilla attacks in Palestine.... This will definitely lead to war; we know it, we accept it." To many Arabs, however, Shukiary dealt more with words than with concrete actions. Another terrorist group. El Fatah, was created and in 1965 actively engaged in terrorism in Israel, usually infiltrating

Israel from Jordan and the Lebanon.

The activities of the terrorist groups helped to worsen relations between Israel and her Arab neighbours, but they also exacerbated hostile relations within the Arab world. Jordan and the Lebanon had both refused to allow the terrorist groups to operate from their territory. Hussein came under particularly heavy attack from Syria and from the terrorist groups for this action, which was taken to be a pro-Zionist measure. Israel's response to the terrorist activities was one of massive retaliatory and punitive raids. The worst of these was directed against the Jordanian village of Samu, the nearest village to an incident within Israel, although the terrorists were receiving support and aid from Syria. While this reprisal angered the Arab nations, it was not sufficient to create unity among them. It was a crucial step in the events leading up to the June war, but it did not allow one particular relational structure to dominate over the others. Hussein's action against the activists within Jordan was condemned by other Arabs at the same time as messages of solidarity against Israel were being delivered.

On 7th April 1967, there was a violent clash between Israel and Syria in which six Syrian aircraft were destroyed and the Israeli pilots flew on to Damascus. Again a military clash in the favour of Israel did not bring the Arabs together. The other antagonisms remained and were sometimes confused with the relational structure defined with respect to Israel. Radio Amman jubilantly broadcast details of the Syrian reverse, and both Amman and Damascus taunted Nasser for hiding behind the United Nations' peace keeping force. Undoubtedly those taunts figured in Nasser's subsequent actions as he could not afford in terms of his prestige to remain inactive when another Arab nation was threatened for a third time, by Israel.

Nasser's move to prevent the alleged Israeli attack on Syria and his closure of the Straits of Tiran, removing the last of the fruits of Israel's 1956 victory, were seen in the Arab world as political triumphs. Nasser's prestige soared and Arab public opinion was inflamed. "There was hardly an Arab city from Casablanca to Baghdad where demonstrations of some kind did not occur. No Arab government, whatever its political complexion, could afford to be backward in pledging moral and material support in the battle apparently provoked by aggressive Zionism."[22] By 27th May all the member countries of the Arab League had pledged their support in one way or another. However, even after the diplomatic success of Nasser and the pledges of solidarity against Israel, the Damascus press and radio were attacking Hussein with a new intensity. There was a terrorist bomb explosion on a frontier town in Jordan which led Jordan to break off diplomatic relations with Syria. The position of Syria should have become intolerable according to the principle of balance on 30th May when Egypt and Jordan made their dramatic rapprochement. Nasser and Hussein embraced in Cairo, and the Radio propaganda against each other ceased immediately. Hussein and Shukiary ceased their public antagonism and Shukiary was allowed to set up his PLO headquarters in the old sector of Jerusalem.

At first sight this could be taken as evidence for the
balance hypothesis, but this rapprochement was not accepted
either by Syria or by Algeria. Saudi Arabia was also
disquieted by the pact but, significantly, for the opposite
reasons. In such a situation, while balance is not achieved,
the structure theorem can be used to facilitate the
description of certain of the lines and points in the graph.
In a graph that is nearly balanced there will be two
coalitions except that negative lines may appear within them,
or positive lines between them, or both. Such lines may be
significant for understanding change in a structure. If we
consider the two coalitions of conservative and revolutionary
Arabs, the positive bond forming between Egypt and Jordan is
a positive line between the two coalitions. The criteria used
to evaluate this by other Arab nations will to some extent
determine whether other "liaison" lines will appear, or
whether negative lines will appear within one of the
coalitions or both.

In terms of signed graphs the situation shown in Fig. 6
changed with the establishment of a positive link between
Egypt and Jordan to that shown in Fig. 8.

This is clearly imbalanced. Syria may still have
attempted to see the I-J link as positive, but this would then
make the positive E-J link even more intolerable. According
to the balance principle the S-J link should have become
positive. There is little or no evidence that it did so.

However, the graph of Fig. 8 is obtained by collapsing
two different types of relations. While it is possible that
the structure defined over one relation may constrain the
structure defined over another, it is possible that the
incongruences remain between the structures. The question of
whether there will be congruence is an empirical question, and
one requiring further theoretical elaboration. It is
necessary to examine both the conditions under which
incongruence is seen as incongruence and the extent to which
it is tolerated. It may well be the case that the interaction
between structures is not simply one of a particular
relational structure constraining others. The possibility
that the achievement of balance in one structure generates
imbalance, or even the need for imbalance, in another
structure cannot be overlooked. There also may be a need for
imbalance in a structure as much as a need for balance, and
postulating simply a tendency towards balance will be
insufficient. By examining separate signed structures, which
are defined over different relations, it is possible to
provide a framework in which to analyse relational structure.
In this way a more useful application of balance theory can be
made.

In 1.3.1 the possibility of extending this approach to
consider larger structures was mentioned. While there are
many suggestive instances where the framework of signed graphs
appears to be fruitful, the relaxing of the ceteris paribus
restriction raises too many problems to be considered here.
Nevertheless the use of signed graphs is useful for analysing
small structures, and the discussion involved in the attempt
to extend their application should raise many interesting
questions. Even if the effect of balance is small compared

with the effects of other variables in larger structures, the
study of these variables will be enriched through developing
an approach that is useful under more restricted conditions.

2 VALUED GRAPHS

This section of the paper is concerned with the problems
of mapping out the structure of a set of relations where
additional information about intensity of the relations is
available. A valued graph is defined as
(i)   a set X of points; (X = $\{x_i\}$)
(ii)   a set P of ordered pairs of points; P = $<x_i, x_j>$ for
some   (i,j)
(iii) a set of valuations V and
 (iv) a mapping from V onto P.

Among the concepts used to characterize structure is the
notion of clique. A clique is defined as a maximal subset of
elements, each in reciprocal relation to the others. As has
been pointed out elsewhere, one drawback with this definition
is that it does not permit the identification of cliques-
within-cliques.   Furthermore,   the   requirements   for   a
collection of units to form a clique are stringent.
In order to allow an analysis of structure in more detail
the following technique was developed for graphs where the
valuations are from a finite linearly ordered set.[23] For
ease of presentation the valuations are considered as
integers.

2.1   Cliques-within-cliques

Let V be a valued graph and let V be a non-valued graph
defined over the same point set as V and obtained by the
following operations:

(i) If the valuation on an arc in V is greater than or
equal to n, then the valuation on the corresponding are in V_n
is put equal to 1,

(ii) If the valuation on an arc in V is less than n then
the valuation on the corresponding arc in V_n is put equal to
0.
Now by definition V and V_n have the same point set and it is
easy to prove the connectedness of a graph at some level n[24]
is the same connectedness as the graph V_n.
Using the construction outlined above, it is possible to
obtain a more thorough examination of the clique structure by
using the algorithm of Ross and Harary[25] at each level n.
Essentially this technique is useable because there is more
information in the graph. If at successive levels n the
clique structure is obtained then changes of clique structure
can be observed. It is clear that as higher levels of n are
considered, the arcs with low valuations are eliminated and as
the lines in the graph become fewer, the cliques in general
become smaller. Thus, what at a low level n is a large
clique, gradually has the peripheral members determined until
finally the clique core is obtained.

313

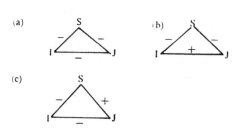

Figure 7

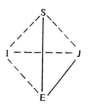

Figure 8

	To/From								
	A	R	B	P	C	E	N.V.	S.V.	NLF
A	—	30	40	18	13	23	17	37	7
R	35	—	11	18	24	21	30	1	13
B	50	12	—	14	24	15	3	7	4
P	19	34	13	—	10	19	14	4	14
C	3	31	20	7	—	17	22	0	19
E	28	43	16	21	44	—	14	3	14
N.V.	20	46	5	14	41	10	—	0	46
S.V.	34	3	14	7	0	5	2	—	1
NLF	10	28	12	17	37	20	45	0	—

Figure 9   Communication Matrix

314

Cliques

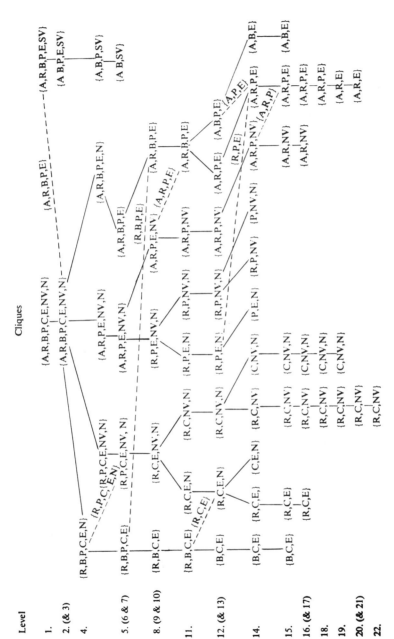

FIGURE 10: Clique Structure

315

The technique outline requires a linear ordering on the valuations, so consequently it has not yet been applied to data on international relations[27]. It is applied here to a communication matrix for nine[27] units involved in the simulation of the Vietnam situation. I do not wish to enter into a debate on the merits of simulation at this juncture. The communication matrix is used solely to illustrate this particular technique. However, it is hoped that if difficulties of operationalism can be overcome, and if the data can be presented in this form, that the technique will then be of use to both students of international relations and to those running simulations.

The data matrix generated by the simulation in given in Fig. 9. The clique structure for this group of nine units is given in Fig. 10. One problem involved in the analysis with such a large range of valuations is the meaning, if any, of each level. In Fig. 10 only those levels are shown where this is a change in the clique-structure. Thus, for example, the clique structure of levels 12 and 13 are the same although two lines present at level 12 drop out at level 13. The only significance given to a particular level is its structural significance derived from changes in the particular aspect of structure that we are interested in.

In order to apply this technique it is necessary that the definition of clique is a meaningful one for the phenomena being investigated. If, in fact, a less restrictive definition of clique is required, then Luce's generalized n-clique[28] can also be determined for each level. A generalized n-clique is identified by identifying a clique in the "pseudo-structure". The pseudo-structure is the graph whose matrix is

$$S = \sum_{i=1}^{N} H_i$$

where G is the structure matrix.

The approach characterized by the identification of cliques is one mapping out the microstructure of some configuration. In contrast to this it is possible to analyse graphs in terms of parameters defined over the whole graph. There are many such parameters that theorists might be interested in, and conceivably the value of such parameters could also be determined at each level. For instance, the connectedness class at each level of the graph might be considered.[29] While one would expect the connectedness of a graph to become weaker as successively higher levels are considered, this does not mean that little or no further information is gained than when the clique structure is considered. As has already been pointed out, the notion of connectedness and clique structures are directed towards problems of macrostructure and microstructure respectively. Also, it is easily demonstrated that there is no necessary relation between the connectedness of a graph and the existence of cliques in that graph. There exist graphs with cliques in each connectedness class and there exist also graphs without cliques in each connectedness class.

Any of the characteristics of structure that find an interpretation in a graph theoretical formulation can also be examined at each level, for example, the various measures of group structure suggested by Høvik and Gleditsch.[30]

All such uses of valued graphs, while using more information than non-valued graphs and allowing a far more detailed analysis of structure, treat valued graphs by breaking them into various non-valued graphs and applying techniques appropriate to the non-valued graphs. This is because the valuations are assumed to be ordered only. If in fact it is possible to use, in a meaningful way, higher forms of measurement, then more powerful techniques can be developed. Nonetheless, the procedures outlined here will be useful for analysing structure with valued arcs.

3 CONCLUDING REMARKS

This paper has sought to demonstrate that the use of graph theory in international relations is neither irrelevant nor invalid. Certainly when signed graphs were used to analyse the structure of relations in a situation like that of the Middle East it was necessary to specify the conditions under which they were applicable. But all theoretical statements apply with the bounds laid down by various assumptions and conditions. Specifying those conditions also facilitates a more adequate discussion of the uses and limitations of a particular theory. The techniques outline in the latter part of the paper are not irrelevant simply because it is difficult to obtain data in the required form. Clearly there are phenomena that cannot be dealt with the means of graph theory. However, graph theory deals with structure and when aspects of structure are germane to the enquiries of the student of international relations, graph theory is potentially useful.

1.Dorwin Cartwright and Frank Harary, "Structural Balance: A Generalization of Heider's Theory," Psychology Review, 63, 1956, pp. 277-293.

2.F. Heider, "Attitudes and Cognitive Organization", Journal of Psychology 21 (1946), 107-12; and The Psychology of Interpersonal Relations, Wiley, 1958.

3.Ibid., p. 174.

4.Cartwright and Harary, op. cit.

5.Frank Harary, "On the Measurement of Structural Balance", Behavioral Science 4 1959, 316-323.

6.Frank Harary, "A Structural Analysis of the Situation in the Middle-East," J. Conflict Resolution, 5, 1961, pp. 167-178.

7.Ibid.

8.See James A. Davis, "Clustering and Structural Balance in Graphs," Hum. Rel., 20, No. 2, 1967, 181-188.

9.Ibid.

10.C. Flament, in Applications of graph theory to group structure, Englewood Cliffs, Prentice Hall, 1963, points out that the difficulty of defining balance stems from the difficulty of giving balance any meaning (p. 92). Even for non-valued graph the suggestion he makes of defining

$$B = \frac{\sum\limits_{i=3}^{n} f(i)\, c_i^{+}}{\sum\limits_{i=3}^{n} f(i)\, c_i}$$

where $f(x)$ is a monotonic decreasing function, the difficulties of determining the form of $f(x)$ are considerable.

11.It is not always clear how this distinction is made, as an actor's perception is part of the situation being analysed.

12.For example, Russia and America with negative links have diplomatic relations, whereas Israel and Egypt also with negative links do not. Refusal to establish diplomatic relations or breaking them, indicates a negative relation, but here the reasons for this are more useful as an indicator. Even the re-establishment of diplomatic relations are not a necessary indication of positivity; compare Egypt and Tunisia with Egypt and Britain, where diplomatic relations were re-established in each case.

13. I have already indicated that the major nations misread the Middle East situation by assuming that more global issues were relevant to the Arabs. These local issues were dominant, which satisfies some of the conditions for applying balance theory.

14. I wish to thank Vera West for her helpful comments and research assistance in the preparation of this section. The sources of information used in this section are the following: Keesing's Contemporary Archives. Michael Howard and Robert Hunter, "Israel and the Arab World: the crisis of 1967", Aldephi paper, No. 41, October, 1967; Walter Laqueur, The Road to War 1967, London; Wiedenfeld and Nicolson, 1968, and Maxime Rodinson Israel and the Arabs, Harmondsworth; Penguin, 1968.

15. Rodinson, Ibid, p. 103.

16. Howard and Hunter, op. cit., p. 11.

17. Bourguiba has made great efforts to secularize Tunisia.

18. S.A. – Saudi Arabia, J – Jordan, In – Iran.

19. Peter Abell, "Structure in Dynamic Structures," Sociology, Vol. 2 (1968), 333–352.

20. This is not a contradiction of my argument that different relations should be kept separate. It may well be that units themselves do collapse different structures which would then need to be taken into account. The a priori collapsing of structures prevents them from being analysed in conjunction with each other and it is this that I am objecting to.

21. Among the various alternatives are the following:
(i) E-+-I and S-+-I, (ii) E-+-J and S-+-J, (iii) E-+-I and S-+-J, (iv) E-+-J, (iv) E-+-J and S-+-I. (All these lead finally to balance if I---J), (v) E-+-I, S-+-I, E-+-J, S-+-J, I-+-J, (vi) I-+-J.

22. Howard and Hunter, op. cit., p. 17.

23. Patrick Doreian, "A Note on the Detection of Cliques in Valued Graphs," Sociometry, Vol. 32 (1969), 237–242.

24. e.g. A graph is strongly connected at level n if each pair of points are mutually reachable by paths where no valuations on arcs in these paths are less than n.

25. Ian C. Ross and Frank Harary, "A Procedure for Clique Detection using the Group Matrix", Sociometry, 20, 1957, 205–215.

26. My thanks are due to Robin Jenkins for making available this data. However, as I am not fully aware of all the objectives and procedures used in the simulation, it is not possible for me to discuss this technique fully in the context of the simulation

27. Those nine units are: A--the US, R--the USSR, B--Britain, P--Poland, E--Egypt, N.V.--North Vietnam, S.V.--South Vietnam, and N--the N.L.F. (The UN has been deleted from the initial data matrix.)

28. See R.D. Luce: "Connectivity and Generalized Cliques in Sociometric Structure," *Psychometrika*, 15, 1950, pp. 169-190.

29. See, F. Harary, et al, *Structural Models: An Introduction to the Theory of Directed Graphs*, New York, Wiley, 1961, Ch. 7.

30. Tord Hoivik and Nils Peter Gleditsch, "Structural Parameters of Graphs: A Theoretical Investigation," *Int. Peace Res. Inst.*, Oslo (mimeo).

8 Participation and Information Models

A.   Decentralization Process

Since World War II, a significant event on the international scene has been the emergence of a large number of new nations, particularly in Asia and Africa. However, in most of these countries, the differences in religion, language, ethnicity and culture have created internal dissension and often violence, despite the desire of the people involved to secure a better future. One basic factor which accentuates the friction is the allocation of decision making authority in the governmental system to different levels in the hierarchy of centre, zone, state, local and other administrative areas. Thus, a study of the proper spatial organization of decision making is vital.

In a country with a federal structure of government, the administrative system is usually a tree-like one. Fig. 8.1 serves as an example with four sample modes, namely 1) Centre; 2) Zone; 3) State; and 4) Local.

Each node, starting from the peak, leads to four subordinate nodes. The "tree" itself consists of four orders; the number of nodes of the first, second, third and fourth orders being 1, 4, 16, and 64, respectively. They are identified by the following numbers: 1 in the first order, 2 to 5 in the second, 6 to 21 in the third, and 22 to 85 in the fourth. It is not necessary for this to be a symmetrical four-node hierarchy. However, for simplicity, let us assume that this is the case.

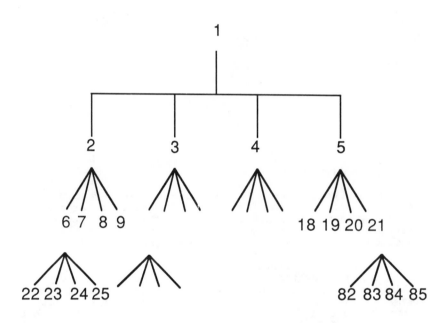

Figure 8.1   A Symmetrical Treelike Hierarchy

For each member of the hierarchy (e.g. at i), we can attach a mass 1,2,...85. This mass can be considered a vector having, say, k components as follows:

$$M_i = (M_{1i}, M_{2i}, \ldots M_{ki}) \qquad (1)$$

The components of this vector can denote different social, economic and political characteristics of the nodes; and geometrically, they can be mapped as a point in a k dimensional space. At this stage, we will not be concerned with measuring of these components. As a crude approximation, a system with a meaningful base can be utilized for this purpose.

Instead of dealing with all these variables in their totality, we can conduct a factor analysis study to identify a number of factors F_1, F_2,....F_m and express the original variables M with the following relation:

$$M_{ji} = a_{j1}F_{1i} + a_{j2}F_{2i} + \ldots + a_{jm}F_{mi}, \qquad (2)$$

i refers to node

j refers to variable

When the factor equation (2) has been estimated, the factor score for any node can be used in place of the variable.

In what follows, we shall assume either that the measurement of k component mass vector have been obtained directly or that they have been replaced by factor scores resulting from a factor analysis study. For any component, e.g. e, we define:

$$I_{ij} = \frac{G \cdot W_{ie}(M_{ie})^{\alpha}W_{je}(m_{je})^{\beta}}{d^b_{ije}} \qquad (3)$$

$$I_i^e = I_{i1}^e + \ldots + I_{in}^e = \sum_{j=1}^{n} \frac{GW_{ie}(M_{ie})^{\alpha}W_{je}(M_{je})^{\beta}}{d^b_{ije}}$$

or

$$= GW_{ie}(M_{ie})^{\alpha} \sum_{j=1}^{n} \frac{W_{je}(M_{je})^{\beta}}{d^b_{ije}} \qquad (4)$$

Dividing both sides of definitional equation (4) by the weighted adjusted mass at i, e namely, $w_{ie}(M_{ie})$ we obtain:

$$_iV^e = \frac{I_i^e}{W_{ie}(M_{ie})^{\alpha}} = G \sum_{j=1}^{n} \frac{W_{je}(M_{je})^{\beta}}{d^b_{ije}} \qquad (5)$$

By definition $_iV^e$ represents total interaction at i, per unit of weighted mass at i. The term $_iV^e$ is designated as potential at i. For each component of the mass vector, M, a potential can thus be computed. The total potential may be obtained by summing these individual potentials, i.e.:

$$_iV = \sum_{e=1}^{k} {_iV^e} \qquad (6)$$

In equation (6), $_iV$ gives the total potential (with respect to all characteristics) generated at i by all other members in the system (following Isard, 1960).

Let us say that a federal constitution clearly defines the jurisdiction of authority in Central, State and Common Lists. The total potential is thus generated at the following levels:

(1)   Between the Centre and the Zones: $_cV_z^e$

(2)   Between Zones: $_zV_z^e$

(3)   Between the Centre and the States: $_cV_s^e$

(4)   Between States within a Zone: $_zV_s^e$

(5)   Between State and State: $_sV_s^e$

(6)   Between Local units and the State; $_LV_s^e$

following (5), we can arrive at the following definitions:

$$_cV_z^e = G \sum_{j=2}^{5} \frac{W_{je}M_{je}^2}{d_{jce}^b}$$

$$_zV_z^e = G \sum_{\substack{z=2 \\ z \neq j}}^{5} \sum_{j=2}^{5} \frac{W_{je}M_{je}^2}{d_{zje}^b}$$

$$_cV_s^e = G \sum_{j=6}^{21} W_{je}M_{je}^2/d_{jce}^b$$

$$_zV_s^e = G \sum_{j=6}^{21} W_{je}M_{je}^2/d_{jze}^b$$

For any component, for example, language, the potential for the country as a whole can be obtained by summing the individual potentials generated at the above levels.

After computing the potential at the <u>Centre</u> created by the Zones, we can consider the potential created by the Zones among themselves. The procedure is similar except that we calculate the potential at each Zone (with respect to populations created by the remaining three Zones) and then take the sum.

We now wish to consider participation and influences with respect to the regular hierarchy, as shown in Fig. 1. We are interested in defining a concept of participation potential which might be directly related to and testable in terms of some operational measure of participation. For example, we may wish to employ a measure of the degree of

1. Participation of any individual in any given decision.
2. Participation of a population of the system in this given decision.
3. Participation of a population of a system in all decisions of that system.

For item 1 we might, for example, define degree of participation in terms of number of votes cast for a political party with a given ideology, number of letters published in newspapers, number of meetings attended, or some other act of communication. If the individual participated in, say, 4% of all communication acts taken by all individuals, then his or her degree of participation in that decision would be 4%. For item 2 we might, for example, measure the average participation of individuals, where the participation of any one individual is defined and where total population numbers are explicit. For item 3 we might measure the average degree (or probability) or participation by any individual in any decision, which is simply the mean of the average population participation in each decision, keeping explicit the total number of decisions and population.

Whatever the level of abstraction, we will define the participation potential P for a system as the sum of the products of the potential generated by each node and the amount of decisions made therein. This can be explained with reference to the hierarchical structure assumed in Figure 7.1. For simplicity let us assume that a given component of the mass vector, the mass = 1, with weights = 1 at all nodes. Further, we assume d_{fg} = 1 when f > g, and d_{fg} = 0 when f < g. The sense of the last assumption is that only the upward flow of participation and exercise of influence are permitted. A person cannot affect decisions at any node of higher order than the one at which he/she is located. Consider all decisions made in their totality and without any loss of generality. The total number of decisions is assumed to be unity.

With these assumptions, the participation potential P is defined as the sum of the product of the potential generated at each node and the amount of decisions to be made at that node. Symbolically,

$$P = \sum_{i=1}^{n} r_i \cdot {}_iV \qquad (7)$$

where r_i is the proportion of all decisions to be made at node i, and $_iV$ is the participation potential generated at the ith node defined in equation (7). Choosing different values for r_i at i(i=1, 2, ...n), we shall get different patterns of decentralization. For example, for r_i = 1 at i = 1, and r_i = 0 elsewhere, we have absolute centralization. Similarly, when r_j = 1 where j is the lowest order node, and r_j = 0 elsewhere, we have absolute decentralization. Between these extremes, different patterns of decentralization will be obtained by assigning different values of r_i at i = 1,2...n.

Regarding this scheme of analysis, a number of remarks are in order. In the measurement of centralization or decentralization, we are using the percentage of decisions made at different nodes. But it is the nature of the

325

decision, and not its number, which is relevant. Again, when we have more than two nodes, it is difficult to decide which pattern is more decentralized, since (a) we shall be comparing two sets, each containing more than two numbers, and (b) each type of decision is not made by all nodes of different orders. Of course, the masses and instances need not be 1 for all nodes. The scope of the previous analysis can be extended by relaxing these assumptions. For example, the decisions can be divided into the following groups:

(1) International; e.g. defence, foreign policy, foreign trade, etc.

(2) National; e.g. language, industrial policy, transportation, national planning, taxation, etc.

(3) Regional and inter-regional; e.g. sharing of resources, inter-regional industrial venture, zonal trade, mutual problems, etc.

(4) State; e.g. local self-government, village development, etc.

In the case of international decisions, it is conceivable that all the decisions will be made by the Central Government. However, in some international decisions, participation by a State may be necessary. For example, when the defence of the country is at issue, a border State's opinion with respect to some decisions may be of value. Even in this case, some decision making power with respect to military training, etc. can be entrusted to the local people.

Similarly, all national decisions need not be made by the Central Government alone. For example, in the case of language, participation by different zones may be of crucial importance. On the other hand, where regional and inter-regional decision making is concerned, as in a boundary dispute, the sharing of river water, and so on, the Central Government need not be left out completely. Similarly, although it is desirable to keep the Centre out of all State decisions, it is always easy to identify some State decisions where the Centre must have some power in order to protect democracy and union. The same type of argument applies in the case of local decisions. The following matrix will explain the argument:

	Type of Decision		Authority	
	Centre	Zone	State	Local
International	0.7	0.1	0.1	0.1
National	0.6	0.2	0.2	0
Regional	0.3	0.3	0.4	0
State	0.1	0	0.6	0.3
Local	0	0	0.2	0.8

Table 1   Hypothetical Decision Matrix

Each cell of the above-mentioned matrix shows the percentage of a particular type of decision made at a given level. For example, with respect to international decisions, 70% of them are made by the Central authority. Admittedly, the use of percentages is quite crude. However, in terms of resource dollars, Table 1 shows that 70% of the total resources will be controlled by the Centre. Again, if there is a joint committee to administer the decision, then 70% of the members will be appointed by the Centre and so on. Obviously, different numbers can be put in the cells of the above matrix, indicating different degrees of decentralization.

The decision matrix in more general form is as follows:

	Type of Decision		Authority	
	Centre	Zone	State	Local
International	r_{Ic}	0	r_{Is}	0
National	r_{cc}	r_{cz}	r_{cs}	r_{cL}
Reg. and Inter-reg.	r_{zc}	r_{zz}	0	0
State	r_{sc}	0	r_{ss}	r_{sL}
Local	0	0	r_{Ls}	r_{LL}

Table 2 General Form of a Decision Matrix

For each decision matrix, a certain value of the participation potential (P) will result, and this value will reflect a certain amount of productivity of the system. It is true that the measurement of the productivity will be difficult since it has to be a combination of growth of income, internal peace, social welfare, national integration, etc. Although choosing a pattern for which this productivity is maximum is a
desirable objective, it may not be feasible since a certain amount of social, political and economic costs have to be incurred. For example, if the Central Government makes a decision which is completely local, due to lack of information and the Centre's distance from the local area, it is likely to make a wrong decision. On the other hand, for a zonal decision, as in a dispute over river water, the Central Government may have an unbiased solution, while the contending parties may not. There is no denying the fact that (1) a major portion of the costs involved may be <u>qualitative</u> in nature, and (2) expressing the cost function in terms of visible policy parameters is an immensely burdensome job. Assuming that such an estimate of the cost had been made, a programming interpretation of the model can be given.

The problem is to choose the level of the decision parameters r_{Ic}, r_{cc}, r_{sc}, r_{zz}, r_{zs}, r_{SL} for each time period (say, at five-year intervals) in such a manner that the total participation potential generated at the terminal year T (say, 2000) is maximum, subject to the fact that the cost of decentralization in each period does not exceed a given amount. Good decisions will decrease the distance and increase the force of integration. Symbolically, this can be stated as follows:

Choose the decision parameters r_{Ic}, r_{cc}, r_{sc}, and so on in such a manner that at time period t,

$$D = [(r_{Ic} + r_{cc} + r_{zc} + r_{sc}) \, (_cV_z + _zV_z + _cV_s) + (r_{cz} + r_{zz}) \, (_zV_z +$$

$$_cV_s) + (r_{Is} + r_{ss} + r_{Ls} + r_{sc}) \, _sV_L$$

$$+ (r_{LL} + r_{SL} + r_{CL}) + {_L}V_L]$$

maximum, subject to, for each t,

Total cost < C_o

$1 > r_{Is}, r_{Ic}, r_{cc}, r_{cz}, r_{sc}, r_{cc}, r_{zz} > 0$, etc.

It is true that the model in this form is too theoretical to be of any practical value. Even the theoretical notions should also be improved in many respects. However, this model is only a suggestion. It is hoped that its critical evaluation and modification will lead to a more refined and operational procedure.

B.   Learning Theory

As the cumulative knowledge base about conflict increases, the cost of misjudgement decreases. The knowledge gained from many conflict situations helps the decision maker to avoid mistakes. Thus, learning through experience permits the decision makers to make decisions more efficiently. The savings (avoidance of cost due to miscalculation) can be computed by fitting appropriate functions with cost as the dependent variable and cumulative decision to the independent variable. The learning rate can be compiled by using the formula

$$\text{Learning Rate} = (1 - \frac{AC_2}{AC_1}) \times 100$$

where AC_2 and AC_1 are the cost (of misjudgement) in two successive periods.

C.   Artificial Intelligence and Expert Systems

Conflict management is a complex model of interconnected components. The connections are so intricate that it is hard to handle them through flow charts and mathematical equations. However, the computer has unlimited potential for handling the problem at hand. If we can properly codify events, a computer can through analogy, compare two situations using the programming languages of artificial intelligence and knowledge engineering, and generate new knowledge. Very few applications of artificial intelligence in political science have been attempted although business applications abound. Considerable work is possible using artificial intelligence in the comparative study of foreign policy.

D.   Asymmetric Information Theory

In a conflict situation, contesting parties do not have equal amounts of information. One country may be larger or stronger, or may have a wider information base than the other. This is similar to a stock market, where the insiders have more information than the ordinary stockholders. Considerable developments in finance have been made in the area of agency theory which may be very useful in finding the best way to extract information through agents who may have a superior information base.

E.   Fuzzy Set Theory

Recently, a new area called Fuzzy Set Theory has been developed. Here the idea is, that oftentimes, the situation is not always "black" and "white". In health care, a person is not always considered "well" or "ill". Sometimes the diagnosis is in between the two poles. There have been some applications of the fuzzy set theory to the social sciences. However, its contribution to conflict studies is rare.

F.   Delphi Method

In many decision processes, interviewing knowledgeable persons and combining the resulting information with those obtained from analytical methods improves the efficiency of the decision process. In political decisions, although vast amount of data are available with respect to expert opinion, very few studies have been successful in integrating it with those obtained from analytical models. Due to limitation of space, I could not discuss the above-mentioned techniques and their application. I plan to do that in a separate study. I would like to present the following articles to show how sophisticated techniques can be used to analyse predicted problems.

G.   Supplementary Examples (Reprinted by permission of editor).

(i)   A POLITICAL ECONOMY OF THE VIETNAM WAR, 1965-1972 Jong Ryool Lee and Jeffrey S. Milstein. Peace Research Society (International) Vol. 21, 1973.

(ii) THE MAJOR POWER CONFRONTATION IN THE MIDDLE EAST: SOME ANALYSIS OF SHORT-RUN, MIDDLE-RUN AND LONG-RUN CONSIDERATIONS Walter Isard and Tony Smith Papers. Peace Research Society (International) Vol. XV, 1970.

(i) A POLITICAL ECONOMY OF THE VIETNAM WAR, 1965-1972

Jong Ryool Lee and Jeffrey S. Milstein. Peace Research Society (International) Vol. 21, 1972.

Since the signing of the cease-fire in Vietnam and the withdrawal of US military forces has changed the nature of the Vietnam conflict, there is no point in forecasting the future of the war in terms of US involvement. Yet the model presented in this paper will shed a macroscopic light on one of the puzzling problems that concern the students of foreign policy: what is the interrelation of political leaders and their constituency?

A recent emphasis among students of international relations on intranational processes stems not only from the observation that national leaders make decisions, but also from the fact that decision makers are dependent upon domestic support. Decision makers do not respond exclusively to external stimuli. Internal political pressures are also important--if not paramount--in constraining the limits of choice of political leaders, even when they are engaged in a conflict with hostile forces. It is well known that widespread dissatisfaction among the American public was a major influence on President Johnson's reversal of military policy in South Vietnam.

There is still little appreciation among political scientists, as well as economists, however, as to how the domestic economic environment interacts with political and military decisions. The war in Vietnam amply illustrates how the war affects the economic environment, and how the economic effect in turn contributes to erosion of political support of the nations leadership. It is the basic thesis of this research that the impetus toward the resolution of military conflict mainly comes from the economic and political impact of the war on the belligerents involved.

2. Model of the Vietnam War

The war in Vietnam was basically a limited local war conducted in the international environment in which a total victory for either side was impossible without much greater sacrifices or risks. Since subtle strategic balance is maintained with limited resources and other constraints, it will not be the point of this article to explain the process of escalation and decommitment in terms of capabilities, ideologies or policy goals. These variables are certainly crucial in explaining why the US became involved in the first place, but these variables are one step removed in explaining and predicting in retrospect why the level of hostilities changed.

The basic unit of analysis of the research reported here is flow of actions of governments or other political entities such as the combined forces of the communists in South Vietnam. Generally actions of government are defined as "the various acts of officials of a government in exercises of governmental authority that can be perceived outside the government" (Allison and Halperin, 1972). Another focus of analysis will be the outcomes, that is, selectively delimited states of the real world importantly affected by the actions of the government or actors. It will be the operational milieu that will determine the actual outcomes whatever the relevant actor may perceive or intend in contemplating his decision. How actions and outcomes affected the political positions of decision makers is not well known.

The influence of foreign events on domestic politics and the influence of the domestic environment on the output of decision making has been a major theme in a framework of linkage politics laid out by Rosenau (1969) in a series of essays. The idea of linkage stems from the observation of domestic politics. This formulation suggests that an analysis of an international chain of relationships should also contain some elements of the comparative study of foreign policy, since each government may react differently to foreign stimuli. Empirical literature on the war in Vietnam abounds in the theme that the US foreign policy is influenced by domestic opposition and that military operations in South Vietnam influenced domestic cohesion in Vietnam and support of Vietnam policy in the United States. Indeed, it can be said that the Vietnam War was as much a domestic issue as a foreign event in US politics.

More generally, we have made the assumption that there is some interaction between decision makers and mass publics regarding foreign events. Broad approval by the majority of a national public of the visible policies of its leaders or at least assent to these activities seems to be a sine qua non for continuous execution of the policy and for the maintenance of the governing power itself. In any political system, the leaders try to meet the demands or desires of their citizens in one way or another. If these demands are not satisfied to a certain extent, the likely result will be the withdrawal or erosion of political support. This premise is not to be equated with arguing that all nations meet the demands of the masses in a democratic way. On the contrary, it is often the case that leaders react to the opposition or demands of the subjects with coercion or propaganda. The demands may be expressed in democracies by voting or public opinion polls, and in totalitarian states by some other means of disloyalty to their leaders (Coplin, 1971, 60-92).

This argument begs one important question: what are the determinants of political support? One simple hypothesis one can entertain is that the mass public responds positively to positive outcomes of governmental actions, and negatively to negative outcomes. In a context of military conflict in which their leaders are involved, we expect a significant relationship between outcomes of the military operations and public support or morale. One analytic theory by Downs (1957) suggests that the mass public responds to the economic well being provided by alternative teams of leadership. An effort at a general theory along this line is proposed by Oran Young among others (Frohlich, Oppenheimer and Young, 1971; Key, 1964; Kramer, 1971). As far as American politics is concerned, we can find reasonable empirical evidence for the politico-economic hypotheses in the literature on voting behaviour and Presidential popularity. In the public's reaction to or judgement of its leaders, the economic impact of military policy may be of greatest importance to the average citizen. Therefore, we posit that the public reaction depends upon not only the military outcomes, but also on the objective state of the economy for each political system.

The foregoing analysis has focused on economic influences on politics. But a final complication is necessary: to incorporate the influence of military decisions on the state of the national economy. We know that every military movement in a foreign land makes a claim on national economic resources and expenditures. These expenditures in turn demand a share of the individual citizen's means of livelihood, more immediately in the form of taxes, but ultimately in terms of real goods he is able to consume (Russett, 1970). For instance, the average US citizen feels the impact of foreign policy--which would otherwise be something remote and nebulous--more in terms of economic costs than in military service. In this study we emphasize the influence of large troop commitments on the stability of the US economy in terms of inflation and unemployment rather than the resources foregone (Lee, 1973). In the United States in particular, it is likely that the perverse effects of troop commitments on the economy erode public confidence in the leadership, and that the decision makers feel obliged to pay attention to that erosion.

This brief advanced above is a simplification of a complex reality. But the general model that one arrives at after this discussion is even more complex than it appears. The causal linkage for a single political unit we posit in the model can be put heuristically in a diagram as follows.

The arrows in the diagram indicate the direction of causality we hypothesize. Very simply put, the chains of actions and reactions are influenced by the military outcomes of the actions, economic effects of actions and degree of domestic political support. Political support in turn is influenced by the military outcomes and economic environment. Since we posit that this process applies to each of the political units which interact with each other, the resulting model is a really complex chain of causal linkages.

Actors in the war in the Vietnam War are identified as the United States, South Vietnam and the combined forces of North Vietnam and the Viet Cong. Although further research may find it more meaningful to take up a four-actor interaction model as is common in other historical and analytic researches of the war, we fail to discriminate between North Vietnamese forces and Viet Cong forces in actual military operations and effects in South Vietnam. Thus this research is based on a "three-actors in interaction" model, by allowing the Communist forces the status of a combined political system. As Oran Young argues, the "mixed-actor model" will provide a ground for a fruitful research (Young, 1972).

On the basis of the theoretical framework laid out above, we collected monthly aggregate data for the period from January 1965 through May 1972, giving 89 data points in total. Many of the military statistics are the same as one of the authors has analysed in various works for parts of the period (Milstein and Mitchell, 1969; Milstein, 1973). We chose key variables for three concepts--military actions, military outcomes and political support--for each of the three belligerents. Likewise we chose a few economic variables to reflect the objective economic environment. Aggregate economic variables are so interrelated that a few economic variables are often sufficient to indicate overall economic conditions for a given economic system.

We have explored with alternative formulations the dynamics of the Vietnam War in this research, within the causal framework laid out above, by simply changing the time lag and the number of independent variables. No prior information was assumed for the military and political variables except some initial values of the first few months. Pure exogenous variables that cannot be explained by our model include the average rainfall in Saigon (abbreviated RN), and a "dummy variable" to distinguish the Johnson and Nixon administrations (abbreviated NX). Among a few simultaneous equation models that we have experimented with, we report the one that we consider theoretically most relevant and parsimonious. This model specifies the hypothesized relationship among "representative variables" of military and political indicators for our conceptual clusters.

MILITARY ACTIONS AND REACTIONS

It can be stated in general that each side's military actions will be approximated as a response to its adversary's actions, previous military outcomes, availability of alternatives, and degree of domestic support. The first hypothesis is that the US troop level will be largely predicted if we have information about the amount of hostile military actions by the NV + VC, amount of military action by SV forces, previous US casualties, and the degree of public approval of the President. In other words, additions to US troop levels were positively related to additional communist armed attacks, US casualties, and US public support, and negatively with SV ground operations.

In formulating this hypothesis in regression form, another important factor in the decision making process should be taken into consideration. The bureaucratic paradigm of decision making suggested by Allison and Halperin emphasizes that policy output if often based on incremental decisions rather than a sharp departure from past policy or actions (Allison and Halperin, 1972). We thus hypothesize that the marginal increase in US troop commitments is associated with the external and internal stimuli. For instance, if no decision is arrived at on the troop level in the current month, the level of troops stays as it was the last month. Thus the level of US troops in South Vietnam can be put as a regression equation:

$$UT - UT_{-1} = t_1 \, LUK_{-1} + t_2 \, (LVA_{-1} - LVA_{-2}) + t_3 \, LSG + t_4 \, US_{-1} + t_5 + u_1$$

In this linear formulation, the t_2 can be interpreted as a "reaction" coefficient in the tradition of the Richardson arms race model, whereas the t_1 is a "reinforcement" coefficient, since a reinforcement of additional forces is required to offset military disadvantages or attrition. If either coefficient is positive, then there is a tendency toward a spiral of military actions and interactions, because casualties as a military outcome are also a function of military actions. This is true of many conflict situations, and the spiral of escalation and counter-escalation is but one particular case of this. Only in the case that both coefficients are negative, will the war wane with one side winning total victory.

The t_3 is called a "substitution" coefficient, since the number of US troops required for the US policy objective of having a non-communist regime in South Vietnam is in part dependent upon the capacity of the endogenous forces to fight the NV + NC forces. We should remember that the reason for US military involvement was the inability of the South Vietnamese forces to sustain the war against the communist guerrilla units without the intervention of US combat troops. The policy of Vietnamization and the Nixon Doctrine in general indicate that the US military forces would be decommitted the sooner the South Vietnamese forces were able to assume the major combat responsibilities. Thus we expect a negative value for this coefficient.

The coefficient t_4 may be called a "viability" coefficient since erosion of domestic political support is hypothesized to influence the will of principal decision makers, particularly the President of the United States, to continue unpopular local involvements such as in Korea and Vietnam.

The same model can applied to the military behaviour of the South Vietnamese and communist forces with only a minor modification. First, it is difficult to say whether the bureaucratic process is operating in military decisions in a war-devastated country. Many important decisions may be made by commanders of relatively small combat units, which are dispersed in the whole area without adequate information about the whole situation or effective communication among the leaders. Thus we hypothesize that the absolute frequency of the communist armed attacks, rather than the monthly difference, will be associated with military outcomes, hostilities by each of allied forces, and the degree of political support.

$$LSG = g_5\ UT + g_6\ LVA + g_7\ NX + g_8\ LSK_{-1} + g_9\ LVS_{-1} + u_2$$
$$LVA = a_1\ UT + a_2\ LSG + a_3\ LVS_{-1} + a_4\ LVK_{-1} + a_5\ RN + u_3$$

MILITARY OUTCOMES

We use as an overall indicator of military outcomes the casualties of each side. In any armed conflict casualties are expected by both decision makers and soldiers. Casualties are a meaningful indicator of outcomes because there has been no chance of total victory for either side throughout the period of protracted conflict. Moreover, both sides fought the Vietnam War as a war of attrition, in which one of the strategic objectives was to kill as many enemy forces as possible--as a test of will to persist, as the rhetoric of the war goes. "Kill ratios" or other military statistics were used by defence analysts as indicators of relative military gains or advantages, yet the absolute number of killed in action is a more vivid indicator of the outcomes, since no side won militarily. It is intuitively clear that the number of troops killed depends upon the number of military actions by both sides, ignoring tactical superiority or intensity of fighting.

$$LUK = UT + k_2 \, LVA + k_3 \, LSG + K_4 + u_4$$
$$LSK = k_{11} \, LSG + k_{12} \, UT + k_{13} \, LVA + k_{14} + u_5$$
$$LVK = k_6 \, LVA + k_7 \, LSG + k_8 \, UT + k_9 + u_6$$

Political Support

In spite of pessimistic accounts of the ability of the American public to give sustained support to their leadership in pursuing foreign policy objectives (Almond, 1968; Lee, 1972) there is no lack of empirical findings that reveal a "responsible" public that rewards or punishes its leaders for objective performance in a systematic manner, while the public's role is considered as largely reactive. We can hypothesize that public approval of the President's handling his job is significantly associated with military outcomes and the state of the domestic economy. For instance, John Mueller reports finding that during the Korean War and the early Vietnam War, public attitude toward the war was significantly associated with the US casualties (Mueller, 1970; 1971).

The variable for "political support" in the United States we use is the yes-minus-no vote to the Gallup Poll question, "Do you approve or disapprove the way the President is handling his job?" What is important for a President and his advisors is not merely public approval of a given Vietnam policy, but the overall political support, since a citizen may disagree with a particular policy yet still approve of the President in terms of other policy performance, given the criss-crossing nature of public opinion. During the Vietnam War period, public approval of Vietnam policy and overall approval is highly associated. We allowed one "dummy" variable, taking 1 for President Nixon's term and 0 for President Johnson, reasoning that President Nixon's role is different from President Johnson's since he is not directly responsible for the initial involvement in Vietnam and he is a different person, with his idiosyncratic characteristics and circumstances. We believe that the three variables chosen reflect the overall state of the national economy.

$$US = s_1 \, LUK_{-1} + s_2 \, UE_{-1} + s_3 \, UC_{-1} + s_4 \, UR_{-1} + s_5 \, NX - s_6 + u_7$$

The same model can be applied to the North Vietnamese and Viet Cong forces. While we do not have an accepted measure of political support such as Gallup Polls, it can be argued that the number of defectors indicates a lack of loyalty among the forces engaged in a conflict for political legitimacy. In this "war of national liberation", military successes are only a means to the end of controlling the populations of the country and winning their allegiance. A plausible assumption is that as the South Vietnamese regime gained support, the Viet Cong would lose support, and vice versa. An indicator of popular support for the South Vietnamese government is the number of political and military defectors. Defecting can be viewed as "voting with one's feet", reflecting a voluntary decision on the part of those who defect. Thus we can hypothesize that the number of defectors will be determined by the number of killed in action of the communist forces, number of killed in action in the South Vietnamese forces, and the objective state of the war-devastated economy.

$$LVS = d_1 \, LVK + d_2 \, LSK + d_3 \, SC_{-1} + d_4 \, SS_{-1} + d_5 + u_8$$

Economic Effect

Though our purpose is not the forecasting of economic variables, we feel it necessary to establish the empirical validity of the economic effect of the military involvement. What makes the economic impact relevant is that public support of national leaders tends to be influenced by the performance of the national economy in the United States, as discussed above. Heavy and abrupt commitment of national resources to the war must have had an adverse effect on the sound operation of the national economy. Since economic variables are often serially correlated, the value of the previous month for each economic variable is expressed along with military variables in the following predictive equations.

$$UC = c_1 \, UC_{-1} + c_2 \, UT + c_3 + u_9$$
$$UE = e_1 \, UC_{-1} + e_2 \, UT + e_3 \, UT_{-1} + e_4 + u_{10}$$
$$UR = r_1 \, uE_{-1} + r_2 \, UC + r_3 \, UT + r_4 + u_{11}$$
$$SS = s_{10} \, LSK + s_{11} \, SC_{-1} + s_{12} \, (UT - UT_{-1}) + s_{13} \, LVS + s_{14} \, SS_{-1} + U_{12}$$
$$SC = c_4 \, SC_{-1} + c_5 \, UT + c_6 \, LSG + c_7 + u_{13}$$

The system of equations that consists of 13 equations presented above comprises the structural model of the war in Vietnam.

3. Structure of the Conflict

Since the system of equations described above deals with a very complex set of relationships, it will be useful to present components of the system of the Vietnam conflict in a simplified diagram. The solid arrows indicate the hypothesized direction of causality, whereas the dotted arrows suggest possible lines of feedback from military outcomes and political consequences. The idea of linkage as emphasized by Rosenau is apparent when one carefully follows the causal loop. For instance, the US economic situation may eventually influence the political or economic situation in Vietnam after a few months in an indirect manner. As evident in this diagram, we postulate that relations between some variables are reciprocal, implying that the system is interdependent. Assuming that the errors in each equation are random with constant variance, the two stage least squares method was applied to estimate the parameters on the overidentified equations by using all the predetermined variables in the system as instruments (Johnson, 1963, 231-274; Theil, 1971, 429-483). In our theoretical structure, no military, political, or economic variable is purely exogenous. Thus the instrument consists of the one-month lagged values of all of 13 variables plus the two dummy variables.

Each regression is based on the data for the seven-year period between May 1965 and March 1972. Note that Nixon's term in office is indicated by a "dummy" variable only in two equations. Essentially we postulate that the processes of escalation and descalation were generated from the same underlying dynamics of the political economy. The variables actually used in estimation are as follows:

Military Actions:
1. UT = US troops levels in South Vietnam (in thousands)
2. LSG = log (South Vietnamese ground operations of battalion-size or larger)
3. LVA = log (North Vietnamese and Viet Cong armed attacks)

Military Outcomes:
4. LUK = log (US troops killed in action)
5. LSK = log (SV troops killed in action)
6. LVK = log (NV + VC killed in action)

Political Support:
7. US = Gallup Poll index of public approval (yes minus no response)
8. LVS = log (NV + VC defectors)

Economic Effect:
9. UC = Annual percentage change in US consumer price index (computed over the same month of the previous year)
10. UE = Rate of unemployment per 1000 civilian force
11. UR = Annual percentage change of real personal income
12. SC = Annual percentage change in SV consumer price index
13. SS = SV black market piaster value weighted by the cost of living index and money supply

Exogenous:
14. NX = A dummy variable, taking 1 for the Nixon administration and 0 for the Johnson administration.
15. RN = Average rainfall in Saigon (cm.)

The estimated structure is as follows (with standard errors in parentheses):

Military Actions and Reactions:

1. $UT - UT_{-1} = 4.1\ LUK_{-1} + 2.6\ (LVA_{-1} - LVA_{-2})$
    $\quad\quad\quad\quad\quad (0.9)\quad\quad (3.8)$
    $\quad\quad - 26.3\ LSG + 31\ US_{-1} + 130$
    $\quad\quad (2.6)\quad\quad (10)\quad\quad (17)$

2. $LSG = 0.00062\ UT - 0.9\ LVA + 0.8\ NX + 0.63\ LSK_{-1}$
    $\quad\quad (0.0003)\quad\quad (0.12)\quad\quad (0.07)$
    $\quad\quad (0.09)$
    $\quad\quad + 0.31\ LVS_{-1}$
    $\quad\quad (0.04)$

3. $LVA = 0.00096\ UT + 0.33\ LSG - 0.22\ LVS_{-1}$
    $\quad\quad (0.00035)\quad\quad (0.14)\quad\quad (0.09)$
    $\quad\quad + 0.52\ LVK_{-1} - 0.00058\ RN$
    $\quad\quad (0.09)\quad\quad (0.04)$

Military Outcomes:

4. $LUK = 0.0077\ UT - 0.13\ LVA - 0.98\ LSG + + 9.9$
    $\quad\quad (0.0005)\quad\quad (0.15)\quad\quad (0.17)$

5. $LSK = 0.16\ LSG - 0.00099\ UT + 0.63\ LVA + 3.3$
    $\quad\quad (0.09)\quad\quad (0.00023)\quad\quad (0.08)$

6. $LVK = 0.61 \quad LVA + 0.5 \quad LSG + 0.00089 \quad UT + 5.1$
        $(0.08) \qquad\qquad (0.09) \qquad\quad (0.00024)$

Political Support:

7. $US = -5.4 \, LUK_{-1} - 1.6 \quad UE_{-1} - 9.4 \quad UC_{-1}$
        $(2.4) \qquad\quad (0.3) \qquad\quad (2.5)$
        $- 0.03 \quad UR_{-1} + 46 \quad NX + 140$
        $(1.90) \qquad\quad (7) \qquad (33)$

8. $LVS = 1.5 \, LVK - 2.3 \, LSK - 0.014 \quad SC_{-1}$
        $(0.3) \qquad (0.4) \qquad (0.005)$
        $- 0.00005 \quad SS_{-1} + 12$
        $(0.00001) \qquad (2)$

Economic Effect:

9. $UC = 0.94 \quad UC_{-1} + 0.00047 \quad UT + 0.10$
        $(0.02) \qquad\quad (0.00018) \qquad (0.08)$

10. $UE = 0.87 \quad UE_{-1} - 0.08 \quad UT + 0.083 \quad UT_{-1} + 7.0$
        $(0.007) \qquad\quad (0.044) \qquad (0.041) \qquad\quad (4.3)$

11. $UR = -0.11 \quad UE + 0.10 \quad UC - 0.00031 \quad UT + 13.7$
        $(0.02) \qquad\quad (0.11) \qquad (0.0012) \qquad\quad (0.8)$

12. $SS = -70 \, LSK + 4 \quad SC_{-1} + 18 \quad (UT - UT_{-1})$
        $(270) \qquad (11) \qquad (25)$
        $+ 190 \, LVS + 0.92 \, SS_{-1} + 194$
        $(260) \qquad\quad (0.05) \qquad (92)$

13. $SC = 0.86 \quad SC_{-1} - 0.0012 \quad UT - 2.8 \, LSG + 23$
        $(0.06) \qquad\quad (0.0058) \qquad (2.3) \qquad (15)$

As a whole, the estimated coefficients tend to have statistical significance in the hypothesized direction. In a simultaneous system of equations, the causal meaning of a coefficient is not clear until one has the reduced form of equations in which each of the endogenous variables are expressed as a function of exogenous variables or past values of endogenous variables. Yet some comments on the estimated structure can be made. First, US and South Vietnamese military actions respond to their own outcomes and to the effect of Vietnamization, rather than to the hostile actions of the communist forces. The effect of the US policy of withdrawal is apparent in the magnitude of the dummy variable in the equation of South Vietnamese military actions.

On the other hand, the communist armed attacks are a response to military actions by the US as well as South Vietnam. What is striking is that in the result of military action equations, the coefficient of political viability turns out to be as significant as hypothesized. In each equation, the erosion of political support is, besides the effect of substitution, virtually the only variable that constrains the escalatory tendency of the war implied in the model.

This model does not lend support to the widely held belief that "the President makes the public opinion, does not follow it" (Lipset, 1970, 74). The war in Vietnam is a case which paradoxically demonstrates that the President is as much limited in his choice of foreign policy by the internal political environment as by the external events. The political environment includes the bureaucratic politics and the constraints of public opinion (Gelb, 1971; 1972; Ellsberg, 1972). It is notable that the President of the United States acted in a hawkish direction whenever public support for such action was high.

Secondly, military casualties are the result of one's own actions. When one's own military actions are allowed, the additional effect of hostile actions by the adversary seem to be minimal.

Thirdly, political support of the US public tends to be associated with outcomes of both the war and of the economic environment. The regression equation 7 indicates that the public approval of the President is systematically affected by the number of the casualties and objective state of inflation and unemployment. That is, once an idiosyncracy is allowed, public approval increases when there are fewer casualties and economic conditions are good. All the coefficients turned out to be significant with expected signs, with the exception of real personal income, which proves to be redundant because of its intercorrelation with inflation and unemployment.

The same thing can be said of South Vietnam. South Vietnamese government and the communist forces were in conflict to win support at the grass roots level. The data shows that NV + VC defections tend to increase when the NV + VC casualties increase and SV casualties decrease. Inflation also turns out to affect political allegiance of the South Vietnamese people; the South Vietnamese government loses support when there is high economic instability.

Finally, regarding the simple equations of the economic effects: using the values of the previous month of the dependent variables as independent variables, we can demonstrate a significant impact of US troop commitments on the American economy. In equations 9-11, coefficients of US troops are consistent. However, in the two economic equations on South Vietnam, the effect of military actions are not significant. One can speculate that the war-devastated economy is hard to predict by the use of political variables alone, particularly since the possible effect of huge amount of US expenditures in South Vietnam is not well understood.

4.   Computer Simulation

The above estimated model was simulated in a computer run by predicting monthly values from May 1965 and onward using as the only values those from January-April 1965. Given the small number of predictors and the simplicity of the model, it is hard to expect a high degree of accuracy for simulating as many as 80 months. In this type of experiment, it is usually the case that simulated values give a poorer fit than the regressions on which the coefficients are based. A model more often diverges from reality when it is first simulated. The immediate objective is to see whether we can tap the general direction of the war from the estimated structure of relationships among variables.

The 13 equation model does not work very well when all the equations are used in a simulation. However, the simulation predicts the military and political variables quite well when the economic equations from 9 to 13 are assumed to be exogenous and actual values used for the economic variables in other equations. The prediction from the eight-equation model is presented in the following graphs where monthly simulated values (dotted line) are compared with actual values (solid lines). It is not necessary to give the graphs of military casualties because they are in a sense trivial, once the military action variables are well predicted.

Allowing that we have a small number of variables in each question, the degree of fit between actual and simulated values of political and military variables using the model is remarkably good. We could have improved the accuracy of the forecasts by adding more variables, but we wish to be theoretically relevant and parsimonious.

These forecasts were obtained from the estimated structure of relationships with prior information from only five economic variables and two dummy variables. Economic variables never appear in equations predicting military variables in our system, and are in only two political equations. These forecasts demonstrate how closely the economic and political variables were intermixed in determining the courses of events in the Vietnam War. One can say that the policy of withdrawal by the US was basically derived from domestic forces and that the process of decommitment was facilitated by the communist side, which had a similar problem of its own.

The domestic political implications of these findings are clear: (1) greater public approval for the President and his Vietnam policy was dependent upon fewer American casualties and improvement of the domestic economy; (2) fewer casualties depended upon fewer American troops in Vietnam; (3) lower inflationary pressure also depended upon military costs of the maintenance of US troops in South Vietnam. Then, President Nixon's policy of decreasing US involvement in the war was a correct for his purpose of keeping the popular support necessary for his reelection.

A qualification is in order. It will not be realistic to believe that the economic situation is totally determined by troop commitments. That is why we used economic variables as a block of factors exogenous to the military-political dimensions of the war at the macro-level analysis. An economic study might further reveal to what extent the defence cost stemming from the war commitment influenced unemployment, inflation and real personal income (Eisner, 1970). When data become available for the later developments, the accuracy of our model can be finally evaluated. Since economic variables are important prior information for forecasting of military and political variables, it will be useful to report further evidence on the military-economic linkage.

A simple hypothesis is that US troop level is correlated with economic indicators. The following diagram describes the politico-economic linkage during the period under study. Coefficients given are bivariate product-moment correlations between the variables connected by arrows.

Fig. 7 indicates that the US troop levels had a mixed effect on the American economy. It hurt the price stability and personal income, but a quick withdrawal of troops was also associated with increased unemployment, indicating a post-war conversion problem in the economy. It would be misleading, however, to interpret this finding as meaning that foreign troop commitments can help solve the unemployment problem in the US economy. For any given level of troops, both unemployment and inflation rates were higher during the decommitment period than for the period during which US troops were being committed to Vietnam, as illustrated in Fig. 8.

US involvement in the war started to have a significant impact on the economy in the summer of 1965, when major commitments of US ground forces first began. At that time the US economy was remarkably well-balanced, was in the longest period of peacetime expansion in its history, and was operating at full capacity.

The new military expenditures required by the Vietnam War generated a demand-push inflation in the economy, an inflation not dampened for political reasons. The Johnson Administration was initially unwilling to level new taxes to finance the additional war costs because additional taxes would have to be approved by the Congress. Congressional scrutiny of a proposed war tax would also have involved a Congressional and public awareness of the deepening US involvement in the war, something the Johnson Administration sought to avoid.

The resultant imbalance between fiscal and monetary policy is apparent in the positive correlation between inflation and unemployment during the early war period. The inflationary effect of the war costs on the national economy is visible in the cross plot shown above in Fig. 8 of US troops levels in Vietnam and the rate of inflation computed over the same month of the previous year.

It should be noted that the burdens of inflation and unemployment fell disproportionately on the young, the poor and the Black — the same social groups who bore a disproportionate share of military service and personal sacrifice in Vietnam. It is not surprising that anti-war movements first started among leaders of civil rights (Okun, 1970). Yet these groups wield the least political influence in the United States. We may speculate that only after other more politically influential sectors of the society also began to feel the economic impact of inflation and made their feelings known that the political leaders in the US perceived the erosion of public support for their Vietnam policy.

Both Vietnamization and the gradual withdrawal of US troops from Vietnam could be seen as policies designed to win popular support in the United States on two grounds. American casualties were reduced and eventually ended. And inflation tended to be reduced as the involvement of US troops and war costs declined. The Nixon administration had been plagued by a generally higher rate of inflation than the Johnson Administration was for any given number of troops in Vietnam. President Nixon, however, was able to keep his popular support in spite of the higher rates of inflation by reducing the US troops commitments and American casualties.

We might note that the US economy was improving in 1971 and the first half of 1972. Our model predicts that President Nixon would have been under more intense and earlier popular pressure to withdraw US forces from Vietnam had economic conditions in the United States not been improving. As the economy improved, President Nixon's political position was strengthened. He was therefore politically more able to withdraw US troops more slowly. The slower US withdrawal and the Vietnamization policy gave the South Vietnamese government more time to strengthen itself politically and militarily, thus increasing its capacity to cope with the Communist forces after the US withdrawal. Thus President Nixon was more successful politically (perhaps because he was luckier economically) in managing his Vietnam policy than President Johnson had been.

An additional pressure on the Nixon administration to reduce US involvement in the Vietnam War came from the worsening US international economic position relative to the industrialized countries in Western Europe, Japan and Canada. Wage inflation in the United States outpaced gains in industrial productivity to a degree greater than most other industrialized countries, especially during the 1965-70 period of the war-generated inflation. In the absence of exchange rate adjustments, the US dollar became over-valued relative to the currencies of the other major industrialized countries, and US goods became relatively more expensive (McCarthy, 1969).

As it became increasingly cheaper to buy imported goods than similar US goods (when the latter were available), US imports grew at a faster rate than US exports. The result has been that the US balance of trade fell from a positive $4.9 billion in 1960 to a negative $6.9 billion in 1972. This trade deficit, along with the balance of payments deficits due to the direct war costs plus foreign military and economic aid, severely weakened the position of the US dollar. Two devaluations of the dollar have been the result. This damage to the US international economic position certainly constituted one pressure on the Nixon administration to reduce the financial drain and other economic costs which US involvement in the Vietnam War required.

5.   Conclusion

Our theoretical model and the remarkably good forecasts derived from it, especially of US actions and political support, lend empirical support to the propositions that the mutual escalation of military actions in Vietnam resulted in domestic and international economic and political costs for the political leaders on both sides of the war. Moves to reduce at least the military part of the conflict, including the withdrawal of US troops, the reduction of fighting, and the signing of the cease-fire agreement, were thus more due to these economic and political costs, especially in their domestic ramifications, than to the military defeat or exhaustion of either side.

Table 1

Empirical Indicators of Analytic Concepts

System Actor / Analytic Concepts	United States	South Vietnam	North Vietnam and Vietcong
I. Military Actions	*UT* U.S. Troops in South Vietnam	*LGS* SV Ground Operations	*LVA* Communist Armed Attacks
II. Military Outcome	*LUK* U.S. Killed in Action	*LSK* SV Killed in Action	*LVK* NV + VC Killed in Action
III. Economic Effect	UR = Real Personal Income UC = Inflation UE = Unemployment	SC = Consumer Price SS = Black Market Piaster Value	
IV. Political Support	*US* U.S. Public Approval	LVS = NV + VC Defectors	

(The capital characters in each cell indicate the abbreviation used in our model specification)

343

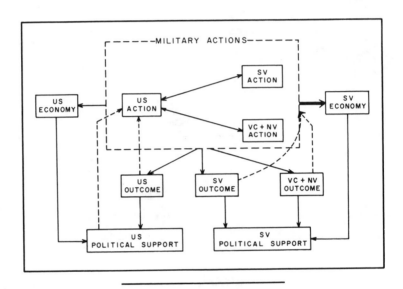

Figure 1
Simplified Diagram of the Model

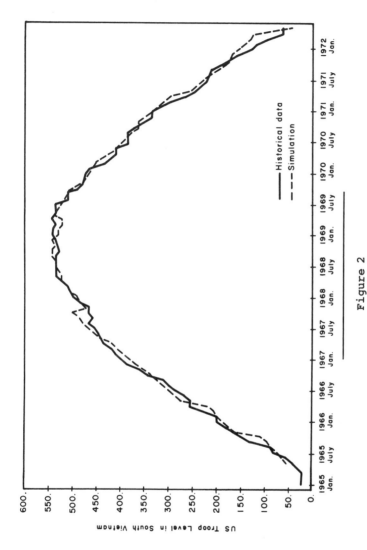

Figure 2

United States Troops in South Vietnam, 1965–1972

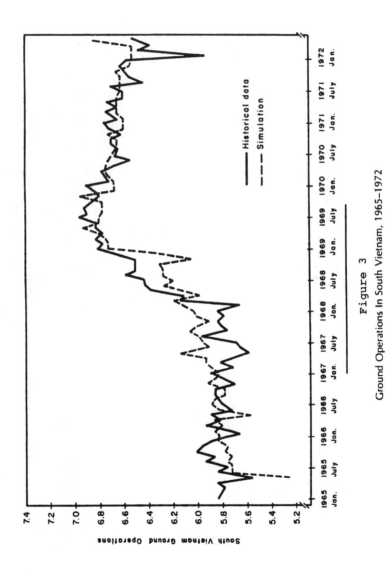

Figure 3
Ground Operations In South Vietnam, 1965–1972

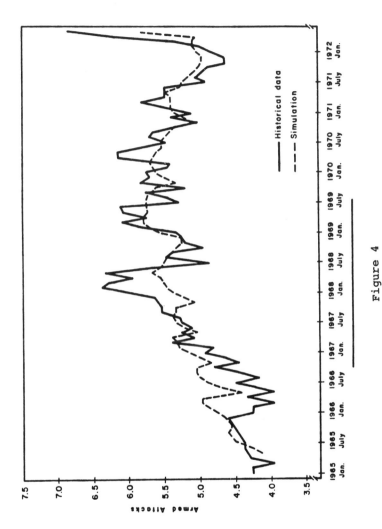

Figure 4
North Vietnamese and Viet Cong Armed Attacks in South Vietnam, 1965–1972

347

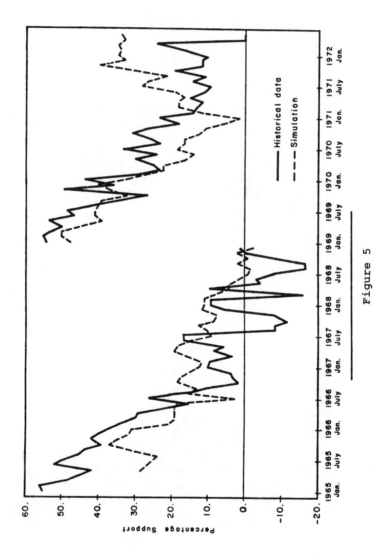

Figure 5

Domestic Political Support for U.S. Policies, 1965–1972

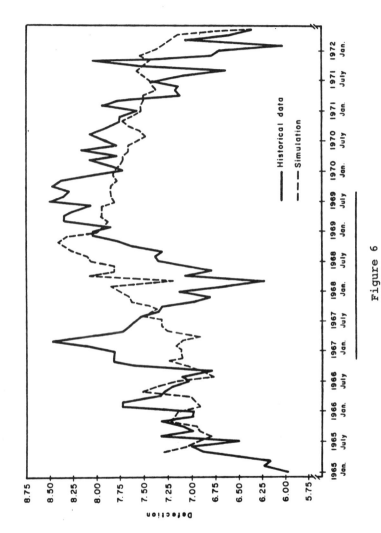

Figure 6

Defections from North Vietnamese Army and Viet Cong in South Vietnam, 1965–1972

349

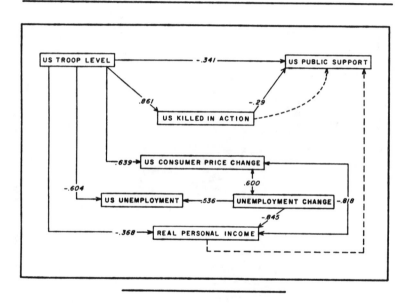

Figure 7
Military-Economic Linkages in the United States, 1965–1972

350

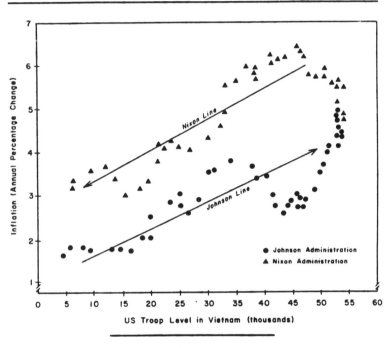

Figure 8a
Scatter Plot of Troop Level and Inflation

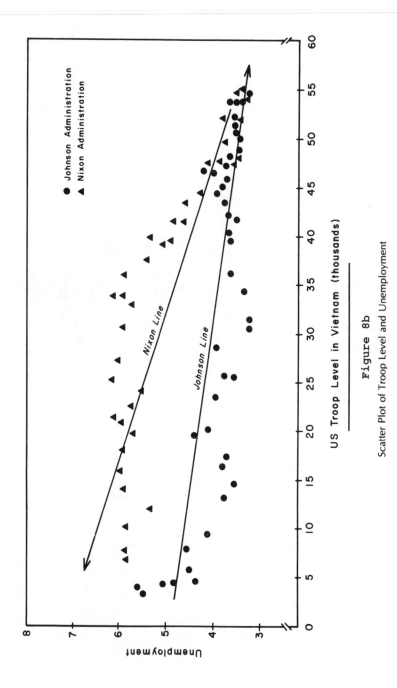

US Troop Level in Vietnam (thousands)

Figure 8b

Scatter Plot of Troop Level and Unemployment

352

References in Lee and Milsteins' Article

Graham Allison and Molton Halperin. 1972. Bureaucratic politics: a paradigm and some policy implication. In Raymond Tanter and Richard Ullman (eds). Theory and policy in international relations. Princeton University Press.

Gabriel Almond. 1968. The American people and foreign policy. Frederick A. Praeger.

William D. Coplin. 1971. Introduction to international politics. Markam.

Anthony Downs. 1957. An economic theory of democracy. Harper and Row.

Robert Eisner. 1970. The war and the economy. In Sam Brown and Len Ackland (eds). Why are we still in Vietnam? Random House.

Daniel Ellsberg. 1972. Papers on the war. Simon and Schuster.

Norman Frohlich, Joe Oppenehimer and Oran Young. 1971. Political leadership and collective goods. Princeton University Press.

Leslie Gelb. 1972. The essential dominoe: American politics and Vietnam. Foreign affairs.
    1971. Vietnam: the system worked. Foreign policy.

Wolfram Hanrieder. 1971. Comparative foreign policy. David McKay.

J. Johnston. 1963. Econometric methods. McGraw-Hill.

V.O. Key, Jr. 1964. Public opinion and American democracy. Alfred A. Knopf.

Gerald Kramer. 1971. Short-term fluctuation in U.S. voting behavior. American political science review.

Jong Ryool Lee.
    1973. Changing national priority of the United States: budgets, perceived needs, and political environment. In Bruce Russett and Alfred Stepan (eds). Military force and American society. Harper and Row.
    1972. Limits of leadership in foreign policy. Typescript.

Seymour Martin Lipset. 1970. The president, the polls, and Vietnam. Readings on the international political system. Prentice-Hall.

Terence McCarthy. 1969. The garrison economy: the new politics of American policy. Holt. Rinehart and Winston.

Jeffrey S. Milstein. 1973. Dynamics of the Vietnam war: a quantitative analysis and predictive computer simulation. Ohio State University Press.

Jeffrey S. Milstein and William C. Mitchell. 1969. Dynamics of the Vietnam War. (In) Vietnam: Issues and alternatives. Shenkman.

John Mueller.
    1971. Trends in popular support for the wars in Korea and Vietnam. American political science review 65.
    1970. Presidential popularity from Truman and Johnson. American political science review 64.

Arthur M. Okun. 1970. The political economy of prosperity. W.W. Norton.

James Rosenau. 1969. Linkage politics. Free Press.

Bruce M. Russett. 1970. What price vigilance? Yale University Press.

Henri Theil. 1971. Principles of econometrics. John Wiley and Sons.

Oran Young. 1972. The actors in world politics (In) The Analysis of international politics. The Free Press.

THE MAJOR POWER CONFRONTATION IN THE MIDDLE EAST:
SOME ANALYSIS OF SHORT-RUN, MIDDLE-RUN
AND LONG-RUN CONSIDERATIONS

Walter Isard and Tony Smith Papers.   Peace Research
Society (International) Vol. XV, 1970.

The Middle East conflict is without question a conflict
as complicated as any we have yet confronted in our world.
Hence, it is presumptuous of scholars with as little knowledge
on the Middle East as we possess to attempt any specific
analysis of this conflict.   Yet, a basic component of this
conflict is a major power confrontation whose elements are
subject to some analysis.   Such analysis can provide insight
helpful with regard to the developments of proposals which aim
at partial resolution of the conflict.   (We do not envisage
that there can be proposals which will achieve full resolution
of this conflict.)   The basic component of interest to us is
the involvement of both the formerly USSR and the USA as
highly competitive major powers.   With regard to the Middle
East, they are clearly in direct competition for control of
whatever resources (economic and political) the Middle East
may represent to them.   But their Middle East actions are also
indirectly affected by their competition for the support of a
world constituency - a competition which must be constantly in
the minds of the leaders of these two powers and their close
allies.   We wish to make explicit certain of the indirect
effects of the competition for world support and to examine
some of their implications for both independent and joint
actions which the US and the formerly USSR might take in the
Middle East.

We view the world constituency as a single, heterogeneous
constituency, differentiated in a multitude of ways, and
cultivated by more than two major powers.   The Union, USA and
Mainland China represent three of these major powers.   In a
real sense, this world constituency may be viewed as a market
for which these three and other powers compete in an
oligopolistic manner, where the existing situation may be
characterized as an interdependent decision situation.[1,2]

In section 2, we briefly review, in the context of the
Middle East, certain analyses covered elsewhere pertaining to
the resolution of a conflict with regard to short- and middle-
run considerations.   In section 3, we develop analysis for the
interdependent decision situation with regard to long-run
considerations of world constituency support.   Finally, in
section 4, we examine implications of the world constituency
game for cooperative solutions in the short- and middle-run.

THE MIDDLE EAST CONFLICT: SHORT- AND MIDDLE-RUN CONSIDERATIONS

We have elsewhere examined game (interdependent decision)
situations which in the Middle East context might be
characterized as follows.[3]   There exist two participants, the
Soviet Union and the USA.   Each chooses an action
(alternative) from an action space (the set of alternatives).

An action is defined in terms of a (continuous) index of equivalent military aid (based on military equipment and supplies, number and type of military personnel, etc. to be provided annually) which is stated in terms of standard currency units. The set of actions available to the Soviet Union is indicated along the vertical axis in Fig. 1; it involves aid ranging from a level of 0 to a level of 100 million. The set of actions available to the USA is indicated along the horizontal axis; it also involves aid ranging from a level of 0 to a level of 100 million.

Associated with each participant is a (quasi-concave; ordinal) preference function for the outcomes associated with each joint action, where outcomes may be defined as "perceived political-military control after discounting for cost of military aid", which we may abbreviate to PPMC. The preference function is representable by a set of indifference curves on the joint action space depicted by the box of Fig. 1. Each indifference curve is a locus of joint actions equally desired by a participant in the sense that each yields the participant the same PPMC, however measured. In Fig. 1, the undashed indifference curves are those of the Soviet Union and they increase up to the Soviet Union Union's most desired joint action – that represented by point F (the numbers associated with the indifference curves of Fig. 1 are employed to indicate an ordering of preference only; any other set of numbers which preserves the ordering can be used). The dashed indifference curves are those of the USA, and they increase up to the USA's most desired joint action – that represented by point G.[4]

Where each participant is motivated strictly to achieve the outcome which he most prefers, and where each behaves as a Cournot maximizer, it is clear that they end up at the globally stable equilibrium point E in Fig. 1. For if the participants are at some other position, say T, at some point of time, one participant, while recognizing that eventually the other will react, senses that there will be a lag in this reaction and judges that he can achieve certain short-run gains by increasing his military aid. For example, he may thereby be able to control certain day-to-day decisions for a while. Hence, if the Soviet Union is the first participant to "defect", it will increase its aid to the level indicated by its best reply curve FF',[5] thereby yielding the new joint action T'. In turn, the USA reacting to the joint action T', will, after some lag, increase its aid to the appropriate level indicated by its best reply curve GG', thereby yielding the new joint action T". And so on, until the Soviet Union and the USA reach a joint action which is indistinguishable by each party from the globally stable equilibrium point E.

If, however, the participants come to recognize the inevitability and undesirability of the equilibrium joint action E (which involves a high annual cost of military aid, as well as the risk of a costly war), and if they can be induced to adopt some cooperative procedure, such as the incremax,[6] or a procedure involving equal decrements of military aid over a series of rounds,[7] we may imagine that they may come to agree to a joint action close to or on the locus of efficient solutions described by the efficiency frontier FG[8]. In particular, we may imagine that they come to agree to a joint action corresponding to or close to point S, a prominent reference point in that it represents a joint action in which both participants provide the same amount of aid annually.[9]

However, note one property of all solutions that lie on or close to the efficiency frontier. They are unstable. If short-run considerations become sufficiently paramount, (for example, the desirability of controlling certain political-military decisions to be made during the next week or two,) one of the participants may be easily tempted to, and may actually defect. He may do so even though he is aware that his defection will lead to subsequent reactions which lead them once again to the inefficient equilibrium (stalemate) position E, where annual costs of military aid will be much greater for a period of at least the several years which he estimates will be necessary to break the new stalemate and to achieve successful negotiations. It is with regard to this undesirable defection property that we now wish to examine the implications of the competition for world constituency support.

3. THE WORLD CONSTITUENCY GAME:
THE INTRODUCTION OF THE LONG-RUN CONSIDERATIONS
IN MIDDLE EAST POLICY

We postulate that the Soviet Union, the USA and other major powers compete over the long run for support by the world constituency. We define this constituency to comprise the entire world's human population. Some of this population, being completely or effectively isolated, such as a tribe at the source of the Amazon, is uncommitted and politically irrelevant. Other populations are fully committed, such as most of the US population and Soviet Union population, and those of the non-Middle East countries who receive significant economic and military aid from either the USA or Soviet Union, etc., or who need to affiliate with the USA or Soviet Union in order to maintain and continue to reaffirm their identity, etc. The rest may be defined as uncommitted, and correspond to the world constituency relevant for competitive action; we will characterize this constituency as the issue-orientated, henceforth to be designated the i-world constituency. We posit that its support is built up over the long-run. It is based upon the development of favourable attitudes, channels of political-economic-social interaction, and commonly-shared institutions. Once favourable attitudes and effective channels of interaction and institutions are disturbed, they are reestablished only gradually over the long run.[10]

Since we are limited to two dimensions in graphic analysis, for the moment we imagine that the world constituency is being "wooed" by both major powers with regard to two major policy issues. One issue relates to the total annual budget of the United Nations, the level of which may be taken generally to reflect the amount of political authority granted this world government agency. The other relates to military involvement in the Middle East conflict (as measured by monthly aid in equivalent standard currency units). We therefore measure along the vertical axis of Fig. 2 the proposed total annual UN budget as a percentage of 1969 level, where we assume that the contributions to this budget by both the Soviet Union and the USA are according to some fixed ratio previously agreed upon. We also measure along the horizontal axis the proposed military aid to the Middle East in equivalent standard currency units as a percentage of February 1970 aid, where both the Soviet Union and the USA are assumed to contribute in the ratio of 1 to 1 (ruble-to-ruble, or dollar-to-dollar). Recall that this second policy issue is with respect to the long-run situation, where the Soviet Union and the USA may take as axiomatic that any short-run deviation in the balance of military aid will be rectified as soon as is feasible by appropriate independent actions on the part of one or both of them. Finally, we assume that expenditure levels on these two issues are sufficiently independent to permit all points in the box of Fig. 2 (at least in the range of possibilities depicted) to be considered as potentially relevant policy proposals. We designate this set of policies as the policy space for the "world constituency" game.

Having specified the two policy dimensions of the game,[11] and having defined the action of any participant as the statement of a proposed policy on each of the two issues of interest, we now turn to an examination of the preferences of the i-world constituency. First, we posit that each member of the i-world constituency (where a "member" may be regarded as a national group, an ethnic group, or a special interest group) defines some most preferred position for itself on these two issues. For example, some constituents may prefer to maintain the present state of affairs, and hence may advocate the "status-quo" position denoted by S in Fig. 1. Next we assume that the members of the i-world constituency are sufficiently numerous and diverse in their interests to permit the distribution of their most-preferred positions to be characterized as a continuous function over the policy space – which we designate as the constituency density function for the world constituency game. As to the specific form of this distribution, we assume that the density of most-preferred positions falls off symmetrically in all directions about the average most-preferred position, represented by the point M in Fig. 2[12] – which, in terms of some current position, corresponds to a policy advocating a level of aid at 85% of the current level, and a level of budget at 125% of the current level. Finally, we assume that the fall-off in density from M is quite gradual in the region around M and increases sharply outside this region – as shown in Fig. 3. While this "symmetric unimodal" constituency density cannot be said to characterize reality, it may approximate the reality as perceived by Soviet Union and US leaders. In any case, the assumption of such a distribution does facilitate the computations and graphic presentation of the analysis to follow.[13]

Now consider any world constituent. He can give (in terms of a single vote or single voice) support either to the Soviet Union or the USA, or to neither.[14] If one of these powers proposes a policy combination which coincides with the constituent's most preferred combination, we can expect the constituent to support that world power wholeheartedly. However, if no world power proposes such a policy combination, then we assume that for the given constituent there is a positive probability that he will support no world power at all.

More specifically, we assume that each constituent evaluates all policies in terms of their "perceived distances" from his most preferred policy. Moreover, we assume for simplicity that this "perceived distance" is some increasing function of Euclidean distance.[15] In terms of this distance concept, we assume that if given a choice between more than one policy proposal, the constituent whose proposal is closest to his most preferred policy combination.[16] Finally, we assume that the probability that he will support the major power whose proposed policy combination is the closer decreases with perceived distance from his most preferred policy combination.

If for each constituent we now designate the function defining these probabilities of supporting each possible (closest) policy combination as his individual support probability function, we may depict this function as follows. Suppose a given constituent's most preferred policy is T, as shown in Fig. 4. Then let the curve of Fig. 4 represent the cross-section through his individual support probability function along the line in the policy space corresponding to proposed policy combinations involving 100% as the level of UN aid. According to this function, the given constituent will never support a proposal of policy combination X (i.e. his support probability for X is zero) and he will support with probability 0.5 a proposal of policy combination R (assuming no other competitive proposal is closer to T than R).

With these basic assumptions, we imagine that both major powers attempt to estimate the percentage support of the i-world constituency which they each would expect to receive, given any pair of policy proposals. We assume for simplicity that the stated positions of the i-world constituents are sufficiently well-known to ensure that the estimates of the constituency density function by each major power can be taken to be the same. We next suppose that in estimating support probability functions for the i-world constituents, each major power estimates a single "average" or "representative" form for the individual support probability functions of constituents. Moreover, we assume that each power uses this average form to approximate all individual support probability functions, and thus considers the individual support probability functions for all constituents as identical in all respects other than the position of their most preferred policy combinations. Finally, designating this representative function for each major power as its support probability function, we assume that the estimates of the support probability functions for the USA and the Soviet Union are the same.[17]

With these estimated functions, we may imagine that each major power, given the policy combination proposed by the other, can calculate the support it can expect to receive for any policy combination it proposes. For example, suppose the USA has proposed a policy combination given by point U in Fig.

2. Then the Soviet Union knows that for any policy combination V, it (the Soviet Union) proposes, all those i-world constituents with a most preferred policy combination closer to U will support its (the Soviet Union's) proposal with zero probability. Also, it knows that all i-world constituents with a most preferred policy combination closer to V than to U will support the Soviet Union proposal, each with a probability defined by his support probability function. Hence, using this information, the Soviet Union can compute the expected percentage of the i-world constituency which will support V given U.[18] Likewise, the Soviet Union can estimate its expected percentage support for each policy combination which it can propose, given U. We shall take these levels of expected percentage support to be the payoffs for the major powers in this world constituency game.

Now suppose that given policy combination U proposed by the USA, the Soviet Union wishes to find that policy combination to propose which will maximize its own payoff. To do so, the Soviet Union need not compute the payoffs for all possible policy combinations V which it could choose. Given the specific functional forms we have taken for the constituency density and support probability functions, it can be shown that the policy combination V which maximizes the Soviet Union's expected support for a given policy combination U by the USA must always lie on the diameter coursing through U and M, as shown in Fig. 2. Moreover, this optimal policy response must always lie on the opposite side of M from U, in the region designated as the "optimal response region, given U" in Fig. 2.[19] Hence we may conclude that given U, the Soviet Union need consider only policy combinations in this region.

The payoffs for the Soviet Union corresponding to policies in this optimal response region, given U, can be depicted as in Fig. 5. Along the vertical axis of Fig. 5 we measure the distance of any proposed policy combination by the USA on the diameter to the left of the centre M, where zero distance corresponds to the proposed policy combination represented by M. The position U is indicated on the vertical axis in Fig. 5. Along the horizontal axis of Fig. 5, we measure the distance of any proposed policy combination by the Soviet Union, which we assume will be on the diameter to the right of M, where again zero distance corresponds to the proposed policy combination represented by M. If we now determine the Soviet Union's payoff for each possible policy combination by the USA and the Soviet Union in the respective regions shown, and if we plot the corresponding "iso-payoff" lines as shown in Fig. 5, then we may easily determine the policy V which maximizes the Soviet Union's payoff given U. This policy V yields the Soviet Union an expected percentage support of 37%, shown in the Figure.

In a similar manner, the Soviet Union can determine the policy which maximizes its payoff given any policy choice by the USA on the left half of the diameter in Fig. 2. The locus of all these optimal policy responses is designated the Soviet Union's best reply curve (see Fig. 5). Note finally that using this best-reply curve, the Soviet Union can determine its optimal policy response for any policy choice by the USA.

This point follows since our symmetry assumptions on the constituency density and support probability functions imply that the position of the best-reply curve shown in Fig. 5 is independent of the diameter through M which is being considered. Hence for any other policy choice by the USA, say U in Fig. 2, we can apply the best-reply curve of Fig. 5 to the diameter passing through U (the dashed line in Fig. 2), and thereby determine the Soviet Union's best policy response to U'. Thus the information in Fig. 5 completely determines the Soviet Union's optimal response to any policy by the US. In a similar manner, we assume that the USA also determines its optimal policy response to any policy proposal of the Soviet Union. By symmetry, the best-reply curve for the USA is precisely the same as in Fig. 5 when the labelling of the axes is reversed.

Given these two best-reply curves, we may consider a series of optimal-policy responses by the USA and Soviet Union to one another, in a manner which parallels the series of military-aid responses examined in connection with Fig. 1. To depict such a response sequence, observe first that since each response must always lie on the same diameter as the previous policy proposal, every possible sequence of policy responses is necessarily restricted to that diameter defined by the initial policy proposal of the sequence. Hence, given such a policy, say V' by the Soviet Union, we may depict the resulting sequence of responses on the diameter through V" by superimposing the relevant payoff surfaces for the US and Soviet Union as shown in Fig. 6. Here the US and Soviet Union iso-payoff lines are shown respectively as dashed and solid lines. Similarly, the respective best-reply curves for the USA and Soviet Union are depicted by the lines UU* and VV*, respectively. Hence, given the initial policy proposal V', the resulting sequence of responses would follow the points $P_1, P_2, P_3, \ldots$ converging to the equilibrium point E', as in Fig. 6. Moreover, since E' is the unique equilibrium point to which all response sequences on this diameter converge, and since E' lies on the diagonal of the box in Fig. 6, we see that for all initial policy proposals on this diameter, the USA and the Soviet Union will eventually end up with policy proposals on this diameter at the same distance d to either side of M. Finally, observing again that this distance d is independent of which ever diameter is involved, for all initial policy proposals in the policy space the US and Soviet Union will end up on the opposite side of the dotted circle in Fig. 2 - which we now designate at the equilibrium locus for the world constituency game.

It is not necessary to repeat here analyses which have been developed in previous papers. For any equilibrium configuration E' on this equilibrium locus, it is easily seen from Fig. 6 that E' is an inefficient equilibrium, since there exist joint policy proposals which both the USA and Soviet Union would prefer to E'. Hence, assuming that both parties are concerned with the possible competition by other third world powers (such as Mainland China), they can each improve their position, relative to a third powers, that is, obtain a greater payoff corresponding to a greater percentage support by the i-world constituency. They can do so by adopting some cooperative procedure - such as equal percentage increments, or incremax -which enables them to reach some joint action close to or on the efficiency frontier as depicted by the arc $J*_1J*_2$ in Fig. 6. The analysis of such cooperative possibilities in situations involving interdependent decision making with interdependent constituencies is too long for presentation in this manuscript. What we wish to do now is to examine the implications of the analysis of this long-run consideration (support by world constituency) for the short-run and middle-run Middle East conflict problem.

4. THE CREDIBILITY FACTOR:
IMPLICATIONS OF LONG-RUN CONSIDERATIONS
FOR SHORT- AND MIDDLE-RUN PROBLEMS

To establish one possible linkage between the long-run (section 3) and the short- and middle-run considerations of section 2, observe that in the world-constituency game there are in fact two relevant policy combinations for each power. One is the powers' proposed policy combination (as treated in section 3 above) and the other is the actual combination which that power is presently carrying out - i.e. its present UN budget expenditures and Middle East military aid expenditures. Recall that in Fig. 1 the present expenditure levels by the USA and Soviet Union are denoted by the status quo position S, which indicates in particular that the military aid expenditures by each power are equal. Let us suppose that this status quo position corresponds to a period of relative quiet in the Middle East involving, say, a tacitly agreed upon balanced-power position of 35 million (standard currency units) in military aid by each power. Then the actual military aid position corresponding to the status quo position S is given by the point H in Fig. 1.

Now suppose that for some reason the USA is tempted to "defect" from this tacit agreement position, and that it contemplates an increase in its actual military aid from 35 million to a level of 65 million, i.e. it contemplates a new joint action H' which lies on its best reply curve in Fig. 1. The immediate increase over the short run in PPMC that would result is apparent from Fig. 1; the USA's position shifts from an indifference curve of less preferred positions to one of more preferred positions. But what would be the effect on the long-run payoff of the US as depicted in Fig. 6?

To estimate the effect of a short-run defection, it is necessary to introduce a "credibility factor" into the long-run payoff functions of both the Soviet Union and USA. This credibility factor relates payoff to the discrepancy between actual and proposed actions. We may imagine that a world constituent expects a certain amount of discrepancy between an actual and a proposed action on the part of any major power - say, for example, because of the impossibility of projecting accurately the full range of needs of the immediate short run. But when the discrepancy exceeds some level, then in the eyes of a world constituent the credibility of a major power's proposal decreases, and continues to decrease regularly to zero as this discrepancy increases. For example, suppose that such discrepancies are viewed by the constituents in terms of some "perceived distance" function (as in section 3), where the relevant "reference" policies are now taken to be the actual policies of the major power, rather than the most preferred policies of the constituents. If we assume then that "credibility" falls from 1.0 (fully credible) to 0.0 (not credible) in any given direction as this perceived discrepancy increases, then a cross-section of such a credibility function might be depicted as in Fig. 7. Here we denote by P the relevant actual policy position for a major power and depict the credibility levels for policy proposals at various perceived distances along a given direction from P. Notice that we assume that policies which are no further from P in a given direction than a perceived distance of d are considered to be "fully credible". Hence we designate the set of policies which are within a perceived distance d from P as the P-credible region in the policy space along the given direction. If the direction of discrepancy has no effect on the credibility function, then the region will be circular about P (as was the case in section 3). Otherwise the P-credible region will be asymmetrical, as is likely to be the case in most situations of actuality, and the slope of the credibility function will fall off at different rates in different directions from P.

Now to incorporate this credibility factor into our analysis, we must give such a credibility function an explicit operational interpretation. To do so, let us now suppose for example that each constituent considers a given policy to be either "credible" or "not credible". We might then interpret the above function as representing the probability that any given constituent considers a major power's policy to be credible, with respect to an actual policy of P. If in addition we assume that a constituent will only support a policy proposal if he considers it to be credible, and if we reinterpret the support probability function of section 3 as representing his probability of support given that he considers a policy to be credible, then we may construct a new support probability function for the constituents by taking the product of the above two functions. This new function represents the probabilities of support after taking into account the credibility factor. Hence, if the USA and Soviet Union then estimate "average" or "representative" credibility functions (now interpretable as behavioural probabilities) and thereby construct new support probability functions, they may incorporate this credibility factor into their calculations as follows.

Suppose that in the world constituency game of section 3 an equilibrium pair of policy proposals is reached, say P_{US} for the USA and P_s for the Soviet Union, as shown on the equilibrium locus in Fig. 8. Here both powers concur in advocating a reduction of military aid expenditure by each power to 85% of their present level, and differ only slightly in advocating increases of UN budget expenditures to 130% and 115% of their present level, respectively. Hence, if we now assume for simplicity that the estimates of credulity functions by the USA and Soviet Union are the same, and if we recall that the actual policies for both powers are given by the status quo position S, then the S-critical regions for both powers can be represented by the oval-shaped area about S as shown in Fig. 8. Here we see that both policies P_{US} and P_S lie within the s-critical region, and hence that (on the basis of the estimated credibility function) they are taken to be fully credible by the constituents. Moreover, since this implies that the estimated payoffs for these policies are unaffected by credibility considerations, the equilibrium properties of these policies are also unaffected.[20] Hence, the outcome of this world constituency game is apparently unaffected by the credibility factor.

Recall, however, that we suppose that the US is considering a possible defection from the military aid position H (associated with S) to a new position H' in order to achieve short-run gains in PPMC. If the USA should defect, then the actual military aid expenditures by the USA would no longer be 35 million, but rather 65 million. Since this would represent an increase in expenditures to approximately 185% of the current level (35 million), this defection by the USA would in a short period of time shift the actual status quo position from S to S' in Fig. 8. If we then construct the S'-credible region about S', the figure indicates that the USA proposal P_{US} would no longer be considered fully credible by the constituents. More specifically, if we take the direction from S' to P_{US} is that which would be associated with a credibility of only 0.20. Hence, the USA can now expect that (on average) only 20% of the world constituents would consider the policy P_{US} to be credible.[21] Hence, given policy P_S of the Soviet Union, the payoff of policy P_{US} to the USA (in terms of expected support percentages) would be lower if the USA were to defect, and the Soviet Union were to follow suit. Moreover, if the USA were to defect, it can be shown that, given policy P_S, the USA can find no policy proposal which yields it as high a payoff as P_{US} would without defection. Hence, while the USA would increase its level of PPMC in the short run, it could do so only at the cost of i-world constituency support in the long run. Thus, we see that in many situations the explicit consideration of this credibility factor may weigh against the possibility of a defection and thereby help stabilize an otherwise unstable cooperative solution.

The analysis just presented is obviously oversimplified. For example, it assumes that credibility is solely a function of proposed and actual policy discrepancies, thereby ignoring the multitude of other factors which may influence credibility.[22] Moreover, it assumes that constituents view the credibility of both major powers in roughly the same way. In addition, many important questions are left unanswered by this analysis. For example, what are the potential feedback effects of short-run decisions on long-run policy positions? Moreover, what are the actual trade-offs between short-run and middle-run payoffs on the one hand, and between short-run and long-run payoffs on the other? Finally, how important are considerations such as i-world constituency support when weighed against the host of other possible long-run goals of a major power?

Yet while there are numerous shortcomings to such simplified analyses as ours, there are also numerous shortcomings to relatively loose and unstructured verbal discussion of short-run, middle-run and long-run behaviour and payoffs when there exists among scholars no common set of accepted definitions concerning alternatives, relevant outcomes, gains and losses, and when there is no analytical framework with which to test for consistency of assumptions and hypotheses. It is with regard to such a framework, wherein these elements are more precisely defined--namely short-run considerations of PPMC, middle-run considerations of higher annual levels of military aid, and long-run considerations of i-world constituency support – that we hope to have made some small contribution to the analysis of an exceedingly complex conflict situation.

Notes

1.See W. Isard, T. Smith, et. al., General Theory: Social, Political, Economic and Regional, M.I.T. Press, Cambridge, MA 1969, pp. 222-227.

2.While we may visualize the current world as one in which major powers may form coalitions, at the moment we wish to pursue analysis for those world situations where such coalitions are unattainable or precluded by cultural or other factors.

3.W. Isard, T. Smith, et. al. op. cit., Chapters 6-7; and W. Isard, "The Veto Incremax Procedure: Potential for Vietnam Conflict Resolution", Papers, Peach Research Society (International), Vol. 10, 1968, pp. 149-162.

4.To facilitate the analysis, the ordinal preference functions are assumed to be roughly of the same form for each participant. The results of the analysis are by and large unaffected for a large range of dissimilar preference functions which we may adopt. For fuller discussion, see W. Isard and T. Smith, op. cit., Chapters 6-7.

We also make the assumption that these preference functions (and thus aspirations, values, perception and information, etc.) remain essentially unchanged as the major powers act and react to each other – admittedly a strong assumption. We also make the assumption that each major power is a monolithic "team" in the sense that all its constituent individuals and interest groups have the same (or agree to use a common) preference ordering, and that, in particular, the industrial-military establishment of any major power is not a discernible subgroup with respect to preferences – clearly, another strong assumption.

5.For every possible action of one participant, the best reply curve indicates the action of the second participant which yields his most preferred outcome of all those achievable, given the first participant's action.

6.W. Isard and T. Smith, op. cit., pp. 309-327

7.Ibid, pp. 446-447

8.Note that the efficiency frontier does not contain the (0,0) point and that for every joint action in the area below and to the left of the efficiency frontier there is a joint action on the efficiency frontier which both participants prefer even though it corresponds to greater aid by both. This preference might, for example, be taken to reflect a conviction on the part of both powers that some military aid must be provided annually in order to help keep third powers, such as Mainland China, out of the Middle East – an objective which is assumed by both parties to be highly desirable over, say, the next five years. They may act on the belief that the greater the combined military aid of the Soviet and the USA, the greater the probability that no third party will enter the Middle East conflict in a major way.

9. However, for a number of reasons, point S may be rejected as a possible agreement point. For example, it may represent unequal percentage-wise contributions of resources when the two major powers possess greatly different initial resource endowments.

10. As Ismael Serageldin has pointed out, sharp lines of distinction are not possible between categories, such as between issue-orientated and committed world constituency, and between middle-run and long-run considerations. For example, the population of certain countries may be committed to a major power in the long-run, like Turkey is to the USA, or Romania to the Soviet Union, and yet at any moment of time, on any specific set of issues, their support cannot be counted upon. Qualification of our analysis and extension of it in other directions are thus suggested by these remarks.

11. By considering only the two policy dimensions defined, we necessarily assume that constituents are not orientated to such issues as: "who controls?", "who has the power to make decisions?", etc.

12. In statistical terms, our assumptions may be characterized as follows. If we let the random variables P_1 and P_2 denote the most preferred position of a randomly sampled constituency member with respect to the two policy issues, and let $f(p_1$ and $p_2)$ denote the joint probability density of P_1 and P_2 on the policy space, then we assume that (1) the density $f(p_1, p_2)$ is unimodal with respect to the mean point $M = (E[P_1], E[P_2])$ and (2) the conditional density of P_1 and P_2 given $p_1 + p_2 = r$ depends only on the value of r[i.e. $f(p_1, p_2/p_1^2 + p_2^2 = r) = g(r)$]. These assumptions imply in particular that P_1 and P_2 are statistically uncorrelated.

13. It is important to emphasize, however, that while the above assumptions help to simplify the computations and graphic presentations, they are in no way essential for the analysis. We could, with the aid of computers and numerical methods, analyse problems with any well-defined distribution of most-preferred positions. However, all of the major ideas can be depicted within the context of these simplifying assumptions, and hence we view them as illustrative devices rather than essential behavioural hypotheses.

14. For simplicity we assume that each constituent supports at most one major power. While relaxations of this assumption are easily achieved, they would complicate the present analysis unnecessarily.

15.The remarks in footnote 13 are relevant here as well.

16.When the two major powers' proposals are at the same distance from the most preferred policy combination of a subset of constituents, we assume that they share equally in any support given by this subset.

17.As in the discussion of footnote 13, the assumptions of identical estimates for constituency densities and support probability functions are in general not essential for the analysis. However, in those situations treated below which involve the total percentage support achieved by both powers it is necessary that the same estimate of the constituency density be used by each power.

18.Formally, this computation involves an integration of the product of the constituency density and support probability function over the region of positive support probability for V given U. The details of such a computation procedure are presented in a forthcoming manuscript by T. Smith

19.The fact that the optimal response to U lies on this diameter follows basically from the symmetry conditions postulated in the density and support functions. This simplification is useful for illustrative purposes in that it permits the relevant policy space to be reduced to one dimension (and hence permits joint policy choices to be illustrated in two dimensions). The fact that the optimal response always lies on the other side of M from U is a very special property of the functions chosen.

20.Observe that the credibility function can only serve to reduce the payoffs computed in section 3. But since the payoffs associated with P_{US} and P_s remain the same, they must by definition still be equilibrium policies with respect to all other policy.

21.To motivate this interpretation, observe that a credibility level of 0.20 indicates that the probability of any given constituent considering P_{US} credible would be 0.20. Hence, if we associate a random variable X_1 with each constituent i, which assumes the value 1 if i consider P_{US} credible, and, if not, then for any finite number of constituents, say N, the percentage of constituents who considers P_{US} credible would be precisely the realization of the random variable $Z_N = \frac{100}{N} \Sigma x_i$. But since ΣZ_N is easily seen to be 20 (for all N), we see that on average, 20% of the constituents would consider P_{US} credible.

22.Deutsch has pointed out for example that the credibility of policy proposals involving "reassurances" may involve very different considerations than the credibility of policy proposals involving "threats".

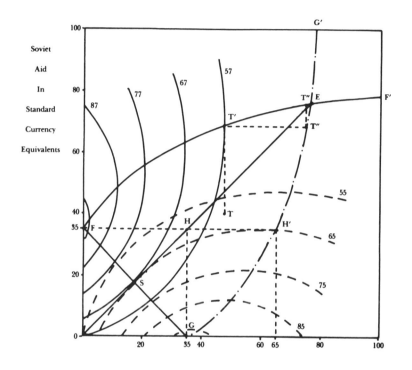

U.S. AID IN STANDARD CURRENCY EQUIVALENTS

FIGURE 1
JOINT ACTION SPACE
AND PREFERENCE ORDERINGS

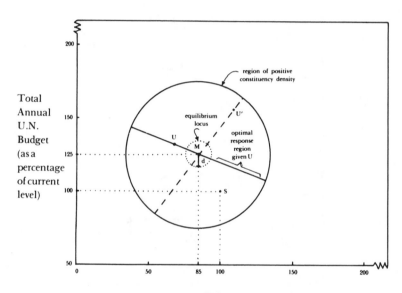

FIGURE 2
EACH POWER'S MILITARY AID EXPENDITURES
(AS A PERCENTAGE OF CURRENT LEVEL)

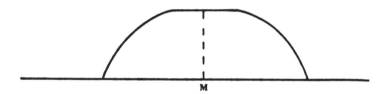

FIGURE 3
DIAGONAL CROSS SECTION
OF DENSITY FUNCTION
OF MOST PREFERRED POLICY COMBINATIONS

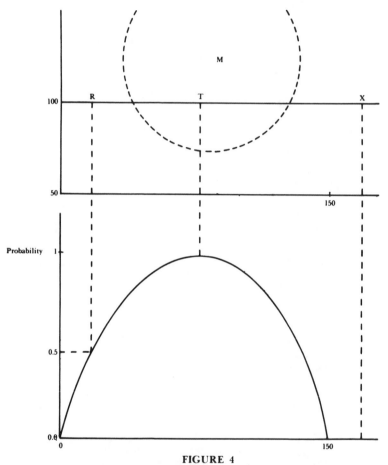

FIGURE 4
INDIVIDUAL SUPPORT PROBABILITY FUNCTION
(FOR THE SUBSET OF POLICIES CONSTRAINED BY $P_{UN} = 100$)

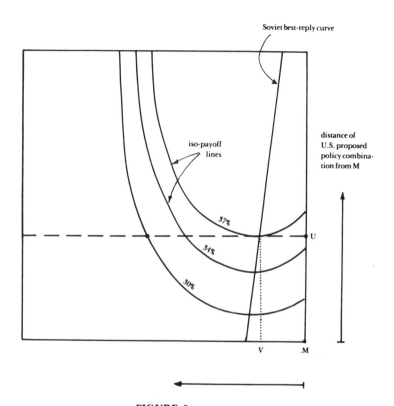

Soviet best-reply curve

distance of
U.S. proposed
policy combina-
tion from M

iso-payoff
lines

37%

34%

30%

U

V   .M

FIGURE 5
DISTANCE OF SOVIET'S PROPOSED
POLICY COMBINATION FROM M

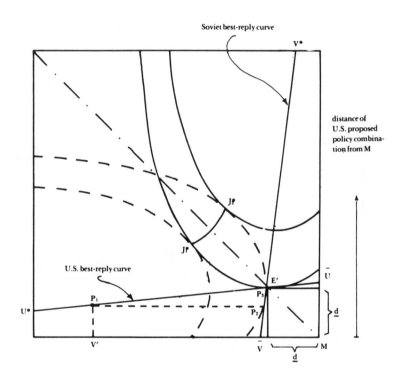

FIGURE 6
DISTANCE OF SOVIET PROPOSED
POLICY COMBINATION FROM M

374

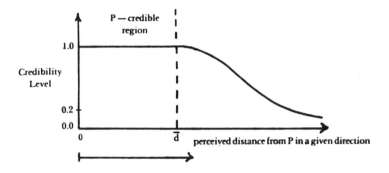

FIGURE 7

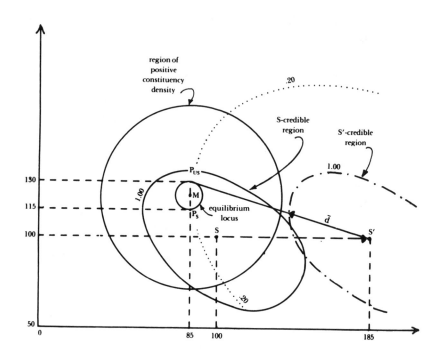

FIGURE 8

Bibliography

Acharya, B.K. "India and China." Indian and Foreign Review, 2, No. 11, 9-10, 19-20, March 15, 1965.

Adams, G. and J.R. Behrman. "Defense Expenditures and Economic Growth in the LDCs: Reconciling Theory and Empirical Results," in Disarmament, Economic Conversion and Management of Peace, New York: Praeger Publishing, 1990 (forthcoming).

Agarwala, A. and Singh, S. The Economics of Underdevelopment, New York: Oxford University Press.

Agee, Marvin H., R.E. Taylor and P.E. Torgersen. Quantitative Analysis for Management Decisions, Englewood Cliffs, New Jersey: Prentice-Hall, 1976.

Aggarwal, L. "Conflicts and Management Strategies in Business" in Organizational Conflict and Peace Science, Vol. 3, 1981.

Alvares, Peter. "Kashmir and Power Balance in Asia," Janata, 20, November 14, 1965, No. 43, 3-4, 6.

Anderton, C. "A New Look at the Relationship Between Arms Race Disarmament and the Probability of War," in Disarmament, Economic Conversion and Management of Peace, edited by Manas Chatterji and Linda Forcey, New York: Praeger Publishing, 1991.

Appadorai, A. and M.S. Rajan. India's Foreign Policy and Relations, New Delhi: South Asian Publishers, 1985.

Appadorai, A. The Domestic Roots of India's Foreign Policy, 1947-1972, Delhi: Oxford University Press, 1981.

Ayub-Khan, Mohammed. Pakistan Perspectives: A Collection of Important Articles and Excerpts from Major Addresses, Washington, D.C.: Embassy of Pakistan, 1965.

Azar, Edward E., R.A. Brady and C.A. McClelland. International Events Interaction Analysis: Some Research Considerations, Beverly Hills: Sage Publications, 1972.

Azar, Edward. "COPTAB: Conflict and Peace Data Bank Center for International Development," College Park: University of Maryland.

Babichev, M. "Perestroika, Disarmament and the Problems of Economic Conversion in the U.S.S.R.," edited by Manas Chatterji and Linda Forcey, New York: Praeger Publishing, 1990.

Barnds, William J. India, Pakistan, and the Great Powers, New York: Published for the Council on Foreign Relations by Praeger, 1972.

Benoit, E. and Boulding, K. (Editors). Disarmament and the Economy, New York: Harper and Row, 1963.

Berelson, B., and Steiner, Gary. Human Behavior: An Inventory of Scientific Findings, New York: Harcourt, Brace and World, Inc., 1966.

Bernstein, R.A., and P.D. Weldon. "A Structural Approach to the Analysis of International Relations," Journal of Conflict Resolution, 1968, 12 (2 June) 159-81.

Bharadwaj, Ranganath. Structural Basis of India's Foreign Trade, University of Bombay, India.

Bloomestein, H.J. and P. Nijkamp. "A Comparison of Some Analytical Procedures for Nonmetric Information in Conflict Analysis," in Disarmament, Economic Conversion and Management of Peace, edited by Manas Chatterji and Linda Forcey, New York: Praeger Publishing, 1991.

Biggs-Davison, John Alec. Pakistan and Western Interests, London: Foreign Affairs Research Institute, 1979.

Boulding, Kenneth E. Conflict and Defense - A General Theory, New York: Harper and Row, 1963.

Boulding, Kenneth. "Towards a Theory of Peace," in Roger Fisher, ed., International Conflict and Behavioral Science, New York: Basic Books, 1966.

Bremer, Stuart A. Simulated Worlds, Princeton, NJ: Princeton University Press, 1977.

"The British Press and the War with Pakistan," Virdura, 2, No. 4 (November 1965), 11-18.

"The British Press on the India-Pakistan Conflict," Foreign Affairs Report, XIV, No. 12, (December 1965, 161-170.

Bryen, Stephen D. The Application of Cybernetic Analysis to the Study of International Politics, Martinus Nijhoff Publishers, The Hague, 1971.

Burke, S.M. Mainsprings of Indian and Pakistani Foreign Policies, Minneapolis: University of Minneapolis Press, 1974.

Cartwright, D., and Harary, F. "Structural Balance: A Generalization of Heider's Theory," Psychological Review, 63 (1956), 277-93.

_____. "A Note on Freud's "Instincts and Their Vicissitudes," International Journal of Psychoanalysis, 40, (1960), 287-90.

Catell, R.B. "An Introduction to Personality Study," London and New York: Hutchinson's University Library, 1950.

Cattell, R.B. and M. Adelson. "The Dimensions of Social changes in the United States as determined by P-Techniques," Social Forces, 30: 1951, pp. 190-201.

Chakroborty, S. The Logic of Investment Planning, Amsterdam, Holland: North-Holland Publishing Company.

Chatterjee, Partha. Arms, Alliances and Stability, New York: John Wiley & Sons, 1975.

Chatterjee, Partha. Arms, Alliances and Stability - The Development of the Structure of International Politics, New York: John Wiley & Sons, 1975.

Chatterji, Manas. "A Game Theoretic Approach of Coalition Politics in an Indian State." International Interactions, Vol. 5, No. 1, 1978.

Chatterji, Manas, A. Rima, H. Jager, Eds. Economics of International Security, London: MacMillan, 1992 (forthcoming).

_____. "A Model of Resolution of Conflict between India and Pakistan," Papers, Peace Research Society, Vol. XII, pp. 20-30, 1969.

_____. "A Model of Resolution of Conflict Between India and Pakistan." Papers, Peace Research Society (International), Vol. 12, November 1968.

_____. "Conflict and Socio-Economic Structure -- A Factor Analysis Study" in Northeast Peace Science Review, Vol. 1, 1978.

_____. Analytical Techniques in Conflict Management. A report submitted to the National Institute of Dispute Resolution, Washington, D.C., 1990.

_____. "Conflict and Socio-economic Structure: A Factor Analysis Study." Mathematical Modeling, Vol. 8, 1986.

_____. On the Use of Conflict Resolution Techniques in Indian Problems. Indian Journal of Regional Science, Vol. 2, 1970.

_____. "Prospects and Problems of a Change from Military to Civilian Industrial Complex," in Disarmament, Economic Conversion and Management of Peace, edited by Manas Chatterji and Linda Forecy, New York: Praeger Publishing, 1991.

_____. "Rhode Island and Defense Expenditure," Rhode Island Quarterly, Spring 1965.

_____. "Third World Disarmament and Economic Development," in Disarmament, Economic Conversion and Management of Peace, edited by Manas Chatterji and Linda Forcey, New York: Praeger Publishing, 1991.

_____. "Use of Management and Peace Science Techniques for Dispute Resolution," in Disarmament, Economic Conversion and Management of Peace, edited by Manas Chatterji and Linda Forcey, New York: Praeger Publishing, 1991.

_____. and L. Forcey (eds.) Disarmament, Economic conversion and Management of Peace, edited by Manas Chatterji and Linda Forcey, New York: Praeger Publishers, 1991.

Cheema, Pervaiz Iqbal. Conflict and Cooperation in the Indian Ocean: Pakistan's Interests and Choices, Canberra: Strategic and Defense Studies Centre, Research School of Pacific Studies, Miami, FL., 1980.

Chiang, Alpha C. Fundamental Methods of Mathematical Economics, New York: McGraw-Hill, Third Edition, 1984.

Choudbury, Golam Wahed. India, Pakistan, Bangladesh, and the Major Powers; Politics of a Divided Subcontinent. G.W. Choudbury, New York: Free Press, 1975.

Chow, Gregory C. Econometrics, McGraw Hill, New York, 1983.

Cioffi-Revilla, Claudio, R.L. Merritt and D.A. Zinnes. eds. Communication and Interaction in Global Politics, Beverly Hills, CA., Sage Publications, 1987.

Cohen, Stephen Philip (editor). The Security of South Asia: American and Asian Perspectives. Urbana: University of Illinois Press, 1987.

Cooley, William W., and P.R. Lohnes. Multivariate Procedures for The Behavioral Sciences, New York: John Wiley & Sons, 1962.

Crane, Robert. "A Critique of Approaches: A Review of K.S. Murth and A.C. Boquet, Studies in the Problems of Peace, [Bombay, Asia Publishing House, 1960]." Journal of Conflict Resolution, Vol. 3, 1961, pp. 336-39.

Domar, E.S. Essays in the Theory of Economic Growth, New York: Oxford University Press.

Donaghy, K. "Some Comparative Dynamics of Economic Conversion," in Disarmament, Economic Conversion and Management of Peace, New York: Praeger Publishing, 1990.

Dorfman, Robert, P. Samuelson and R. Solow. Linear Programming and Economic Analysis. New York: McGraw-Hill, 1958.

Dunbar, William. India in Transition, Sage Publications for Center for Strategic and International Studies, Washington, DC, Georgetown University, 1976.

Duncan, K. and S. Gale. "Notes on a Third Paradigm: Well Formed Event Texts as a Data Model of Terrorist Actions," in Disarmament, Economic Conversion and Management of Peace, edited by Manas Chatterji and Linda Forcey, New York: Praeger Publishing, 1991.

Dutt, Vidya Prakash. India's Foreign Policy, New Delhi: Vikas, 1984.

Dutt, Vidya Prakash. July–October 1966. "China and Indo-Pakistani Relations," International Studies, 8, No. 1–2, 126–133.

Elhance, A. "A Conceptual Framework for the Study of Arms Production in the Third World," in Disarmament, Economic Conversion and Management of Peace, New York: Praeger Publishing, 1990.

Fischer, D. and R. Schwartz. "Economists and the Development of Peace," in Disarmament, Economic Conversion and Management of Peace, New York: Praeger Publishing, 1990.

Fishmann, L. "Disarmament and Full Employment," Rocky Mountain Social Science Journal, March 1965.

Fogarty, T. "Issue of Disarmament in the Context of European Integration," in Disarmament, Economic Conversion and Management of Peace, New York: Praeger Publishing, 1990.

Forcey, L. "Coming to Terms with Two Cultures: Approaches to Disarmament, Economic Conversion and Management of Peace," in Disarmament, Economic Conversion and Management of Peace, edited by Manas Chatterji and Linda Forcey, New York: Praeger Publishing, 1990.

Freud, S. "Instincts and Their Vicissitudes," First published in Internationals Zeitschrift für artztliche Psychoanalyse, Vol. 3, 1915, Translation by C.M. Baines in Collected Papers, Vol. 4, Metaphychology, London: The Hogarth Press, 1925.

Frisch, Ragnar. Planning for India: Selected Explorations in Methodology, Bombay, India: Asia Publishing House.

Gangal, S.C. "The Commonwealth and Indo-Pakistani Relations," International Studies, 8, No. 1–2, July-October 1966, 131–149.

Gamson, William Al. "Coalition Formation at Presidential Nominating Conventions," The American Journal of Sociology, Vol. LXVIII, 1962, pp. 157–171.

381

Garrido, L. Dynamical Systems and Chaos: Proceedings of the Sitges Conference on Statistical Mechanics, Sitges, Barcelona, Spain, September 5-11, 1982, Berlin and New York: Springer-Verlag, c1983.

Ghatate, Narayan Madhav. "Disarmament in India's Foreign Policy, 1947-1965," unpublished Ph.D. dissertation, American University, 336 pages, 1966.

Gillespie, John V., and D.A. Zinnes, eds. Mathematical Systems in International Relations Research, New York: Praeger Publishers, 1977.

Goodman, Leo A. The Analysis of Cross-Classified Data Having Ordered Categories, Cambridge, MA.: Harvard University Press, 1984.

Graybeal, Ronald. "The Impact of Arms Control Upon the Hawaiian Economy," Stanford University (mimeo), December 1961.

Guetzkow, H. "Isolation and Collaboration: A Partial Theory of International Relations, The Journal of Conflict Resolution, 1, (1957), 48-68.

Guha, Samar. "When East Bengal Breaks Off," Janata, 21, No. 2 (January 30, 1966), 7-8, 12.

Guilford, J.P. Fundamental Statistics in Psychology and Education, Fourth Edition, New York: McGraw-Hill, 1965.

Gundevia, Y.D. Outside the Archives, Hyderabad, (India): Sangam Books: Distr. by Orient Longman, 1984.

Gupta, Sisir. "India's Policy Towards Pakistan," International Studies, 8, No. 1-2, (July-October 1966), 29-48.

Haendal, Dan. The Process of Priority Formation: U.S. Foreign Policy in the Indo-Pakistani War of 1971, Boulder, CO: Westview Press, 1977.

Haldane, J.B.S. "The Maximization of National Income," Sankhya-The Indian Journal of Statistics, Vol. 16, December 1955.

Harary, F. A Structural Analysis of the Situation in the Middle East in 1956, Journal of Conflict Resolution, 1961, 5, (2, June) 167-78.

_____. Graph Theory. Reading, MA: Addison-Wesley, 1969.

_____. R. Norman, and D. Cartwright. Structural Models: An Introduction to the Theory of Directed Graphs. New York: Wiley, 1965.

_____. "Structural Duality," Behavioral Science, 2 (1957), 255-65.

_____. "On the Measurement of Structural Balance," Behavioral Science, 4 (1959), 316-23.

_____. and Norman, R.Z., Graph Theory as a Mathematical Model in Social Science. Ann Arbor, Mich: Institute for Social Research, 1953.

Hattori, A. "The Scope and Limits of International Cooperation for World Peace: A Lesson from International Economic Policy Coordination," in Disarmament, Economic Conversion and Management of Peace, edited by Manas Chatterji and Linda Forcey, New York: Praeger Publishing, 1991.

Heermann, Emil F., and L.A. Braskamp. Readings in Statistics for the Behavioral Sciences, New Jersey: Prentice-Hall, Inc., 1970.

Heider, F. "Attitudes and Cognitive Organization," Journal of Psychology, 21 (1946), 107-12.

Holden, Arun V. Chaos, Princeton, N.J.: Princeton University Press, 1986.

Holsti, Ole R., R.C. North, and R.A. Brody. "Perception and Action in the 1914 Crisis," in Quantitative International Politics: Insights and Evidence, by J. David Singer ed., New York: The Free Press, 1968.

Howard, Nogel. "The Arab-Israeli Conflict: A Metagame Analysis Done in 1970," Papers, Peace Research Society, Vol. XIX, 1972, pp. 35-60.

Intriligator, M. "Soviet 'New Thinking' and the Prospects for a New East-West Relationship," in Disarmament, Economic Conversion and Management of Peace, edited by Manas Chatterji and Linda Forcey, Praeger Publishing, New York, 1991.

Isard, W. Methods of Regional Analysis, Cambridge, Mass. The M.I.T. Press, 1960.

Isard, W., and Tony Smith. "On Social Decision Procedures for Conflict Situations," Papers, Peace Research Society, Vol. VIII, pp. 20-50, 1967.

_____. and Smith T., "A Practical Application of Game Theoretical Approach to Arms Reduction," Papers, Peace Research Society, (International), IV, 1965.

_____. and C. Smith, Conflict Analysis and Practical Conflict Management Procedures, Cambridge, MA: Ballinger Publishing Co., 1982.

_____. and Y. Nagao, International and Regional Conflict, Cambridge, MA: Ballinger Publishing Co., 1983.

_____. and C. Smith et al., Arms Races, Arms Control, and Conflict Analysis, New York: Cambridge University Press, 1988.

_____. and Czamanski, S., "Techniques for Estimating Local and Regional Multiplier Effects of Changes in the Level of Major Governmental Programs," Peace Research Society (International) Papers, Vol. III.

_____. and Karaska, G., Unclassified Defense and Space Contracts: Awards by County, State and Metropolitan Area, United States, Fiscal year 1964, World Friends Research Center, Inc., Philadelphia.

_____. and Schooler, E., "An Economic Analysis of Local and Regional Impacts of Reduction of Military Expenditures," Peace Research Society (International) Papers, Vol. 1, 1964.

_____. "Models for Projecting Economic-Ecologic and Inter-Nation Conflict," in Disarmament, Economic Conversion and Management of Peace, edited by Manas Chatterji and Linda Forcey, New York: Praeger Publishing, 1990.

Jain, Rajendra K. (editor). U.S.-South Asian Relations 1946-1982, Atlantic Highlands, NJ: Humanities Press, 1983.

_____, R.K. China-South Asian Relations, 1947-1980, Atlantic Highlands, NJ: Humanities Press, 1981.

_____. Soviet-South Asian Relations, 1947-1978, Atlantic Highlands, NJ: Humanities Press, 1979.

Joint Economic Committee, Congress of the United States, Background Material on Economic Aspect of Military Procurement and Supply - 1964.

Kapur, Harish. "The Soviet Union and the Indo-Pakistan Relations," International Studies, 8, No. 1-2 (July-October 1966), 150-157.

Karanakaram, K.P. "China in India's International Relations," China Report 2, No. 6, November/December 1966, 35-39.

Kashyap, S. The Politics of Defection: A Study of State Politics in India. Institute of Constitutional and Parliamentary Studies, New Delhi, India, 1968.

Kaushik, Devendra. Soviet Relations with India and Pakistan, Delhi, Vikas Publications, 1971.

Klein, L. and M. Gronicki. "Trade-Offs Between Military and Civilian Programs in Warsaw," in Disarmament, Economic Conversion and Management of Peace, edited by Manas Chatterji and Linda Forcey, New York: Praeger Publishing, 1990.

Klecka, William R. 1980, <u>Discriminant Analysis</u>, Beverly Hills, CA: Sage Publications.

Kumari, V. "Regional Imbalances of Central Assistance," <u>Eastern Economist</u>, Vol. 53, pp. 1917-1923, 1969.

Kumar, Mahendra. <u>Current Peace Research in India</u>, Rajghat, Varanasi, India, 1968.

Lall, Betty. "Reduction of Defense Expenditure and Economic Conversion," in <u>Disarmament, Economic Conversion and Management of Peace</u>, edited by Manas Chatterji and Linda Forcey, New York: Praeger Publishing, 1990.

Leontief, W.W. "Disarmament, Foreign Aid and Economic Development," <u>Peace Research Society (International) Papers</u>, Vol. II, 1964.

_____. "The Structure of Development," <u>Scientific American</u>, September 1963.

_____. and Fay Duchin, <u>Military Spending</u>, New York: Oxford University Press, 1983.

Luce, R.D. & A.A. Rogow. "A Game Theoretical Analysis of Congressional Power Distribution for a Stable Two Party System," <u>Behavioral Science</u>, Vol. 1, pp. 83-95, 1956.

Mahalanobis, P.C. <u>The Approach of Operation Research to Planning in India</u>, Bombay, India: Asia Publishing House, 1963.

Marascullo, Leonard A. and J.R. Levin. <u>Multivariate Statistics in the Social Sciences: A Researcher's Guide</u>, Monterey, CA: Brooks/Cole Publishing Co., 1983.

Mason, Edward S. <u>Foreign Aid and Foreign Policy</u>, New York: Harper and Row, 1964.

Melman, S. "Two Futures for the American Economy: The Role of Economic Conversion," in <u>Disarmament, Economic Conversion and Management of Peace</u>, edited by Manas Chatterji and Linda Forcey, New York: Praeger Publishing, 1990.

Miller, J.G. "Toward a General Theory for the Behavioral Sciences," <u>American Psychologist</u>, 10 (1955), 513-31.

Millikan, M. and Rostow, W.W. <u>United States Foreign Policy: Economic, Social and Political Change in the Underdeveloped Countries and its Implications for United States Policy</u>, Cambridge, MA, M.I.T., 1960.

Misra, K.P. "The Indo-Pakistan Conflict," <u>Afra Quarterly</u>, V, No. 3, October-December 1965, 203-217.

Mitra, A. "A Note on the Mahalanobis Model," <u>Economic Weekly</u>, Bombay, India.

Modelski, George. "War and the Great Powers," Papers, Peace Research Society, Vol. XVIII, pp. 45-59, 1972.

Morissette, J.O. "An Experimental Study of the Theory of Structural Balance," Human Relations, 11 (1958), 239-54.

Murphey, Rhoads. "Economic Conflict in South Asia," Journal of Conflict Resolution, Vol. 4, pp. 83-95, 1960.

National Aeronautics and Space Administration, NASA Annual Procurement Report Fiscal Year 1964.

Nayar, Baldev Raj. American Geopolitics and India, New Delhi: Manohar, 1976.

Newcomb, T.M. "An Approach to the Study of Communicative Acts," Psychological Review, 60 (1953), 393-404.

Nie, Norman H., C.H. Hull, J.G. Jenkins, K. Steinbrenner and D.H. Bent. SSPSS (Statistical Package for the Social Sciences, Second Edition, New York: McGraw-Hill, 1970.

Palmer, G. "The Chicken's Dilemma: American Strategic Policy and NATO," in Disarmament, Economic Conversion and Management of Peace, edited by Manas Chatterji and Linda Forcey, New York: Praeger Publishing, 1990.

Peterson, R.S. and Tiebout, C.M. "Measuring the Impact of Regional Defense-Space Expenditures," Review of Economics and Statistics, November 1964.

Pilsuk, M. and Anatol Rapaport. "A Non-Zero-Sum Game Model of Some Disarmament Problems," Papers, Peace Research Society, Vol. 1, pp. 20-30, 1963.

Polachek, S. and J.A. McDonald. "Strategic Trade and the Incentive for Cooperation," in Disarmament, Economic Conversion and Management of Peace, edited by Manas Chatterji and Linda Forcey, New York: Praeger Publishing, 1990.

Prasad, Bisheshwar. "Foundations of India's Foreign Policy: Imperial Era, 1882-1914," Calcutta, Nyad Prokash, 1979.

Rahman, A. "Regional Allocation of Investment," in Quarterly Journal of Economics, February 1963.

Rao, P. Chandrasekhara. "Indo-Pakistan Agreement on the Rann of Kutch: Form and Contents," Indian Journal of International Law, 5, No. 2 (April, 1965), 176-185.

Rao, V.K.R.V. and Dharm Narain. Foreign Aid and India's Economic Development, Bombay, India: Asia Publishing House.

Rapaport, Anatol, and A.M. Chammah. Prisoner's Dilemma, Ann Arbor: University of Michigan Press, 1965.

Rapaport, Anatol. Mathematical Models in the Social and Behavioral Sciences, New York: John Wiley & Sons, 1983.

Rapaport, Anatal. "Lewis Fry Richardson's Mathematical Theory of War," The Journal of Conflict Resolution, 1, November 3, 1957.

Ray, Asmini K. "Pakistan as a Factor in Indo-Soviet Relations," Economic and Political Weekly, 1, No. 12, November 5, 1966, 503-06.

Ray, Jayant Kumar. "India and Pakistan as Factors in Each Other's Foreign Policies," International Studies, 8, No. 1-2, July-October 1966, 49-63.

Richardson, L.F. Arms and Insecurity, Pittsburgh: The Bonwood Press, 1960.

Riggs, James and Thomas West. "Essentials of Engineering Economics, New York, McGraw-Hill, Boston Co. 1986.

Riker, W.H. The Theory of Political Coalitions, New Haven: Yale University Press, 1962.

Rossa, P.J. "A Q-Factor Analysis of the State Attribute Domain," Department of Government and Politics, University of Maryland, College Park, Maryland (mimeo), 1977.

Rosen, S.M. "A New Orthodoxy on Disarmament Economics," The Correspondent, Winter 1965.

Rosenstein-Rodan, Paul. "International Aid for Underdeveloped Countries," Review of Economics and Statistics, May 1961.

Rostow, W.W. The Process of Economic Growth, New York: W.W. Norton Company, Inc.

Rummel, R.J. "Dimensions of Conflict Behavior Within and Between Nations," General System, 8: 1963, pp. 1-50.

Sager, Peter. "Moscow's Hand in India: An Analysis of Soviet Propaganda," Berne, Swiss Eastern Institute (1966), 224 pages, 24 plates.

Seiglie, C. "Internal and External Factors Affecting Military Expenditures," in Disarmament, Economic Conversion and Management of Peace, edited by Manas Chatterji and Linda Forcey, New York: Praeger Publishing, 1990.

Sen, Chanakya. The Fulcrum of Asia; Relations Among China, India, Pakistan, and the USSR <by> Bhabani Sen Gupta, New York: Pegasus, 1970.

Sengupta, Jati K. Applied Mathematics for Economics, Dordrecht, Holland: R. Reidel Publishing Co., 1987.

387

Seth, Nareshavern Dayal. "India's Policy Towards China and Pakistan in the Light of Kautilya's Arthasastra," Modern Review, CXX, No. 3, Whole No. 717, September 1966, 200-203.

Shah, A.B. ed., "India's Defense and Foreign Policies," Manaktala, Bombay (1966) ix, 169 pages.

Shubik, Martin. Game Theory in the Social Sciences, Cambridge, MA: The MIT Press, 1982.

Sigler, John H. "Cooperation and Conflict in United States-Soviet-Chinese Relations, 1966-71: A Quantitative Analysis," Papers, Peace Research Society, Vol. XIX, pp. 107-128, 1972.

Singh, Amar Kaur Jasbir. Himalayan Triangle: A Historical Survey of British India's Relations with Tibet, Sikkim, and Bhutan, 1795-1950. London, British Library, 1988.

Singh, Balgit. "The United States and the India-Pakistan Conflict," Parliamentary Studies, 9, No. 12, December 1965, 15-19.

Singh, Kuldeep. India and Bangladesh, Delhi, India: Annual Publications, Distr. by Anupama Publishers, Distributors, 1987.

Smoker, Paul. "The Arms Race as an Open and Closed System," Papers, Peace Research Society (International), VII, 1967.

SPSSX User's Guide, 2nd Edition, McGraw-Hill, New York 1986.

Starobin, L. "Convergence (New Look at U.S. - U.S.S.R. Relations)," in Disarmament, Economic Conversion and Management of Peace, New York: Praeger Publishing, 1990.

Stein, Arthur. "India's Relations with the U.S.S.R. 1953-63," Orbis, Philadelphia, Summer 1964, 357-373.

Stevens, Benjamin. "Interregional Linear Programming," Ph.D. dissertation, University of Pennsylvania, Philadelphia, 1959.

Suits, Daniel B. "Econometric Analysis of Disarmament Impacts," in Disarmament and the Economy, edited by Emile Benoit and Kenneth Boulding, Harper and Row, 1963.

_____. "Forecasting and Analysis with an Econometric Model," American Economic Review, March 1962.

Tarbell, David S., and T.L. Saaty. "The Conflict in South Africa: Directed or Chaotic," Journal of Peace Science, Vol. 4, No. 2, pp. 151-168, Spring 1980.

Tewari, S.C. Indo-U.S. Relations, 1947-1976, New Delhi: Radiant
Publishers, 1977, University of Lucknow.

Tharoor, Shashi. Reasons of State: Political Development and
India's Foreign Policy Under Indira Gandhi, 1966-1977, New
Delhi: Vikas Pub. House, 1982.

Tinbergen, J. "Parallel Ways of Integrating the World," in
Disarmament, Economic Conversion and Management of Peace,
edited by Manas Chatterji and Linda Forcey, New York:
Praeger Publishing, 1990.

Tryon, Robert C. and Daniel E. Bailey. 1970, Cluster Analysis,
New York: McGraw-Hill.

Vaidyanathan, R. "Some Recent Trends in Soviet Policies Towards
India and Pakistan," International Studies, VII, No. 3,
January 1966, 429-447.

van Gastel, R., and J.H.P. Paelinck. "Hypergraph Conflict
Analysis," Conflict Management and Peace Science, Vol. 10,
No. 1, pp. 59-86, Spring 1988.

van Gastel, R., and J.H.P. Paelinck. "Computing the Solution to
a Conflict Situation by Means of Continuous Multicriteria
Analysis, in Disarmament, Economic Conversion and
Management of Peace, New York: Praeger Publishing, 1991.

Vertzberger, Yaacov. Misperceptions in Foreign Policy Makeup:
The Sino-Indian Conflict, 1959-1962, Boulder, CO:
Westview Press, 1984.

Wallace, T. Dudley and J.L. Silver. Econometrics an
Introduction, Addison-Wesley Publishing Co., Reading, MA,
1988.

Wolpert, Stanley A. Roots of Confrontation in South Asia:
Afganistan, Pakistan, India, and the Superpowers, New
York: Oxford University Press, 1982.

Yapp, Malcolm. Strategies of British India: Britain, Iran, and
Afghanistan, 1798-1850. Oxford, Clarendon Press; NY,
Oxford University Press, 1980.

Zafar Shah, M.A. India and the Superpowers: India's Political
Relations with the Superpowers in the 1970's, Dhaka,
Bangladesh: University.

Zeeman, E.C. Catastrophe Theory, Reading, MA: Addison-Wesley
Publishing Co., 1977.

Zimmerman, Charles, and Milton Leidenberg. "Hiroshema On,"
Mazingora 9.

About the Author

Manas Chatterji, is Professor of Management and Economics at the State University of New York at Binghamton. He previously taught in the Wharton School at the University of Pennsylvania. He has held many visiting appointments in American and European universities and has lectured at international meetings in China, Soviet Union, Japan, India, Europe and Latin America. He is the author and co-author of numerous books and has published about 80 scholarly articles in the areas of urban-regional, energy-environmental, health and technology management. He has been the co-editor (with Walter Isard) of the journals Conflict Management and Peace Science and Papers: Peace Science Society (International). He is a member of the Board of Directors of the international association, Economists Against Arms Race.